GW00482899

The C I.R.A. in Meath

First Published by

Owen McFadden, Baile Ghib

in 2015

Cover Images: Martry Company of Irish Volunteers assembled outside "The Hall" in Oristown Co. Meath on their way to the annual St. Kieran's Well Festival in Carnaross on 4th September 1914. Original photography kindly provided by Sib Rooney the proud owner and resident of "The Hall" and copy of image produced by Aubrey Martin, Perfect Stills Photography, Navan. Image modified to suit book cover by the author, Owen McFadden. An un-modified copy of Sib Rooney's original photograph can be seen on page 197

ISBN: 978-0-9933809-0-7

Disclaimer

The Author has taken all reasonable care to ensure that this publication is a true and accurate reflection of the reported information in the Primary Sources. The Author can not be held responsible for damages due to errors or omissions contained within this book or for defamatory statements contained within the Primary Source. It is not the Author's intention to publish any defamatory statements. For a full and accurate transcript of the information contained within this book please refer to the Primary Sources.

Printed in the Republic of Ireland by: Anglo Printers Limited, Mell Industrial Estate, Mell, Drogheda, Co. Louth. Tel: 041 9835000 www.angloprinters.ie

This book is dedicated to my wife Fiona, my son Stephen and my daughter Clare who patiently put up with me.

Contents

	Page
Sources	
Acknowledgements	
Introduction	1
Chapter 1: The main players	2
Chapter 2: The run up to the 1916 Easter Rising	10
Chapter 3: The 1916 Easter Rising in Co. Meath	13
Chapter 4: 1917, 1918, 1919 and 1920	33
Chapter 5: 1921, 1922 1923	46
Chapter 6: Policing and Justice	69
Chapter 7: Irish Volunteer Companies in Meath	78
Ardbraccan Company	78
Ardcath Company	84
Athboy Company	85
Ballinacree Company	92
Ballinlough Company	94
Ballivor Company	101
Bective and Kilmessan Company	103
Boardsmill Company	108
Bohermeen Company	109
Carnaross Company	115
Castletown Company	125
Cloncurry Company	127
Clongill Company	128
Commons Company	131
Creewood Company	132
Crossakiel Company	133
Culmullin Company	133
Curragha Company	136
Drumbaragh Company	137

Drumconrath Company	140
Duleek Company	142
Dunboyne Company	143
Dunderry Company	152
Dunmoe Company	155
Dunshaughlin Company	156
Enfield Company	158
Fennor Company	160
Fordstown Company	161
Johnstown Company	163
Julianstown & Laytown Company	168
Kells Company	169
Kentstown Company	176
Kilbeg Company	177
Kilberry Company	179
Kilbride Company (near Mulhuddart)	183
Kilcloon Company	185
Kildalkey Company	187
Kilmainhamwood Company	191
Kilmore Company	191
Kiltale Company	191
Killyon Company	193
Lobinstown Company	194
Longwood Company	194
Martry Company	196
Meath Hill Company	201
Moylagh Company	202
Moynalty Company	206
Navan Company	211
Newcastle Company	229
Nobber Company	232
Oldcastle Company	234
Rathkenny Company	240
Ratoath Company	242
Skryne & Killeen Company	243
Slane Company	245
Stackallen Company	246
Stonefield Company	246
Summerhill Company	251
Trim Company	253

Whitegate Company 263
Yellow Furze Company 265

Chapter 8: Volunteer's final resting places 267
Ashbourne – Kilbride Cemetery 268
Athboy – Church of Ireland Churchyard Cemetery 269
Athboy – Saint James's Cemetery 270
Athboy – Rathmore - Saint Lawrence's Cemetery 273
Batterstown – Ballymaglassan Churchyard Cemetery 274
Drumconrath Cemetery 275
Dunboyne – Loughsallagh Cemetery 278
Dunboyne – Rooske Cemetery 281
Dunshaughlin Churchyard Cemetery 284
Dunshaughlin – Kilmessan – Church of the Nativity 285
Dunshaughlin – Knockmark Cemetery 288
Kells – Ballinlough - Church of Assumption Cemetery 290
Kells – Carnaross Cemetery 293
Kells – Carnaross – Dulane Cemetery 297
Kells – Cortown Cemetery 298
Kells – Fordstown – Girley Old Cemetery 299
Kells – Kilskyre Church Cemetery 300
Kells – Martry Graveyard 302
Kells – Moynalty – Saint Mary's Cemetery 304
Kells – St. Colmcille's Cemetery 306
Kells – St. John's Cemetery 312
Kells – Stahalmog Cemetery 313
Navan – Ardbraccan Churchyard Cemetery (includes R.I.C.) 314
Navan – Ardmulchan Churchyard Cemetery 316
Navan – Bohermeen Churchyard Cemetery 317
Navan – Boyerstown Cemetery 322
Navan – Castletown Kilpatrick Cemetery 323
Navan – Donaghmore Cemetery 324
Navan – Donaghpatrick Church Cemetery 325
Navan – Dunderry Cemetery 327
Navan – Dunderry – Churchtown Cemetery 329
Navan – Kentstown Churchyard Cemetery 330
Navan – Kilberry Cemetery 331
Navan – Kilcarne Cemetery 333
Navan – Skryne – St. Colmcille's Churchyard Cemetery 335
Navan – St. Mary's Cemetery. (Also includes R.I.C.) 336

Navan – Wilkinstown – Fletcherstown Cemetery 349
Oldcastle – Ballinacree Churchyard cemetery 352
Oldcastle – Moylagh Churchyard Cemetery 354
Oldcastle – Old Loughrew Cemetery 358
Oldcastle – St. Bridget's Cemetery 359
Slane – Gernonstown Graveyard 363
Slane – Hill of Slane Cemetery 364
Slane – Monknewtown Cemetery 366
Slane – Rathkenny New Churchyard Cemetery 368
Slane – Rathkenny Old Churchyard Cemetery 369
Summerhill New Churchyard Cemetery 371
Trim – Ballivor – Killaconnigan Cemetery (includes R.I.C.) 372
Trim – Ballivor – New Cemetery 374
Trim – Garadice – Coole Churchyard Cemetery 376
Trim – Kilbride - Moymet Cemetery 377
Trim – Longwood – Kilglass Cemetery 378
Trim – Longwood – St Mary's Cemetery 379
Trim – St. Loman's Cemetery 381

Chapter 9. Looking for Someone? 385

Love to hear your feedback 406

Sources:

The following books, newspapers, websites and research material was used to compile material for inclusion in this book, in alphabetical order:

A History of the Parish of Clonmellon / Killallon by Eugene Sheridan, Clonmellon.
An Toglac newspapers, (the official newspaper of the Volunteers).
Dunderry A Folk History by Dunderry History Group & John Keely.
Faithful to Ireland, North Meath F.C.A. and its Origins by Tony Brady.
Ireland's Rebels by Morgan LLywelyn.
Politics and War in Meath 1913-23 by Oliver Coogan.
Prisoners of War, Ballykinlar Internment Camp 1920-1921 by Liam O'Duibhir.
Revolutionary Ireland by George Morrison.
Riocht Na Mi Volume XXVI - 2015
Royal and Loyal, Meath's G.A.A. History by Michael O'Brien.
Sinn Fein Rebellion Handbook, Easter, 1916 published by the Irish Times.
Stories from around Ballinacree by Ballinacree Local Community.
Stories from Eskaroon, by Paddy Keely.
The Irish Times Book of the 1916 Rising by Shane Hegarty and Fintan O'Toole.
The Oldcastle Centenary Book by John Smith.
The Meath Chronicle newspapers.
The Meath War Dead by Noel French.
When the Clock Struck in 1916 by Derek Moulyneux & Darren Kelly.
Wielding the Ash, Kicking the Leather by Frank McCann & Seamus Brennan, Trim.
With the Irish in Frongoch by W.J. Brennan-Whitmore.

Abbreviations of Sources:

Due to space constraints sources identified as MM9.1.1/KM3L-F23 or MM9.1.1/KM79-BS2 or MM9.1.1/KMQR-5RQ or similar format refer to "Ireland, Prison Registers, 1790-1924," index and images, FamilySearch citing "Irish Prison Registers 1790-1924," Brightsolid; Dundalk, Louth, Ireland, Dundalk Prison, item 2, book 1/16/1, National Archives, Dublin; FHL microfilm 2356848.

Numbers beginning with with the letters "RO" refer to Military Archives, Military Service Pensions Collection, Roinn Cosanta (Central Registry, I.R.A. Nominal Rolls)

Numbers beginning with with the letters "WS" refer to Bureau of Military History, 1913- 21, Witness Statements.

Acknowledgements:

I would like to acknowledge with thanks the help provided by the following people and groups, in alphabetical order:

Carol Owens, Navan, formally of Carrick Street, Kells, Co. Meath.

Eileen Sheils, Gibbstown, Navan, Co Meath.

Ethna Cantwell, Navan.

Eugene Sheridan, Clonmellon, Co. Westmeath.

Evans (Jeff) Miller, Silverlawns, Navan.

Facebook: 1916 Irish Easter Rising.

Facebook; Kells Republican Graves and Monuments Committee.

Jimmy Dunphy, Gibbstown, Navan.

Joe McFadden (my uncle) who died before the completion of this book – R.I.P.

John Maguire, Dunboyne - son of James, 1st Meath Brigade, Quartermaster, I.R.A.

John McNamara, Cloncarneel, Kildalkey, Co. Meath.

Kells Archaeological & Historical Society (KAHS), particularly Willie.

Liam Moran, Navan, Co Meath.

Malachy Hand, Moylagh, Oldcastle. Co. Meath

Michael (Mixer) Collins, Coole, Summerhill, Co. Meath.

Michael O'Brien, Johnstown Navan, Co. Meath.

Nancy McFadden, Gibbstown, Navan, Co. Meath.

Navan Historical Society.

Noel French, Trim, Co. Meath.

Owen Heaney, Castletown, Kilberry, Co. Meath.

Patrick Curtis, Boyerstown, Navan, Co. Meath.

Perfect Stills Photography, Navan, particularly Aubrey Martin LIPF

Seamus Smith, Ballinacree, Oldcastle, Co. Meath.

Sean Collins, Liscarton, Navan.

Sean Craughan, Oldcastle, Co. Meath.

Sean Fay, Moymet, Kilbride, Trim, Co. Meath.

Sebastian (Sib) Rooney, Oristown, Kells, Co. Meath.

Stephen Ball, New Line, Bohermeen, Navan, Co. Meath.

Tom French, Meath County Library, Navan, Co. Meath.

Tony Brady, Cherryhill Road, Kells, Co. Meath.

With a special mention of thanks to the proof readers:

> Fiona my wife.
> Clare my daughter.
> My mother-in-law, Anna Smith.
> My sister-in-law, Fiona Smith

Introduction

It is true to say that the 1916 Rising was not as big an operation in Meath as it was in Dublin, but to the people involved it was huge. The Volunteers from Meath displayed dedication and loyalty, as you will see. For an organisation like the Irish Volunteers or the Old I.R.A. to exist and succeed it was necessary for secrecy to be maintained. 'Walls have ears' and 'loose tongues cost lives' so Volunteers and their families kept their mouths shut. Later came the Irish Civil War which left a bitter taste in the mouths of the Irish people. As in most wars, both sides were involved in atrocities and dirty tricks. Mothers lost sons, children lost fathers, wives lost husbands and people's lives were destroyed and changed forever. These terrible events were inflicted on the Irish People by their own countrymen. It was a particularly difficult time in Ireland and I understand why people would prefer not to talk about it. Some local events were never revealed by the men involved, not even on their death beds. Understandably some families who did know did not pass on their memories or knowledge of events. These obstacles make writing a book like this very difficult. Consequently some people have the misperception that the Rising only happened in Dublin. This is fuelled by books targeting the bigger market of Dublin and ignoring the rest of the country. There are people who never heard of the events in their locality related to the War of Independence and the Irish Civil War because of the secrecy, the social circles that they lived in, maybe they did not grow up in their current locality or because they were too young. Others have a romantic notion that the Old I.R.A. in Meath were no more than a 'Dad's Army' or that they were harmless and that there was no war in Meath other than in the minds of the few. Others think that the Old I.R.A. were only engaged in war with the British not their own countrymen. I intend that this book will help address these issues and that the reader will understand events from a local point of view. It is not my intention to drag people kicking and screaming back to the heartbreak and pain of the past for the sake of a story but to reflect and learn from the past. To remember and honour the Volunteers and their supporters and to record the events of a local historical nature. On this, their centenary, I hold the men and women of 1916 and the Old I.R.A. in great respect. I salute them and I am honoured to tell their story in Co. Meath. I hope this book does everyone justice, maybe more justice than they received one hundred years ago. I hope we can put the past in the past and move forward together united. Enjoy.

Owen McFadden
Baile Ghib

Chapter 1
The Main Players

Why did the 1916 Rising occur?

Well it did not happen overnight and like most significant events in life it did not happen for one single reason alone. A series of events or actions occurred running up to Easter 1916, which created the environment in which a spark would ignite it. Here we are going to explore those events and actions. We have to go back a little bit in history first to see what happened running up to 1916. First let me introduce you to the organisations and people who played some significant role in events:

The Irish Republican Brotherhood (I.R.B.):

The Irish Republican Brotherhood (I.R.B.) was formed about 1858. It was financially supported by an Irish American group called The Fenian Brotherhood. Members of the Fenian Brotherhood and the Irish Republican Brotherhood in Ireland became known as "Fenians." Like its counterpart in America the I.R.B. was a secret organisation. As you will see in this book they secretly joined the ranks of the Irish Volunteers with the intention of using them to achieve their aims and objectives which was to separate Ireland from the United Kingdom and to establishing a Republic by armed rebellion.

The Ulster Volunteer Force (U.V.F.):

In 1912 the Ulster Volunteers was formed. They comprised of North of Ireland based Protestant militia groups locally organised by the Orange Order. Their aim was to block any attempts to introduce Home Rule in Ireland, to maintain British Rule and to ensure that Ireland remained within the British Union. These militia groups became known as the Ulster Volunteer Force (U.V.F.) and they publically stated that they would use force if necessary. The British Government were aware that a large number of British Army would not take action against the U.V.F. Ordering the British Army to do so would lead to a massive breakdown in British military discipline. For that reason the British Government never took any action against the U.V.F. and they were allowed to do as they wished.

The National Volunteers:

We will cover them later in this book.

The Ulster Volunteer Force (U.V.F)

The Irish Volunteers:
In November 1913 the Irish Volunteers were formed in the South of Ireland in direct opposition to the Ulster Volunteer Force (U.V.F.) in the North. Their primary aim was "to secure and maintain the rights and liberties common to the

The Irish Volunteers.
Source of photograph, author unknown from Public domain via Wikimedia Commons

whole people of Ireland." The Irish Volunteers included members of the Gaelic League, Ancient Order of Hibernians, Sinn Fein and secretly the Irish Republican Brotherhood (I.R.B.) mentioned earlier. Initially the Irish Volunteers were not a secret organisation and it was supported by many County Councils, businessmen and politicians.

The Commanding Officer of the Irish Volunteers was a schoolmaster named **Pádraig Pearse.** A Dublin man, formally a barrister and an Irish teacher, Pearse was a writer, a poet, a nationalist and a politician with a deep love for the Irish language.

Eoin McNeill was the main man in the formation of the Irish Volunteers. An Antrim man, he was well-educated with a deep knowledge of Irish History. He was described as a nationalist, a revolutionary and a politician. A believer in the preservation of the Irish language and culture and a member of the Gaelic League

and also a member of Sinn Fein. He held the position as chairman of the Irish Volunteers and Chief-of-Staff. His knowledge of Irish History and of the strength of the British Military made him aware that full hand to hand engagement between ill-equipped and untrained Volunteers with

Eoin McNeill. Picture courtesy of Irish Volunteers http:irishvolunteers.org

British Crown Forces was suicidal. He believed the Irish Volunteers needed to be fully armed and highly trained to take on Britain and until all those elements were in place he would not allow them to engage in combat unless it was in a defensive action. Defensive action means to defend against any attempt to disarm the organisation, to counter any attempt to impose conscription and to oppose any attempt by the U.V.F. or others to force the abandonment of Home Rule. This "defence only" policy did not suit the I.R.B. plans.

The Irish Citizen Army:

Also in 1913 employers in Ireland refused to recognise workers unions which caused workers to go on strike. In August 1913 the employers locked out members of the union from their businesses causing all-out strikes of 25,000 workers bringing Dublin's industry to a grinding halt. This became known as the

Irish Citizen Army photo courtesy of Irish Volunteers
http:irishvolunteers.org

lock-out. During union rallies, rioting between strikers and Dublin Metropolitan Police became vicious resulting in the deaths of several strikers and injuries to several hundred. The workers union formed a small army of militia to protect strikers and workers from police. This small army became known as the Irish Citizen Army. It was almost entirely a Dublin army although they had small branches in Tralee and in Killarney. In October 1914 **James Connelly** took over command of the Irish Citizen Army. Connelly was born in Edinburgh, Scotland to Irish parents from Co. Monaghan. He began work at eleven years of age. In 1882 he joined the British Army with papers falsifying his name and age enabling him to enlist. There he gained a knowledge of discipline and military tactics. He served in Ireland in 1889 for one year and he developed a hatred for the British Army. He deserted the army, married and got involved in Trade Union activities. He moved to Ireland and in 1912 he and others formed, what is now known as the Irish Labour Party. In 1914 he became the Trade Union Secretary and Commandant of the Irish Citizen Army.

The Royal Irish Constabulary (R.I.C.):

The Royal Irish Constabulary were an armed British police force in Ireland and they were here from the early 1800's until 1922. There were thirty six R.I.C. barracks in County Meath with an overall strength of 150 men. R.I.C. men were paid about three pounds 10 shillings per week.

Auxiliaries:

The Auxiliaries were a division of the R.I.C. The force was made up of ex-British Army servicemen who were recruited into the R.I.C. as temporary police Constables. The Auxiliaries were used by the British Government to immediately strengthen the R.I.C. when they came under pressure rather than having to train more R.I.C. recruits. Auxiliaries were paid £7 per week. They had a strength of 100 men in County Meath and they were distinct from the Black and Tans.

What is the difference between the Irish Volunteers and the I.R.A.? There is no difference. In January 1919 the 1st Dail assembled in Dublin and took over responsibility for the Irish Volunteers. They renamed them the Irish Republican Army (I.R.A.). We will cover this a bit more later in the book.

Auxiliaries

Cumann na mBan Photo courtesy of Irish Volunteers http:irishvolunteers.org

Cumann na mBan:

In April 1914 Cumann na mBan were formed with the aim of supporting and working with the Irish Volunteers, to assist in arming and equipping them for the defence of Ireland and to form a fund for these purposes. This volunteer force were mainly wives and sisters of Irish Volunteers. In 1916 the President of the organization was Constance Markievicz. She was born in London, grew up at Lissadell House in Co. Sligo. During the Rising she was Second in Command to Michael Mallin in St. Stephens Green. Cumann na mBan looked after I.R.A. Volunteers "on the run", fed them and gave them a place to rest. They trained in first aid and administered field dressings to wounded Volunteers. They visited Volunteers in prison. They cooked for I.R.A. Police Guards and also for the prisoners of the I.R.A. Police. They scouted areas prior to attacks reducing the risk of British Army ambushes or capture of Volunteers. They relayed positions of military forces back to Volunteers steering them out of harm's way. They carried dispatches from place to place, gathered intelligence by cycling round and keeping their eyes and ears open.

The British Army:

The strength of the British Army in County Meath varied at different times but their maximum strength was:

Navan: 450 British Troops (300 Leinster Regiment and 150 Cameronians).
Kells: 150 British Troops (South Wales Borderers)
Dunshaughlin: 100 British Troops (South Wales Borderers)
Oldcastle: 50 British Troops (Regiment unknown)

The Black and Tans:

When ex-British Army Servicemen arrived back to Britain from the First World War

A Black and Tan in Dublin with a Lewis Gun.
Photo courtesy of The National Library of Ireland
(Public domain) via Wikimedia Commons

they faced unemployment. Many of them had no skills other than fighting. The British Government came under pressure to do something to accommodate them. In 1919 the British Government were also coming to terms with the fact that the R.I.C. were not an adequate force to deal with the I.R.A. so they decided to form an armed force of these ex British Servicemen and send them to Ireland to support the R.I.C. and to put the fight up to the I.R.A. This force became known as the Black and Tans because of the colour of their uniforms. The first Black and Tans arrived in Ireland in March 1920 and in all about 8,000 of them arrived. They became known as a very undisciplined force who often got drunk before going on terrifying raids, indiscriminately killing innocent people, looting and burning towns, homes and businesses. They had a strength of 50 men in County Meath and they were paid ten shillings per day.

Chapter 2
The Run Up to the 1916 Easter Rising in Co. Meath

Let's set the scene. The majority of the people in Ireland wanted Home Rule (the right to govern themselves in Ireland) and they looked for it in a democratic and peaceful way for many years. In 1886 Home Rule was denied to the Irish because Liberal Unionists rebelled against it. In 1893 it was denied again because the House of Lords objected to it. In 1914 it was denied yet again due to threats by the Ulster Unionists and the looming World War One was a higher priority for the British Government. It looked unlikely that Ireland would ever get Home Rule. The Union with Britain was doing nothing for the average Irish person. Working conditions were poor. Workers had no rights. Dublin was full of tenement slums. Irish people lived in horrible conditions and we had the highest infant mortality rate in Europe.

In July 1914 the First World War had started and England committed to engage in the Great War as it was called. The I.R.B. were asking themselves is this our opportunity to start the Rebellion? Irish Nationalists had long prophesied that England's difficulties would be Ireland's opportunity. The Irish Parliamentary Party had been campaigning for Home Rule in Ireland and had become very popular. They had the support of many of the Irish Volunteers. The Irish Parliamentary Party leader was John Redmond. The leaders of the Irish Volunteers asked Redmond for his public approval of the Irish Volunteers. Redmond had no involvement in forming the Irish Volunteers, but he seen how popular they were, the growing strength of the organisation, and the common objectives of the two organisations so he moved to take control of the Irish Volunteers. The leaders of the Irish Volunteers resisted but they knew that if they refused he would probably call on his supporters to withdraw from the Irish Volunteers. In June 1914 the Leaders of the Irish Volunteers reluctantly allowed Redmond to nominate half of the membership of the Irish Volunteer Executive. Redmond already had supporters in the Volunteer Executive so this effectively gave him control of the organisation. This was a great boost to the Irish Volunteers as young Irish men flocked into their ranks. The Volunteers had a strength now of 151,700 men. A huge body of men. In August 58 companies were formed in six months in County Meath alone. Places like Finucane's draper shop in Ludlow Street in Navan were advertising the sale of volunteer's uniforms, caps, belts, and marching boots etc. Public opinion was all in favour of the Volunteers. The gentry were making their support for the Volunteers known in the newspapers. The I.R.B. could see that a perfect opportunity to stage the Rising was on the horizon. Then on 20th September 1914 a spanner was thrown in the works when John Redmond made a speech in which he called on the

Volunteers to enlist in his new army called the National Volunteers. He pledged his support to the Allied cause and said that the new National Volunteers would fight in the Great War alongside the British Army. The Leaders of the Irish Volunteers and the I.R.B. rejected and condemned Redmond's call. Militant nationalists reacted angrily against Redmond and nearly all of the original leaders of the Irish Volunteers grouped together and dismissed Redmond's appointees to the Irish Volunteer Executive. However it was too late, the vast majority of the Irish Volunteers (142,000) supported Redmond. Many naive young men excited with the prospect of becoming a real soldier in a real army, carrying a real gun and becoming a war hero did follow Redmond. They left the Irish Volunteers, became known as National Volunteers, joined the British Army and went to fight in the World War, where many of them were killed. The ranks of the Irish Volunteers were decimated. They were down now to 9,700 men and in many cases whole companies just ceased to exist all over the country. This changed things dramatically for the I.R.B. and their plans for a Rising. Reassessing their position now:

- The Irish Volunteers have been weakened by the split in the organisation.
- The U.V.F. had recently landed 20,000 German rifles at the Port of Larne in the North of Ireland as the British Government turned a blind eye. The I.R.B. may have considered the possible risk that if the U.V.F. mobilised and came south during a rebellion they could have upset their plans.
- The Irish Volunteers had just landed 900 Mauser rifles at Howth, but they were still inadequately armed and in many parts of the country they had no arms at all which was the case in Co. Meath.

Considering these points the I.R.B. decided they would wait. They would let the British get well engaged in the Great War and when they were stretched and unable to react with full force the I.R.B. would seize the moment and strike them hard and fast with a Rebellion. They decided that until the time was right they would re-double their efforts in building a strong, well trained, well armed fighting army of Irish Volunteers. Soon after it became apparent that the U.V.F. were joining the British Army and going to war for Britain which took them out of the picture.

All positive publicity went to Redmond and the National Volunteers depicting the brave young men going to war. Crying mothers, wives and girlfriends waving to ship loads of young men leaving Ireland was the news of the day. Irish public opinion swung against the Irish Volunteers who were depicted as cowards who would not go to war and fight.

The loss of all of those Volunteers to the British Army was only a temporary setback to the I.R.B. but they did not realise this at the time. The men who did go to war had an awful time but they received the very best training and experience and it made good soldiers and officers out of them. Some rose in rank and gained very useful military experience. Many of the soldiers and officers who survived World War 1 returned to Ireland and joined the Irish Volunteers. You will find that some of the top men in I.R.A. General Head Quarters (G.H.Q.) were in fact ex-British Army. Even some of Michael Collins trusted advisors were ex-British Army. You will find in this book that was also the case right through the Volunteer organisation to the individual companies. Ex-British Army men formed local Irish Volunteer companies or they trained Volunteers. They contributed greatly to the I.R.A. in the War of Independence. It was in later years that it became a black and white case of a British Soldier was an enemy soldier.

Irish Volunteers drilling (training). Photo courtesy of Irish Volunteers http:irishvolunteers.org

1915 saw recruiting of Volunteers progressing at a furious pace. Sean Boylan cycled from Dunboyne to all parts of County Meath attending meetings, forming companies, drilling, training and organising Volunteers into an army. He dud this on a daily basis often cycling throughout the night and staying in areas with Volunteers for days at a time. For background information on Sean Boylan see Dunboyne Company page 144.

In Easter 1915 The Irish Volunteers participated in large scale manoeuvres in Dublin. The rationale behind this was that it would leave the authorities off their guard when the same manoeuvres would occur next year, Easter 1916.

Chapter 3
The 1916 Easter Rising in Co. Meath

The I.R.B. Master Plan: In January 1916 the Irish Volunteers had been established about three years. Despite the major split caused by Redmond, companies of Irish Volunteers were steadily growing and gaining strength again. The I.R.B. had identified the Irish Volunteers as one of the key elements in their master plan for the defeat of British Rule in Ireland. Since the establishment of the Irish Volunteers the I.R.B. had secretly instructed all their members to join the Volunteers. Volunteers who rose in rank to officers were secretly offered a place in the I.R.B. By now the I.R.B. were well established as high ranking officers within the Irish Volunteers so they were progressing towards gaining almost full control of the organisation and apparently the Irish Volunteer's Chief-of-Staff was unconcerned. The I.R.B. were also building up relationships with the Irish Citizen Army and Cumann na mBan as part of their overall master plan. The I.R.B. along with **Pádraig Pearse** engaged with **James Connolly's** Irish Citizen Army and Cumann na mBan President **Constance Markievicz** to prepare for a Rebellion. They planned the Rebellion or Rising to commence on Easter Sunday 1916. Part of the plan was that for several weeks prior to the Rising Irish Volunteer companies were to arrange regular weekend parades and route marches to take place throughout the country culminating in three days of nationwide parades and route marches on Easter Sunday. Volunteers were to go on route marches fully kitted out including food and rations each weekend. They were to assemble in towns on Sunday mornings in the face of R.I.C. The plan was that the authorities would become accustomed to these regular parades and route marches and would not be alarmed to hear of a nationwide mobilisation of Irish Volunteers for the Easter weekend 1916. The element of surprise would be with the Volunteers. Hostilities near Easter were to be avoided until the Dublin Brigade make the first strikes in the Capital. The co-ordinated Master Plan also included:

- A shipment of German arms to be landed in Ireland by Roger Casement and to be quickly distributed throughout the country.
- Irish men to arrive from England over a lengthy period prior to the Rising and to be in readiness to engage in the Rising.
- Break out of German Prisoners of War held in Irish jails to be planned and the prisoners to engage in the Rising.
- Dublin to be surrounded by a chain of Volunteers isolating it from the rest of the country.
- Rail links to Dublin to be broken to cut off supplies to British Troops and to prevent arrival of British reinforcements and artillery.

In Co. Meath the Hill of Tara was to be choreographed into the Irish Rebellion. The Hill of Tara was of no significant strategic military importance, but it was the place where 400 Irish Rebels died when they were attacked by British Troops on 26th May 1798. For that reason its inclusion in the Irish Rebellion was purely of a symbolic importance to the I.R.B.

The assembled Volunteers at Tara were to march across to Slane where they would meet with the Louth Volunteers. There, they would jointly take control of the Bridge over the Boyne until all units had crossed, then they were to blow up the Bridge. Volunteers were to capture an Artillery Train which was expected to arrive from Athlone. German Prisoners of War held in Oldcastle, which included Engineers who were proficient in the use of this artillery had agreed to operate the Artillery in exchange for their freedom. The Louth and Meath men were then to make their way to Blanchardstown Flower Mills keeping in touch with Fingal, South Dublin, Kildare and Wicklow. There they would form a large part of the chain that would surround Dublin. The British Troops at the Curragh in Kildare would be isolated from the battle in Dublin. All R.I.C. barracks in the country were to be attacked for their weapons and ammunition. Orders were issued on a need to know basis. Sources: Lecture by Alphie Monaghan, Volunteer Organiser, published in The Anglo-Celt dated 9th April 1966 page 14. "Historoma" presentation arranged by Lt. Col. Kane O.C. Columb Barracks Mullingar as reported in the Westmeath Examiner dated 23rd April 1966, page 3.

All companies began weekly route marches and parades marching increasingly long distances each week followed closely by R.I.C taking notes and writing reports. Sure enough the R.I.C. did get used to the laborious task of having to cycle round the countryside observing these parades every weekend in all weathers.

On Saturday 1st April 1916 Sean Boylan (see Dunboyne Company) was summoned to a meeting with Pádraig Pearse at St Enda's in Dublin. At the meeting Pearse introduced him to Donal O'Hannigan. Pearse said that he had appointed O'Hannigan, Officer Commanding Meath, Louth, South Down, South Armagh and Monaghan areas for the Rising. He told Sean Boylan to quietly prepare the Meath Volunteers, but to await the order to mobilise. He was told that when he got the order that he was to have all companies in Meath prepared and he was to mobilise with his men in Dunboyne, that he was to send out scouts to get in touch with O'Hannigan and that he was to await O'Hannigan's arrival and fall in under O'Hannigan's command. He was also told that a German ship would land arms in the country. Pearse was of course referring to Roger Casement's plan to land arms at Kerry.

In early April Donal O'Hannigan and Gary Byrne arrived in Kells to take over control and to make final arrangements for the start of the Easter Rising. For background on Gary Byrne see Drumbaragh Company. Commanding Officers were instructed on a need to know basis only. They were told to prepare the

Volunteers secretly and to instruct them to be prepared to assemble at the Hill of Tara at short notice carrying arms and three days of rations. The actual date of the Rising was not released yet and the only ones who even knew there was a Rising on the cards were R.I.B. men, who were all in commanding positions within the Irish Volunteers as explained earlier.

On April 18th 1916 twenty two year old Patrick Loughran (see Navan Company) from Market Square Navan had been working in Dublin as a draper for the past two years. Patrick was an Irish Volunteer in the Kimmage Company in Dublin for the past year. He had been in a company of Irish Volunteers in Tralee for about two years before that. On 18th April he was present when his company were addressed by Commandant Kent who instructed them to stay at home on Good Friday and to be ready to fight for Ireland at the Easter weekend. Patrick Loughran stated in his Witness Statement that the first shots of the rebellion were fired at about 10pm that night. Patrick goes on to say that his company were in an old mill owned by Count Plunkett which the Volunteers regularly used as a drill hall and a meeting place. He said that at that time the old mill was housing about 100 men who had arrived from England to engage in the Easter Rising. Detectives arrived at the scene and an Irish Volunteer guard open fire on them as they approached. The Detectives withdrew from the scene. If that account is true this happened about six days before the official date of the Rising. It is difficult to understand why the authorities did not follow up on this incident.

The I.R.B. feared that Eoin McNeill would not allow the Irish Volunteers to engage in an open rebellion. On April 19th 1916 they showed McNeill a letter from Dublin Castle, supposedly intercepted, indicating that the British were about to arrest McNeill and all other National and Republican leaders. The I.R.B. told Eoin McNeill that Roger Casement was about to land a shipment of German rifles in Kerry. They convinced McNeill that all Republican forces needed to be mobilised immediately otherwise years of building them up would be lost. McNeill reluctantly agreed to the mobilisation of the Irish Volunteers as part of what he thought was a "defensive" act. Historians for years believed that letter was forged and maybe it was.

On Good Friday, April 21st 1916, Patrick Loughran was mobilised at 11am, this must be why he was told to stay at home on Good Friday, so that they could contact him. He reported to Weavers Hall on Donore Avenue, Dublin where the rest of his company gathered. Shortly afterwards they were dismissed without explanation. This might have been a dry run to see how the mobilisation would go on the day, to iron out any problems that arose and provide the I.R.B. with timing data etc. for the real Rising. Later that evening Patrick Loughran and other Volunteers were out again, this time they carried dispatches to and from high ranking officers in the City. They were also instructed to deliver revolvers and ammunition to various houses around the Islandbridge area.

In Dunboyne, Sean Boylan received a written order from Pádraig Pearse to mobilise his men at 6pm on Sunday next and this would mark the start of the Easter Rising. However, also on that day, April 21st, Roger Casement was captured and the 20,000 rifles, ten machine guns and ammunition were lost.

On Holy Saturday, April 22nd 1916, Eoin McNeill learned that Roger Casement was arrested and that the German rifles were lost. He contacted the newspapers including the Sunday Independent with the following notice:

"Owing to the very critical position, all orders given to Irish Volunteers for tomorrow, Easter Sunday, are hereby rescinded, and no parades, marches, or other movements of Irish Volunteers will take place. Each individual Volunteer will obey this order strictly in every particular.
EOIN MACNEILL,
Chief of Staff, Irish Volunteers" Source: The Sunday Independent dated 23rd April 1916

He also sent dispatches to several Commanding Officers with the same message. This threw another spanner in the works for the I.R.B. They quickly convened a meeting and along with the Irish Citizen Army and Cumann na mBan, they agreed to go ahead with the Rising but a day later. Delaying the Rising until Easter Monday would give them time to get the word out to the Volunteers and it would avoid conflicting with the countermanding order that McNeill sent out. They sent out dispatches through the I.R.B. command structures advising the Commanding Officers of the Volunteers of this change of plan. At this stage the Leaders must have known that this Rising was going to be a failure. Why did they go ahead with it?

The ordinary Irish Volunteers around the country knew nothing of these events. They were receiving mixed messages, one to mobilise, another to cancel mobilisation and another to change the date of the mobilisation. Some officers, who were mostly I.R.B. now, went out to the various companies and told Commanding Officers to make final preparations for the Rising to commence. In Meath shotgun cartridges were filled with buckshot and the few available guns and ammunition were got ready. Final arrangements were discussed and orders to mobilise in Meath at 6pm tomorrow evening, Easter Sunday, were issued to individual Volunteers present. They were all to carry whatever arms were available and three days rations. They were not told any further details. Not all Volunteers received the orders, some had seen the newspapers and followed the orders issued by Eoin McNeill and stayed at home. Some Volunteers and officers lived in remote areas and some were only too happy to have the long Bank

Holiday weekend off after marching every weekend for weeks. Some of them socialised for the weekend in the pubs and dances. Some were out all Sunday night and had a lie in on Bank Holiday Monday morning. Some had planned to go to the races in Fairyhouse on the Bank Holiday Monday.

On Easter Sunday morning, April 23rd 1916, Patrick Loughran, (Navan Company) who was in Dublin, was one of those who had seen Eoin McNeill's notice in the Dublin newspapers. He followed the orders and went home to Navan and had no further involvement in the 1916 Rising. Later in the afternoon the Meath Volunteers were informed that they were to mobilise in a stealth fashion. Dunboyne Volunteers were told to assemble near Sean Boylan's House in Dunboyne. Carnaross and Drumbaragh companies were told to quietly make their way to the Hill of Tara without drawing attention to themselves. They were told they would be joined there by other detachments and they were all to await further orders. They made their way to the Hill of Tara in various modes of transport and in small groups.

Drumbaragh Company – Seven men mobilised after lunch on Easter Sunday. They were Gary Byrne from Dublin wo was in charge, Willie Byrne, Hugh Smith, Frank O'Higgins, Joseph Power, Sean Dardis and Sean Hayes. They met outside the Chapel in Kells and keeping a low profile they quietly set off to Navan on foot. Between them they were armed with three ancient revolvers, a point 38 automatic and a point 22 rifle and some ammunition. Outside Kells town Gary Byrne had arranged for a couple of cars to take the men to Navan. From Navan they travelled the rest of the way to the Hill of Tara on foot.

Carnaross Company – Travelled by horse drawn sidecars carrying a football creating the impression that they were going to play a football match. The Carnaross Company were a bigger company and they were armed with about twelve point 22 revolvers.

All 30 or 40 Volunteers arrived at Tara at about 7pm and all carried three days rations which they had prepared themselves. When they assembled at Tara, Gary Byrne told them to keep a low profile and to stay quiet and that that they would be joining up shortly with Donal O'Hannigan accompanied by Volunteers from Co. Louth. He told Volunteers of instructions from General Head Quarters (G.H.Q.) that there was to be no engagement in Meath until the Dublin Brigade had used the element of surprise in Dublin. You will find all available details of the above men in Chapter 7 under their respective companies.

Around the same time in the evening the Louth men, under the Command of Donal O'Hannigan, crossed into County Meath, they arrived in Slane. They had spent the afternoon marching from Dundalk through Ardee to Slane as part of their weekly route march and being watched by a few unsuspecting R.I.C. men on bicycles. Donal O'Hannigan had orders to take the Bridge at Slane and to hold it until other Volunteer forces crossed. But now Donal was not sure if the Rising was cancelled or not. When he set off from Dundalk earlier he had confirmed orders that the Rising was on and he knew his mission but while on the route march he received a message by a dispatch rider from Eoin McNeill saying that the Rising was off. He was not sure if the second message was genuine or not. He had sent out several dispatch riders to Dublin to confirm but none of them had returned yet. When the route march arrived in Slane they did not go as far as the bridge so as not to raise suspicions, they generally hung around the village keeping an eye on the bridge and awaiting the arrival of dispatch riders or the Meath men from the Hill of Tara.

While all of this was going on, a man called Benson arrived at Sean Boylan's house in Dunboyne with a message that the Rising was off and to stop the mobilisation. Boylan told whatever men were available in Dunboyne to spread the word and he tried to get a car to go to the Hill of Tara but there was none to be got. As the night wore on they eventually got a taxi and they headed for the Hill of Tara. The Volunteers at the Hill of Tara had waited and waited for orders to move. Evening turned into night and then, sometime before midnight, a

taxi arrived carrying Sean Boylan and Benson. Sean Boylan told Gary Byrne that the Rising was off and to quietly disperse the Volunteers and await further orders. The men dispersed and found their way home in ones and twos and in small groups so again not to raise suspicions. On their way home they felt dismayed and downhearted and were wondering what was going on. Sean Boylan stayed that night in Larry Clarke's house at No. 13 Brews Hill Navan.

Early next morning, April 24th 1916, Easter Monday, the Irish Citizen Army Volunteers assembled at Liberty Hall in Dublin for the Rising and to receive their orders. Amongst those present were four Volunteers from Co. Meath. They were Luke Bradley, Patrick Bradley, Patrick (P.J.) Fox and his son James Fox. Volunteers Luke Bradley and Patrick Bradley are brothers from Newtowngirley, Fordstown, Kells, Co. Meath.

Volunteer Luke Bradley, Newtowngirley, Fordstown, Kells. Irish Citizen Army. Photo from Meath Chronicle dated 16th April 1966.

They had both been in the Irish Citizen Army since its inception in 1913. Luke was working in the Inchicore Foundry where he became a member of the Irish Trade & General Workers Union and a member of the Irish Citizen Army. Volunteer Patrick Fox aged 43 years and his son James aged 16 years were natives of Drumree, near Dunshaughlin Co. Meath. P.J. used to run the Spenser Arms Hotel in Drumree but he ran into hard times and they moved to Dublin in 1912 looking for work. P.J. had been a Republican activist all of his life and was a member of the I.R.B. He became involved with the Irish Citizen Army while in Dublin. His young son James went to school in Dunshaughlin before they moved to Dublin and he was a member of Na Fianna Eireann. During this period his mother had moved back to her parents in England leaving young James with his dad.

Volunteer Patrick Bradley, Newtowngirley, Fordstown Kells. Irish Citizen Army. Photo from Meath Chronicle dated 16th April 1966.

On the same morning, 24th April, two more Meath men, Irish Volunteers Philip Clarke and Thomás Allen reported for duty and were assigned to the Four Courts with a section of men. Philip Clarke from Monknewtown near Slane Co. Meath had been with the Irish Citizen Army since he moved to Dublin about two and a half years previously. Philip was the eldest son of ten children, aged about 41 years he had a job as a van driver in Dublin and he lived in Cork Street, Dublin with his wife and eight children. Thomás Allen was born in 1883 in the parish of Moyvalley, Longwood Co. Meath. He was 33 years of age, married with four children. He was a member of A Company, 1st Battalion, Dublin Brigade, Irish Volunteers.

Back at Liberty Hall, all of the Volunteers were divided into sections with the Meath men, Luke and Patrick Bradley, PJ. and James Fox in one section under the command of Michael Mallin. The orders for all Volunteers in that section was to take St. Stephen's Green and hold it. Volunteer Patrick Fox quietly got Michael Mallin's ear for a few minutes to tell him that he did not feel he was young enough, strong enough or well enough to continue. He bowed out of the operation and he put his son James in Michael Mallin's charge. The Volunteers got into action, made their way to St. Stephens Green, evacuated civilians from the Green, closed the gates and began barricading the perimeter with cars, carts, bicycles, metal drums, wooden poles, anything that was available. They began taking up positons behind the barricades, building defences and digging trenches in the Green. War quickly raged on the streets of the Capital. They came under sustained attack from British forces and they had to call for support. Philip Clarke was one of the Meath men who was reassigned from the Four Courts to support the battle for St. Stephens Green. Patrick Bradley and Luke Bradley were assigned to opposite ends of the Green. The Irish Citizen Army battled all day and secured their objectives with little losses. Later that night the Volunteers reflected on the fairly successful day and what might happen tomorrow, but the main thing was that they had made it through the first day.

Meanwhile back in Dunboyne Sean Boylan got back from Navan. He found that all the Dunboyne Volunteers seemed to have got the message that the Rising was called off. It was Bank Holiday Monday and the Fairyhouse races were on. Many of the Dunboyne Volunteers were gone for a day at the races. Then as the day wore on Sean Boylan heard rumours that there was fighting in Dublin. He raced round the locality alerting Volunteers, Christopher Lynam, Francis Lownes and Peter Keating. They rounded up other available Volunteers including Edward (Ned) Boylan, Christopher Keating, James Keating, Hughie Farrell, Owen King and Daniel Madden. They set about blowing up a bridge over a railway and destruction of railway tracks, but before they did Boylan received word from a local girl that a man was around earlier and left a message that he was to do nothing other than to go to Leixlip with his men and join up with men from Maynooth. They immediately set out on foot to Leixlip, which was about six miles away, with about fourteen men armed with two rifles, some single barrel shotguns and a few revolvers, but they were too late. The Maynooth men had passed through earlier. They headed back to Dunboyne and Boylan sent men out in several directions to scout and report back.

Meanwhile back in Kells, the Volunteers that were sent home from Tara the previous night knew nothing of these events. Now they were hearing rumours that the Rising had started in Dublin without them. As the day wore on they were hearing wild rumours and stories of events in Dublin. Why were they sent home? Was it because the orders from General Headquarters were messed up? How could this be happening? Disappointment and disbelief set in, quickly turning to frustration, defiance and anger. What were they supposed to do now? Listening for every word of news from Dublin. The area was crawling with R.I.C. men watching every move now. Some Volunteers set out on bicycles from Kells and from Athboy to do something or to find out what was happening only to be stopped at R.I.C. roadblocks and sent back home. Sean McGurl from Athboy did somehow manage to get to Dunboyne. He joined up with the Dunboyne Company according to Sean Boylan's witness statement and I cover that event later on page 23. Some Volunteers flew tricolours on prominent vantage points to keep up morale only to have them torn down by R.I.C. The Rising would be a total failure and there was nothing they could do. That night in Kells, Gary Byrne learned from the other Volunteers where they had encountered police road blocks and he set off in the dark on his bicycle. Cycling all night he somehow managed to avoid the roadblocks.

Other Meath men, but not living in Meath at the time and who were mobilised for the Rising on Monday 24th April were:

Patrick Cole, Arodstown, Summerhill, Co. Meath, see Summerhill Company.

Joseph Kennedy, Raytown Ashbourne. He was a fitter working in Broadstone Railway and was an active Volunteer in B Company, 1st Battalion, Dublin Brigade. He had been mobilised and dismissed on the Sunday. On Monday he was mobilised and engaged in the fighting in Colmcille's Hall, North King Street, Moore's Coach Builders, North Brunswick Street, Four Courts Hotel, Father Matthew Hall and Church Street Dublin. Source: MSP34REF43598

Liam O'Regan, Climber Hall, Kells, Co. Meath was a Member of the Maynooth Company of Irish Volunteers since 1914. He was mobilised on Monday and set out with eighteen men plus officers towards Dublin that evening. They waded over the freezing Tolka River with their Rifles held over their heads. They spent the night in Glasnevin Cemetery and arrived at the G.P.O. at 8 a.m. on Tuesday morning. He was detailed for Parliament Street. He was on the roof of the Royal Exchange Hotel covering the party in the Mail Office and fired on military who were attacking the Mail Office. He also fought in the G.P.O. until the surrender. In 1941 Liam received one of the medals struck to commemorate the 25th Anniversary of the 1916 rising.

Sources: MSP34REF46881. http://www.freewebs.com/duleekmonument/meathhistory1916.htm

James Russell, Ballymahon, Ashbourne, Co. Meath. He was a member of B Company 4th Battalion, Dublin Brigade in 1916. Mobilised on Monday and engaged in fighting at South Dublin Union. Arrested after the surrender and imprisoned until end of July or August. Source: MSP34REF96281

Matthew Maguire, Brownstown Dunboyne, Co. Meath. He was a member of the Maynooth Company, 3rd Battalion, Meath Brigade in 1916. Source: 34E2145

Back at St. Stephen's Green, under the cover of darkness on that Monday night the British Army took over the Shelbourne Hotel and the United Services Club. Both buildings were four stories high and had good vantage points overlooking St. Stephens Green. The British Army managed to position machine guns on the top floor or roof of both buildings and had them trained over St. Stephen's Green waiting for first light. At dawn the next morning, Tuesday April 25th 1916, Philip Clarke, unaware of the British Army move overnight emerged from his position moving heavy chains which were taken from around St.

Volunteer Philip Clarke from Monknewtown, Slane Co. Meath, Irish Citizen Army. Photo kindly provided by his Grandniece Jean McBee, Greensboro, North Carolina, U.S.A.

Stephen's Green to strengthen a barricade. A short burst of machine gunfire rang out from the roof of the Shelbourne Hotel and he was killed instantly.

The second machine gun opened up from the top of the United Services Club and between them they had the Volunteers at their mercy. Bullets were churning up the soil in the park while the Volunteers clung to the sides of their trenches. Young James Fox panicked and made a dash for it but he was cut to pieces by machine gunfire from the top of the United Services Club. The Volunteers had to retreat and evacuate the Green. One half, including Patrick Bradley took shelter in the Royal College of Surgeons Building while the others including Luke Bradley took shelter in the Jacob's Factory. Luke managed to evade arrest after the surrender and he made his way to Fordstown. See more about Luke Bradley on page 162. Philip Clarke's name is engraved on the family plot headstone in Monknewtown Cemetery, Slane, see page 366 but he was buried in St Brigid's Cemetery Glasnevin. A monument in his honour was erected on Rosin Bridge near his home in Co. Meath in 1937. Young James Fox was buried in Knockmark Cemetery, Drumree, near Dunshaughlin, see

page 288   Source: Presentation by Mr Jim Gilligan on James Fox 1899-1916 at Dunshaughlin Pastrol Centre on 20th April 2015. http://www.independent.ie/regionals/droghedaindependent/localnotes/slane-27165976.html http://irishmedals.org/rebels-killed-in-1916.html Shootout at the Battle of St. Stephens Green by Paul O'Brien. When the Clock Strikes in 1916 by Derek Molyneux & Darren Kelly.

Volunteer James Fox, Drumree, Irish Citizen Army

Meanwhile back in Dunboyne, Sean Boylan and his men observed a British Army troop train arrive at the Railway Station carrying artillery field guns from Athlone and about 500 British Army Cavalry Troops. They observed the train being unloaded and in the afternoon they watched them move in towards the city by road with their field guns. Sean Boylan's scouts eventually made contact with a company of Louth men at the Red House on the Dunshaughlin Road. They brought back a note to Sean Boylan saying that they proposed to go into the city through Finglas and to throw out a screen of scouts there. Boylan and the rest of the men made their way to the Red House. There they found Donal O'Hannigan in charge and he was able to provide some of the unarmed men with rifles and ammunition. Sean McGurl, a Volunteer from Athboy arrived and joined the group. Under the command of O'Hannigan they all moved towards Tyrrelstown House near Blanchardstown. They set up camp there and during their time there O'Hannigan sent out scouts looking for other Volunteers and gathering intelligence. He also sent messengers to General Head Quarters (G.H.Q.) to advise them of their position and to send orders. Gary Byrne arrived at Tyrrelstown House after cycling from Kells. He managed to send a message back to his brother William Byrne in Kells to let him know that he got through, where he was and that he was OK. There was 30 or 40 Volunteers in Tyrrelstown House at this stage. A continuous flow of scouts were in operation and they reported back that the centre of the city was cordoned off by British Forces, there was no way through.

Meanwhile back in Carnaross, a dispatch was delivered to the Farrelly household by Jack Dardis of Kells ordering the Carnaross Company to be prepared to march at short notice. All weapons and rations were prepared and ready to go. In Kells, William Byrne received the message from his brother Gary that he was in Tyrrelstown house and he also set of on his bicycle from Kells that night. Using the same route as his brother he managed to avoid the road blocks as well.

Other Meath men, but not living in Meath at the time and who were mobilised for the Rising on this day Tuesday 25th April were:
Patrick O'Malley, Mointireoin, Ratoath, Co. Meath. Patrick had been a member of the Irish Volunteers and I.R.B. prior to 1916. On Easter Tuesday 25th April while on route to mobilise with Irish Volunteers in the Connemara area of County Galway he was arrested by British forces. He was subsequently interned until December

of that year. He was rearrested in February 1917 and he was deported to England from which he escaped the following May. Source: MSP34REF16495

Michael Commins of Kilgraigue, Dunboyne, Co. Meath was active in Clarinbridge Company, Galway Brigade. He had been mobilised a few times on Easter Sunday and Monday but no further orders arrived. On Tuesday morning he was involved in an attack on Clarenbridge Barracks. Later in the day he was sent scouting towards Aranmore Railway Station where a train of military and police arrived. He fired on the police while they were on the platform. Source: MSP34REF43972

Back at Tyrrelstown House on Wednesday 26th April 1916 William Byrne Drumbaragh Company Commanding Officer arrived also after cycling from Kells. He got involved in setting up defences at the house.

Other Meath men, but not living in Meath at the time and who were mobilised for the Rising on this day Wednesday 26th April were:

William J. Murphy, Brews Hill, Navan. He was working at Atheneum, Enniscorthy, Co. Wexford. Prior to the Rising he was the Manager of the Arms Department of J. O'Donoghue Ltd, through which arms and ammunition were bought. He was mobilised on Wednesday 26th April 1916 and was on duty in the atheneum and was sent to Turrett Rocks on the Thursday where he sniped the R.I.C. barracks. He was posted in the atheneum until the surrender. He was arrested and interned in Frongoch, Wales for fourteen weeks. Source: MSP34REF40121

Back at Tyrrelstown House again on Thursday 27th April 1916 scouts eventually reported back the position of Commandant Tom Ashe and the Fingal Battalion. They were near Ashbourne. See also Gary Byrnes witness statement
http://www.bureauofmilitaryhistory.ie/reels/bmh/BMH.WS0143.pdf

In Kells the Carnaross Company and the Drumbaragh Company received orders which were quietly relayed from Volunteer to Volunteer to reassemble at the Ball Alley crossroads near Sylvan Park within the hour. They were told that they were going to Athboy to link up with German Internees who were to jail break from Oldcastle and they all would be proceeding from there to Dublin City. But before mobilisation could be completed another order came to cancel the mobilisation and to go home again and to be prepared to go at short notice. On Thursday evening the Carnaross Company arranged for the local priest to hear all their confessions. There was a real fear now that if they could get out, some of the men would not come back alive.

On Friday April 28th 1916 there were still no orders from General Head Quarters to the men at Tyrrelstown House but Donal O'Hannigan managed to make arrangements for a meeting with Commandant Thomas Ashe near Ashbourne.

Meanwhile Commandant Thomas Ashe and about 35 Volunteers of the 5th Battalion, Dublin Brigade also known as the Fingal Brigade made their way over the Dublin Meath border to Ashbourne at about 10:30 a.m. Their mission was to hamper British reaction to the Rising by blowing up railway tracks and bridges leading to Dublin. To cut communication lines. To generally draw some military attention away from hard pressed Volunteers in the City and to gather arms where possible. Commandant Thomas Ashe was born in 1885 in Lispole, Co. Kerry. He was the School Principal at Corduff National School in Lusk, Co. Dublin. A tall man with a commanding presence. He was said to be a charismatic public speaker. He became Brigade Commandant shortly before the Rising. He was a member of the I.R.B., the Gaelic League and an accomplished performer on the traditional bagpipes. His second in command on the day was Richard Mulcahy. Mulcahy was born in Waterford in 1886, raised in Co. Tipperary, he worked in the Engineering Department of the post office in Thurles, Bantry, Wexford and Dublin. He was also a member of the I.R.B. and the Gaelic League.

Thomas Ashe photo courtesy of Irish Volunteers http:irishvolunteers.org

They arrived at the R.I.C. barracks at Rath Cross on the Slane side of Ashbourne and Ashe decided that they were going to take the barracks mainly for the weapons and ammunition. They had already successfully taken a couple of smaller R.I.C. barracks on their way there and had secured weapons and ammunition. The Ashbourne R.I.C. Barracks was normally manned by four constables and a Sergeant, but due to the Rising in Dublin, the heightened activities of the Fingal Brigade in the area over the past few days and the likelihood that the barracks would be attacked, reinforcements had been called in from the neighbouring districts of Navan, Dunboyne and Slane to strengthen the barracks. That morning the barracks had a strength of sixteen R.I.C. men and a District Inspector. While still some distance from the barracks the Volunteers broke into columns and some left the road. Leaving a column in reserve, they spread out widely. Using the cover of ditches and hedges they worked their way through the fields until they were able to take up positions surrounding the barracks.

While all of this was going on in Ashbourne the R.I.C. in Navan, Kells, Slane and surrounding areas were organising to travel to Ashbourne to further reinforce and defend the barracks there. County Police Inspector Alexander Gray and District Police Inspector Harry Smyth had knowledge that a group of Volunteers were operating in the Ashbourne area and that an attack on the Ashbourne R.I.C. Barracks was imminent. County Inspector Alexander Gray was aged 57 and he had been serving with the R.I.C. for over 33 years. Harry Smyth was an ex-British Army man aged 41 years. He was from Baldock in Hertfordshire. He had served with the R.I.C. for more than sixteen years and he was based in Navan R.I.C. Barracks for the past five years. The R.I.C. Police Inspectors had acquired cars from local "well to do" people. One of the cars, a model "T" Ford belonged to Spicers of Navan and the driver was R.I.C. Constable Eugene Bratton from Navan. Bratton was in plain clothes that day and unknown to the R.I.C. he regularly supplied information to the Irish Volunteers. Another car that the R.I.C.

A typical Model T Ford

had that day belonged to the Marchioness of Conyngham who lived in Slane Castle. Only a few months previously she was announcing her support for the Volunteers. Now her concern was that the Volunteers might arrive in Slane and maybe burn the Castle down. So when the R.I.C. asked for her car to confront the rebels she gladly gave it along with her chauffeur Mr. Keating to drive it. No one really knew the strength of the rebels at the time. Information was scarce and rumours were circulating like wildfire. County Police Inspector Gray and District Police Inspector Smith assembled sixty R.I.C. men armed with rifles in Slane that morning. They then set off in a convoy of about 17 or 18 cars in the direction of Ashbourne with R.I.C. Sergeant Shanaher from Navan travelling in one of the cars near the front of the convoy and District Police Inspector Smith travelling at the rear of the convoy in Spicers model "T" Ford driven by R.I.C. Constable Eugene Bratton.

Meanwhile back in Ashbourne the Volunteers under the command of Commandant Thomas Ashe and Richard Mulcahy had surrounded Ashbourne R.I.C. Barracks. Ashe shouted to the R.I.C. men inside the barracks to lay down their weapons and to surrender, which was answered with a volley of shots from within the barracks. The Volunteers opened fire and the gun battle continued for about a half hour. Volunteer Jerry Golden threw a homemade explosive device at one of the lower windows which was protected by a steel shutter. Although the device did not explode inside the barracks, the noise of the blast frightened the occupants. Waving a white handkerchief, the R.I.C. men were heard shouting that they would be killed and that they wanted to surrender.

Almost at exactly the same time the convoy of 17 or 18 cars arrived from Slane and immediately came under fire from a couple of Volunteers who were manning Rath Cross a short distance from the R.I.C. barracks. This alerted the Volunteers at the barracks who then saw the convoy of cars coming from Slane. R.I.C. Sergeant John Shanaher from Navan, in one of the leading cars, was shot dead immediately. He was aged 48 and been with the force for over 25 years. The R.I.C. men took cover behind their cars and returned fire. R.I.C. Constable Eugene Bratton who was driving the last car in the convoy managed to see what was happening up at the front of the convoy. He alerted District Police Inspector Smith and he abandoned Spicer's car in time to avoid being shot and he ran back in the direction of Kilmoon. He was in civilian clothes so Volunteers who had the road covered let him pass. He got a bicycle from a house and cycled to Balrath Barracks where he phoned Navan and Drogheda R.I.C. Barracks and told them what was happening.

Back at Ashbourne Barracks, the Volunteers were outnumbered now due to the arrival of the sixty R.I.C. men from Slane. The gun battle raged for a further five hours in which John Crennigan, aged 21 from the Irish Volunteers Fingal Brigade was shot dead by District Inspector Harry Smyth from Navan. At first the Irish Volunteers were under pressure and almost going to retreat but with some smart thinking and out manoeuvring by Richard Mulcahy, Thomas Ashe and the Volunteers they slowly turned the tide. They got the upper hand by positioning a small number of Volunteers where they could keep the R.I.C. on the road pinned down while a larger group of Volunteers using the dykes, drains and ditches managed to outflank the R.I.C. convoy. On realising that their numerical advantage was being eroded by guerrilla strategy some of the R.I.C. men panicked and broke away isolating themselves from the rest of the force and were picked off by Volunteer fire. These small groups then found themselves with no option but to surrender and hand over their weapons. R.I.C. resistance began to crumble and more began to panic. As District Police Inspector Harry Smyth was shouting orders to his men and telling them to keep up the fight he was shot dead by Volunteer Frank Lawless. That ended the battle and the R.I.C. men surrendered. Smith was aged 41 and had been with the force for over 16 years.
The R.I.C. men suffered eight deaths including County Inspector Alexander Gray and District Inspector Harry Smyth and fifteen wounded while the Volunteers

suffered two deaths and five wounded. The dead Volunteers were John
Crinnegan aged 21 from Swords and Thomas Rafferty aged 22 from Lusk.
The R.I.C. men killed and wounded were:
Connelly, Patrick, Constable, wounded, aged 30.
Cunningham, Patrick, Constable, Lismullen, wounded, age 30.
Cleary, James, Constable, Moynalty, killed, aged 23.
Drinan, Patrick, Constable, wounded, aged 26.
Duggan, Michael J., Constable, Crossakiel, wounded, age 19.
Finan, Tim, Constable, wounded, aged 28.
Glennon, Francis P., Constable, wounded age 37.
Gormley, James, Const., killed, aged 25, buried in Navan, see page 348.
Gray, Alexander, County Inspector, killed, age 57.
Hickey, James, Const., Kells, killed, aged 49, buried in Navan, see page 348.
Kenny, Francis, Constable, Athboy, wounded, aged 23.
Johns, William E., Constable, wounded, aged 20. See also page 49.
Leckey, Henry, Constable, Oldcastle, wounded, aged 36.
McGann, Henry, Constable, Oldcastle, wounded & permanently disabled, aged 23.
McHale, Richard, Const., killed, aged 22, buried in Navan, see page 348.
McKeon, Patrick, Constable, wounded, aged 24.
Mulvihill, Martin, Constable, wounded, aged 31.
Murphy John, Constable, wounded, aged 26.
Murtagh, Peter, Constable, wounded, aged 41.
Scully, Patrick J., Sergeant, wounded, aged 48.
Shanaghan, John, Sergeant, killed, aged 48.
Smyth, Harry, District Inspector, killed, age 41, buried in Ardbraccan see page 315.
Young, John, Sergeant, killed, aged 42, buried in Navan, see page 348.
Four civilians were also killed, two of them were driving cars in the R.I.C. Convoy,
one of which was Mr. Keating, the Marchioness of Conyngham's chauffeur. The
other two civilians killed were unfortunately just passing through the area at the
wrong time. All weapons and ammunition were gathered up by the Volunteers
which amounted to 96 Rifles and ammunition. Their R.I.C. prisoners were told
never to take up weapons against the Irish Republic again and they were released.
R.I.C. Constable Eugene Bratton who had evaded the battle and had gone to
Balrath Barracks to get help cycled back to the scene at Ashbourne. With
permission from Commandant Thomas Ashe he put the body of District Police
Inspector Harry Smith into Spicers model "T" Ford and drove it to back to the
Inspector's house outside Navan where he handed the body over to his wife.
Later Bratton was awarded The King's Police Medal "in recognition of his
conspicuous gallantry during the Irish rebellion." The bodies of the two
Volunteers were taken away by the Volunteers. With the help of locals, the R.I.C.

men gathered up the bodies of the eight R.I.C. men using a horse and cart. Their bodies were placed in the wash-house at the end of the barracks for the night. The R.I.C. men then hobbled back to Navan in whatever vehicles were still fit to drive where their injuries were treated in the County Infirmary, Navan. The following day coffins arrived at the Ashbourne Barracks. The bodies were put into the coffins and they were taken away in a lorry. R.I.C Sergeant William O'Connell was also later awarded The King's Police Medal "in recognition of his conspicuous gallantry during the Irish Rebellion"

Later, a Civil Action was taken by the chauffeur's wife, Mrs. Sarah Keating against the Marchioness of Conyngham. Mrs. Keating took the action under the Workman's Act claiming that her husband was employed by the Marchioness of Conyngham as a motor car driver and during the course of that work he was killed leaving his wife and two children. The court in Slane found in favour of the widow and she was awarded £300. The Judge directed that £150 be paid to Mrs. Keating directly and £150 to be invested in the war loan for the children until they become of age. Sources: Bureau of Military History, 1913- 21, Witness Statement No 904 on 23rd November 1953, Witness: John Austin, Ashbourne, Co. Meath. Eye-witness of Battle of Ashbourne, 28th April, 1916.
http://www.freewebs.com/duleekmonument/meathhistory1916.htm
http://www.militaryheritage.ie/news/special_folder/The_Fingal_Battalion.pdf
http://www.bureauofmilitaryhistory.ie/reels/bmh/BMH.WS0904.pdf http://thecricketbatthatdiedforireland.com/2013/04/17/bicycle-pump-the-battle-of-ashbourne-1916/ Sinn Fein Rebellion handbook, Easter, 1916 published by the Irish Times.
http://irishconstabulary.com/topic/1260/Easter-Monday-1916#.VPMgPvmsVzI Faithful to Ireland, North Meath F.C.A. and its Origins by Tony Brady. "The Battle of Ashbourne" presentation by the Ashbourne Historical Society in Dunshaughlin Library on 26th February 2015.

On the same day 28th April things were not going so good for the Volunteers in

Lieutenant THOMAS ALLEN
"C" Coy., 1st Battalion. Irish Volunteers.

Shot in Action at Four Courts,

April 28th, 1916.

Dublin City. Lieutenant Thomás Allen, mentioned on page 19, was defending the West wing of the Four Courts when he was shot in the chest by a British Army sniper or machine gunner. He died shortly afterwards in the Richmond Hospital.

He was initially buried in Glasnevin Cemetery but on 6th January 1917 he was removed to Kilglass Graveyard, Longwood, County Meath where the remains were interred in his native parish of Moyvalley, Longwood near the Hill of Down, see page 378.

Sources: the National Library of Ireland 1916 online exhibition (O'Mahony Album).
https://broadsidesdotme.wordpress.com/2012/04/25/357/ on 28th June 2015. Thomás Allen Meath 1916 Society
www.facebook.com/Meath1916Society
http://www.irishmedals.org/rebels-killed-in-1916.html
A 1916 commemorative postcard for Lieutenant Thomas Allen.

Extract from the National Library of Ireland 1916 online exhibition (O'Mahony Album) and also https://broadsidesdotme.wordpress.com/2012/04/25/357/ on 28th June 2015.

Back in Ashbourne the following day, Saturday April 29th 1916, Ashe and his men were at Newbarn, Ashbourne near Kilsallaghen. Three police officers in plain clothes approached in a car flying a white flag of truce. They asked I.R.A. sentry guards to take them to see Ashe where they handed him a letter from Pearse ordering him to surrender. Ashe could not believe it and he wanted to verify it. Arrangements were made between Ashe and the police to provide safe passage for Richard Mulcahy to go to Dublin and see Pearse. He returned and confirmed that the surrender had taken place. Ashe demobilised the Battalion and sent the Volunteers home. Ashe was arrested, tried by court-martial and sentenced to death. The sentence was commuted to penal servitude for life.

Sources: Irish Independent dated 9th April 1966, page 5.

Richard (Dick) Mulcahy was also arrested and interned in Knutsford and at Frongoch Camp in Wales. When he was released in December 1916 he took the Pro-Treaty side. He became Commanding Officer of the Dublin Brigade, Irish Volunteers. Dick Mulcahy's career continues on page 36.

Late on Saturday night April 29th 1916 word reached Tyrrelstown House that the 1st Battalion under the command of Edward Daly from Limerick had surrendered in Dublin that day. On Sunday morning April 30th all arms at Tyrrelstown House were oiled and buried locally and some Volunteers dispersed across country.

On Monday May 1st 1916 the rest of the Volunteers at Tyrrelstown House dispersed across country, Gary and William Byrne cycled back to Kells. On Tuesday May 2nd 1916 Sean Boylan arrived home from Tyrrelstown House and was arrested along with his brothers Ned, Joe, Peter and Christy Lynam. They were taken to Richmond Barracks and locked in the gym.

In November / December 1951 in a letter to the Military Pension Board Sean Boylan listed the names of men who occupied Tyrrelstown House during the 1916 Rising:

Dublin / Drumbaragh Company: Byrne Gary.

Dunboyne Company: Byrne Peter, Boylan Peter, Boylan Sean, Crean Aidan, Farrell Frank, Farrell Hugh, Keating James, King Owen, Lowndes Frank, Lynam Christopher, Madden Dan, Maguire James, Mullally James, Mullally Patrick and Newman Peter.

Carnaross Company: Byrne William.

Athboy Company: McGurl Sean.

On May 3rd 1916: Execution of Thomas Clarke, aged 59. Treasurer and Supreme Council member of the I.R.B.

Execution of Thomas MacDonagh, aged 38. Irish Volunteers Director of Training and Commander of 2nd Battalion and a member of the I.R.B.

Execution of Pádraig Pearse, aged 37. Founder Member of the Irish Volunteers. Commander in Chief of the Irish Forces during the Easter Rising.

On May 4th 1916: Execution of Joseph Plunkett, aged 29. A member of the I.R.B. and the Irish Volunteers. Director of Military Operations.

Execution of Edward Daly, aged 25, Irish Volunteers 1st Battalion Commanding Officer.

Execution of Michael O'Hanrahan, aged 39. A member of the Irish Volunteers.

Execution of William Pearse, (brother of Pádraig), aged 35. A member of Irish Volunteers.

The prisoners at Richmond Barracks were paraded in the barracks square. They were marched to the North Wall and loaded on a cattle boat. They sailed to Holyhead where they were loaded on a train and taken to Wandsworth Prison, London where they were treated very badly. They were later sent to internment camps in Scotland and England.

On May 8th 1916: Execution of Eamonn Ceannt, aged 59. Founder member of the Irish Volunteers, 4th Battalion Commanding Officer.

Execution of Con Colbert, aged 28. Irish Volunteers, Company Commanding Officer, F Company, 4th Battalion.

Execution of Sean Heuston, aged 25. Leader of a section of the 1st Battalion during the Easter Rising.

Execution of Michael Mallon, aged 42. Irish Citizen Army Chief of Staff.

On May 9th 1916: Execution of Thomas Kent, aged 51. Executed in Cork. A member of the Irish Volunteers.

On May 12th 1916: Execution of Sean MacDiarmada, aged 32. A member of the I.R.B. and the Irish Volunteers.

Execution of James Connelly, aged 48. Commandant-General of the Dublin Forces during the Easter Rising. A founder of the Irish Citizen Army.

On August 3rd 1916: Roger Casement who attempted to land the shipment of Arms in Ireland was hanged in England, aged 52. A member of the Irish Volunteers.

The 1st battle in the War of Independence had been lost, but the war was not over.

Why didn't more Volunteers mobilise in Meath and elsewhere for the Rising?

1. Communications:

    Obviously there was huge confusion amongst the Irish Volunteers when McNeill countermanded the orders to mobilise on Easter Sunday. That problem was compounded by the fact that communication at the time were poor and the Irish Volunteers had to rely on verbal communications and dispatch riders to communicate day to day operations. That system is reasonably effective in an urban environment where there is a high density of people who regularly see each other and large numbers of people can be contacted by a short journey of a dispatch rider. That system is much slower in the rural setting where a Volunteer's nearest neighbour can be miles away. And a dispatch rider might travel a half day only to alert a very small group of Volunteers.

2. Weapons:

    Remember that at the time the British had one of the largest Empires in the world. The Irish Volunteers had little or no weapons to take on a professional well armed British Army. What were they supposed to fight with? It was absolutely necessary that they landed Roger Casement's weapons in Ireland and that the weapons got into the hands of the Volunteers to have any chance. Volunteers and officers saw in the newspapers that Roger Casement's shipment of arms was lost. If they saw that, they would have seen the order from McNeill not to go out on Easter Sunday. The individual Volunteer was not a fool, he was not going on a suicide mission. He simply complied with the order not to mobilise.

3. Live to Fight another day:

    When the shipment of guns from Germany were lost and McNeill countermanded the order to mobilise, the Leaders knew then that this was a failed Rising before it even started. At this stage they knew and accepted their fate, that they would be executed. They were not anxious to die and I am sure they wanted to win, but I believe they decided to spare as many Volunteers as possible and to become martyrs themselves to inspire future Volunteers to finish their work to achieve an Irish Republic.

Chapter 4
1917, 1918, 1919 and 1920

Immediately after the Easter Rising the majority of the citizens of Ireland were not at all in favour of the Irish Volunteers. They held the view that the Irish Volunteers were responsible for the deaths of all civilians and the destruction of Dublin City. Morale was very low within the Volunteers. Then the execution of the leaders of the Rising aroused the feelings of the public all over the country as well as those of the Volunteers. As the executions occurred the majority of the public changed their opinion about the Volunteers. They were disgusted, particularly with the execution of James Connelly who was so badly wounded that he had to be put sitting in a chair to be executed. For months after the failed rising the ordinary Irish Volunteer in Meath did not know what had happened. Why they were not all mobilised or why the Rebellion was such a failure. The officers who did know were either dead or in English jails. Volunteers lost the fighting spirit and determination. They made little effort to re-engage, they did not see the point of it anymore. They had done all that was asked of them. When they were mobilised for the Rising they thought this is it, this would be their chance to hit back. But then the bitter disappointment came and continued to hang over them for a long time, in fact some would say they never got over it. The surviving officers made efforts to re-motivate, reorganize and lift the spirits of Volunteers. Sometimes this was done in the form of Irish Language classes and Irish Dance classes. Officers who tried to talk to the men were met with resentment. In Co. Meath as probably elsewhere, the Volunteers displayed very little interest or enthusiasm at these meetings. Some Meath Volunteers expressed their anger. Meetings were vocal and participants were slow to put their names forward or to participate in a meaningful manner. But the change of public opinion in favour of the Irish Volunteers in Ireland continued to grow and was felt by the British Government. As a result, they carried out a general release of all 1916 prisoners which commenced in December 1916 and continued for the first half of 1918. This changed everything. Eamon De Valera was seen as the hero who was going to lead the Volunteers home from the English and Scottish prisons. The huge change in public opinion to the Irish Volunteers could be felt everywhere. There was no more sneering at them, they were seen as heroes who stood up for what they believed in. The Volunteers felt that the mystery of the failed Rising might be unveiled at last. Meath's Sean Boylan would be back soon. The dark cloud of depression lifted, the air was filled with enthusiasm. The Volunteers suddenly could see that they needed to pick themselves up, regroup, reorganize and generally put foundations in place in preparation for the release of the prisoners. New recruits started coming in as well, many of them through

G.A.A. circles. Prisoners eventually returned home to a hero's welcome, a far cry to when they went in.

On September 25th 1917 Thomas Ashe, who led the attack on Ashbourne R.I.C. Barracks (see chapter 3) died as a result of forcible feeding while he was on hunger strike in Mountjoy Prison.

Irish Volunteers fire a volley at the funeral of Thomas Ashe. Photo courtesy of the Irish Volunteers http:irishvolunteers.org

Sean Boylan, the Brigade Commanding Officer issued an order prohibiting the holding of fairs as a mark of respect. The next day a fair that was planned to be held in Mullagh was stopped by the Moynalty Company of Irish Volunteers.

At a subsequent inquest into the death of Thomas Ashe, the jury condemned the staff at the prison for the "inhuman and dangerous operation performed on the prisoner, and other acts of unfeeling and barbaric conduct." Source: O'Connor, Ulick (2001). *Michael Collins and the Troubles*. Mainstream Publishing. p. 124. ISBN 1-84018-427-2. Bureau of Military History, 1913- 21, Witness Statement No WS1625 on 4th June 1957, Witness: Michael Govern, Clooney, Moynalty, Kells, Co. Meath. Quartermaster, Kells Battalion, 3rd Brigade.

In the spring of 1918 conscription was introduced in England and the British Government decided to apply it to Ireland as well. This would mean that young men would be forced to join the British Army and to fight in World War 1. The ordinary man who did not want to be involved in Irish politics found himself in a position where he would be likely to be shot at the front line of a war in a foreign country and if he survived that he could be shot when he came home for wearing a British uniform. I guess the better of two evils was to join the Irish Volunteers. The effect on the Irish Volunteers in Meath as elsewhere was that there was a sudden rush of people wanting to join up. This caused some disorganisation as un-disciplined Volunteers joined the ranks but this was quickly corrected with more drilling and training of the new recruits. When the conscription scare subsided most of these new recruits left the Volunteers as quickly as they appeared. There were of course exceptions to that rule.

By this time Larry Clarkes at No 13 Brews Hill, Navan had now become the Volunteers Battalion Head Quarters. At least one meeting per week was held there and in many cases two meetings per week. Dispatches came into the house from Dublin Volunteers H.Q. and Annie Clarke looked after them. Weekly she delivered messages to Pádraig DeBurca in Kells School, see Carnaross Company. Clarkes took in men "on the run" for weeks at a time and looked after them. Source: MSPCFN: MSP34REF60242

The Meath Volunteers supported Sinn Fein candidates by providing policing and defensive services during canvassing, at electoral public speeches and appearances at electoral rallies. Consequently in the by-election in Cavan in June 1918 the Meath Volunteers played an important role in ensuring that Arthur Griffith of Sinn Fein won his seat, see more about these events in chapter 6.

In August 1918 a strike by farm labourers was in force for a few months. Word reached the Navan Volunteers that Pro-British Farmers had requested additional British Troops to be sent to Meath to protect farmers' interests. This was discussed at a Brigade Committee Meeting in Larry Clarkes in Brews Hill, Navan. A contingent of British Military were supposed to arrive in Navan by train on a specific date. The night before the expected arrival a column of Volunteers were selected, three from Navan Battalion, four from Trim and five from Athboy Battalion to remove a section of the railway track near Beauparc, Navan. The section of track selected was on a bend where the track was about twelve feet higher than the surrounding ground. A train with empty wagons came along, was derailed and wrecked. The driver and train officials were slightly injured. The contingent of British Military did not arrive.

Source: Bureau of Military History, 1913- 21, Witness Statement No 901 on 7th November 1953, Witness: Seamus Finn, Athboy, Co. Meath. Adjutant, Meath Brigade, Vice Commanding Officer & Director of Training, 1st Eastern Division, I.R.A.

In November 1918 World War 1 ended. The naive young boys who joined the British Army four years earlier and had survived the Great War were coming home experienced, battle hardened and wiser men. They were viewed upon with suspicion by Volunteers and their supporters. The majority of them stayed out of the conflict in Ireland and worked their way into civilian life without any problems. However, some continued to support the British Army or to serve with the British Army making them enemy soldiers in their own towns. Others joined the Irish Volunteers and were able to set up training regimes similar to British Army training. They were able to pass on their knowledge about weapons and tactics. They provided great service and received promotion within the ranks of the Irish Volunteers. This training, advice and leadership stood to the Irish Volunteers in future years.

In December 1918 Sinn Fein won the General Election in the South of Ireland. They refused to take their seats in the British Parliament and instead they set up the 1st Dail Eireann and declared Ireland an Independent state. Richard (Dick) Mulcahy (one of the leaders of the attack on Ashbourne R.I.C. Barracks mentioned in Chapter 3) was appointed Minister of Defence taking control of the Irish Volunteers. Sources: http://www.1916rising.com/pic_timeline.html

A few weeks later in January 1919 the 1st Dail assembled in Dublin. Richard (Dick) Mulcahy renamed the Irish Volunteers the Irish Republican Army (I.R.A.). Oaths of Allegiance to the Irish Republic were taken by all I.R.A. Volunteers and officers. Dick Mulcahy became the I.R.A. Chief of Staff.

Source: Sean Boylan's witness statement No 1715 on 16/12/1957.

The 21st January 1919 became the start date of the Irish War of Independence when the I.R.A. began attacks on British Army and R.I.C. all over Ireland. The U.V.F. took up arms along with the British Army and R.I.C. in the North of Ireland for what they saw as the defence of British Territory. Meath was not really affected until September 1919 when the British Government outlawed Dail Eireann and Sinn Fein and a series of police raids at the homes of Sinn Fein and I.R.A. Volunteers began. The War of Independence intensified. Black and Tans and Auxiliaries were sent over from England to support the R.I.C.

R.I.C. barracks dotted around the rural communities were a hindrance to Volunteers training and activities. There were R.I.C. barracks in Ballivor, Lismullen, Moynalty, Trim, George's Cross, Longwood, and Robinstown. The R.I.C. were able to gather local intelligence from these barracks and feed it to their General Head Quarters (G.H.Q.) where an overall intelligence picture could be formed. The barracks were also a means of communication for the R.I.C. A message could be relayed or distributed to several barracks quickly by carrying it a short distances to the neighbouring barracks. These lines of communication stretched all over the country carrying information and messages to and from their General Head Quarters in Dublin. At the end of 1919 orders came from the I.R.A. Head Quarters for all companies to focus on attacks and closures of all rural R.I.C. barracks. These attacks increased in early 1920 and were fairly successful which fired up the Volunteers to continue. However, in some instances planned attacks were aborted at the last moments due to signs or local word that Crown Forces were waiting for them. It was suspected that these events were more than coincidence, that there were informers around. Were the informers within the ranks of the Volunteers? These regular late cancellations of attacks did disappoint and annoy Volunteers. However in hindsight a cancellation was for their own good. Better to live and fight another day.

On 31st October 1919 **Ballivor R.I.C. Barracks** was attacked. In response to a knock on the door R.I.C. Constable William Agar opened the barracks door and then realising his error tried to stop the I.R.A. getting in. In the struggle he was shot dead and another R.I.C. man was wounded. This marked the first real casualty of the War of Independence in County Meath. The I.R.A. captured the barracks and they seized weapons and ammunition during the operation. The Bishop of Meath put the curse of God on the perpetrator who shot an R.I.C. constable in Ballivor. Agar was aged 35 and was survived by his widow and nine year old daughter. He was buried at St. Mary's Church, Rathvilly, Co. Carlow. This attack in particular focused minds on how vulnerable the R.I.C. were to attacks of this nature. The I.R.A. men alleged to have been involved in the attack were:

From Trim Company: Paddy Mooney, Paddy Fay, Harry O'Hagan, Joe Lawlor, Mick Giles, John Mooney, P. Duignan, Paddy Lawlor, Joe Kelly, Stephen Sherry.

From Longwood Company: Pat Giles, Larry Giles, M. Fagan and McEvoy.

Source: http://archiver.rootsweb.ancestry.com/th/read/IRL-CARLOW/2012-10/1351522310

On 2nd November 1919 there was a failed attack on **Lismullen R.I.C. Barracks** also

known as Dillon's Bridge. Prior reconnaissance of the barracks was done by Annie Clarke from Brew's Hill Navan by gathering information from friends and neighbours living near the barracks and by taking notes while cycling near the barracks on a few occasions. Annie was not an affiliated member of the Navan I.R.A. Company but she was a prominent member of Cumann na mBan. During the actual attack on Lismullen R.I.C. Barracks there was an exchange of gunfire in which R.I.C. Sergeant Matthews was severely wounded in the head and lost an eye. The I.R.A. did not succeed in taking the barracks and they did not seize any weapons during the operation. But the R.I.C., realised how vulnerable they were, abandoned the barracks shortly

Annie Clarke
Photo kindly provided by her granddaughter Teresa Clarke

afterwards and moved to the safety of the larger towns. The I.R.A. Volunteers alleged to have been involved in the attack were:

From Navan Company: Joe Bailey, John Boland, Annie Clarke (nee Grace), Pat Fitzsimons, Tom Gavigan, Michael Gaynor, James German, James Hilliard, Patrick Keating, Thomas Kinsella, Matt Loughran, Pat Loughran, William Lougheran, James Lynch, James Mackey, Michael McKeown and Joseph Woods.

From Commons Company: Patsy Bennett, Patrick Boyle, James Byrne, Richard Byrne, Michael Hyland, Loughlin O'Rourke,

Paddy Stapleton, Thomas Walsh and Pat Waters,

From Johnstown Company: James Boylan and other un-named Volunteers.

From Bective, Kiltale & Dunderry Companies: Several un-named Volunteers blocked the roads in their areas to delay arrival of support to the R.I.C. barracks. A planned attack on **Summerhill R.I.C. Barracks** did not take place because the timing of the plan just did not come together on the night. The I.R.A. men alleged to have been involved in the planned attack were:

From Summerhill Company: Michael Grehan, Peter Dolan, Patrick Grogan and Edward Kearney

Dunboyne Company: Several un-named Volunteers.

Likewise a planned attack on **Bohermeen R.I.C. Barracks** did not take place because the timing of the plan just did not come together on the night. The I.R.A. men alleged to have been involved in the planned attack were:

From Delvin Company: Commandant M. Fox, Captain James Kiernan, James Bray, Captain W Doyle, Lieutenant James Doyle, James Ward, L. Sherlock.

From Athboy Company: Pat Murray, Peter Reilly, Thomas Martin, P. Carey, Seamus Finn, Captain J. Martin and B McConnell.

The attack on **Bohermeen Barracks** was rescheduled but the R.I.C. had evacuated the building before it took place. Local Volunteers burned the barracks to prevent the R.I.C. returning.

Sources: Bureau of Military History, 1913- 21, Witness Statement No 901 on 7th November 1953, Witness: Seamus Finn, Athboy, Co. Meath. Adjutant, Meath Brigade, Vice Commanding Officer & Director of Training, 1st Eastern Division, I.R.A. WS1723. Freeman's Journal, 3rd N o v 1919. Dunderry A Folk History by Dunderry Historical Group & Johnny Keely.

George's Cross R.I.C. Barracks built in 1840 by Arthur Hill Cornwallis Pollock of Mountainstown House. Photographed here with kind permission of the current proud owner, Alan Myler.

Almost all rural R.I.C. barracks were evacuated by Easter Sunday 4th April 1920 due to attacks and R.I.C. men had moved to the safety of bigger towns. There was a plan drawn up for an attack on **Georges Cross** but the R.I.C. evacuated the barracks before the attack. At an I.R.A. Brigade Council Meeting at John Newman's (see Bohermeen Company) a list of all evacuated R.I.C. barracks in Meath was compiled and orders were issued for all of them to be burnt down to ensure the R.I.C. did not return. This order was carried out Easter Week 1920.
On May 12th 1920 **Moynalty R.I.C. Barracks** and **Mullagh R.I.C. Barracks** were burned down by local Volunteers on the same night. Source: WS1650
On May 23rd 1920 the **Drumconrath R.I.C. Barracks** was burned with assistance from Moynalty I.R.A. Company. Source: WS1650.
In July 1920 the R.I.C. abandoned the **Crossakiel Barracks, the Carnaross Barracks and the Stirrupstown Barracks.** Source: Bureau of Military History, 1913- 21, Witness Statement No W.S. 1615 on 16th May 1957, Witness: Seán Keogh, Smithstown, Ballinlough, Kells, Co. Meath. Commanding Officer 5th Battalion, Meath Brigade
Duleek and Kilmoon R.I.C. Barracks were also burned around this time. About Mid-November 1920 **Lismullen or Dillon's Bridge R.I.C. Barracks** and **Robinstown R.I.C. Barracks** were burned by local Volunteers.
Now, apart from the bigger towns, there were only two rural R.I.C. barracks left, one at Longwood and one at Crossakiel. Defences of these and town R.I.C. barracks were increased with barricades and barbed wire.

In the spring of 1920 a large number of I.R.A. prisoners went on hunger strike in Mountjoy demanding special political status. They received huge support from the general public. On the 13th / 14th April a general strike closed shops and businesses. Trains and buses did not run. School were closed and public meetings were held to support the prisoners. As a result about 70 prisoners were released amongst them were three Volunteers from Co. Meath:
Frank Loughran, see Bective and Kilmessan Company.
Patrick Clynch, see Navan Company.
John Mangan, see Bective and Kilmessan Company.

It was in 1920 that training in the art of manufacturing mines and grenades and in the handling of explosives began.
It was also in early 1920 that, in the absence of the R.I.C., a lawless trend emerged in many areas. Numbers of burglaries and robberies increased. Locals were frightened. Crime became a big problem. The already stretched I.R.A. companies now had to deal with Community Policing and Justice issues and the administration of law and order. They had so much to deal with I had to give it a Chapter of its own, see Chapter 6, Policing and Justice.
In May 1920 all I.R.A. companies in Meath were formed into Battalions. Source: WS1659

In August or September 1920 the I.R.A. General Head Quarters (G.H.Q.) issued orders to all companies to gather up all available guns and ammunition from private owners in their areas. In most cases the local people handed over the guns and ammunitions without any question or hesitation but in some cases they did not and they had to be taken by force. Source: Bureau of Military History, 1913- 21, Witness Statement No W.S. 1539 on 4th December 1956, Witness: David Hall, Knutstown, Garristown, Co. Dublin. Officer Commanding 1st Brigade, 1st Eastern Division, I.R.A.

In September 1920 the I.R.A. in Cork and other Counties were coming under serious pressure from Crown Forces. I.R.A. G.H.Q. issued orders to Sean Boylan to initiate attacks from Meath Battalions on Crown Force targets in Meath. The general idea was to draw some British Crown Forces away from other hard pressed parts of the country as they were severely impacting on I.R.A. activity. Sean Boylan arranged a Special Battalion Council Meeting to be held in Carnaross. Those who attended the meeting were:

Meath Brigade Commanding Officer Sean Boylan, see Dunboyne Company.
Moynalty Company Commanding Officer - Paddy O'Reilly, see Moynalty Company.
1st Battalion Intelligence Officer - Patrick Clinton, see Dunboyne Company.
4th Battalion Commanding Officer – Patrick Farrelly, see Carnaross Company.
4th Battalion Vice commanding Officer - Tommy O'Reilly, Mullagh.
5th Battalion Commanding Officer -Tom Manning, see Ballinlough Company.
5th Battalion Adjutant - Peter O'Higgins, see Ballinlough Company.
5th Battalion Quartermaster – Barney Harte, see Ballinlough Company.

Sean Boylan said that ambushes of enemy forces would have to commence in all Battalion Areas and that plans were to be drawn up immediately. 1st Battalion and 4th Battalion representatives agreed to commence planning but 5th Battalion representative Tom Manning opposed the idea. He said that they had insufficient weapons or ammunition to deal with the likely reprisals from Crown Forces. Tom Manning was supported by Peter O'Higgins and Barney Harte. Sean Boylan got very annoyed by this and he had the three men court-martialed on a charge of Mutiny. The following day Tom Manning was removed from his post, reduced in rank and he was replaced by David Smyth, Mullagh as 5th Battalion Commanding Officer. Peter O'Higgins was removed from his post and replaced by Peter O'Connell (see Stonefield Company) as the 5th Battalion Adjutant. Barney Harte was also reduced in Rank and all three men were sentenced to two lashes of a horse-whip each. At the same time Matt Tevlin, see Carnaross Company, was appointed 2nd Battalion Engineer.

On 30th September 1920 the I.R.A. Brigade Quartermaster Michael (Mick) Hynes of Tullyard (see Trim Company) managed to recruit an R.I.C. man named Constable Patrick Meehan from Trim R.I.C. Barracks. He was a native of Co. Clare and he had been in the R.I.C. for about ten years. He provided Mick Hynes with valuable information including sketches of the layout of the inside of the barracks. A week of surveillance was put in place with numbers and movements of police in and around the barracks noted. The I.R.A. carried out a co-ordinated attack in which they set the R.I.C. barracks on fire. During the operation the R.I.C. Head

Constable White was seriously wounded when he was shot through the lung. The I.R.A. saw to it that he received medical attention and he was attended to by Dr. T.J. Lynch who had him removed to the Hospital section of the local Workhouse. One I.R.A. Volunteer had his face and hands burned when a container of petrol exploded as he was setting fire to the barracks. The I.R.A. seized twenty rifles and carbines, twenty shotguns, six revolvers, a box of grenades, bayonets and ammunition during the attack. At the moment that the attack begun all available I.R.A. Volunteers in surrounding districts blocked all roads to Trim with felled trees. It took seven hours for the authorities to clear the trees and to come to the aid of the Trim R.I.C. Barracks by which time it had burned to the ground. The success of the attack was soon overshadowed when reinforcement troops including drunken Black and Tans descended on the town of Trim firing shots indiscriminately, burning homes, shops and businesses, plundering, looting and destroying everything in their wake. There were savage scenes of brutality as they generally terrorised the townspeople. 25% of the town was burned that night. These acts frightened everyone but opinions of the townspeople was divided. Some people venting their anger on the I.R.A. Their view was that these awful scenes would not have happened if the I.R.A. did not attack the R.I.C. barracks. Others vented their anger on the British Forces and either joined the Volunteers or helped the Volunteers in any way they could. For a more detailed account of the attack I would recommend that you read Politics and War in Meath 1913-23 by Oliver Coogan or Witness Statements from the Irish Bureau of Military History which are available online free of charge. The I.R.A. Volunteers and officers allegedly involved in the attack were:

Athboy Company: Willie Doyle.

Ballinlough Company: Nick Gaynor.

Bective & Kilmessan Company: Michael Brady, Christopher Caffrey, John Mangan, Jack O'Brien, James Quinn, Patrick Quinn and Christopher Reid.

Dunboyne Company: Sean Boylan, Frank Carolan, Bernard Dunne, Kit Lynam, James Maguire, Nicholas Moran and Mary Connell.

Kells Company: Bob Mullen, and several unnamed Volunteers knocked trees to cut off roads to Trim.

Kilcloon Company: Michael Phoenix.

Kildalkey Company: Patrick McGurl, and several unnamed Volunteers knocked trees to cut off roads to Trim.

Longwood Company: Larry Giles, Pat Giles and several unnamed Volunteers who knocked trees to cut off roads to Trim.

Navan Company: James Byrne, Patrick Keating, Mick Hilliard and several
                        unnamed Volunteers who knocked trees to cut off roads to
                        Trim.

Trim Company: Christopher Andrews, Matthew Andrews, Phil Doggett,
                        Patrick Duigenan, Patrick Fay, Mick Giles, John Healy,
                        Mick Hynes, Pat Hynes, Joe (Poultice) Kelly, Joe Lalor,
                        Pat Lalor, Mattie Mathews, John Mooney, Paddy Mooney,
                        Joseph Nolan, Harry O'Hagan, Pat O'Hagan, Pat O'Hara,
                        Seamus O'Higgins, Sean O'Higgins, Patrick Proctor,
                        James (Jim) Sherry, John Sherry, Luke Sherry,
                        Stephen Sherry, Tom Sherry.

In all, there was about 150 Volunteers involved in the operation. Mary Connell, listed above under the heading "Dunboyne" was not an affiliated member of the Dunboyne I.R.A. Company. She was in fact a member of the Dunboyne Cumann na mBan and she played a large part in the Dunboyne I.R.A. Company. Her role in this operation was conveying messages to Company Commanding Officers in the Dunboyne area to co-ordinate the blocking of roads at the precise time of the attack. Immediately after the attack the haul of arms and ammunition were taken by car to a safe house in Eskaroon, Dunderry, Navan where they were dumped in a loft in a yard behind Dick Keely's house.

In 1922, during the establishment of the Irish Free State, Patrick Meehan, the R.I.C. man mentioned above, was appointed Inspector to An Garda Síochána. He was later promoted to Superintendent and he was stationed at Granard, Co. Longford. The Trim R.I.C. Barracks is now the Castle Court Hotel. Sources: Bureau of Military History, 1913- 21, Witness Statement No 478 on 21st February 1951, Witness: Superintendent Patrick Meehan, Garda Siochana, Granard, Co. Longford. Former Constable R.I.C. 1910-1921 and Member of Garda Siochana 1922. Bureau of Military History, 1913- 21, Witness Statement No WS1539 on 4th December 1956, Witness: David Hall, Knutstown, Garristown, Co. Dublin. Officer Commanding 1st Brigade, 1st Eastern Division, I.R.A. Bureau of Military History, 1913- 21, Witness Statement No WS1715 on 16th December 1957, Witness: Sean Boylan, Edenmore, Dunboyne, Co. Meath. Commanding Officer Meath Brigade and Commanding Officer 1st Eastern Division, I.R.A. Stories from Eskaroon by Paddy Keely. Dunderry A Folk History by Dunderry History Group & Johnny Keely.

In October 1920 the U.V.F. were failing in the defence of the R.I.C. in the North of Ireland. To counteract this an armed reserve police force was set up in the North called the Ulster Special Constabulary and their primary role was to bolster the R.I.C. and to fight the I.R.A. Protestant militia groups and U.V.F. were encouraged to join this police force to legitimise themselves.

On 1st November 1920 Kevin Barry was hanged. He was 18 years of age. On 21st November 1920 fourteen British Intelligence men were shot dead in Dublin. R.I.C. retaliated by shooting fourteen people dead at a Football Match in Croke Park. So nationally, things were very heated in the whole country.

In January 1921 an I.R.A. Active Service Unit (A.S.U.) was operating in the general Trim Area. It consisted mostly of Trim Company and Battalion men who were still wanted men "on the run". From their camp in a place called Ciarogue House in the Kilmessan district they entered Trim under the cover of darkness and ambushed a military foot patrol at Haggard Street using hand grenades and gun fire. There were unconfirmed reports that some Military were wounded and one later died. The ambush party escaped unharmed. The I.R.A. Volunteers and officers allegedly involved in the ambush were:

Bective Company: Christopher Caffrey, Patrick Quinn, Christopher Reid.
Dunderry Company: Christopher Coffey and Michael Kiernan.
Trim Company: Mick Hynes, Pat Hynes, Joe (Poultice) Kelly,
Michael (The Gale) McArdle, Paddy Mooney,
Seamus O'Higgins, Sean O'Higgins,
James (Jim) Sherry, John Sherry

After the ambush the authorities put up a reward of £1,000 each for Hynes, Mooney and O'Higgins.

Source: Bureau of Military History, 1913- 21, Witness Statement No WS1696 on 11th November 1957, Witness: Patrick Quinn, Ringlestown, Kilmessan, Co. Meath. I.R.A. Battalion Commanding Officer, 1st Battalion, 2nd Brigade, 1st Eastern Division. Bureau of Military History, 1913- 21, Witness Statement No WS1060 on 11th January 1955, Witness: Seamus Finn, Athboy, Co. Meath. Adjutant Meath Brigade 1916-1917. Vice Commanding Officer & Director of Training 1st Eastern Division.

In late 1920 defences on Longwood R.I.C. Barracks had been increased due to heightened attacks on other barracks so much so that there was little hope of taking it. The Longwood I.R.A. Company decided that it should be attacked anyway. One night in late 1920 the I.R.A. opened fire on the building which lasted for about 20 minutes. They then called on the R.I.C. within the building to surrender. They refused and the firing started again until the I.R.A. ran out of ammunition. When the report of this attack went back to I.R.A. General Head Quarters (G.H.Q.) they were not impressed with the quantity of ammunition that was wasted on an operation that returned no positive results. They directed that there were to be no more such operations or attacks on targets in Meath in future unless detail plans were reviewed and sanctioned by G.H.Q. in advance. The I.R.A. Volunteers and officers allegedly involved in the attack were:

Longwood: Larry Giles, Pat Giles, Moss Fagan, William Murray, P. Corrigan,
C McEvoy, Michael McEvoy, Thomas Donnelly, John Grogan,
Peter Grogan, P. Heavy, Edward Bird, John Costello and Chris Boylan.

Source: Bureau of Military History, 1913- 21, Witness Statement No W.S. 1060 on 11th January 1955, Witness: Seamus Finn, Athboy, Co. Meath. Adjutant Meath Brigade 1916-1917. Vice Commanding Officer & Director of Training 1st Eastern Division.

In early 1921 many of the Volunteers were "On the Run" including all of the men from the Trim Company who were on the Crown Forces most wanted list. The weather of early 1921 turned very cold and raids by British Forces increased. Large forces of British troops, Black and Tans and R.I.C. men would quickly swoop and encircle an area, searching every building and tightening the circle in the process. This was a very effective technique for the British and a huge headache for the I.R.A. Volunteers and the local people as well. The same houses could be raided daily or nightly in some cases. Safe houses which normally would not be searched were being searched now. Men "on the run" had to keep moving all the time. The raids meant that they could not rest. Some of the Trim Company stayed around Kilmessan and Dunderry. Others got scattered and many of them became ill with pneumonia and complete exhaustion. If you look at the gravestones of the Volunteers you will notice that many of them died very young possibly caused by these harsh conditions.

Commandant Pat McDonnell from Stonefield, Oldcastle (see Ballinlough Company) was the Intelligence Officer of the 5th Battalion (Oldcastle). He was "on the run" himself along with his brother Tom when he issued a report on a recent upsurge in raids by British forces. His report linked the raids to information being leaked to the enemy some of which was probably unintentional via loose talk in public houses. General Head Quarters issued a warning to all Volunteers in this regard. About a month afterwards, on 23rd March 1921 Pat McDonnell and his brother Tom found themselves encircled by one of these search swoops, they were trapped. As they tried to escape Pat McDonnell was shot dead by Black and Tan Troops and his brother Tom narrowly escaped. He was buried in Ballinlough Church of Assumption Cemetery, see page 291. Source: Bureau of Military History, 1913- 21, Witness Statement No W.S. 1060 on 11th January 1955, Witness: Seamus Finn, Athboy, Co. Meath. Adjutant Meath Brigade 1916-1917. Vice Commanding Officer & Director of Training 1st Eastern Division. Bureau of Military History, 1913- 21, Witness Statement No W.S. 1615 on 16th May 1957, Witness: Seán Keogh, Smithstown, Ballinlough, Kells, Co. Meath. Commanding Officer 5th Battalion, Meath Brigade. Headstone Inscription.

In August 1920 availability of arms and ammunition was a big problem. The few arms they had in arms dumps could not be touched due to the continuous raids. Word came from General Head Quarters to Brigade Officers to focus on demolition of bridges and creating road blocks as a countermeasure to the swooping raids. This turned out to be an effective solution. British Troops and raiding parties needed to use the roads to sweep quickly in on an area. So the local Volunteers resorted to demolishing bridges and blocking the roads by cutting trenches across them. This was an inconvenience for the local people and the Volunteers but not as big an inconvenience as having a British Army raiding party going through your house. Volunteers could move round in fields and behind road ditches, hop over road trenches and streams and find a way across rivers if necessary. British raiding parties would come to a grinding halt. The most significant bridges targeted were Carlanstown Bridge blown up around the 2nd week of December 1920 under the command of Commandant Eamon Cullen (see Summerhill Company). Moynalty Bridge was blown up around the 1st week in December 1920. The nine-eyed bridge over the River Blackwater near Virginia Road and Mahonstown Bridge was blown up at the end of December 1920.

Rockview Bridge and McCormack's Bridge between Delvin and Mullingar were destroyed under the Command of Commandant Fox of Delvin. Tandy's Bridge on the main Athboy to Oldcastle Road was destroyed by Athboy Company. Joe Martin (see Athboy Company) who trained the men on the demolition of bridges with explosives, said in his Witness Statement that six river bridges in the Athboy area were destroyed and roads were extensively trenched. The 2nd Brigade failed to demolish the Boyne Bridge at Kilcarne and Dillon's Bridge near Tara due to lack of explosives. Likewise the destruction of the bridge on the Navan Dublin Road at Clonee failed due to lack of explosives as well. Many other smaller bridges were destroyed all over Co. Meath and where a road did not have a bridge, the road was trenched. Trenching was hard work done with picks and crowbars. R.I.C. and British Army patrols had to fill in the trenches to get through and in some cases they acquired help of some local British subjects to help them during the day. But where this occurred the I.R.A. would visit them and force them to dig the trenches out again at night. Cavalry movements started to come back into fashion. R.I.C. and British Army raiding parties would go out on horseback across country. The final solution for the Military was to carry heavy strong planks with them and plank each road trench as they came to it.

Source: Bureau of Military History, 1913- 21, Witness Statement No W.S. 1060 on 11th January 1955, Witness: Seamus Finn, Athboy, Co. Meath. Adjutant Meath Brigade 1916-1917. Vice Commanding Officer & Director of Training 1st Eastern Division. http://www.bureauofmilitaryhistory.ie/reels/bmh/BMH.WS1650.pdf

The rebuilding and destruction of the bridges continued and in late February 1921 a local man named John McMahon, Newtown House, Kilmainhamwood was cycling from Kells in the dark. He was unaware that the I.R.A. had blown up the Bridge and he fell to his death. He was aged 58 and father of twelve children. His wife had died two years earlier. Source: The Meath Chronicle dated 26th June 2013, Obituary of his daughter, Elizabeth Kaczmarek nee McMahon. WS1615.

Chapter 5
Years 1921, 1922 and 1923

On 9th February 1921 Crown Forces descended on the public house of Bob Chandler at Robinstown searching for arms and ammunition. Bob was questioned and he told them that he did not have any arms or ammunition. Bob was not in the I.R.A. or Sinn Fein but they seemed to think he was. He was beaten and kicked down the stairs. During the search of the premises Bob's invalid mother was mistreated. Valuables were stolen. Furniture and clothing was stacked up outside and set alight. They drank their fill and smashed the rest of the stock and fittings before leaving. Bob Chandler passed the details of this incident to the Volunteers and he went "on the run". Two of the men involved in the looting of the premises went to Dublin and reported the incident to the British Head of the Force, Brigadier General Crozier. As a consequence a number of the looters were suspended from duty. In a statement by Brigadier General Crozier in mid-February he said that this was not the first time this happened. That there were dozens of occasions, some more serious, where officers were dismissed and subsequently reinstated. He said that conditions have become so impossible that he felt he had to resign. And resign he did. This incident received quite a bit of publicity at the time, increased by the resignation of Crozier.

About February 1921 Kells I.R.A. Commanding Officer, Bob Mullen had been arrested and was in jail. His role was taken over by Benny Carolan. Around the same time it came to Eamon Cullen's attention that a telegraph machine was installed in Kells Post Office. Compared to a dispatch rider, this machine would be a huge step in improved communication speed. Kells R.I.C. were probably using it to communicate with their General Head Quarters (G.H.Q.). The I.R.A. had an ambition to have the machine as well, so either way it was not going to be left in Kells Post Office for long. Eamon Cullen got approval from I.R.A. G.H.Q. to put an operation together to remove the machine from the post office. This would be the 1st operation for Benny Carolan as Kells I.R.A. Company Commanding Officer. The operation involved sixteen I.R.A. Volunteers from Kells and four Volunteers from Kilbeg Company. The plan was that six Volunteers would make up the actual raiding party while fourteen Volunteers would protect them. A van which arrived at Kells Post Office every night was to be hijacked before it reached Kells. The raiders would drive the van to the post office at the usual time. The post office would not suspect anything they would just open the door as usual and the six raiders would take over. The rest of the Volunteers would ensure that an R.I.C. patrol would not interfere with proceedings, but of course it didn't work out that way. The I.R.A. were only setting up the road block when the van drove through. The van was early and the I.R.A. did not recognise it until it was too late.

So now twelve of the Volunteers made their way across fields, back gardens walls and fences to reach the back of the post office. That left only eight Volunteers to cover them. The raiding party had to break their way through the back door, taking so long and causing such a racket that the post office staff had time to ring the R.I.C barracks. By the time they got in, took control and dismantled the telegraph machine the post office was surrounded by R.I.C. men. A gun battle ensued. One I.R.A. man, Farrell Tully, was injured and captured and several I.R.A. were slightly wounded but managed to escape with the telegraph machine. The R.I.C. suffered no casualties. Over the next few days the R.I.C. made further arrests and most of the Volunteers spent the rest of 1921 in jail. The I.R.A. Volunteers and Officers allegedly involved in the raid were:

Cork: Brennan (he was "on the run" from Cork and active in Meath)

Kells Company: Patrick Brady, Thomas Brady. Benny Carolan, Bill Connell, Michael Cumiskey, Patrick Dolan, William Donegan, Bernard Flynn, Michael Fox, Jack Hegarty, Patrick Maguire, James McDonnell, John McGillic, Farrell Tully, Nicholas Tully.

Kilbeg Company: Four Volunteers, unfortunately un-named.

Summerhill Company: Eamon Cullen.

Source: Bureau of Military History, 1913- 21, Witness Statement No W.S. 1060 on 11th January 1955, Witness: Seamus Finn, Athboy, Co. Meath. Adjutant Meath Brigade 1916-1917. Vice Commanding Officer & Director of Training 1st Eastern Division.

On 23rd February 1921 an R.I.C. motor patrol was ambushed in Carnaross. In March 1921 road trenching was still ongoing by I.R.A. Volunteers at night while the military forces were filling them in again by day.

The focus of attacks turned from barracks to road ambushes. I.R.A. Volunteers from Carnaross noticed that a patrol of two military trucks of R.I.C. travelled from Kells to Oldcastle on Friday mornings at between 10am and 10:30 a.m. This information was relayed to a meeting of the 5th Battalion held in Farrelly's of Clongowney, Crossakiel. The route of the trucks was watched for a few weeks and it emerged that the patrol was not regular but it did follow the same route on most Fridays. After careful planning the ambush was sanctioned by the 5th Battalion Council for 1st April 1921 at Sylvan Park, just outside Kells on the road to Oldcastle. The man in charge of the operation was the 5th Battalion (Oldcastle) Commanding Officer Davie Smith under the supervision of the Brigade Vice Commandant and Adjutant Seamus Finn, see Athboy Company. There were possibly forty five I.R.A. Volunteers and officers involved in this operation but unfortunately I do not have all their names. On the night prior to the planned ambush the ambush party stayed in a disused house belonging to a man named Terence Bennett. The disused house was selected because it was near the ambush position. A local man, Jimmy Shields, saw the ambush party moving into the disused house and he had to be arrested by the I.R.A. in case he spread the word overnight. Another local man named John Daly noticed the I.R.A. party and arrived with his shotgun to lend a hand. He was not an I.R.A. Volunteer but wanted to be involved in the ambush. In the early hours of the morning, under the cover of darkness, the ambush party dug a hole in the road and a landmine was concealed in the hole by the Carnaross Company Engineer Matt Smith (see Carnaross Company) under instructions of the 5th Battalion (Oldcastle) Engineer Matt Tevlin, see Carnaross Company. Signal men took positions on Drumbaragh Hill where they could signal the ambush party of the approaching military trucks. The rest of the ambush party took up positions with rifles, shotguns and revolvers. The trucks did not come and the ambush party stayed in position until 3 pm. During the day they had to take a few civilian prisoners who discovered the ambush and they were held prisoner behind a house known as Rowleys. At 3pm they decided to abort the ambush and Matt Smith and Matt Tevlin had to disarm the mine and lift it. The ambush party were just up and stretching themselves when they spotted the signal from Drumbaragh Hill that a military truck was approaching. They were only back in their positions when it arrived. There was no mine in the road now so they opened fire immediately. The R.I.C. returned fire and the truck accelerated through the ambush. The I.R.A. claimed that three R.I.C. men were wounded in the attack and an R.I.C. rifle was discovered on the road after the truck had passed. Some of the I.R.A. Volunteers and officers allegedly involved in the ambush were:

Athboy Company: Seamus Finn.

Ballinlough Company: Patrick Conway, Sean Keogh, Harry Lee.

Carnaross Company: James Dunne, Pat Dunne, Sean Farrelly, James Lynch,
                             Thomas Lynch, Matthew or Michael McInerney,
                             Ned O'Connor, Matt Smith, Matt Tevlin, Philip Tevlin.

Mullagh Company: Davie Smith.

Stonefield Company: Mick Boylan, Charles Conaty, Thomas Mulvany,
                             Peter O'Connell, Thomas O'Connell, Matt Tobin,
                             Mick Wynne.

Whitegate Company: Patrick Tobin.

Local Civilian: John Daly. Not a Volunteer, a local rebel.

Sources: WS1060

An Toglac, the official newspaper of the Volunteers which aimed to provide guidance and develop the Volunteer movement nationally printed an article on 6th May 1921, on page 3 entitled *"The Proper Employment Rifle."* The column describes how a rifle should be used and gives an example of how a sniper in Co. Meath recently killed or wounded three R.I.C. men. It goes on to say that *"he had a post from which he was able to take under fire a long stretch of road. The enemy party were in a Crossley and our sniper shot one as it approached, one as it was passing and a third as it was going away"* The article does not give sufficient detail to link it to a particular incident but it could possibly be referring to the ambush at Sylvan Park, Kells on 1st April. The Crossley Company did produce a military truck.

In April 1921 Dublin Castle banned all fairs, markets and public assemblies including G.A.A. activities but excluding Horse Race Meetings and Hunts. The reason they were excluded was that they were favourite sports of Unionists, upper classes and high ranking British Army officers.

On 7th April 1921 R.I.C. Sergeant William E. Johns was shot and wounded at a Horse Race meeting in Boyerstown. The attack was carried out by Volunteer William Rooney of Ardbraccan Company and formally of Commons Company, see his profile in Ardbraccan Company. Incidentally, this is the second time that William E. Johns was wounded in Co. Meath. He was shot five years previously as a Constable at the Battle of Ashbourne, see paragraph 3. He survived on both occasions. Sources: Dunderry A Folk History by Dunderry History Group & Johnny Keely.

There was a heightened intensity of I.R.A. activity and attacks in 1921 which resulted in new command structures having to be put in place In April – May 1921. Michael Collins was personally involved in this and it was Collins himself who showed Sean Boylan the map of the country marked out showing all 9 Division Areas. The 1st Eastern Division was formed and Meath became the 1st Brigade and was made up of six Battalions. Each battalion was made up of four or more companies and each company was made up of twelve or more Volunteers. Similar was done for the other divisions of the country. Although these new structures would mean big changes for officers particular Battalion Officers and Division Officers, it would not make much difference to the individual Volunteers. However, it would have brought renewed enthusiasm and activities to the whole army and a hope that orders and decisions would flow a bit more quickly. R.I.C. noticed this increased activity in the areas so they intensified their surveillance and intimidation on individual Volunteers. People were regularly stopped by R.I.C. men and asked where they were going and what they were doing. R.I.C. men approached the young Volunteers' parents and asked them did they know where your young lad was and what he was doing. What he might be involved in, and did they know what could happen to him as a result. R.I.C. men went to employers telling them what their employees were involved in. R.I.C. men went to the Clergy advising them to inform their congregation of the risks of being involved with the Volunteers. Some Volunteers were very intimidated by these acts, some found themselves with no other choice but to cease. However, the majority of Volunteers kept going and I.R.A. work continued uninterrupted.

In June 1921 Flying Columns were organised in all Brigades. Flying Columns are made up of about twenty men selected for their skills and abilities and were selected from all the companies in a Brigade. These men would receive specialist training. Flying Columns could also be described as Special Operations Forces or Special Task Forces or Active Service Units.

Similar to the ambush at Sylvan Park described earlier, an ambush of a military truck at Drumbaragh was planned in June 1921 and again a road mine was deployed. This was a smaller ambush party and the man in charge of this one was Matt Tevlin, see Carnaross Company. This ambush party was mainly made up of Carnaross Company. The ambush was going as planned in that the military truck arrived and the mine exploded causing severe damage to the truck. The ambush party immediately opened fire on the truck from a high wall overlooking the scene. The occupants of the military truck returned fire. What was not planned was that a second military truck appeared on the scene and also opened fire on the ambush party leaving them with no option but to retreat across what was described as Sweetman's gardens in the direction of Kieran and Carnaross. During the retreat I.R.A. Volunteer Jack Lynch was wounded, see Carnaross Company. The ambush party dispersed across the fields. A widespread search for the ambush party took place immediately and Matt Tevlin found himself surrounded by military who were closing in on the field where he was hiding. Matt took of his coat and hid it. When the military arrived at the field he was walking around in his shirt sleeves pretending to be counting cattle. He later walked back to the scene of the ambush. The military were still there and he talked to one of the soldiers about the awful events that were going on.

Source: Bureau of Military History, 1913- 21, Witness Statement No WS1659 on 26th August 1957, Witness: Peter O'Connell, Crosswater, Carnaross, Kells, Co. Meath. I.R.A. Battalion Adjutant, 5th Battalion, Meath Brigade.

The I.R.A. General Head Quarters (G.H.Q.) had heard of trench mortars being used by the British Army in the Great War. They were being used to fire mortars out of the trenches across the battlefield and when they hit the ground they exploded. I.R.A. G.H.Q. could see that these would be very useful for lobbing mortars into barracks. There was no chance of getting any so they asked Dick McKee, Commanding Officer of the Dublin Brigade and his Vice Commanding Officer, Peadar Clancy, to take charge of the G.H.Q. Engineering Section and to produce an experimental trench mortar gun. They took on the task and decided on producing a copy of the British Stoker Gun. The main reasons they selected the Stoker was that they had British military text books and manuals which described the gun in reasonable detail. When the experimental mortar gun was ready they obviously couldn't test it in Dublin so they decided to test it at Lustown, Batterstown, Dunboyne, Co Meath a short distance from the home of Mary Connell. Mary Connell was not an affiliated member of the Dunboyne I.R.A. Company. She was in fact a member of the Dunboyne Cumann na mBan and she played a large part in the Dunboyne I.R.A. Company. Her isolated residence was probably an influencing factor in the selection of the test site. The test date was set for approximately 21st June 1921. All the necessary security was put in place to ensure a British patrol would not arrive unexpectedly during testing. Mary acted as a scout ensuring the area was secure prior to the arrival of the mortar gun and the commencement of the test. The Gunner operating the mortar gun was Captain Matt Furlong. Unfortunately during the tests the gun exploded severely injuring him. Using a mattress from Mary Connell's bed and a gate which was taken off its hinges a makeshift stretcher was quickly constructed and he was carried to Mary's house. They could not get him inside the house so Mary covered him with her blankets and coats while waiting for an ambulance to arrive from Dublin. Dr. Grogan attended to Matt Furlong before the ambulance arrived but he died from his injuries shortly afterwards. The mattress, blankets and coats were so badly saturated in blood that they had to be burned. Parts of the experimental mortar gun and shells were dumped in the Tolka River.

Source: Bureau of Military History, 1913- 21, Witness Statement No WS1043, Witness: Colonel Joseph V. Lawless, "C" House, Cathal Bruagh Barracks, Dublin. Lieut. Swords Coy., up to 1916. Brigade Engineer Officer Fingal Brigade later; commissioned officer National Army & member of investigating staff of Bureau, 1954. Subject: National Activities, North Co. Dublin, 1911 - 1922. Bureau of Military History Military Service Pension Collection, file reference No MSP34REF38375 of Mary Connell, Lustown, Batterstown, Co Meath

About mid-June 1921 the Brigade Commanding Officer, Patrick Kelly (see Johnstown Company) under instructions from Divisional Commanding Officer Sean Boylan (see Dunboyne Company) instructed companies in the Battalion area to hand over all non-essential arms and ammunition. Bective Company Commanding Officer Patrick Quinn (see Bective Company) collected the arms in the Battalion Area of Trim, Kiltale, Bective and Dunderry. He then sent them via pony and trap, driven by a young lady named Miss Kiernan who was a sister of Michael Kiernan (see Fordstown Company) and accompanied by James Quinn (see Bective Company) to the Battalion Quartermaster Jack O'Brien (see Johnstown Company). From there the arms were secretly moved to Kildare. A few nights later, 29th June 1921 an I.R.A. Battalion Council meeting was held at a house on the Athlumney-Beauparc Road. Brigade Commanding Officer Patrick Kelly attended as did Commandant Matthew Barry (see Johnstown Company) and Battalion Vice Commanding Officer Patrick Stapleton (see Navan Company). Kelly revealed that a top secret operation was about to be launched and he was looking for Volunteers. About 11 to 14 local I.R.A. men volunteered to participate. Details were not revealed. On 1st July 1921 as a result of the I.R.A. meeting in Navan about 11 to 14 local Volunteers separately travelled by bicycle and on foot to a meeting place near Dunboyne. When night fell they travelled across country on foot to Stacumney near Hazelhatch, Celbridge, Co. Kildare secretly joining up with about 100 more Volunteers and officers from various other companies of the Eastern Division. Included were the Fingal men in the charge of Paddy Mooney from Trim. The Dunboyne men in the charge of Bernard Dunne from Dunboyne and the Navan men in the charge of William Booth from Navan. They eventually arrived at a large house situated near a railway line. The house belonged to a Mr. Wardell. The Wardell family had been taken prisoner by the I.R.A. some time earlier and had been locked away under guard in an outhouse. The whole area had been previously scouted by Mary Connell and other ladies from Cumann na mBan. They had extensively cycled the surrounding area ensuring that it was free of British Crown Forces ensuring safe passage for I.R.A. Volunteers to take up their positions unnoticed. When the Meath I.R.A arrived the main house was buzzing with I.R.A. Officers and Volunteers. Arms, ammunition and explosives were coming in and being distributed to the men. Some of these arms were gathered in Co. Meath as mentioned earlier. Under directions of Eamon Cullen (see Summerhill Company) explosives were laid alongside the tracks by about 10 or 12 Engineers. It soon emerged that the intention was to carry out a large scale attack on a passing troop train. The train was travelling from Belfast carrying about 1,000 British Troops and officers who were returning to the Curragh after providing security for the King of England's visit to Belfast at the opening of the Northern Ireland Parliament. But a small reconnaissance plane flying above the troop train must have spotted the I.R.A. ambush party and alerted Gormanstown or Baldonnel. The train was stopped long before it reached the ambush point. A British Military patrol arrived on the scene and opened fire on the I.R.A. ambush party and a gun battle ensued. The I.R.A. suffered some casualties and were forced to retreat. One of the wounded I.R.A. men was William Goodwin, see Kilcloon Company. He managed to hide himself in a nearby field of corn. He was later rescued by Mary Connell and other members of Cumann na mBan who moved him to safety where they treated him for his injuries. The ladies also recovered two Thompson Machine Guns which were lost by I.R.A. Volunteers during the operation. Cumann na mBan were back on their bicycles immediately after the I.R.A. retreated. They gathered information on the positions of British patrols and search parties and they managed to pass the information to the various I.R.A. groups so that they could plan their escape routes. The I.R.A. Volunteers and officers from Meath allegedly involved in the failed troop train ambush planning and or operation were:

Ardbraccan Company:	Patsy Bennett.
Athboy Company:	Seamus Finn.
Dunboyne Company:	Pat Clinton and Barney Dunne.
Dunboyne Cumann na mBan:	Mary Connell and several unnamed ladies.
Johnstown Company:	Matthew Barry, Patrick Kelly and others but unfortunately I have no more names.
Kilcloon Company:	William Goodwin
Summerhill Company:	Eamon Cullen.
Trim Company:	Seamus O'Higgins, Paddy Mooney.
Navan Company:	William Booth, and others but unfortunately I have no other names.

Notably Sean Boylan was not mentioned in this operation. He said in his Witness Statement that he was told by Michael Collins to be involved in the planning but not to be involved in the actual operation. Why? Within ten days of the failed troop train operation a Truce was announced so the Irish and British must have been discussing the possibility of a Truce at this time. In that case it seems likely to me that this troop train operation was put in place in a last-ditch effort to give the illusion that the I.R.A. were well armed and capable of pulling off an operations with the potential of causing large scale casualties. The truth was that the I.R.A. were never well armed and now their levels of arms and ammunition were at their lowest, as was evident from the rounding up of guns from Meath for the troop train Ambush operation in Kildare. Strategically, if the troop train operation was a success it would give the I.R.A. a stronger hand in negotiation talks. On the other hand if the I.R.A. lost high ranking officers in a failed operation it would weaken their hand. In my opinion that was why Sean Boylan and probably other high ranking officers were told to take a back seat in this operation. Even as a failed operation, but with no loss of high ranking officers it would have demonstrated to the British that they were not winning the war and that they were becoming as vulnerable as the R.I.C. were in their rural barracks. This planned operation was probably the last operation conducted by the I.R.A. as a united force. Bureau of Military History Military Service Pension Collection, file reference No MSP34REF38375 of Mary Connell, Lustown, Batterstown, Co Meath. Sean Boylan WS1715 Seamus Finn 1060.

On 11th July 1921 a Truce was announced. The people of the country saw the fighting stop but the I.R.A. looked upon it as a temporary situation and an opportunity to regroup and get prepared for the Truce to break. I.R.A. General Head Quarters made plans that in the event of renewed hostilities that the Dublin Brigade and all G.H.Q. Staff would immediately evacuate Dublin and the city would be cut off from the country. The 1st Eastern Division, which of course includes the Meath Brigades, would immediately cut off all enemy communications North and West of Dublin. British Troops would be isolated in Dublin. In preparation for this, training was intensified in all areas. Proper training manuals were issued from I.R.A. G.H.Q. to Battalions. Trainers were sent round all areas. Training camps were established in several places such as Ballymacoll House, Dunboyne and at Baileboro. A very good trainer named Pat Garrett went round the Meath areas training officers who in turn trained Volunteers. Some officers were selected and sent for more advanced or more specialised training. Again the officers trained the Volunteers. This training and knowledge building continued on an ongoing basis right through to Christmas 1921.

But why was Britain interested in a Treaty? Britain was almost bankrupt as a result of World War 1 and in the early 1920s they were in a deep recession. They could not afford the cost of the troubles in Ireland anymore.

In the 2nd half of 1921 the Truce was still holding. Talks between Irish and British Politicians were ongoing. Hostilities had more or less stopped. An Irish negotiations delegation including Eamonn De Valera were in London full time. But in the North of Ireland a mob of Orangemen started attacking Nationalist families. The newspapers told of daily lootings and attacks where people were being burned out of their houses and killed by mobs. There was a sudden countermove by the I.R.A. Volunteers in the Northern Divisions and they arrested about 30 leading Orange mobsters who were suspected of being heavily involved in organising and participating in these attacks on the Nationalist people. The 30 Orangemen were transferred to an "unknown destination" which is now known to have been Trim, Co. Meath where they were held prisoner. The attacks by Orangemen in the North reduced considerably. After being held in Trim for a few weeks I.R.A. G.H.Q. ordered for the Orangemen to be released. The attacks on Nationalist families stopped. Sources: Meath Chronicle dated 18th February 1922 page 1.

Details of a possible Treaty:
- The 26 Counties in the South of Ireland would become a self-governing state or a free state within the British Commonwealth.
- The British Crown Forces would withdraw from the 26 Counties of Ireland over the next year.
- The disestablishment of the Irish Republic declared in 1919.
- The abandonment of the First Dáil.
- The King of England would be the Head of State of the Irish Free State and he would be represented by a Governor General.
- Members of the new Free State's Parliament would be required to take an Oath of Allegiance to the Irish Free State and to His Majesty the King.
- Britain would continue to control a limited number of Shipping Ports in Ireland.
- The Irish Free State would assume responsibility for a proportionate part of the United Kingdom's debt, as it stood on the date of signature.
- The Treaty would have superior status in Irish law so that it would take precedence in the event of a conflict between it and the new 1922 Constitution of the Irish Free State.

Volunteers would be happy to see an end to the War of Independence but not happy with British Forces remaining in the six Counties and not happy with an Oath of Allegiance to the King or the betrayal of the Irish Republic which had been proclaimed during the Easter Rising. Two main opinions formed:

On one side you had Volunteers who were in favour of the Treaty who became known as the Pro-Treaty I.R.A. Their view was that the I.R.A. could not keep up this sustained level of engagement against the British Crown Forces indefinitely and that they should take the 26 Counties as part of the Treaty. They ultimately became politically represented by the Fine Gael party.

On the other side you had Volunteers who were opposed to the Treaty who became known as Anti-Treaty I.R.A. Their view was that they could continue the struggle, that the British were nearly beaten and that there never was a better time to dig deeper and push the British Forces completely out of all 32 Counties of Ireland. They ultimately became politically represented by the Sinn Fein Party which split also creating the Fianna Fáil Party.

Treaty Talks went on between the Irish and British for a further five months. On December 6th 1921 Eamonn De Valera would not go to the final talks in London, instead he sent a high level five man delegation. The British Government would not talk with a delegation that did not have the power to make decisions. De Valera said that the delegation had the necessary power but he secretly told the delegation that he wanted them to refer back to his cabinet on the main points and he wanted to see the complete text of the Draft Treaty before it was signed. When all the negotiations were done and the final document was in front of the Irish Delegation for signing the British did not want to hear that they had to review it in Ireland first. They threatened to withdraw the whole Treaty and go back to full scale war. The Irish delegation took a break from the meeting to consider their position. The British told them to be back and sign the Treaty by a specific hour that night or the Treaty was off the table. The Irish delegation felt that after five months of negotiations that this was the best deal they would get and they would never be forgiven for refusing it so they came back that night and reluctantly signed it. Michael Collins remarked that he might have signed his death warrant. Did they have the authority to sign it or not? Was it their last chance to accept the Treaty or were the British bluffing. Did De Valera's negotiation tactic backfire? Were the British smarter than the Irish? They were certainly more experienced.

The Irish signatories to the Treaty were Arthur Griffith (mentioned earlier in this book see Chapter 4), Michael Collins, Robert Barton, George Gavin Duffy and Eamonn Duggan from Longwood, Co. Meath. Duggan was the son of an R.I.C. man. He joined the I.R.A. and was previously sentenced to three years penal servitude for his involvement in the 1916 Rising. He qualified as a solicitor and became involved in Politics. The Irish delegation returned back to Dublin with the signed Treaty. De Valera was furious that his instructions were not followed. On 8th December 1921 Eamonn De Valera called a Cabinet Meeting to review the Treaty in which he made it known that he was opposed to the Treaty. On 9th

January 1922 the Dail ratified the Treaty by a very narrow majority causing a major split in the Irish Government and in the I.R.A. Eamonn De Valera resigned and he formed the Fianna Fail party who politically represented the Anti-Treaty side while Fine Gael represented the Pro-Treaty side. These two parties have dominated politics in Ireland since then. The Irish Free State came into existence on the signing of the Treaty on 6th December 1921. The Irish were required to defend all the terms of the new Anglo Irish Treaty which meant they needed an army and police force.

On 31st January 1922 the I.R.B. chose to support the Pro-Treaty side and they issued instructions to their men to that effect. As we explained throughout this book the vast majority of officers in the I.R.A. were members of the I.R.B. Many Volunteers were not sure which side they should take, if any. They looked to their company Commanding Officers for guidance. Company Commanding Officers were generally regarded as leaders in their community and were generally fairly highly regarded and respected men. Therefore a company Commanding Officer had great influence over the Volunteers in his company. For that reason, as the majority of the officers took the Pro-Treaty side so did the majority of the Volunteers. Whether through the influence of others or not, individual I.R.A. Volunteers started falling into Pro-Treaty and Anti-Treaty sides.

Which side did the majority of Volunteers in Meath take? Shortly after the announcement of the Treaty, Bobby Byrne (Navan Company) arranged a public meeting in Commons, Navan on a Sunday afternoon to gauge feelings and to hear opinions. Over 1,000 men attended and voted in favour of the Treaty with a majority of ten to one. Of course this is not very scientific or indisputable evidence but it is a good indicator of the feelings of the Volunteers in Navan and surrounding districts at the time. It might also be representative opinion of the majority of Volunteers in County Meath at the time. So the vast majority of Volunteers in Meath took the Pro-Treaty side and the majority of them joined the Free State Army. The Anti-Treaty side were in the minority and many of them took up arms to continue the battle against British occupation of Ireland and against anything that stood in their way, including the Pro-Treaty I.R.A. Some Volunteers and officers could see that this was going to turn into a bloody war of Irish men against their fellow brothers in arms and they just went home, put away their guns and got on with their lives as civilians. Some men went further than that as was the case with Paddy Fay of Kilbride, Trim and Stephen Sherry of Dunderry who were in charge of arms dumps. They refused to tell the rest of the Volunteers where the guns were so as to avoid them being used to shoot fellow I.R.A. men.

As part of the treaty the British agreed to pull out of the 26 Counties and to hand all the barracks and buildings over to the Irish. But the Pro-Treaty I.R.A.

did not have an army or police force large enough or sufficiently equipped to take control of the buildings or to defend them. This left the Irish government in a bit of a predicament. They called on pro-treaty sympathisers and supporters to step up to the mark, which they did. Hundreds of men who, up to now, had not been involved in front line I.R.A. temporarily enrolled into pro-Treaty I.R.A. They were commonly referred to at the time as "Official Forces I.R.A." Their role was to temporarily occupy the buildings handed over after the British Crown Forces departed until such time as the build-up of Free State Army or Civic Guards had reached sufficient capacity that they could occupy these buildings themselves. One of these was a young man from Ethelstown, Kells, Co Meath named Joseph Smyth. Joe had not been a member of any I.R.A. company in Meath, he went straight from being a civilian to being a soldier assigned to occupy and guard Athboy Barracks. Of course the Anti-Treaty I.R.A. were not going to sit back and let all the barracks and buildings be taken over by Pro-Treaty I.R.A. They had secured some of the buildings already and planned to take more. The Pro-Treaty I.R.A. started taking up the role as the Free State Army. Orders came from the Free State G.H.Q. that all Volunteers and officers are to defend the Treaty and anyone who does not will be disciplined. They started rounding up Anti-Treaty I.R.A. and jailing them including Eamonn De Valera. The Volunteers never really had political choices before. British Rule had been imposed on them all of their lives. The only way they ever got to where they were was by force. So it was not

long before it turned to violence again and quickly escalated to shooting one another. Source for Official Forces info: Tony Brady, Cherryhill Road, Kells.

On 13th March 1922 the Kells R.I.C. Barracks was formally handed over to the I.R.A. On 14th March the Trim R.I.C. Barracks and Dunshaughlin R.I.C. Barracks was formally handed over to the I.R.A. The last R.I.C. barracks in Meath to be formally handed over was the Navan Barracks and it was formally handed over on 15th March 1922. On the same day the Auxiliary Barracks at Church

De Valera arrested by Irish Free State Army. Photo courtesy of Irish Volunteers http:irisgvolunteers.org

View Navan was also given up and it was quickly re-occupied by an I.R.A. company of the Fingal Brigade.

Source: Meath Chronicle dated 18th March 1922, page 1.

On 23rd April 1922 two rival groups of Pro-Treaty and Anti-Treaty I.R.A. clashed over possession of Athboy R.I.C. Barracks and it turned into a gun battle. Source: Dunderry a Folk History by Dunderry History Group and & Johnny Keely.

In May 1922 Anti-Treaty I.R.A. Forces tried to take Slane Barracks. A small group of men were awaiting a train at Gormanstown Train Station on Monday 29th May 1922 when they were challenged by R.I.C. Shots were exchanged. One R.I.C. man and one I.R.A. man was shot dead. The I.R.A. man was named as Staff Captain James Flanagan who was a member of the Anti-Treaty Forces. http://irishmedals.org/anti-treaty-killed.html Irishwarmemorials.ie. 2006-03-28. Retrieved 2013-12-09.

28th June 1922 marks the official start of the Irish Civil War.

Since the split, Anti-Treaty numbers were very low, they were only a fraction of the strength that they previously were. Some of their leaders and officers were gone to the Pro-Treaty side and a breakdown of structures and discipline was evident. They were disorganised and not prepared for this dramatic change in their lives. They did not re-adjust as quickly as they should have. Skirmishes broke out wherever they interfaced with the Pro-Treaty side which turned into bitter and terrible war. Pro-Treaty Forces who were now Free State Army were well equipped by the British with whatever they needed. They also had the advantage of knowing the terrain and the safe houses and the people who might support Anti-Treaty men. Anti-Treaty men could not go home they had to stay "on the run" in Active Sevice Units (A.S.U.)

On 5th July 1922 a force of about 200 Free State Army surround Curraghtown House near Dunderry Co. Meath. Inside the house were about 30 Anti-Treaty I.R.A. Volunteers who became known as the Curraghtown Active Service Unit (A.S.U.). A gun battle and a standoff ensued and went on a few days. Volunteer Sergeant George McDermott (see Ardbraccan Company) was shot dead. Free State Army officer Sean Nolan from Kildare was also shot dead. The circumstances surrounding the death of George McDermott remain controversial. One side saying he was shot dead while un-armed and trying to negotiate a ceasefire and the other side saying he was shot as an armed combatant. The I.R.A. men allegedly involved in the Curraghtown Battle were:

Ardbraccan Company: Patrick Boyle, James Byrne, George McDermott, William McGuirk and Valentine Stapleton.

Bohermeen Company: Gerald O'Reilly.

Castletown Company: George Cudden.

Clongill Company: James Hoey, Michael Swan.

Johnstown Company:	James Boylan.
Kells Company:	Dan Sullivan.
Kilberry Company:	James Heaney, Owen Heaney, John McKeon, Peter Shields.
Kildalkey Company:	Christopher Fagan.
Navan Company:	Edward Cahill, Christy Cregan, Richard Doran, Joseph Egan, John Farrelly, John Gaynor, Mick Hilliard, Thomas Kinsella, Laurence McGovern, Michael McKeon, Nicholas Naulty, Daniel Quinn, Patrick Stapleton, William Sullivan.
Rathkenny Company:	James Ginnity, Matthew Ginnity.

The Irish Independent dated 8th July 1922 reports that when the terms of a surrender were agreed the Anti-Treaty I.R.A. men emerged from the house and "Friends on either side, recognising one another, shook hands"

Dunderry A Folk History by Dunderry History Group & Johnny Keely. The Irish Independent dated 8th July 1922, page 5. Hand written Letter in Navan Library by Owen Heaney giving his account of the Battle of Curraghtown as the last remaining survivor dated 12th December 1985.

Now many of the Anti-Treaty I.R.A. were captured and interned all over the country. The Curraghtown A.S.U. were temporarily held in Trim and then interned in Dundalk, Co. Louth on 22nd July 1922. On 27th July 1922 their Comrades from Meath on the outside along with the help of Anti-Treaty I.R.A. forces from the Northern Division detonated a bomb against the perimeter of the prison blowing a hole in the exercise yard wall. More than 100 Anti-Treaty prisoners escaped in this dramatic operation. A truck which had been commandeered by Meath I.R.A. was used to ferry some of the Meath men out of the area before roadblocks were set up. The truck deposited its load of prisoners a safe distance from Dundalk. Incidently one of the Volunteers from the Northern Division involved in this operation was a Newry man called Tommy McGill. In 1940 this same Tommy McGill moved to Gibbstown House.   Source: Owen Heany, Castetown, Kilberry.

Again we were in a time of general unrest. The thuggish element that we saw during the breakdown of law and order in 1920 re-emerged. People took advantage of the situation to become involved in criminal activity which led to an increase in lawlessness including robberies, burning of houses and farm sheds for no good reason other than spite and jealousy between rival neighbours.

Michael Collins shot dead - The Meath Connection:
A young man named William Moran from Navan Co Meath was a member of the
Free State Army and he was stationed in Cork on the tragic day when Michael
Collins was shot dead.

William Moran, Navan. Picture kindly provided by his son Liam Moran

William Moran was the son of Eddie & Annie Moran who were Lockhouse Keepers and lived at Rowley's Lock Bridge, Navan. Picture kindly provided by Liam Moran, Navan.

William Moran was a member of the Bective and Kilmessan I.R.A. Company. After the Treaty he took the Pro-Treaty side. He joined the Free State Army and he was stationed in Cork in August 1922.

On 22nd August 1922 Michael Collins was shot dead when his convoy drove into an Anti-Treaty I.R.A. ambush at Béal Na Bláth in Co. Cork. William Moran is pictured here guarding Shanakiel Hospital in which lay the body of his Commander-in-Chief, Michael Collins after the fatal ambush. William was also a member of the army detail who accompanied Michael Collins body back to Dublin for the State Funeral.

William Moran, front row 2nd from left, guarding the Hospital in which lay the body of his Commander-in-Chief, Michael Collins. Picture kindly provided by his son Liam Moran.

Joseph Smyth

Meanwhile an Anti-Treaty A.S.U. made up of the Curraghtown A.S.U. and other escapees from the Dundalk jail break became active in Co. Meath. On 7th September 1922 about twenty members of the A.S.U. attacked Athboy Barracks. The barracks was occupied by the "Official Forces I.R.A." who were supporting the Pro-Treaty I.R.A. One of the Official Forces soldiers was killed in the attack. He was Joseph Smyth from Ethelstown, Kells, Co Meath previously mentioned on page 57. He was buried in St. Colmcille's Cemetery, Kells, see page 310. Owen Heaney (see Kilberry Company) said he was one of the men involved in this attack. Also in September 1922 another Free State Army Barracks, this one in Oldcastle was attacked by Anti-Treaty I.R.A. One Free State Soldier was killed. Sources: Photo kindly provided by his Niece Mrs Margaret McGovern, Rodstown House, Ethelstown, Kells, Co. Meah. Faithful to Ireland by Tony Brady, page 76.

Spin Doctors were even on the go at that time. On 15th October 1922 directives were issued to the press by Free State director of communications, Piaras Béaslaí to the effect that in future Free State troops were to be referred to as the "National Army", the "Irish Army", or just "Troops". That Anti-Treaty side were to be called "Irregulars" and were not to be referred to as "Republicans", "I.R.A.", "Forces", or "Troops", nor were the ranks of their officers allowed to be given. Around the same time the Catholic Hierarchy issued a statement condemning the Anti-Treaty fighters and saying that they were guilty of grievous sins that may not be absolved in Confession and therefore not permitted to receive Holy Communion. In effect this meant that the Anti-Treaty I.R.A. would be excommunicated, and if killed could not expect a church burial or to pass on to heaven. I.R.A. Volunteers, like everyone else were part of a population that was 90% devoted Catholics. This was an extremely heavy burden on Volunteer's minds. Now the Free State had legislation, the support of the Church, much of the Press and they were prepared to treat the Anti Treaty I.R.A. Volunteers as criminals rather than as combatants.

Richard Mulcahy I.R.A. Chief of Staff and leader of Fine Gael. Photo courtesy of Irish Volunteers http:irishvolunteers.org

In November 1922 the Irish Minister of Defence Richard (Dick) Mulcahy described earlier in this book (see pages 25 and 36) ordered that any Anti-Treaty activists found carrying arms were to be executed. Seventy Seven Anti-Treaty I.R.A. prisoners were officially executed as a result of that order. One of them was only 16 years of age. Unofficially far more were executed when and where they were captured. There were unofficial reports from different parts of the country of terrible atrocities such as groups of Anti-Treaty I.R.A. being tied to landmines before they were exploded, and captured men beaten to death with rifle butts. Young men and boys who gave up everything to support the Irish Government in the fight for independence and who took the

Oath of Allegiance to defend the Republic were slaughtered by their own countrymen and by the 1st Irish Government that they helped to put in place. Why? Because they had a difference of opinion on how to defend the Republic. Volunteers who were trained by people like Dick Mulcahy were betrayed by him. Could they not talk to each other? Did it have to be execution?

Anti-Treaty I.R.A. hit back and in early December 1922 they shot dead two TDs in Dublin who were on their way to the Dáil. The Free State government conducted retaliatory executions of Anti-Treaty I.R.A. prisoners. Anti-Treaty I.R.A. retaliated by burning the homes of TDs and Senators, some of which contained children who were perished and so the tit for tat reprisal continued on both sides. Further attacks by anti-treaty I.R.A. were punished by executing more anti-treaty prisoners. These actions engrained a bitterness in generations of Irish people that is still talked about today. Propaganda campaigns began. One side telling of the terrible atrocities of the other side. All of this senseless killing of Irish people by Irish people did nothing but sicken the public. These actions led to some soldiers deserting the Free State Army in disgust. Some of them just took off their uniforms and went home. Others defected to the side of the Anti-Treaty I.R.A. which was the case in the following story.

Laurence Skeeky, Lobinstown in Free Stater Army Uniform 1922. Photo kindly provided by Tom French, County Library, Navan.

Patrick Mullaney, a native of Balla, Co. Mayo was a school teacher. During the War of Independence he operated with the Meath/Kildare A.S.U.s and was involved in a number of attacks on R.I.C. barracks, railway lines and bridges. He sided with the Anti-Treaty I.R.A. forces in Kildare. On 28th June 1922 he was arrested by the Free State Army and imprisoned in the Curragh. He escaped on 20th August and he took command of the Anti-Treaty forces, 1ˢᵗ Brigade, 1ˢᵗ Eastern Division. The 1ˢᵗ Brigade's area of operations was from Dunboyne to Celbridge and from Lucan to Maynooth. He immediately set up what became known as the Lexlip Flying Column or Active Service Unit (A.S.U.) which was made up of 25 or 30 Volunteers. Five of those Volunteers were previously in the Free State Army and based at Baldonnel. The five had deserted or defected from the Free State Army and two of the five were from County Meath. The two men from Meath were

➤ Private **Laurence Sheeky**, aged 21 years, from Braystown, Lobinstown, Navan, Co. Meath.

➤ Private **Terence Brady**, aged 18 years, from Fletcherstown, Wilkinstown, Navan, Co. Meath.   Previously a member of the Castletown I.R.A. Company, see page 125.

Although the Leixlip A.S.U. only operated for three months, it was a well-disciplined, heavily armed, guerrilla fighting force. They engaged in the repeated destruction of railway lines and communications between Dublin and Maynooth and they were responsible for several ambushes and sniping attacks on Free State Army Troops in Maynooth and Lucan. This A.S.U. became of great concern to the Free State Army.

Volunteer Terence Brady, Fletcherstown, Wilkinstown, Navan, Co Meath in Free State Army Uniform. Photograph kindly provided by his Grandniece Nancy McFadden, Gibbstown, Navan.

On 1ˢᵗ December 1922 a lorry carrying provisions for the Free State Army at Maynooth was seized by the Leixlip A.S.U. near Collinstown and burned. Three Free State soldiers in the lorry were taken prisoner and a fourth escaped unnoticed. He made his way back to Maynooth Barracks where he raised the alarm. A detachment of Free State Army soldiers marched across country towards the scene and as they neared Grangewilliam House near Maynooth they came under rifle and machine-gun fire and they returned fire. Private Moran, a Free State Soldier, was killed in this exchange. More Free State troops arrived from Portobello Barracks,

Naas, Trim and Lucan supported by armoured cars. An exchange of fire began and

Typical Rolls Royce Armoured Car

the Free State Army forced the A.S.U. to abandon the house and retreat. Three Volunteers and two Free State Soldiers were wounded in the ensuing running gun-battle which lasted several hours until the Free State Army surrounded and captured the A.S.U. of twenty two Volunteers. Twenty one rifles, one Lewis Machine Gun, one Thompson Machine Gun, five revolvers, one Peter and Painter Automatic Pistol, five grenades and about 1,000 rounds of ammunition were also recovered. On 11th December 1922 the five ex-Free State Soldiers including the two Meath men were taken to Kilmainham Jail where they faced a court-martial on charges of "Treachery." All five men were found guilty and sentenced to death. On 8th January 1923 the five men were executed by Free State Army firing squad at Keogh Barracks. They were buried within the confines of the barracks. Around the same time a third man from Meath, **Thomas Murray** from Kilcarne, Navan but originally from Whitecross Co, Armagh was arrested in Dundalk along with two other men. On 9th January 1923 the three men were tried on a charge of being in possession of a revolver and ammunition. They were also found guilty and sentenced to death. On 13th January 1923 the Free State Army executed them in Dundalk Jail by firing squad and they were also buried within the confines of the jail. In October 1924 the bodies of seventy seven executed I.R.A. Volunteers were exhumed and handed back to their families for burial. The bodies of the three men from Meath were brought by their families to the Mortuary Chapel in Navan where they remained overnight. Mass was said in St Mary`s Church in Navan before the tricolour draped coffins of Volunteers Laurence Sheeky and Terence Brady were laid to rest with full military honours in the Republican Plot in St. Mary's Cemetery Navan. Their comrade Volunteer Thomas Murray was buried with full military honours later that day in the Republican Plot in Dundalk. The names of all three men are written on the large white monument over the grave in Navan but Thomas Murray is not buried there, see page 345.

The rest of the Leixlip A.S.U. captured Volunteers were also tried, convicted and sentenced to death but due to legal issues their sentence was commuted to ten years in jail and they were later released under the terms of the General Amnesty.

Sources: Ages are provided in the National Army Census of November 1922. Cahir Davitt BHM.WS1751, p.32. Ernie O'Malley Military Notebooks U.C.D. Archives. Freemans Journal dated 9th January 1923 page 5. Hunger Strike Monument in Duleek. James Dunne BMH.WS1571. J. Durney, The Civil War in Kildare, (Mercier Press, 2011) p.102. Kildare Observer dated 9th December 1922. Meath Chronicle dated 1st November 1924 p.1. Meath Chronicle dated 11th April 1931 p.1. Meath Chronicle dated 15th April 1933 p.5. Meath Chronicle dated 27th April 1957 p.7. Meath Chronicle dated 4th April 1973 page 9. N. O'Sullivan, Every Dark Hour. A History of Kilmainham Jail, (Liberties Press, 2007), p.224. South Star dated 13th January 1923 p.7. The Irish Independent, 2nd December 1922 p.7. The Irish Independent 9 December 1922 p.4. The Irish Independent 9th January 1923 p.5. Ulster Herald. www.irishmedals.org/anti-treaty-killed.html. www.stairnaheireann.com/2013/12/01/1922-irish-civil-war-2/. www.theirishstory.com/2015/01/08/a-damn-good-clean-fight-the-last-stand-of-the-leixlip-flying-column/#_ednref18. www.nli.ie/1916/pdf/7.12.pdf

Another man who suffered a similar fate was **Cornelius (Con.) McMahon,** a familiar face in Navan and a native of Co. Clare. Con spent many years working in Navan and was a member of the Navan I.R.A. Company. In February 1923 Con was arrested in his home county and then taken from his cell in Limerick Prison and executed by the Irish Free State Army. See his profile on page 224.

Source: http://freepages.genealogy.rootsweb.ancestry.com/~ccfgpw/ban-191.jpg

Volunteer Con. McMahon

On 27th of February 1923 Michael Greally, a Volunteer in the Oldcastle I.R.A., see page 237, and another man named Luke (Leo) Burke, Keady, County Armagh took part in an armed raid on the Hibernian and Northern Banks in Oldcastle. Both men were captured by Free State Troops from Ceannanus Mor, Kells, County Meath. They were charged with taking part in an armed raid and with being in possession of £385 19s 11d of stolen money. They were found guilty and sentenced to death. On 13th March 1923 they were taken from their cells in Mullingar Barracks and executed by Irish Free State Army firing squad. Michael was buried in Cloontuskert Cemetery, Curraghroe, Co. Roscommon.

The following is a transcript of a letter that Michael wrote to a young lady at 2:30 a.m. on the morning of his execution:

Dear Miss O'Brion,
I know you will be surprised to hear of our capture at Oldcastle and charged with taking part in raid of Banks and we have been told about two hours ago we will be shot at 8 O'clock this morning, myself and Leo. We have had Father Kelly and we have arranged to serve at our last Mass tomorrow fully resigned to Gods all powerful will but there is one thing you can rest assured we will die like all true Soldiers of the Republic which must live on because great men have made it. So we die true to our Oath, true to Ireland and true to the dead. May God give the boys strength to carry through, to realise the hopes of Pearse, Connelly, poor Mellows and the rest of the glorious dead. My reward for travelling to Dublin in 1916 and for suffering unknown hardships since in prison and out on the hillside is execution at the hands of my own countrymen. I am sending my few things on to there and my Brother may call for them later on. When you can, give him all if you don't wish to take a souvenir in remembrance. If Paddy comes out remember me to him I knowing he is true. Pray for me and I will pray for you when I go to heaven. Tell your mother and Josie also to pray for me. Good bye in this world from your dear friend.

> *Michael Greally.*
> *God save the Republic.*

Note that Michael's surname was spelled differently in various record and newspapers i.e. Greely, Grealy etc. but in the above letter the man himself spells his name Greally. <small>Sources: Copy of above transcribed letter kindly provided by Sean Craughan, Oldcastle. http://www.irishmedals.org/anti-treaty-killed.html</small>

By May 1923 the executions of the Volunteers had taken such a heavy toll on the Anti-Treaty I.R.A. that they agreed to a ceasefire and ceased this terrible war. The executions stopped but the Free State Army continued to apply pressure rounding up and imprisoning men. By June 1923 there was over 11,000 republican prisoners being held in Irish jails and they continued to be held for the rest of the year.

Chapter 6
Policing and Justice

In 1918 Arthur Griffith, a leading figure in Sinn Fein was running for election in East Cavan. During the election campaign his opposition candidates, Ancient Order of Hibernians and members of the Orange Order put up some confrontation and were alleged to have assisted in drafting British Troops and Auxiliaries into the areas where he was addressing the electorate. It was alleged that the British Troops and Auxiliaries intimidated Griffith's listeners and supporters. The Cavan Irish Volunteers did not have sufficient numbers to deal with this and they called on the Meath Volunteers for assistance. The Meath Brigade sanctioned it and under directions from Seamus O'Higgins (see Trim Company) Meath Irish Volunteers attended campaign speeches by Arthur Griffith at Baileboro, Virginia and Cootehill in a policing and patrol capacity. Their mission was to maintain and preserve order and to protect the electorate from intimidation. On Polling day they also policed the Polling Stations to ensure that voters were allowed to vote without intimidation. Seamus Cogan played a leading part in organising the Meath Volunteers for the campaign which ended in a huge victory for Arthur Griffith and following Sinn Fein Candidates. This was the first time that the Meath Volunteers were asked to perform a Policing Role.

As described earlier, by April 1920 nearly all rural R.I.C. barracks in County Meath had been evacuated and burned. This sudden absence of R.I.C. Police presence incited an increase in criminal activity and general lawlessness in rural areas. Mick Hilliard described in his Witness Statement that acts of "looting and robbery of shops, churches and private houses as well as other offences" took place. Criminals formed gangs which even included individuals from the I.R.A. Their aim was to profit from running some farmers off their land. Shots were fired into farmhouses and in one instance a house was blown up. To counteract this and to enforce some sort of crime control, Dáil Éireann issued instructions to the I.R.A. to take over community district policing duties and Sinn Fein conducted regular parish court sittings. Courts were set up and court sittings were regularly held in Carnaross and in Kildalkey. One of the problems that the I.R.A. had with this work was that they themselves were wanted men. When they arrested a suspect they had the problem of detaining him until trial and if the suspect was later convicted and received a custodial sentence the I.R.A. had to find somewhere for the offender to serve his sentence, all while the I.R.A. and the offender were being sought by British Crown Forces and so the whole lot had to be done while "on the run". There were no fixed locations for detaining a suspect or a convicted prisoner. To keep ahead of British swoops and searches the place of detention would change regularly and at very little notice.

These places of detention became known as "unknown destinations" and they would contain only a small number of prisoners at each one. Cumann na mBan and I.R.A. Volunteer's wives and sisters cooked the food for the prisoners and for

Typical Parish Court Hearing. Two I.R.A. policemen standing guard in centre of picture. Picture courtesy of Irish Volunteers http://irishvolunteers.org/

the Volunteers who guarded them. I.R.A. Volunteers fed the prisoners and guarded them 24 hours a day and provided escorts to move them to Sinn Fein parish court hearings or to other "unknown destinations". This put great strain on the Volunteers and all of this was done at the risk of losing their own liberty in the process. Only one or two of the "unknown destinations" in Co. Meath were ever found by the British Crown Forces and that was after the I.R.A. had released the prisoners and the Volunteers had abandoned the location. After a time the words "unknown destinations" was enough to put the fear of God into would-be criminals and made them think twice before they engaged in a crime. However, there were always a few people that would take the chance.

It was around May 1920, there was a land dispute in Rosemount, Newcastle, which is in North Meath, along the Meath-Cavan border. A gang of men, who became known as the Cormeen Gang, were intimidating anyone interested in buying a particular farm that was for sale in Rosemount, Newcastle. Despite this a man named Phil Smith from Coole, Kilmainhamwood bought the farm. The gang decided they were going to force Smith off the farm. When threats and verbal abuse failed, they hired a killer named Gordon. Gordon was an ex-British Army man who had served in France as a sniper in the 1914-1918 war. One day Mark Clinton, who was a nephew of Phil Smith, was helping his uncle by ploughing a field with a team of horses. Mark was an I.R.A. Volunteer. It was alleged that Gordon shot the two horses dead one after the other from a long range of several hundred metres before he shot Mark Clinton dead as well. After a local outcry for justice Gordon was arrested by R.I.C. on a charge of possession of arms and ammunition without a permit and he was taken to Navan. After a short hearing he was released by the court. Sean Boylan (see Dunboyne Company) was immediately informed of this development and he contacted Pat Loughran (see Navan Company) instructing him to ensure that Gordon did not escape. Pat Loughran mobilized all available Volunteers to be on the lookout on all roads for Gordon. Sean Boylan also mobilised John Kelly, (see Dunboyne company). John Kelly was the Brigade Chief of Police and he mobilized all available I.R.A. Police Volunteers to begin searches of all public premises in Navan. Mick McKeown and James Mackey (see Navan Company) were appointed to keep close observation on Navan R.I.C. Barracks (now known as Navan Town Hall or the Old Garda Barracks). Later that evening McKeown and Mackey observed Gordon leaving the barracks in Navan. They followed him up the town and he entered the Flat House Bar on Railway Street. John Kelly was informed and he went to the Flathouse with Joseph Boyle and Patrick Keating (see Navan Company) to arrest Gordon. Sean Boylan headed to the Flathouse by car. When Sean Boylan arrived McKeown and Mackey were casually making conversation with Gordon. Joseph Boyle and Patrick Keating were keeping observation on two R.I.C. men who were also in the bar. John Kelly was calmly standing inside the door to cover off any attempted escape. Sean Boylan entered and pub, produced a revolver and he arrested Gordon and forced him into the car. He was taken to an "unknown destination" which is now known to have been Peter O'Connor's, Salestown, Dunboyne. After several hours of interrogation Gordon admitted his involvement, he named the rest of the gang involved and he named the gang leader. The information was immediately passed to Pat Farrelly (see Carnaross Company) advising him that most of the gang were in his area. The suspects were arrested by the I.R.A. and taken to an "unknown destination" which is now known to have been Harry Dyas, Bolton House, Boltown, Kilskyre, Kells. The house was un-occupied at the time and the prisoners were held there for a few weeks. When the R.I.C and British Troops realised what was happening they started large scale house to house searches. Before the R.I.C. and Military closed in on their location the prisoners were moved to other "unknown destinations". One is now known to have been at Slan Duff, Kentstown, Navan and another was in Bohermeen, Navan where they were guarded by the Commons I.R.A. Company. Eventually, after some weeks, the searches were scaled down and when the heat was off, the prisoners were moved to Peter O'Connor's, Salestown, Dunboyne where they were held for I.R.A. military trial. During a preliminary trial some of the prisoners broke down and revealed the whole plot. An officer arrived from I.R.A. General Head Quarters (G.H.Q.) to act as Senior Court Officer along with two local I.R.A. Brigade Officers. The case was heard in O'Connor's and the court found Gordon guilty of the murder of Mark Clinton and he was sentenced to death. The Gang Leader was found guilty and sentenced to expulsion from Ireland for life. The rest of the gang were found guilty and they were sentenced to expulsion from Ireland for terms ranging from 7 to 15 years. There was an appeal which was granted by Michael Collins. The case was re-heard and they came to the same conclusion. After the final hearing Gordon was given a few moments with a Clergyman and he was shot at Castlefarm, Dunboyne. The rest of the gang were taken in threes and fours to ports in Dublin, Dundalk and Drogheda where they were loaded on ships and deported under the supervision of John Kelly, Brigade Chief of Police. The means of getting prisoners on to the boat was simply row them out to the ship during the night and hide them in a lifeboat or other hiding place aboard the ship. The ship may not necessarily have been a passenger ship. The prisoner would become a stowaway and I would imagine he would be quite willing to facilitate his deportation rather than the alternative.

Source: Bureau of Military History, 1913- 21, Witness Statement No WS1060 on 11th January 1955, Witness: Seamus Finn, Athboy, Co. Meath. Adjutant Meath Brigade 1916-1917. Vice Commanding Officer & Director of Training 1st Eastern Division. Bureau of Military History, 1913- 21, Witness Statement No WS1622 on 3rd June 1957, Witness: Michael Hilliard, T.D., St. Enda's Villas, Navan, Co. Meath. Navan I.R.A. Company Commanding Officer, I.R.A. Brigade Intelligence Officer. Bureau of Military History, 1913- 21, Witness Statement No WS1627 on 11th June 1957, Witness: Charles Conaty, Ballyhist, Carnaross, Kells, Co. Meath. 1st Lieutenant, Stonefield Company. Commanding Officer of 2nd Battalion, 3rd Brigade, I.R.A. Bureau of Military History, 1913- 21, Witness Statement No WS1659 on 26th August 1957, Witness: Peter O'Connell, Crosswater, Carnaross, Kells, Co. Meath. I.R.A. Battalion Adjutant, 5th Battalion, Meath Brigade.

In July 1920 a number of cattle were stolen from a farm near Oldcastle. Seán Keogh alleges in his Witness Statement that I.R.A. Police investigation led them to a suspect in the Oldcastle area named John Farrelly. He was arrested by I.R.A. Police and taken to a Sinn Fein Court where he was convicted and sentenced to a period of detention. On Thursday 22nd July 1920 at 3am an I.R.A. Police detail were taking the prisoner by car to an "unknown destination" where he was to serve his time. That "unknown destination" is now known to have been Tully Mill, Oldcastle. When travelling through Oldcastle town they were called upon to halt by a British army military patrol comprising of a 2nd Lieutenant and sixteen soldiers of the 1st Battalion of the Norfolk Regiment, British Army. The car accelerated through. There was an exchange of gun fire in which Seamus Cogan was shot dead and Harry Sheridan, Jimmie O'Neill and their prisoner were wounded and at least two British Soldiers were seriously wounded. A short distance further on at Castlecor, Jimmy O'Neill lost control of the car, crashed and ended up in a field. They carried Cogan's body to a place known locally as Gavin's shed. In a follow up operation by Crown Forces Thomas Bardon from Summerbank (see Oldcastle

Company) was arrested at Tully Mill. He was there awaiting Seamus Cogan and the I.R.A. Police detail to arrive with their prisoner. Owen Clarke's clothes were splattered with blood so he had to hide until Charlie Fox, a local merchant in Oldcastle, provided him with new clothes.   Charlie then disposed of the blood stained clothes down a pump hole. The I.R.A. men alleged to have been involved in the incident were:

Ballinlough Company: Seán Keogh.

Drumbaragh Company: Jimmie O'Neill –The driver.

Oldcastle Company: Owen Clarke, Thomas (Tom) Lynch, Harry Sheridan and Thomas Bardon.

Stonefield Company: Seamus Cogan.

Seamus Cogan was buried in the Republican Plot at Ballinlough Cemetery on Sunday 25th July, see page 290. Harry Sheridan spent some time in the Mater Hospital, Dublin where he was treated for a gunshot wound to his shin bone.

Source: Bureau of Military History, 1913- 21, Witness Statement No W.S. 1615 on 16th May 1957, Witness: Seán Keogh, Smithstown, Ballinlough, Kells, Co. Meath. Commanding Officer 5th Battalion, Meath Brigade. Riocht Na Midhe, Volume XXVI . 2015. Personal Interview with Seamus Smith, Ballinacree on 2nd June 2015. Personal Interview with Sean Craughan

Informers and Spies:

In the Bureau of Military History Witness Statements I noticed that the terms spies and informers seem to mean the same thing in many instances. For the purposes of this book I am distinguishing spies from informers. I am defining informers as people who inform on other people to the local police. And I am defining spies as undercover intelligence agents who are secretly mingling with their enemy to gather intelligence information.

There were several rebellions in Irish History where informers were perceived as a problem for the rebels. Seamus Finn, who was a high ranking I.R.A. Officer in the Meath Area, tells us in his Witness Statement that around autumn 1920 Informers began to be a serious problem. British Crown Forces were a step ahead of Volunteers operations. Operations failed or had to be cancelled. Key Volunteers were being arrested or killed. The Volunteers decided they had to take action and they began to carry out surveillance of suspects. In some cases post office mail was raided by the Volunteers, hand written notes were intercepted and generally evidence was gathered. Where evidence of an informer was conclusive it was presented to General Head Quarters for review. When sanctioned by G.H.Q. the suspect was arrested, tried and executed. This was a bitter and gruesome order for a Volunteer to have to carry out. About ten people in Co. Meath were executed by the I.R.A. as informers during the 1920 – 1922 period. An informer's body would be left in a prominent place with a note attached saying something to the effect of spies and informers beware. This had the effect of stopping informants, stopping the casual chat between local people and the local Constable and in some cases suspected informers left the country.

Source: Bureau of Military History, 1913- 21, Witness Statement No W.S. 1060 on 11th January 1955, Witness: Seamus Finn, Athboy, Co. Meath. Adjutant Meath Brigade 1916-1917. Vice Commanding Officer & Director of Training 1st Eastern Division.

Reprieve for Informers did not seem to work according to Patrick O'Reilly, who was the Commanding Officer of the Moynalty I.R.A. and who later became a Battalion Vice Commanding Officer. He said in his Witness Statement that they arrested a suspected informer around December 1920. He faced an I.R.A. trial, was found guilty and released with a warning. He was put under I.R.A. surveillance. This suspect continued to relay any information he could to the R.I.C. He was re-arrested by I.R.A. Police, tried again by a higher court involving I.R.A. G.H.Q. personnel, convicted and shot.

Source: Bureau of Military History, 1913- 21, Witness Statement No WS1060 on 11th January 1955, Witness: Seamus Finn, Athboy, Co. Meath. Adjutant Meath Brigade 1916-1917. Vice Commanding Officer & Director of Training 1st Eastern Division. Bureau of Military History, 1913- 21, Witness Statement No WS1650 on 16th July 1957, Witness: Patrick O'Reilly, Bellair, Moynalty, Co. Meath. Captain Moynalty Company, Vice Commandant Kells Battalion, I.R.A.

Likewise Sean Farrelly, an I.R.A. Vice-Commanding Officer of the Meath Brigade from 1917 to 1921 tells us in his Witness Statement of another young man named Keelin from Kilmainhamwood who was very friendly with the Black and Tans and passed them any information that he could. The I.R.A. thought that by giving him a fright he might realise the gravity of his behaviour, so they arrested him and he was taken to an "unknown destination" which is now known to have been an unused house in Lower Leitrim, the property of a Miss McMahon of Mullagh. After being detained there for a few weeks, he was severely cautioned and released. But after his release he brought the Black and Tans to the house in which he had been detained and they burned it to the ground. He then travelled the countryside with the Black and Tans on their raids. The I.R.A. put him under observation and at the first opportunity they re-arrested him. He was court-martialed, found guilty and executed.

Bureau of Military History, 1913- 21, Witness Statement No WS1734 on April 1958, Witness: Sean Farrelly, Sourlogstown, Trim, Co. Meath. Vice Commanding Officer, Meath Brigade, I.R.A. 1917 – 11th July, 1921.

Spies or British Intelligence Agents were also executed by the I.R.A. David Hall, who was the I.R.A. 1st Brigade Commanding Officer said that they dealt with three Spies in their Brigade area of mainly Co. Meath. Bureau of Military History, 1913- 21, Witness Statement No W.S. 1539 on 4th December 1956, Witness: David Hall, Knutstown, Garristown, Co. Dublin. Officer Commanding 1st Brigade, 1st Eastern Division, I.R.A.

Both sides had spies and both sides had the same way of dealing with them. In September 1920 the I.R.A. suspected a man in Kiltale called Gavigan of being a spy. He was arrested by the I.R.A. Police and while being held to face charges at a court-martial he escaped. He was in fact a Black and Tan spy stationed in Dublin. Shortly afterwards he arrived back in the Kiltale area along with his Black and Tan colleagues and they arrested John McCormack of Pelletstown, James Wildridge of Drumree and Matthew Wallace of Batterstown, see all at Culmullin Company. They were looking for others but they were gone "On the Run". The three were taken to Dublin Castle where they were court-martialed on a charge of abducting Gavigan. John McCormack and James Wildridge were interned in the Curragh. Matthew Wallace was sent to Sandhurst Prison in England, he was only sixteen years of age. Source: Bureau of Military History, 1913- 21, Witness Statement No W.S. 1539 on 4th December 1956, Witness: David Hall, Knutstown, Garristown, Co. Dublin. Officer Commanding 1st Brigade, 1st Eastern Division, I.R.A.

Also in May 1921 a British Army Company Quartermaster Sergeant named Herrod of the South Wales Borderers based in Navan was apparently seen visiting a local girl. Whether it was romance or spying he was captured and killed between Navan and Kells. His body was found in the river Blackwater. Source: Faithful to Ireland by Tony Brady, page 60. Personal Interview with Stephen Ball, Bohermeen on 2nd July 2015.

Sometimes the wrong people were targeted as spies as in the following case: It was February 1921. The War of Independence was raging in Ireland and Co. Meath was in the thick of it. Postal letters was the main means of communication in those times. If the I.R.A. suspected that there was an informer or a spy in a particular area one of the things they would do was raid the mail and see who was sending information to whom. This activity did uncover suspects but the actual raid of the mail would alert an informer or a spy that the I.R.A. were on his trail. A more effective approach was to have a postal worker keep a close eye on mail and intercept suspicious letters addressed to R.I.C. It is alleged in Seamus Finn's and Mick Hilliard's witness statements that this was happening in Navan Post Office and they named the Postal Worker as Patrick Hughes from Dundalk, a member of the I.R.B. Information that Hughes uncovered and passed to Mick Hilliard, the Navan I.R.A. company Commanding Officer (see Navan Company) revealed the identity of at least one spy and helped to identify the whereabouts of several R.I.C. men who were on the I.R.A.'s most wanted list and had been relocated for their own safety. As a result at least one of the alleged spies was shot by the I.R.A. and the information relating to the wanted R.I.C. men was passed to other I.R.A. units who would follow it up in their parts of the country. These events came as a surprise to the R.I.C. and after sometime the R.I.C. Intelligence suspected a security leak at Navan Post Office and that the Postmaster, Mr. Hodgett, could be a possible suspect. Mr. Hodgett, was a native of Dungannon, Co. Tyrone. He was aged 55 years but partially disabled due to the effects of a stroke that he had suffered in recent years. He lived in Academy Street, Navan with his wife Grace since 1917 and they had four children. He was a member of the Church of Ireland. He was regarded by locals as a loyal British subject who had no involvement in politics. An efficient and trustworthy man who had close friends in local businesses. Navan R.I.C. Head Constable Queenan suggested to Hodgett that Constable Queenan's daughter should be employed in Navan Post Office as a Clerk. The young lady was probably being put there to keep an eye on what was going on and to report back to her father if she saw anyone tampering with the mail. However as she had no qualifications or previous experience of post office duties, Mr. Hodgett was not happy about this suggestion and he protested strongly.

On more than one occasion he was advised by the R.I.C. to accept the new girl. He refused and he reported the situation to his post office authorities. This drew more attention to him from the R.I.C. They probably thought he was trying to cover up the leak or that he was the source of the leak himself. On the night of the 18th February 1921, after midnight the Hodgett Family were asleep when there was loud knocking on their front door. Grace Hodgett put her head out the upstairs bedroom window and asked who is there. The reply came back "police." She went down stairs and opened the door. Two men armed with handguns came in saying that they were Sinn Feinners and talking a language that she did not recognise. They took Mr. Hodgett from his home, not even fully dressed. They forced and dragged him up Ludlow Street, through the Square and down Watergate Street, past the R.I.C. barracks to Poolboy Bridge at the bottom of Flower Hill where they shot him and threw him over the bridge into the river Boyne. When his body was recovered the R.I.C. said he had been executed by the I.R.A. The Hodgett family refuted this claim. Mrs. Hodgett said that the attackers were talking gibberish pretending they were speaking Irish, that they took her husband past the R.I.C. barracks to his execution which was itself also a short distance from the R.I.C. barracks. She claimed it was the R.I.C. who had done it. I.R.A. Intelligence conducted their own investigation and said that the R.I.C. did carry out the execution and they got two R.I.C. men from Baileboro to carry out the actual deed so that they would not be recognised. Michael Hilliard, Navan I.R.A. Company Commanding Officer, and later I.R.A. Brigade Intelligence Officer said in his Witness Statement that the two R.I.C. men were in the charge of R.I.C. District Inspector Hunt at the time.

Mr Hodgett's close friend, Mr. Gilbert was the owner of Navan Engineering Works. He was also considered to be loyal British subject. When his suspicions were confirmed he was so disgusted with the behaviour of the R.I.C. that he completely changed his attitude to them and he started making hand grenades in his works and supplying them to the I.R.A. Likewise Mr. Hodgett's son became an I.R.A. Intelligence agent.

Sources: Navan & District Historical Society; Navan Postmasters by Liam McCarthy; http://www.navanhistory.ie/index.php?page=postmasters Bureau of Military History, 1913- 21, Witness Statement No W.S. 1060 on 11th January 1955, Witness: Seamus Finn, Athboy, Co. Meath. Adjutant Meath Brigade 1916-1917. Vice Commanding Officer & Director of Training 1st Eastern Division.

Peter O'Connell from Crosswater, Carnaross, Kells, Co. Meath was I.R.A. Battalion Adjutant, 5th Battalion, Meath Brigade said in his witness statement that there was an I.R.A. man working within Kells Post office as well. His name was Jack Tuite and he was a post office clerk. Jack intercepted a letter from the Virginia Road /

Stonefield district addressed to the authorities in Dublin. It contained a list of names of I.R.A. Volunteers in the Stonefield and Whitegate areas. I.R.A. Police arrested a man named either Nicholas or Bryan Bradley on 2nd January 1921 at the home of his sister at Curragh, Carnaross, Kells, Co. Meath.

Bradley was another postman and an ex-British Soldier who fought in France in the 1st World War. As a postman he got to know the addresses of every active I.R.A. man in the district. He was tried by the I.R.A. and convicted of espionage. A priest from Kilmessan and a curate from Moynalty heard his confession and administered the last rights before he was executed around April 1921 in the Carnaross area. That means he was an I.R.A. prisoner on death row for about four months.

Bureau of Military History, 1913- 21, Witness Statement No WS1659 on 26th August 1957, Witness: Peter O'Connell, Crosswater, Carnaross, Kells, Co. Meath. I.R.A. Battalion Adjutant, 5th Battalion, Meath Brigade. Bureau of Military History, 1913- 21, Witness Statement No WS1734 on April 1958, Witness: Sean Farrelly, Sourlogstown, Trim, Co. Meath. Vice Commanding Officer, Meath Brigade, I.R.A. 1917 – 11th July, 1921. http://www.irishmedals.org/civilians-killed.html

On Monday 28th February 1921 a man arrived in Navan asking in pubs as to the whereabouts of I.R.A. men. He mentioned the names of prominent I.R.A. men from the area who were "on the run". Navan I.R.A. quickly got involved and without alerting him or saying who they were the stranger was casually questioned during the course of the day by several men of the Navan I.R.A. Company including Mick Hilliard, Pat Fitzsimons, John McLoughlin and Hugh Durr. He told them his name was Michael O'Brien from Silvermines, Co Tipperary but he spoke with a Scottish accent. He also told them that he shared a cell with Bob Chandler (the Publican from Robinstown previously mentioned at page 46). The stranger seemed to be under the impression that Bob Chandler was in the I.R.A. or Sinn Fein but he was not. The British soldiers and Auxiliaries had the same impression when they were questioning Bob Chandler in his Pub in the previous February. Did the army send the stranger to Navan to follow up on their poor information? The stranger refused to tell them anything about himself. They told him they would take him to see the men he was looking for. Mick Hilliard obtained a handgun from Loughlin (Jack) Rourke. The stranger was taken to an area near Beechmount House where he was shot as a spy.

It would be interesting to know who this stranger was and what he was doing. If he was a spy it is very difficult to believe that the authorities would send him on such a suicidal mission. If he was not a spy why was he asking these questions and why did he not explain himself before it was too late. Was he just a foolish stranger with a big mouth in the wrong place? Or was he an enemy soldier who thought that the people he was talking to were fools? We will probably never know.

Source: Bureau of Military History, 1913- 21, Witness Statement No WS1622 on 3rd June 1957, Witness: Michael Hilliard, T.D., St. Enda's Villas, Navan, Co. Meath. Navan I.R.A. Company Commanding Officer, I.R.A. Brigade Intelligence Officer.

Ardbraccan Company

The Ardbraccan I.R.A. Company was formed around the end of 1920. For years the Commons area was in the Navan Company Area but when the Ardbraccan Company was formed it took in the area known as Commons and that is the reason you will find I.R.A. Volunteers from Commons in Ardbraccan Cemetery. The Navan Company Commanding Officer at the time was Patrick Stapleton from Commons and he transferred to become Ardbraccan's first Commanding Officer. In 1921 the Ardbraccan I.R.A. Company had a strength of 33 men. In 1922 that strength was reduced to seven men. Sources: WS1622. RO 488.

Patrick (Patsy) Bennett, Neilstown, Ardbraccan, Navan, Co Meath was a Volunteer

in the Commons I.R.A. Company in 1919. He was a brother of Johnny Bennett, see Bohermeen Company. On 2nd November 1919 he was involved in an attack on Lismullen R.I.C. Barracks, see the story on page 37. He transferred to the Ardbraccan I.R.A. Company in 1920. He and Larry Collins stole two guns from the home of the R.I.C. District Inspector at the top of Flower Hill, Navan in the autumn of 1920. He continued as a member of the company in 1921. On the 2nd July 1921, about two weeks before the Truce, he was involved in a failed attack on a troop train near Celbridge, see the story on page 51. He joined the Free State Army but he was only in it a few days when the Civil War was announced. It is said locally in the Ardbraccan area that he was so disgusted that he threw his rifle in the Liffey and he went home. He became a member of the L.D.F. (Local Defence Force) and he is seen here in his L.D.F. uniform. He died on 28th December 1989 aged 89 years and was buried in Bohermeen Cemetery, see page 317. Source: RO 488. Headstone Inscription. Dunderry A Folk History by Dunderry History Group & Johnny Keely. Politics and War in Meath 1913-23 by Oliver Coogan, page 129.

Patrick Boyle, Commons, Navan, Co. Meath was born in Commons about 1902. In 1919 he was a Volunteer in the Commons I.R.A. Company. On 2nd November 1919 he was involved in an attack on Lismullen R.I.C. Barracks, see the story on page 37. He transferred to the Ardbraccan I.R.A. Company in 1920. In 1921 and 1922 he continued as a Volunteer in the Ardbraccan I.R.A. Company. In 1922 he was described as a farm labourer. He became a member of a 30 man strong I.R.A. Active Service Unit who later became known as the Curraghtown A.S.U. On 5th July 1922 he was involved in the Battle of Curraghtown where he was arrested by the Free State Army, see the story on page 58. He was temporarily held in Trim and then interned in Dundalk, Co. Louth on 22nd July 1922. On 27th July 1922 he escaped from Dundalk Jail, see the story on page 59. In 1936 his address was given as New York, U.S.A. Sources: RO 488. MM9.1.1/KM3L-FTT. Louth County Archives http://www.louthcoco.ie/en/Services/Archives/Archive_Collections/ Dunderry A Folk History by Dunderry History Group & Johnny Keely

Peter Bray, Ongenstown, Navan, Co. Meath was a Volunteer in the Ardbraccan I.R.A. Company in 1921. Source: RO 488

Michael Buchannon was a Volunteer in the Ardbraccan I.R.A. Company in 1921. In 1936 his address was given as Australia. Source: RO 488

James Byrne was born in Commons, Navan about 1900. He was a Volunteer in the

Commons I.R.A. Company in 1919. On 2nd November 1919 he was involved in an attack on Lismullen R.I.C. Barracks, see the story on page 37. He transferred to the Ardbraccan I.R.A. Company in 1920. He continued as a Volunteer in the Ardbraccan I.R.A. Company in 1921. In 1922 he was the Ardbraccan I.R.A. Company Commanding Officer. He became a member of a 30 man strong I.R.A. Active Service Unit who later became known as the Curraghtown A.S.U. On 5th July 1922 he was involved in the Battle of Curraghtown where he was arrested by the Free State Army, see the story on page 58. He was temporarily held in Trim and then interned in Dundalk, Co. Louth on 22nd July 1922. He was described in prison records as a labourer. On 27th July 1922 he escaped from Dundalk Jail, see the story on page 59. On 12th September 1922 he was recaptured at Kilberry, Navan and reinterned. In 1936 his address was given as Dublin. Sources: RO 488. MM9.1.1/KM3L-F2F. Louth County Archives http://www.louthcoco.ie/en/Services/Archives/Archive_Collections/ Dunderry A Folk History by Dunderry History Group & Johnny Keely.

Laurence Byrne was a Volunteer in the Ardbraccan I.R.A. Company in 1921. He died before 1938. Source: RO 488

Richard Byrne, Balreask Old, Navan, Co. Meath was a Volunteer in the Commons I.R.A. Company in 1919. On 2nd November 1919 he was involved in an attack on Lismullen R.I.C. Barracks, see the story on page 37. He transferred to the Ardbraccan I.R.A. Company in 1920. He continued as a Volunteer in the Ardbraccan I.R.A. Company in 1921 and 1922. Source: RO 488. Dunderry A Folk History by Dunderry History Group & Johnny Keely.

Francis Coffey, Ardbraccan, Navan, Co. Meath was a Volunteer in the Ardbraccan I.R.A. Company in 1921. In 1925 he was a member of the Martry G.A.A. Football Team who won the Feis Cup that year. He died on 11th August 1965 and was buried in Bohermeen Cemetery, see page 318. Sources: RO 488. Royal and Loyal by Michael O'Brien page 93. Headstone Inscription.

Laurence (Larry) Collins, Liscarton, Navan was originally a Volunteer in the Commons Company of Irish Volunteers. He transferred to the Ardbraccan I.R.A. Company in 1920. In the autumn of 1920 he and Patsy Bennett walked the railway line to Navan to reach the top of Flower Hill unnoticed where they entered the home of the R.I.C. District Inspector and they escaped with two guns. In 1922 Larry took the Pro-Treaty side and he joined the Free State Army. He ran a successful business in Liscarton called Leo Collins Joinery. The site is now occupied by Liscarton Motor Company Ltd. Larry Collins died on 21st October 1988 and was buried in St.

Mary's Cemetery, Navan, see page 336. Source: Politics and War in Meath 1913-23 by Oliver Coogan, page 129 and personal iterview with his son Michael (Mixer) Collins and his grandson Sean Collins in July 2015. Headstone inscription.

Patrick Coogan, Oatlands, Navan, Co. Meath was a Volunteer in the Ardbraccan I.R.A. Company in 1921. His name is engraved on a headstone in Bohermeen Cemetery, see page 319. Source: RO 488. Headstone Inscription.

James Dalton, Knockumber, Navan, Co. Meath was born in Commons, Navan about 1899. In 1921 he was a Volunteer in the Ardbraccan I.R.A. Company but he was arrested and imprisoned in Mountjoy, Dublin for offences under the Defence of the Realm Regulations (DRR) and on a charge of having a revolver. Sources: RO 488. MM9.1.1/KMQR-G5Z. MM9.1.1/KM79-R9G

Louis Dempsey was a Volunteer in the Ardbraccan I.R.A. Company in 1921. In 1936 his address was given as Dublin. Source: RO 488

Michael Foley, Ardbraccan, Navan, Co. Meath was a Volunteer in the Ardbraccan I.R.A. Company in 1921. Source: RO 488

Michael Gerrard was a Volunteer in the Ardbraccan I.R.A. Company in 1921. In 1936 his address was given as England. Source: RO 488

Andrew Halpin was a Volunteer in the Ardbraccan I.R.A. Company in 1921. He died before 1938. Source: RO 488

James Hughes was a Volunteer in the Ardbraccan I.R.A. Company in 1921. Source: RO 488

John Hyland, Ardbraccan, Navan, Co. Meath was a Volunteer in the Ardbraccan I.R.A. Company in 1921. Source: RO 488

Michael Hyland, Hayes, Navan, Co. Meath was a Volunteer in the Commons I.R.A. Company in 1919. On 2nd November 1919 he was involved in an attack on Lismullen R.I.C. Barracks, see the story on page 37. He transferred to the Ardbraccan I.R.A. Company in 1920. He continued as a Volunteer in the Ardbraccan I.R.A. Company in 1921. He was appointed I.R.A. Battalion Engineer, 4th Battalion, 2nd Brigade, 1st Eastern Division in April 1921. He died on 10th November 1970 and was buried in St. Mary's Cemetery, Navan, see page 338. Source: WS1622. Headstone Inscription. Dunderry A Folk History by Dunderry History Group & Johnny Keely.

Patrick Hyland, Ardbraccan, Navan, Co. Meath was a Volunteer in the Ardbraccan I.R.A. Company in 1921. He died on 28th October 1970 and was buried in Boyerstown Cemetery, see page 322. Source: RO 488. Headstone Inscription.

Michael Markey, Balreask Old, Navan, Co. Meath was a Volunteer in the Ardbraccan I.R.A. Company in 1921. Source: RO 488

William Martin was a Volunteer in the Ardbraccan I.R.A. Company in 1921. In 1936 his address was given as England. Source: RO 488

George McDermott, Boyerstown, Navan, Co. Meath attended the old school on the Fair Green in Navan. He joined the British Army in 1914 and he fought in the 1st World War. He returned home after the war in 1918 and he joined the Commons Company of Irish Volunteers. He was a Volunteer in the Ardbraccan I.R.A. Company in 1921. He became a Sergeant of a 30 man strong I.R.A. Active Service Unit who later became known as the Curraghtown A.S.U. On 5th July 1922 he was involved in the Battle of Curraghtown where he was shot dead by Free State Army soldiers, see the story on page 58. He was 35 years of age. He was buried in Ardbraccan Cemetery, see page 314. Source: RO 488. Headstone Inscription. Meath Chronicle dated 16th September 1967, page 13.

William McGuirk was born in the U.S.A. about 1903. He became a Volunteer in the Commons Irish Volunteers. In 1921 and 1922 he was a Volunteer in the Ardbraccan I.R.A. Company. In 1922 he was a farm labourer. He became a member of a 30 man strong I.R.A. Active Service Unit who later became known as the Curraghtown A.S.U. On 5th July 1922 he was involved in the Battle of Curraghtown where he was arrested by the Free State Army, see the story on page 58. He was temporarily held in Trim and then interned in Dundalk, Co. Louth on 22nd July 1922. On 27th July 1922 he escaped from Dundalk Jail, see the story on page 59. On 12th August 1922 he was recaptured at Wilkinstown, Navan. In 1938 his address was given as Philadelphia, U.S.A. Sources: RO 488. MM9.1.1/KM3L-FYS. Louth County Archives http://www.louthcoco.ie/en/Services/Archives/Archive_Collections/ Dunderry A Folk History by Dunderry History Group & Johnny Keely.

James McKenna, Balreask Old, Navan, Co. Meath was a Volunteer in the Ardbraccan I.R.A. Company in 1921. Source: RO 488

Bernard Monaghan, Knockumber, Navan, Co. Meath was a Volunteer in the Ardbraccan I.R.A. Company in 1921. Source: RO 488

Michael Monaghan, Kilmainham, Kells, Co. Meath was a Volunteer in the Ardbraccan I.R.A. Company in 1921. Source: RO 488

William Moore was a Volunteer in the Ardbraccan I.R.A. Company in 1921. In 1938 his address was given as England. Source: RO 488

Loughlin (Jack) O'Rourke, Knockumber, Navan, Co. Meath was a Volunteer in the Commons I.R.A. Company in 1919. He was involved in an attack on Lismullen R.I.C. Barracks on 2nd November 1919, see the story on page 37. His address was given as Shambo, Navan. He transferred to the Ardbraccan I.R.A. Company in 1920. In February 1921 he was involved in the questioning of a stranger in Navan suspected of being a spy, see the story on page 77. In July 1921 he was the Ardbraccan I.R.A. Company 1st Lieutenant. Sources: Politics and War in Meath 1913-23 by Oliver Coogan, page 123. WS1622. RO 488. Dunderry A Folk History by Dunderry History Group & Johnny Keely.

William Rooney, Boyerstown, Navan, Co. Meath and a native of Co. Wicklow was an ex-British Army soldier. He was decorated for his Gallantry in the First World War. He returned home from the War in 1918 and in 1919 he was a Volunteer in the Commons I.R.A. Company. He transferred to the Ardbraccan I.R.A. Company in 1920 where he became Staff Captain. In April 1921 he was the Adjutant of the 8th Brigade (Fingal). On 7th April 1921 he shot and wounded R.I.C. Sergeant William E. Johns aged 25 years at Boyerstown Horse Races. He escaped from the scene but in a follow up operation James Loughran (see Bohermeen Company) and William were engaged by a party of R.I.C. There was an exchange of fire and the two men were chased cross country from Irishtown to Ongenstown where they were captured. William Rooney was charged with endangering the safety of police. He was found guilty and he received fifteen years penal servitude. He suffered from TB and when he was released from prison as part of the terms of the Treaty in 1922 in poor health. On 17th March 1922 he died in Navan Hospital of double pneumonia aged 32 years. He was buried in Roundwood, Co. Wicklow.

Sources: RO 488. Meath Chronicle dated 28th May 1921, page 1. Meath Chronicle dated 4th June 1921, page 1. Dunderry A Folk History by Dunderry History Group & Johnny Keely. Meath chronicle dated 27th April 1935, page 5. Mrs. Margret Conway, Moattown, Kildalkey article published in Meath Chronicle dated 12th March 1966. Michael Hilliard's speech in Ardbraccan Cemetery, see Meath Chronicle dated 2nd April 1932 page 1. WS1060. MM9.1.1/KMQR-TW7. Meath Chronicle dated 18th March 1922 page 1.

Patrick Stapleton, see Navan Company

Nicholas Stapleton, Commons, Navan, Co. Meath was a Volunteer in the Ardbraccan I.R.A. Company in 1921 and 1922. He died on 29th August 1955 and was buried in Donaghmore Cemetery in Navan, see page 324.

Source: RO 488. Headstone Inscription.

Valentine Stapleton was born in Commons, Navan, Co. Meath about 1905. He was a Volunteer in the Commons Irish Volunteers. In 1921 and 1922 he was a Volunteer in the Ardbraccan I.R.A. Company. In 1921 he was arrested and imprisoned in Mountjoy, Dublin on a charge of being in possession of firearms. In 1922 he was a farmer. He became a member of a 30 man strong I.R.A. Active Service Unit who later became known as the Curraghtown A.S.U. On 5th July 1922 he was involved in the Battle of Curraghtown where he was arrested by the Free State Army, see the story on page 58. He was temporarily held in Trim and then interned in Dundalk, Co. Louth on 22nd July 1922. On 27th July 1922 he escaped from Dundalk Jail, see the story on page 59. In 1938 his address was given as Massachusetts, U.S.A. Sources: RO 488. MM9.1.1/KMQR-5RQ. MM9.1.1/KM3L-F2J. Louth County Archives http://www.louthcoco.ie/en/Services/Archives/Archive_Collections/ Dunderry A Folk History by Dunderry History Group & Johnny Keely.

Thomas Walshe, Commons, Navan, Co. Meath was a Volunteer in the Commons I.R.A. Company in 1919. On 2nd November 1919 he was involved in an attack on Lismullen R.I.C. Barracks, see the story on page 37. He transferred to the Ardbraccan I.R.A. Company in 1920. He continued as a Volunteer in the Ardbraccan I.R.A. Company in 1921.

Source: RO 488. Dunderry A Folk History by Dunderry History Group & Johnny Keely.

Patrick Waters, Commons, Navan, Co. Meath was born about 1891.

He joined the Irish Volunteers around 1917. He was a Volunteer in the Commons I.R.A. Company in 1919. On 2nd November 1919 he was involved in an attack on Lismullen R.I.C. Barracks, see the story on page 37. He transferred to the Ardbraccan I.R.A. Company in 1920. He became the Ardbraccan I.R.A. Company Quartermaster in 1921. In November 1936 he attended a meeting to appoint a Brigade Committee for gathering information related to qualifying Volunteers for the Military Service Pensions. He died on 7th March 1973 aged 82 years and was buried in St. Mary's Cemetery, Navan, see page 346. His picture was kindly provided by his grandnephew Evans (Jeff) Miller, Silverlawns, Navan. Source: Headstone Inscription. Dunderry A Folk History by Dunderry History Group & Johnny Keely.

Ardcath Company

In July 1921 Ardcath Company had a strength of twelve men. In July 1922 there were no Volunteers so the company ceased to exist. Source: RO 519

John Andrews, Ardcath, Garristown, Co. Meath was a Volunteer in the Ardcath I.R.A. Company in 1921. Source: RO 519

Thomas Cox, Ardcath, Garristown, Co. Meath was a Volunteer in the Ardcath I.R.A. Company in 1921. Source: RO 519

Fir in Dowling, Ardcath, Co. Meath was the Ardcath I.R.A. Company 1st Lieutenant in 1921. I do not understand the name "Fir in Dowling" I have rechecked it a few times and I confirm that it is correctly transcribed from the official records of Military Service Pensions Collection number RO 519. Source: RO 519

James Dunne, Ardcath, Garristown, Co. Meath was the Ardcath I.R.A. Company Commanding Officer in 1921. Source: RO 519

Thomas Keenan, Clonaly, Garristown, Co. Meath was a Volunteer in the Ardcath I.R.A. Company in 1921. Source: RO 519

James Kelly, Clonaly, Garristown, Co. Meath was a Volunteer in the Ardcath I.R.A. Company in 1921. Source: RO 519

John McCormack, Ardcath, Garristown, Co. Meath was a Volunteer in the Ardcath I.R.A. Company in 1921. Source: RO 519

James McGuinness, Bartramstown, Garristown, Co. Meath was a Volunteer in the Ardcath I.R.A. Company in 1921. Source: RO 519

Patrick Moore, Ardcath, Garristown, Co. Meath was the Ardcath I.R.A. Company Quartermaster in 1921. Source: RO 519

Peter Moore, Ardcath, Garristown, Co. Meath was the Ardcath I.R.A. Company Adjutant in 1921. Source: RO 519

Thomas Wall, Ardcath, Garristown, Co. Meath was the Ardcath I.R.A. Company 2nd Lieutenant in 1921. Source: RO 519

Patrick Walsh, Brienstown, Garristown, Co. Meath was a Volunteer in the Ardcath I.R.A. Company in 1921. Source: RO 519

Peter Walsh, Ardcath, Garristown, Co. Meath was the I.R.A. Fourth Battalion Commanding Officer in 1921. Source: RO 519

Athboy Company:

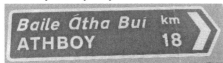

An Athboy Company of Irish National Volunteers was formed in 1913 by Joe Martin, Tom Devine and John McGurl with a strength of 20 men which grew rapidly to a strength of 100 men. Training and drills were conducted by two ex-British soldiers named James Geraghty and Patrick Holland. In July 1914, at the outbreak of World War One, a huge split immerged in the Volunteer movement nationally. John Redmond, who was the leader of the Irish Parliamentary Party, called on the National Volunteers to join the Irish Regiments of the British Army and to fight in the Great War, as it was called. A handful of Volunteers who disagreed left the National Volunteers and the rest of them joined the British Army. As a result by the end of 1914 the Athboy Company of National Volunteers failed to exist. The Athboy Company of Irish Volunteers was formed in 1917 with a strength of twelve men and it was organised by Seamus Finn, Joe Martin and Sean O'Grady. In 1918 the strength of the company rose to 40 men due to the threat of Conscription into the British Army. The company was attached to the 3rd Battalion Meath Brigade. In January 1919 the Irish Volunteers became the I.R.A. In the spring of 1920 the Athboy I.R.A. Company was involved in the burning of the R.I.C barracks in Stirrupstown, Delvin, Bohermeen and Causestown. In June or July of 1920 a Sinn Féin District Court was established in the area. In April 1921 the Athboy I.R.A. Company became attached to the 2nd Battalion, 4th Brigade. The Athboy Company had a strength of 36 men and in 1922 its strength was fifteen men. Sources: RO 496. WS1660. WS1723.

Thomas Barrett, Martinstown, Athboy was a Volunteer in the Athboy I.R.A. Company in July 1921. Source: RO 496

John Broderick, Connaught Street, Athboy, Co. Meath was a Volunteer in the Athboy I.R.A. Company in July 1921 and July 1922. Source: RO 496

George Butterfield was a Volunteer in the Athboy Company of Irish Volunteers in 1916 and he was involved in the Easter Rising. After the failed Rising he got involved in reorganising the company in Athboy. Sources: WS0857. Politics and War in Meath 1913-23 by Oliver Coogan. Page 100

Patrick Butterfield was born in Athboy around 1882. In 1915 he was a Volunteer in the Athboy Company of Irish Volunteers. He attended the funeral of O'Donovan Rossa at Glasnevin Cemetery in August 1915. On Wednesday 26th April 1916 he left Athboy to engage in the rebellion in Dublin but he could not get into Dublin and he returned within a couple of days. After the failed Rising he got involved in reorganising the company in Athboy. In 1918 he was arrested and imprisoned in Mountjoy, Dublin for taking part in an unlawful riot. He continued as a Volunteer with the Athboy I.R.A. Company in 1921 and 1922. In 1921 he gave his address as Bundoggan, Athboy and in 1922 he gave his address as Connaught Street, Athboy, Co. Meath. Sources: WS1723. RO 494. MM9.1.1/KMQR-J1T. MM9.1.1/KM79-KWK. Politics and War in Meath 1913-23 by Oliver Coogan, Page 100.

John Callery, Martinstown, Athboy, Co. Meath was a Volunteer in the Athboy I.R.A. Company In July 1921. He died on 20th February 1975 and was buried in Saint James Cemetery, Athboy, see page 270. Source: RO 496. Headstone Inscription.

Patrick Carey, Knockshangan, Athboy, Co. Meath was a Volunteer in the Athboy Company of Irish Volunteers. After the failed Rising in 1916 he got involved in reorganising the company in Athboy. From 1918 to 1920 he was the Quartermaster of the Athboy I.R.A. Company. Around September 1920 he was arrested. In December 1920 he was appointed the Quartermaster of the 3rd Battalion, Meath Brigade. On his release he continued his I.R.A. activity through to 1922. In early September 1922 he was arrested following an attack on Athboy Barracks in which one of the Official Forces I.R.A. was killed, see page 62. Source: WS1723. WS01060. Faithful to Ireland by Tony Brady, page 78

Bartle Carroll, Connaught Street, Athboy, Co. Meath was a Volunteer in the Athboy I.R.A. Company in July 1921. Source: RO 496

James Cassidy, Greenpark, Athboy, Co. Meath was a Volunteer in the Athboy I.R.A. Company in July 1921. In early September 1922 he was arrested following an attack on Athboy Barracks in which one of the Official Forces I.R.A. was killed, see page 62.
Source: RO 496. Military Service Pension Collection, file reference No. MD-20519. Faithful to Ireland by Tony Brady, page 78

John Cassidy was a Volunteer in the Athboy I.R.A. Company in July 1921.
Source: RO 496

John P. Costigan, Athboy, Co. Meath was a Brigade Intelligence Officer of the 1st Brigade (Meath), 1st Eastern Division in 1921. In 1922 he was the Battalion Adjutant, 2nd Battalion, 1st Brigade (Meath). Source: WS1715. RO 479. RO 481.

Michael Cullen was a Volunteer in the Athboy I.R.A. Company In July 1921. In 1936 his address was given as England. Source: RO 496

Tom Devine, Athboy, Co. Meath was a Volunteer in the Athboy Company of National Volunteers in 1913. His name is engraved on a headstone in St. James Cemetery, Athboy. The inscription says that Tom Devine died on 9th April 1952, see page 270. Source: WS1660. Headstone Inscription

Martin Doherty, Martinstown, Athboy, Co. Meath was a Volunteer in the Athboy I.R.A. Company in July 1921. He died on 21st December 1937 and was buried in the Church of Ireland Cemetery in Athboy, see page 269. Source: RO 496. Headstone Inscription

James Doyle, Bridge Street, Athboy, Co. Meath was a Volunteer in the Athboy Company of Irish Volunteers in 1916 and he remained a Volunteer through to 1922. After the failed Rising he got involved in mustering up disappointed Volunteers and trying to get them to regroup and reorganise. Source: WS0857. RO 496. WS0857

William Doyle from Athboy Co. Meath was the 1st Lieutenant in the Athboy I.R.A. Company in 1918 and 1919. After the failed Rising of 1916 he got involved in reorganising the company in Athboy. In September 1920 he seized fuel which was later used to burn the heavily fortified Trim R.I.C. Barracks in a co-ordinated attack, see the story on page 40. In 1921 he was appointed Athboy I.R.A. Company Commanding Officer and his address was given as Bundoggan, Athboy. Captain William Doyle continued to hold the post of Company Commanding Officer through 1922 and his address was given as Connaught Street, Athboy. Source: WS1723. RO 494. RO 496. Politics and War in Meath 1913-23 by Oliver Coogan, Page 100.

Matthew Eustace, Pluckstown, Athboy, Co. Meath was a Volunteer in the Athboy I.R.A. Company in July 1921. His name is engraved on a headstone in St. James Cemetery, Athboy. The inscription says that Matthew Eustace died on 29th June 1970, see page 271. Source: RO 496. Headstone Inscription.

Peter Falkner, Martinstown, Athboy, Co. Meath was a Volunteer in the Athboy I.R.A. Company in July 1921. Source: RO 496

Patrick Farrelly, Rathcarn, Athboy, Co. Meath was born in Rahoney, Athboy, Co. Meath about 1890. In July 1921 he was a Volunteer in the Athboy I.R.A. Company. In 1923 he was arrested by Pro-Treaty I.R.A. and imprisoned in Mountjoy, Dublin for being a member of an armed organisation. Sources: RO 496. MM9.1.1/KM78-CQ2. Military Service Pension Collection, file reference No. MD-20516

Michael Finn was the 1st Eastern Division Medical Officer Captain in March 1921. His address was given as Co. Dublin. Source: WS1060

Seamus Finn, a native of Athboy, was the Athboy Company Commanding Officer in 1916, 1917 and 1918. He was a keen hurler with the Athboy O'Growney Hurling and Football Club. After the failed Rising he got involved in trying to bolster up disappointed Volunteers and trying to get them to regroup and reorganise. In 1917 he was the only officer in the Athboy Company of Irish Volunteers. On 24th January 1918 he addressed a public meeting in Ballivor to start a Sinn Fein Club. Fifty men enrolled. In October 1919 Seamus was appointed Brigade Adjutant, Meath Brigade, I.R.A. On Sunday 30th September 1920 he was involved in the attack on the heavily fortified Trim R.I.C. Barracks, see the story on page 40. In December 1920 he was appointed Brigade Adjutant and Acting Vice Commanding Officer, I.R.A. On 1st April 1921 he was involved in an ambush of a military truck at Sylvan Park, Kells, see the story on page 47. He was appointed Director of Training and Special Services, I.R.A. In July 1921 he was a Commandant and he was the Divisional Vice Commanding Officer and Director of Training. He was also a member of Meath County Council in 1921 and Chairman of Trim R.D.C. Colonel Commandant Seamus Finn died on 16th July 1974. His funeral mass took place in St. James's Church Athboy. Source: WS0857. WS1723. WS0901. RO 494. The Meath Chronicle dated 20th July 1974, page 1. WS0857. WS1060. WS1715. The Meath Chronicle dated 9th Feb 1918

John Finnegan was the 2nd Lieutenant of the Athboy I.R.A. Company in July 1921. He died before 1936. Source: RO 496

James Geraghty was an ex-British Army Soldier and he was the Athboy Company of National Volunteers Commanding Officer in 1913. His name is engraved on a headstone in St. James Cemetery, Athboy. The inscription says that James Geraghty died on 6th November 1952, see page 271. Source: WS1660. Headstone Inscription.

James Halligan was appointed Engineer of the 2nd Battalion, 4th Brigade, 1st Eastern Division, I.R.A. in April 1921. Sources: WS1723. WS1660.

Michael Hoey was a Volunteer in the Athboy Company of Irish Volunteers in 1915. He attended the funeral of O'Donovan Rossa at Glasnevin Cemetery in August 1915. On Wednesday 26th April he left Athboy to engage in the Rebellion in Dublin but they could not get into Dublin and he returned within a couple of days. After the failed Rising he got involved in reorganising the company of Irish Volunteers in Athboy. He continued as an I.R.A. Volunteer in 1921 and he gave his address as Castletown, Athboy, Co. Meath.
Sources: WS1723. RO 496. Politics and War in Meath 1913-23 by Oliver Coogan, Page 100.

Patrick Holland was an ex-British Army Soldier and he was the Athboy Company of National Volunteers Vice-Commanding Officer in 1913. His name is engraved on a headstone in St. James Cemetery, Athboy. The inscription says that Patrick Holland died on 9th October 1932, see page 271. Source: WS1660. Headstone Inscription

Thomas Keane, Bridge Street, Athboy, Co. Meath was a Volunteer in the Athboy I.R.A. Company in July 1921. He died before 1936. Source: RO 496

Hugh Kelly, Dunderry, Co. Meath was born in Knockshangan, Athboy, Co. Meath about 1898. In 1920 he was a Volunteer in the Athboy I.R.A. Company. About September 1920 he was arrested. On his release he continued as an I.R.A. Volunteer in 1921 and 1922. In 1923 he was arrested by Pro-Treaty I.R.A. and imprisoned in Mountjoy, Dublin for being a member of an armed organisation. Sources: WS1723. MM9.1.1/KM78-CQK.

Christopher Mahon was a Volunteer in the Athboy I.R.A. Company in July 1921. He died before 1936. Source: RO 496

John Martin, Connaught Street, Athboy, Co. Meath was a Volunteer in the Athboy I.R.A. Company in July 1921. His name is engraved on a headstone in St. James Cemetery, Athboy. The inscription says that John Martin died on 11th March 1932, see page 272 Source: RO 496. Headstone Inscription.

Joseph (Joe) Martin, Kilkeelan, Athboy, Co. Meath was born in Athboy in 1897. In his Witness Statement he describes himself as a farmer and a Rate Collector. He joined the Athboy Company of National Volunteers when it was formed in 1913. In 1914 he had a disagreement with the National Volunteers and he left. After the failed Rising he got involved in trying to boost up disappointed Volunteers in an attempt to get them to regroup and reorganise. In April 1917 he was the 1st Lieutenant of the Athboy I.R.A. Company. In 1918 he was the 2nd Lieutenant. During the 1918 General Election he was on police duty at one of the Polling Booths. In late 1918 or early 1919 be became an I.R.A. Battalion Engineer. In 1920 he was "on the run". In December of 1920 he was in Delvin on Christmas Eve when three men armed with a handgun tried to grab him. He drew his revolver and fired wounding one of the assailants twice. He subsequently found out that the assailant was a British Spy and that he was on the I.R.A.'s wanted list. In July 1921 Joe was the I.R.A. Brigade Engineer, 4th Brigade, 1st Eastern Division and he was also the Athboy I.R.A. Company Intelligence Officer. He continued in those roles until the end of 1922. In early September 1922 he was arrested following an attack on Athboy Barracks in which one of the Official Forces I.R.A. was killed, see page 62. He died on 21st July 1963 and was buried in St James Cemetery in Athboy, see page 272. Sources: WS1660. WS1723. WS0901. RO 496. WS0857. WS1623. Faithful to Ireland by Tony Brady, page 78. Headstone Inscription.

Thomas Martin, Connaught Street, Athboy, Co. Meath was a Volunteer in the Athboy I.R.A. Company in October 1919. In July 1921 and 1922 he was the Athboy I.R.A. Company Adjutant. Source: WS0901. RO 494. RO 496.

Bernard (Barney) McConnell, Martinstown, Athboy, Co. Meath was a Volunteer in the Athboy Company of Irish Volunteers in 1915. He attended the funeral of O'Donovan Rossa at Glasnevin Cemetery in August 1915. On Wednesday 26th April he mobilised for the Easter Rising of 1916 but he could not get into Dublin due to roadblocks. After the failed Rising he got involved in reorganising the

company of Irish Volunteers in Athboy. He continued as an I.R.A. Volunteer in 1921. He died before 1936.
Source: WS1723. Politics and War in Meath 1913-23 by Oliver Coogan, Page 100. WS0857.

Christopher McCormack, Bridge Street, Athboy, Co Meath was a Volunteer in the Athboy I.R.A. Company in July 1921. Source: RO 496

Thomas McGuinness was a Volunteer in the Athboy I.R.A. Company in July 1921. Source: RO 496

Patrick McGurl, Frayne, Athboy, Co. Meath was born in Addinstown, Co. Westmeath, in October 1883. His family moved to Athboy in 1893. He was a brother of below Sean. He joined the Athboy Company of National Volunteers when it was formed in 1913. In 1914 he had a disagreement with the company, he left and he joined the Irish Volunteers. In December 1917 he transferred to the Kildalkey Company of Irish Volunteers which had recently been formed and it was nearer to his home. At end of spring 1921 he was appointed I.R.A. Battalion Adjutant, 2nd Battalion, 4th Brigade, 1st Eastern Division. In July 1921 the records show that he still held that role. In May 1966 he attended the 1916 Commemoration in Kildalkey.
Source: WS1660. RO 496. WS1723. Meath Chronicle dated 7th May 1966, page 9.

Sean McGurl, Frayne, Athboy, Co Meath was a Volunteer in the Athboy Company of National Volunteers in 1913. He was a brother of above Patrick. He split from The National Volunteers in 1914. He attended the funeral of O'Donovan Rossa at Glasnevin Cemetery in August 1915. At Easter 1916 he left Athboy to engage in the Rebellion in Dublin. Sean Boylan in his witness Statement confirmed that he was there but Boylan spelt his name McGurrell. He said that Sean was at the Red House in Dunboyne on 25th April 1916 and he served under the command of Donal O'Hannigan at Dunboyne. Along with the Dunboyne Company and others he was part of the column of men who occupied Tyrrelstown House during the Easter Rising, see the story on page 23. In June or July 1920 he was appointed Battalion Chief of Police, 3rd Battalion, Meath Brigade. Sources: WS1660. WS0212. WS1723.

John McKenna, Connaught Street, Athboy, Co. Meath was the Athboy Company Quartermaster in July 1921 and 1922. Source: RO 494. RO 496

Joseph (Joe) Monaghan was appointed I.R.A. Brigade Adjutant, 4th Brigade, 1st Eastern Division at the end of spring 1921. He died before 1936.
Sources: WS1623. WS1715. WS1723. RO 494

Matthew Monaghan, Athboy, Co. Meath was a Volunteer in the Athboy I.R.A. Company in July 1921. In 1936 he was a member of An Garda Síochána.
Source: RO 496

Patrick Monaghan, Clifton, Athboy, Co. Meath was a Volunteer in the Athboy I.R.A. Company In July 1921. He died and was buried in St. James Cemetery, Athboy, see page 272. Source: RO 496. Headstone Inscription.

James Mulvany, Kildalkey, Co. Meath was a Volunteer in the Athboy I.R.A. Company in July 1922. Source: RO 496

Paddy (Pat) Murray, Sherlockstown, Athboy, Co. Meath was a Volunteer in the Athboy I.R.A. Company In October 1919. He was appointed the I.R.A. company Quartermaster in 1921. Source: WS0901. RO 494. RO 496.

Gilchrist O'Byrne was a Volunteer in the Athboy I.R.A. Company in 1915. He attended the funeral of O'Donovan Rossa at Glasnevin Cemetery in August 1915. On Wednesday 26th April he left Athboy to engage in the Rebellion in Dublin but he could not get into Dublin and he returned within a couple of days. Source: WS1723.

Sean O'Grady, a native of Co. Clare, joined the Volunteers in Athboy in 1913. In 1916 he was involved in the Easter Rising. In 1917 he was the 2nd Lieutenant of the Athboy Company of Irish Volunteers. He was an Insurance salesman and after the Rising he travelled round Meath under the guise that he was selling insurance, mustering up disappointed Volunteers and trying to get them to regroup. In April 1921 he was the Battalion Commanding Officer. Later Commandant Sean O'Grady returned to his native Co. Clare and he was succeeded by Commandant Michael Fox as Battalion Commanding Officer. O'Grady was interned in Ballykinlar, in Co. Down. He became a member of Seanad Eireann and then Parliamentary Secretary in a number of Fianna Fail Governments. He lived at The Ward, Co Dublin. He died in April 1966. Source: WS0857. WS0858. WS1660. Politics and War in Meath 1913-23 by Oliver Coogan, Page 100. WS1723. The Irish Press dated 8th April 1966 page 3.

Patrick (Pat) O'Growney was a Volunteer in the Athboy Company of Irish Volunteers in 1915. He attended the funeral of O'Donovan Rossa at Glasnevin Cemetery in August 1915. He was mobilised for the Easter Rising of 1916 but he could not get through the British Security surrounding Dublin. After the failed Rising he got involved in reorganising the company in Athboy. He was a member of Meath County Council in 1921.
Source: WS1723. Politics and War in Meath 1913-23 by Oliver Coogan, Page 100. WS0857. WS1060.

Michael O'Neill, Grennanstown, Athboy, Co. Meath was a Volunteer in the Athboy I.R.A. Company in July 1921. Source: RO 496

Leo Reilly was a Volunteer in the Athboy I.R.A. Company In July 1921. Source: RO 496

Peter Reilly, Connaught St., Athboy was a Volunteer in the Athboy I.R.A. Company in October 1919. In July 1921 and 1922 he was the 2nd Lieutenant of the I.R.A. company. Source: WS0901. RO 494. RO 496

? Rispin, Athboy, Co. Meath was a Volunteer in the Athboy Company of Irish Volunteers in 1918. Rispins of Athboy were blacksmiths and they made pikes from old springs of cars, traps and motors. The pikes were used as weapons by the Volunteers. Source: WS0901.

Joseph Seerey, Pluckstown, Athboy, Co. Meath was a Volunteer in the Athboy I.R.A. Company in July 1921. Source: RO 496

Laurence Sherlock, Sherlockstown, Athboy, Co. Meath was a Volunteer in the Athboy I.R.A. Company in October 1919. In July 1921 and 1922 he was the 1st Lieutenant of the I.R.A. Company. In early September 1922 he was arrested following an attack on the Athboy Barracks in which one of the Official Forces I.R.A. was killed, see page 62. Source: WS0901. RO 494. RO 496. Faithful to Ireland by Tony Brady, page 78

Edward Thornton was a Volunteer in the Athboy I.R.A. Company in 1921. In April 1921 he was appointed I.R.A. Brigade Intelligence Officer, 4th Brigade, 1st Eastern Division. Sources: WS1623. WS1715. WS1723. RO 494. RO 496.

James Ward, Bridge Street, Athboy, Co. Meath was a Volunteer in the Athboy I.R.A. Company in October 1919. He continued in that role until the end of 1922. Source: WS0901. RO 496

Ballinacree Company:

Baile na Críche
Ballinacree

Meath Villages   WELCOME · FÁILTE

The Ballinacree Company was formed about September 1920. When I.R.A. structures were reorganised in April 1921 the Ballinacree Company became attached to the 2nd Battalion, 3rd Brigade, 1st Eastern Division. In 1921 Ballinacree Company had a strength of seventeen men. In 1922 that strength was reduced to five men. Sources: RO 489. WS1627. WS1659.

John Balfe, Ballinacree, Oldcastle, Co. Meath was a Volunteer in the Ballinacree I.R.A. Company In 1921. He died on 12th October 1975 and was buried in Ballinacree cemetery, see page 352. Source: RO 489. Headstone Inscription

Patrick Balfe, Moate, Oldcastle Co. Meath was a Volunteer in the Ballinacree I.R.A. Company in 1921. He died on 2nd March 1973 aged 80 years and was buried in Ballinacree cemetery, see page 352. Source: RO 489. Military Service Pension Collection, file reference No.MD-20425. Headstone inscription.

John Brown, Dungimmon, Mountnugent, Co. Cavan was a Volunteer in the Ballinacree I.R.A. Company in 1921. Source: RO 489

Peter Clarke, Cullentra, Mountnugent, Co. Cavan was a Volunteer in the Ballinacree I.R.A. Company in 1921. Source: RO 489

Peter Connell, Tubride, Oldcastle, Co. Meath was the Ballinacree Company 1st Lieutenant in 1921. In 1936 his address was given as Co. Cavan. Source: RO 489. Photo kindly provided by the Ballinacree Community Centre, thanks to Seamus Smith, Ballinacree.

James Donoghue, Hammondstown, Castlepollard, Co. Westmeath was a Volunteer in the Ballinacree I.R.A. Company in 1921. In 1922 he was an Officer in the Ballinacree I.R.A. Company. In 1936 his address was given as U.S.A. Source: RO 489

Bernard Farnan, Ballymanus, Castlepollard, Co. Westmeath was a Volunteer in the Ballinacree I.R.A. Company in 1921. Source: RO 489. Photo kindly provided by the Ballinacree Community Centre, thanks to Seamus Smith, Ballinacree.

James Heery, Hammondstown, Castlepollard, Co. Westmeath was a brother of below John Heery and he was a cousin of below James Heery. James was the Ballinacree Company Commanding Officer In 1921 and 1922. He died on 23rd December 1973 at his residence. He was buried in Ballinacree Church Cemetery. Source: RO 489. Military Service Pension Collection, file reference No. MD-30466. Irish Press dated 25th December 1973, page 2. Interview with Seamus Smith, Ballinacree in May 2015

James Heery, Tubrid, Oldcastle, Co. Meath was a Volunteer in the Ballinacree I.R.A. Company in 1921. Source: RO 489. Military Service Pension Collection, file reference No. MD-20467. Interview with Seamus Smith, Ballinacree in May 2015

John (Jack) Heery, Hammondstown, Castlepollard, Co. Westmeath was a brother of above James Heery from Ballinacree. Jack was a Volunteer in the Ballinacree I.R.A. Company in 1921 and 1922. Source: RO 489. Interview with Seamus Smith, Ballinacree in May 2015

Michael Heery, Tubrid, Oldcastle, Co. Meath was a Volunteer in the Ballinacree I.R.A. Company in 1921 and 1922. In 1936 his address was given as Dublin. Source: RO 489. Interview with Seamus Smith, Ballinacree in May 2015

Patrick Hennessy, Rasillagh, Oldcastle, Co. Meath was a Volunteer in the Ballinacree I.R.A. Company in 1921. Source: RO 489. Stories from around Ballinacree. Photo kindly provided by the Ballinacree Community Centre, thanks to Seamus Smith, Ballinacree.

Edward Kelly, Hilltown, Castlepollard, Co. Westmeath was a Volunteer in the Ballinacree I.R.A. Company in 1921. In 1936 his address was given as Co. Cavan. He died on 30th October 1960 and was buried in Ballinacree Cemetery, see page 353. Source: RO 489. Headstone Inscription

Richard McGinn, Moate, Oldcastle, Co. Meath was a Volunteer in the Ballinacree I.R.A. Company in 1921. Source: RO 489

Richard (Dick) Murtagh, Ballinacree, Oldcastle, Co. Meath was born in Oldcastle about 1899. In 1921 and 1922 he was the Ballinacree I.R.A. Company 2nd Lieutenant. In 1922 he was a Weaver. He was arrested by Pro-Treaty I.R.A. and interned in Dundalk, Co. Louth on 22nd July. On 27th July 1922 he escaped from Dundalk Jail, see the story on page 59. In 1936 his address was given as England. Source: RO 489. MM9.1.1/KM3L-FLV. Louth County Archives http://www.louthcoco.ie/en/Services/Archives/Archive_Collections/

Thomas Murtagh, Ballinacree, Oldcastle, Co. Meath was a Volunteer in the Ballinacree I.R.A. Company In 1921. His name is engraved on a headstone in Ballinacree Cemetery, see page 353. Source: RO 489. Headstone Inscription.

Thomas Reilly, Hilltown, Castlepollard, Co. Westmeath was a Volunteer in the Ballinacree I.R.A. Company In 1921. He died 23rd April 1976 aged 87 years and was buried in Ballinacree Cemetery, see page 353. Source: RO 489. Headstone Inscription. Photo kindly provided by the Ballinacree Community Centre, thanks to Seamus Smith, Ballinacree.

Ballinlough Company:

A company of Volunteers was formed in Crossakiel in 1914 under the command of

Captain Worship Booker who was an officer of the British Army Reserve. Drilling and training was under instructions of an ex- British Army man named Terence Brady. But Crossakiel Company ceased to exist in 1915 as a result of the national split in the organisation. Seán Keogh formed the Ballinlough Company of Irish Volunteers in July 1916 and the remaining Volunteers from Crossakiel transferred to the Ballinlough Company. At the end of 1916 the Ballinlough Company had a strength of 25 men. There were no officers in the Ballinlough Company at the time. By March 1917 the company strength was 40 men and they appointed Seán Keogh their Commanding Officer. In the Spring of 1918 the British Government threatened to introduce Conscription in Ireland which would mean that young men would be forced to join the British Army and to fight in World War One. This threat drove more young men into the Irish Volunteers and in Ballinlough the strength of the company rose to 100 men. When the Conscription threat passed the company strength went back to 45 men. In January 1919 the Irish Volunteers became the I.R.A. In 1920 the Ballinlough I.R.A. Company was attached to the 5th Battalion, Meath Brigade. By Easter Sunday 4th April 1920 the R.I.C. had evacuated the Crossakiel Barracks due to attacks and R.I.C. men had moved to the safety of bigger towns. The barracks were burnt down by local volunteers to ensure the R.I.C. did not return. In March 1921 an I.R.A. Battalion Meeting was held in Farley's in Clonagrouney, Crossakiel where the Sylvan Park military truck Ambush was planned, see the story on page 47. When I.R.A. structures were reorganised in April 1921 the Ballinlough Company became attached to the 2nd Battalion, 3rd Brigade, 1st Eastern Division. In 1921 the strength of the Ballinlough Company was 53 men and in 1922 it had reduced to 23 men. Sources: WS1715. WS1615. WS1627.

George Beggan, Kells Co. Meath was a Volunteer in the Ballinlough I.R.A. Company In 1921. Also in 1921 he was arrested and interned in Ballykinlar Internment Camp, Co Down. He was held in Compound No 2. In 1936 his address was given as Herbertstown, Clonmellon, Co. Westmeath. Sources: RO 489. Prisoners of War by Liam O' Duibhir, page 315. Photo kindly provided by Eugene Sheridan, Clonmellon, author of A History of the Parish of Clonmellon/Killallon

James Beggan, Saraghstown, Crossakiel, Kells, Co. Meath was a Volunteer in the Ballinlough I.R.A. Company in 1921. Source: RO 489
George Bough, Crossakiel, Kells, Co. Meath was a Volunteer in the Ballinlough I.R.A. Company in 1921. Source: RO 489
Michael Bough was a Volunteer in the Ballinlough I.R.A. Company in 1922. Source: RO 489
Hugh Brady, Ranevogue, Crossakiel, Kells, Co. Meath was a Volunteer in the Ballinlough I.R.A. Company in 1922. Source: RO 489
James Brady, Crossakiel, Kells, Co. Meath was a Volunteer in the Ballinlough I.R.A. Company in 1922. In 1936 his address was given as U.S.A. Source: RO 489
Patrick Conway, Stonefield, Oldcastle, Co. Meath was the Ballinlough I.R.A. Company 1st Lieutenant in 1921. On 1st April 1921 he was involved in an ambush of a military truck at Sylvan Park, Kells, see the story on page 47. In 1936 his address was given as U.S.A. Sources: RO 489. WS1060.
John Cowley, Ballinlough, Kells, Co. Meath was a Volunteer in the Ballinlough I.R.A. Company in 1921. Source: RO 489
Christopher (Cristie) Farrelly, Ardglasson, Crossakiel, Kells, Co. Meath was a Volunteer in the Ballinlough I.R.A. Company in 1921. He died on 11th August 1972 and was buried in the Church Cemetery in Kilskyre, see 300
Source: RO 489. Headstone Inscription.

Michael Farrelly, Seymourstown, Crossakiel, Kells, Co. Meath was the Ballinlough Company 2nd Lieutenant in 1921. Source: RO 489

Nicholas Farrelly, Seymourstown, Crossakiel, Kells, Co. Meath was a Volunteer in the Ballinlough I.R.A. Company in 1921. He was arrested and interned in Ballykinlar Internment Camp, Co. Down. He was held in Compound No 2. On his release he continued his involvement with the Ballinlough I.R.A. Company throughout 1922. Sources: RO 489 and Prisoners of War by Liam O' Duibhir, page 315

Patrick Farrelly, Seymourstown, Crossakiel, Kells, Co. Meath was a Volunteer in the Ballinlough I.R.A. Company in 1921 and 1922.
Source: RO 489. Military Service Pension Collection, file reference No. 34-41394

Philip Farrelly, Balnagon, Crossakiel, Kells, Co. Meath was the Ballinlough Company Quartermaster in 1921 and 1922. Source: RO 489

Christopher (Christie) Farrell, Johnsbrook, Kilskyre, Kells, Co. Meath was the Ballinlough Company Adjutant in 1922. Source: RO 489. Military Service Pension Collection, file reference No. 34-SP-42690

John Fitzgerald, Saraghstown, Crossakiel, Kells, Co. Meath was a Volunteer in the Ballinlough I.R.A. Company in 1921. In 1936 his address was given as U.S.A. Source: RO 489

Patrick Fitzgerald, Saraghstown, Crossakiel, Kells, Co. Meath was a Volunteer in the Ballinlough I.R.A. Company in 1921. Source: RO 489

Bernard Flood, Crevagh, Crossakiel, Kells, Co. Meath was a Volunteer in the Ballinlough I.R.A. Company in 1921. Source: RO 489

Joseph Flood, Balnagon, Crossakiel, Kells, Co. Meath was a Volunteer in the Ballinlough I.R.A. Company in 1921. Source: RO 489

Matthew Flood was a Volunteer in the Ballinlough I.R.A. Company in 1921. In 1936 his address was given as Carracastle PO, Balleyhademeen, Co. Mayo. Source: RO 489

Thomas Flood, Balnagon, Crossakiel, Kells, Co. Meath was a Volunteer in the Ballinlough I.R.A. Company in 1921. Source: RO 489

Patrick Friary, Crossakiel, Kells, Co. Meath was a Volunteer in the Ballinlough I.R.A. Company in 1921. Source: RO 489

John Gargan, Ballinlough, Kells, Co. Meath was a Volunteer in the Ballinlough I.R.A. Company in 1921. In 1936 his address was given as U.S.A. Source: RO 489

John Garry, Milltown, Kilskyre, Kells, Co. Meath was a Volunteer in the Ballinlough I.R.A. Company in 1921. Source: RO 489

Nicholas (Nick) Gaynor, Ballinlough, Kells, Co. Meath was a Volunteer in the Ballinlough I.R.A. Company in 1920. In September 1920 he was involved in the attack on the heavily fortified Trim R.I.C. Barracks, see the story on page 40. In 1921 he was arrested and interned in Ballykinlar Internment Camp, Co. Down. He was held in Compound No 2. On his release he continued as a Volunteer with the Ballinlough I.R.A. Company throughout 1922.
Sources: RO 489. Prisoners of War by Liam O' Duibhir, page 315. WS0858.

James Gillic, Stonefield, Oldcastle, Co. Meath was a Volunteer in the Ballinlough I.R.A. Company in 1921. Source: RO 489

Larry Gillic, was a Volunteer in the Ballinlough I.R.A. Company in 1921. In 1936 his address was given as Brooklyn, New York. Source: RO 489

Patrick Gilsenan, Saraghstown, Crossakiel, Kells, Co. Meath was a Volunteer in the Ballinlough I.R.A. Company in 1921. In 1936 his address was given as U.S.A. Source: RO 489

Bernard (Barney) Harte, Springville, Kilskyre, Kells, Co. Meath was a Volunteer in the Ballinlough I.R.A. Company. In July or August 1920 he was appointed Battalion Quartermaster, 5th Battalion, Meath Brigade. In October, Barney Harte was charged by the I.R.A. with Mutiny. He was court-martialed, found guilty, sentenced to two lashes of a horse-whip and reduced in rank, see page 40. He continued as a member of the I.R.A. until the end of 1922. Source: RO 489. WS1715. WS1734. Military Service Pension Collection, file reference No. MD-10109

Patrick Harte, Springville, Kilskyre, Kells, Co. Meath was a Volunteer in the Ballinlough I.R.A. Company in 1921. Source: RO 489

Frank Higgins was born in Kilskyre about 1891. He was a Volunteer in the Ballinlough I.R.A. Company. In 1920 he was arrested and imprisoned in Mountjoy, Dublin for offences under the Defence of the Realm Regulations (DRR). In 1921 he was arrested and interned in Ballykinlar Internment Camp, Co Down. He was held in Compound No 1. In 1936 his address was given as Haddington Road, Dublin. Sources: RO 489. Prisoners of War by Liam O' Duibhir, page 296. MM9.1.1/KM79-531.

Seán Keogh was a native of Smithstown, Crossakiel, Kells and he was born 1898. He joined the Crossakiel Company of Irish Volunteers in 1914 but due to the nationwide split in the organisation the Crossakiel Company ceased that same year. In 1915 he joined the Irish Republican Brotherhood (I.R.B.). In 1916 he formed the Ballinlough Company of Irish Volunteers. After the failed Rising he got involved in mustering up disappointed Volunteers and trying to get them to regroup and reorganise. In March 1917 he became the Ballinlough Company Commanding Officer. In July or August 1920 he was involved in the burning of Crossakiel barracks by the local I.R.A. Volunteers after the R.I.C. had abandoned it. Later the same night he was involved in the burning of Carnaross Barracks by the Carnaross I.R.A. Volunteers. On 22nd July 1920 he was involved in a shootout with British Troops in Oldcastle in which Seamus Cogan was killed, see page 72. In July 1920 Seán Keogh became I.R.A. Battalion Vice Commanding Officer, 5th Battalion, Meath Brigade as a result of Seamus Cogan's death. Later in 1920 Seán became I.R.A. Battalion Commanding Officer but about October 1920 he was arrested for illegal detention of one of His Majesty's Forces. He was imprisoned in Mountjoy, Dublin for offences under the Defence of the Realm Regulations (DRR). Tom Manning (see Ballinlough Company) took over his position as Battalion Commanding Officer. In February 1921 Seán was released from prison. On 1st

April 1921 he was involved in an ambush of a military truck at Sylvan Park, Kells, see the story on page 47. He was arrested again and interned in Rath Camp in the Curragh, Co Kildare. After an attempted escape from the Curragh he was imprisoned in Kilkenny on a charge of attempting to escape from military custody. Charles Conaty (see Stonefield Company) took over the role as I.R.A. Battalion Commanding Officer. About July 1921 Seán Keogh escaped from Kilkenny Jail. He died on 10th October 1978 and was buried in Ballinlough cemetery, see page 291. Sources: RO 489. WS0857. WS1060. WS1615. WS1627. MM9.1.1/KM79-RV8. MM9.1.1/KM7D-27T. WS1715. WS1734. Headstone Inscription.

Henry (Harry) Lee, Sylvan Park, Kells was the Ballinlough Company Commanding Officer 1921 and 1922. On 1st April 1921 he was involved in an ambush of a military truck at Sylvan Park, Kells, see the story on page 47. In 1936 his address was given as Gormanstown. Sources: RO 489. WS1060.

James Lee, Seymourstown, Crossakiel, Kells, Co. Meath was the Ballinlough Company Adjutant in 1921 and for part of 1922. Source: RO 489

Patrick Manning was a Volunteer in the Ballinlough I.R.A. Company in 1921 and 1922. In 1936 his address was given as Hartsland, Clonmellon, Co. Westmeath. Source: RO 489

Thomas (Tom) Manning, Clonmellon, Westmeath was a Volunteer in the Ballinlough Company of Irish Volunteers. In March 1917 he became the Ballinlough Company 1st Lieutenant. Shortly afterwards he became a member of the I.R.B. About the end of July 1920 he became I.R.A. Battalion Vice Commanding Officer after Seamus Cogan was killed, see the story on page 72. In September 1920 he became the Battalion Commanding Officer, 5th Battalion, Meath Brigade when Sean Keogh was arrested. In October 1920 Tom Manning was charged by the I.R.A. with Mutiny. He was court-martialed, found guilty, sentenced to two lashes of a horse-whip and reduced in rank, see the story on page 40. Within a couple of days he was replaced by Davy Smith, see Mullagh Company. However Tom Manning remained a member of the I.R.A. until the end of 1922. In 1936 his address was given as U.S.A. Sources: RO 489. WS1615. WS1627. WS1715.

Michael Mathews, Crossakiel, Kells, Co. Meath was a Volunteer in the Ballinlough I.R.A. Company in 1921. Source: RO 489

Peter Mathews, Crossakiel, Kells, Co. Meath was a Volunteer in the Ballinlough I.R.A. Company in 1921 and 1922. Source: RO 489

Philip Mathews, Crossakiel, Kells, Co. Meath was a Volunteer in the Ballinlough I.R.A. Company in 1921. He died on 5th January 1976 and was buried in Kilskyre Church Cemetery, see page 300. Source: RO 489. Headstone Inscription.

Padraig (Pat) McDonnell, Stonefield, Oldcastle was a former student of

 Maynooth. In 1917 he was a Volunteer in the Ballinlough I.R.A. Company. In September 1920 the 5th Battalion, Meath Brigade was restructured following a mutiny court-martial, see that story on page 40. As a result Padraig was appointed I.R.A. Battalion Intelligence Officer, 5th Battalion, Meath Brigade and he was also the Battalion Chief of Police. On 23rd March 1921 he was killed in action by Crown Forces at Oldcastle, see the story on page 44. He was buried beside his Comrade Seamus Cogan in Ballinlough cemetery, see his grave on page 291. A monument in his honour stands in Oldcastle town. On his death the position of Battalion Intelligence Officer was filled by Harry Lee. Sources: RO 489. WS1615. WS1659. WS1715. Headstone Inscription. Meath Chronicle dated 2nd April 1921 page 1. Photo kindly provided by Tom French, Meath County Library, Navan and Tony Brady, Cherryhill Road, Kells.

Thomas (Tom) McDonnell, Stonefield, Oldcastle was a Volunteer in the Ballinlough I.R.A. Company. In March 1921 while "on the run" with his brother Patrick above they were cornered by British Military. They made a run for freedom. Patrick was shot dead and Tom escaped arrest, see page 44. His name is engraved on a headstone in Ballinlough Cemetery, see page 291. Source: WS1060. Headstone Inscription.

Michael McGrane, Klskyre, was a Volunteer in the Ballinlough I.R.A. Company. In 1921 and 1922. Source: RO 489 Military Service Pension Collection, file reference No. MD-3180

Daniel McGuinness, Hartstown, Clonmellon, Co. Westmeath was a Volunteer in the Ballinlough I.R.A. Company in 1921 and 1922. In 1922 he took the Anti-Treaty side and in early 1923 he was arrested by the Free State Army during a military raid in Clonmellon. Source: RO 489. Faithful to Ireland by Tony Brady, page 83.

James McGuire, Carlile House, Kildalkey, Athboy, Co. Meath was a Volunteer in the Ballinlough I.R.A. Company in 1921. Source: RO 489

Bernard McKeown, Seymourstown, Crossakiel, Kells, Co. Meath was a Volunteer in the Ballinlough I.R.A. Company in 1921 and 1922. He was arrested and interned in Ballykinlar Internment Camp, Co. Down. He was held in Compound No 2. He was released as part of the Terms of the Treaty in 1922. He took the Anti-Treaty side and in early 1923 he was arrested at his home and interned by the Free State Army. Sources: RO 489. Prisoners of War by Liam O' Duibhir, page 315. Faithful to Ireland by tony Brady, page 83.

Brian McKeown, Crossakiel, Kells, Co. Meath was the Battalion Commanding Officer In July 1922. Source: RO 484

Patrick McKeown, was the Ballinlough Company Commanding Officer in 1921 and 1922. He was arrested and interned in Ballykinlar Internment Camp, Co. Down. He was held in Compound No 2. In 1936 his address was given as Lower Drumcondra Road, Dublin. Sources: RO 489. Prisoners of War by Liam O' Duibhir, page 315

Joseph Moore, Robinstown, Kilskyre, Kells, Co. Meath was a Volunteer in the Ballinlough I.R.A. Company in 1921 and 1922. In 1936 his address was given as U.S.A. Source: RO 489

Edward Muldoon, Saraghstown, Crossakiel, Kells, Co. Meath was a Volunteer in the Ballinlough I.R.A. Company in 1921. Source: RO 489

James Muldoon, Newtown, Killallon, Co. Meath was a Volunteer in the Ballinlough I.R.A. Company in 1921 and 1922. Source: RO 489

Eugene Nulty, Smithstown, Crossakiel, Kells, Co. Meath was a Volunteer in the Ballinlough I.R.A. Company in 1921. In 1936 his address was given as U.S.A. Source: RO 489

Peter O'Higgins, was born in Kilskyre Kells. He was a Volunteer in the Ballinlough I.R.A. Company. He was a brother of Frank O'Higgins, see Drumbaragh Company. He was also a brother of Brian O'Higgins who fought in the 1916 Rising, was a founder member of Sinn Fein and a TD in Dail Eireann from 1921 to 1926. Peter O'Higgins became Battalion Adjutant, 5th Battalion, Meath Brigade in July or August 1920. In October 1920 Peter O'Higgins was charged by the I.R.A. with Mutiny. He was court-martialed, found guilty, sentenced to two lashes of a horse-whip and reduced in rank, see the story on page 40. A couple of days later he was replaced by Peter O'Connell, see Stonefield Company. In 1921 Peter O'Higgins gave his address as Glenamona, Kells and in 1922 he gave his address as Sylvan Park, Kells. He continued as a member of the I.R.A. until the end of 1922. Sources: RO 489. WS1715. WS1734.

James O'Neill, Clonabraney, Crossakiel, Kells, Co. Meath became the Ballinlough Company 2nd Lieutenant in March 1917. He continued as the Ballinlough I.R.A. Company 2nd Lieutenant throughout 1921. In 1936 he was a member of An Garda Síochána. Source: RO 489. WS1615

Bernard Reilly, Balnagon, Crossakiel, Kells, Co. Meath was a Volunteer in the Ballinlough I.R.A. Company in 1921 and 1922. Source: RO 489

John Reilly, Balnagon, Crossakiel, Kells, Co. Meath was a Volunteer in the Ballinlough I.R.A. Company in 1921 and 1922. Source: RO 489

Matthew Reilly, Balnagon, Crossakiel, Kells, Co. Meath was the Ballinlough Company Quartermaster in 1921 and 1922. He died on 15th December 1959 and was buried in the Kilskyre Church Cemetery, see page 301. Source: RO 489. Headstone Inscription

Michael Rourke was a Volunteer in the Ballinlough I.R.A. Company in 1922. Source: RO 489

Ballivor Company:

The Ballivor Company of Irish Volunteers was formed in 1917 with assistance from Athboy Company's Seamus Flynn and Joseph Martin. In 1918 the strength of the Ballivor Company increased to 29 due to the threat of conscription into the British Army. Also in 1918 a Sinn Fein Club was formed at a public meeting in Ballivor on 24th January which was addressed by Seamus O'Higgins, Trim and Seamus Finn, Athboy. Fifty members enrolled in the Sinn Fein Club. In January 1919 the Irish Volunteers became the I.R.A. On 1st November 1919 the Ballivor R.I.C. Barracks was attacked. One R.I.C. man was shot dead and rifles and revolvers were seized by I.R.A. Volunteers during the attack. By Easter Sunday 4th April 1920 the R.I.C. had evacuated the Ballivor Barracks due to attacks and they had moved to the safety of bigger towns. The Ballivor Barracks were burnt down by local Volunteers to ensure the R.I.C. did not return. In 1921 the Ballivor I.R.A. Company Strength was down to 20 men and in 1922 the company had no members so it ceased to exist. Sources: WS1723. WS1715. The Meath Chronicle dated 9th Feb 1918, page 1

Michael Bligh, Portlester, Ballivor, Co. Meath was a Volunteer in the Ballivor I.R.A. Company in July 1921. Source: RO 495

John Brackin, Ballivor, Co. Meath was the Adjutant in the Ballivor I.R.A. Company in July 1921. Source: RO 495

Andrew Brennan was a Volunteer in the Ballivor I.R.A. Company in July 1921. Source: RO 495

Thomas Brown, Muchwood, Ballivor, Co. Meath was the 1st Lieutenant in the Ballivor I.R.A. Company in July 1921. His name is engraved on a headstone in Killaconnigan Cemetery, see page 372. Source: RO 495. Headstone Inscription

Thomas Byrne, Grange, Ballivor, Co. Meath was a Volunteer in the Ballivor I.R.A. Company in 1920. In October 1920 he was arrested and jailed. In July 1921 he was still in jail. Source: RO 495

Christopher Casserly, Cooloran, Ballivor, Co. Meath was a Volunteer in the Ballivor I.R.A. Company in July 1921. Source: RO 495

Daniel Connor, Portown, Ballivor, Co. Meath was born about 1889. He was a Volunteer in the Ballivor I.R.A. Company in July 1921. He died in March 1967 aged 78 years and was buried in Ballivor New Cemetery, see page 374. Source: RO 495. Headstone Inscription

John Cunningham was a Volunteer in the Ballivor I.R.A. Company in July 1921. In 1936 he was a patient in St. Loman's Mental Hospital in Mullingar. His name is engraved on a headstone in Killaconnigan Cemetery. The inscription says that John Cunningham died on 25th March 1979, see page 372. Source: RO 495. Headstone Inscription.

Joseph Cunningham was a Volunteer in the Ballivor I.R.A. Company in July 1921. In 1936 his address was given as Dublin. Source: RO 495

Patrick Dixon was the Secretary of the Ballivor Sinn Fein Club in January 1918. He was a Volunteer in the Ballivor I.R.A. Company in July 1921. He was a former member of the Ballivor Davitts and Rathcormack Football Teams. In September 1941 he collapsed and died while helping a neighbour whose cow had calved.
Source: RO 495. The Meath Chronicle dated 9th Feb 1918, page 1. The Meath Chronicle dated 4th October 1941, page 1

Patrick Donohue, Portlester, Ballivor, Co. Meath was a Volunteer in the Ballivor I.R.A. Company In July 1921. Source: RO 495

Michael Flanagan was a Volunteer in the Ballivor I.R.A. Company in July 1921.
Source: RO 495

Philip Grey was a Volunteer in the Ballivor I.R.A. Company in July 1921. Later that year he was appointed Engineer of the 1st Battalion, 4th Brigade, 1st Eastern Division, I.R.A. In 1936 his address was given as Dublin. He lived at 57 Philipsburgh Terrace, Faiview, Dublin. He died on 9th May 1971 and was buried in Ballivor New Cemetery. Source: RO 495. Headstone Inscription.

James Heny, Ballivor, Co. Meath was the Ballivor Company Commanding Officer in July 1921. Source: RO 495

Peter Kiernan, Carronstown, Ballivor, Co. Meath was the 2nd Lieutenant in the Ballivor I.R.A. Company in July 1921.
In May 1966 he attended the 1916 Commemoration in Kildalkey. He died at his residence in February 1982 and was buried in Killaconnigan Cemetery, Ballivor, Co. Meath, see page 373.
Source: RO 495. Meath Chronicle dated 7th May 1966, page 9. Irish Press dated 24th February 1982, page 2. Headstone Inscription.

Patrick Loughlin, Ballivor, Co. Meath was a Volunteer in the Ballivor I.R.A. Company in July 1921. Source: RO 495

Thomas Maguire was a Volunteer in the Ballivor I.R.A. Company in July 1921. In 1936 his address was given as Dublin. Source: RO 495

Bernard McCabe, Elmgrove, Ballivor, Co. Meath was the Quartermaster of the 1st Battalion, 4th Brigade, 1st Eastern Division, I.R.A. in July 1921. Source: RO 495

Edward McCabe, Elmgrove, Ballivor, Co. Meath was a Volunteer in the Ballivor I.R.A. Company in July 1921 and later that year he was appointed Battalion Commanding Officer. Source: RO 495

John McDonnell, Trim, Co. Meath was a Volunteer in the Ballivor I.R.A. Company in July 1921. Source: RO 495

Thomas McDonnell, Muchwood, Ballivor, Co. Meath was a Volunteer in the Ballivor I.R.A. Company in July 1921. His name is engraved on a headstone in Killaconnigan Cemetery, see page 373. Source: RO 495. Headstone Inscription.

James Miggan, was the Quartermaster in the Ballivor I.R.A. Company in July 1921. In 1936 his address was given as U.S.A. Source: RO 495

Joseph Monaghan, was a Volunteer in the Ballivor I.R.A. Company in July 1921. He died before 1936. Source: RO 495

John Regan, Longwood, Co. Meath was a Volunteer in the Ballivor I.R.A. Company in July 1921. His name is inscribed on a headstone in Longwood Cemetery, see page 380. Source: RO 495. Headstone Inscription

James Rickard, Kilmer, Ballivor, Co. Meath was a Volunteer in the Ballivor I.R.A. Company in July 1921. Source: RO 495

James Rickard, Kilmer, Ballivor, Co. Meath was a member of the Ballivor Sinn Fein Club Committee in January 1918. He was the I.R.A. Battalion Adjutant in July 1921. Source: RO 495

Bective & Kilmessan Company:

The Bective I.R.A. Company was formed at the latter end of 1917. It was organised by Paddy Mooney and Seamus O'Higgins of Trim Company and it was set up as the Bective section of the Trim Irish Volunteer company. The Bective Section had no arms. In 1918 the strength of the Bective Section rose to 20 men mainly due to the threat of Conscription of young men into the British Army. It was at this stage that the Bective section broke away from the Trim Company and stood on its own as the Bective Irish Volunteers company and they elected their own officers. This shortly came to the notice of the R.I.C. who arrested Frank Loughran, the new Bective I.R.A. Company Commanding Officer. Patrick Quinn took over Command of the Bective I.R.A. Company shortly after Frank Loughran's arrest in 1919 and the Bective Company forged ahead. On 2nd November 1919 the Bective I.R.A. Company blocked all the roads in their area as part of the coordinated attack on Lismullen R.I.C. Barracks also known as Dillon's Bridge Barracks, see the story on page 37. In May 1920 the Bective I.R.A. Company took over Community Policing duties in the area and Sinn Fein set up a court for the Battalion Area of Trim, Kiltale, Bective and Dunderry. A man called R.J. Murray was appointed President of the Court. John (Jack) Horan (see Kilbride Company) and another man were nominated District Justices. In the summer of 1920 the Bective I.R.A. Company was attached to the 2nd Battalion, Meath Brigade. In 1921 the Bective Company Strength was 28 men. In April 1921 the Bective Company was attached to the 1st Battalion, 2nd Brigade, 1st Eastern Division. In 1922 the Bective Company ceased to exist. A few remaining Volunteers from the Bective Company transferred to the Kilmessan Company giving the Kilmessan I.R.A. Company a total strength of ten men. Sources: RO 485. WS1696.

Matthew Boyle, Ringlestown, Kilmessan, Co. Meath was a Volunteer in the Bective & Kilmessan I.R.A. Company in July 1921.
Source: RO 485. Military Service Pension Collection, file reference No. 24-SP-4641

Michael Brady, Ennistown, Kilmessan, Co. Meath was involved in an attack on the heavily fortified Trim R.I.C. Barracks in September 1920, see the story on page 40. He was a Volunteer in the Bective & Kilmessan I.R.A. Company in July 1921.
Sources: RO 485. WS0858. Military Service Pension Collection, file reference No 24SP1392

Stephen Brady, Philipstown, Dunderry, Co. Meath was a Volunteer in the Bective & Kilmessan I.R.A. Company in July 1921. Source: RO 485

Christopher Caffrey, Ferry Hill, Kilmessan, Co. Meath was elected the 2nd Lieutenant in the Bective I.R.A. Company in the summer of 1918. In 1920 he had to go "on the run" and in September 1920 he was involved in an Active Service Unit (A.S.U.) while "on the run". At the end of September 1920 he took part in the attack on the heavily fortified Trim R.I.C. Barracks as a member of the A.S.U., see the story on page 40. In March or April 1921 he was appointed I.R.A. Battalion Vice Commanding Officer, 1st Battalion, 2nd Brigade. He died before 1936. Sources: RO 485. WS1696. WS0858. WS1715.

Thomas Durrin, Kilcarty, Kilmessan, Co. Meath was a Volunteer in the Bective & Kilmessan I.R.A. Company in July 1921. Source: RO 485

Christopher Farnan was a Volunteer in the Bective & Kilmessan I.R.A. Company in July 1922. In 1936 his address was given as Dublin. Source: RO 485

William Foley, Ennistown, Kilmessan, Co. Meath was a Volunteer in the Bective & Kilmessan I.R.A. Company in July 1921. Source: RO 485

James Griffin, Colvinstown, Tara, Co. Meath was a Volunteer in the Bective & Kilmessan I.R.A. Company in July 1921. Source: RO 485

Bernard Harris, Tribley, Kilmessan, Co. Meath was a Volunteer in the Bective & Kilmessan I.R.A. Company in July 1921. Source: RO 485

John Harris, Tribley, Kilmessan, Co. Meath was a Volunteer in the Bective & Kilmessan I.R.A. Company in July 1921. Source: RO 485

James Horan, Bective, Navan, Co. Meath was a Volunteer in the Bective & Kilmessan I.R.A. Company in 1920 when he was arrested. He continued as a Volunteer in the Bective & Kilmessan I.R.A. Company in 1921. His name is engraved on a headstone in the Church of the Nativity Cemetery in Kilmessan but I am not 100% sure it is the same James Horan, see page 286. Source: RO 485. WS1696.

James Landy, Follistown, Navan, Co. Meath was a Volunteer in the Bective & Kilmessan I.R.A. Company in July 1922. Source: RO 485

Bernard Lenehan was a Volunteer in the Bective & Kilmessan I.R.A. Company in July 1921. In July 1922 he was a member of An Garda Síochána. Source: RO 485

Edward Losty, Curtistown, Kilmessan, Co. Meath was a Volunteer in the Bective & Kilmessan I.R.A. Company in July 1922. He died on 25th August 1973 and was buried in the Church of the Nativity Cemetery in Kilmessan see page 286.
Source: RO 485. Headstone Inscription.

Frank Loughran was elected the Bective I.R.A. Company first Commanding Officer in the summer of 1918. In 1919 he was arrested and imprisoned in Mountjoy. The role of company Commanding Officer went to Patrick Quinn. Frank took part in a hunger strike within the jail. As result of public pressure Frank was released from prison along with about 70 other I.R.A. prisoners around mid-April 1920, see page 39. He was involved in the burning of Dillon's Bridge or Lismullen R.I.C. Barracks, see page 39. He was appointed I.R.A. Battalion Commanding Officer and shortly afterwards he was re-arrested. He was still an active member of the I.R.A. in July 1921. In 1936 his address was given as Dublin but I don't know if that Dublin address was correctly recorded on the pension records. In 1925 a Francis Loughran was a member of An Garda Síochána and was Garda Sergeant in Loughlin Bridge, Co. Carlow. I am not sure if this is the same Frank Loughran. He died on 12th July 1981 and was buried in the Church of the Nativity Cemetery in Kilmessan, see page 286. Source: RO 485. WS1696. Military Service Pension Collection, file reference No. 24SP1392. Dunderry A Folk History by Dunderry history Group and Johnny Keely. Headstone Inscription.

Thomas Loughran, Tullykane, Kilmessan, Co. Meath was a Volunteer in the Bective & Kilmessan I.R.A. Company in July 1921. Source: RO 485

Thomas Magher, Ennistown, Kilmessan, Co. Meath was a Volunteer in the Bective & Kilmessan I.R.A. Company in July 1921. Source: RO 485

William Magher Ennistown, Kilmessan, Co. Meath was a Volunteer in the Bective & Kilmessan I.R.A. Company in July 1921. Source: RO 485

John Mangan, Tara, Co. Meath was born in Robinstown in 1898. He lived his youth in Bective and his later years in Kiltale, Dunsany, Co. Meath. He became a Volunteer in the Bective Section of the Trim Irish Volunteers in 1917. He was arrested and imprisoned in Mountjoy in 1919. He took part in a hunger strike within the jail. As result of public pressure John was released from prison along with about 70 other I.R.A. prisoners around mid-April 1920, see page 39. In September 1920 he was involved in an attack on the heavily fortified Trim R.I.C. Barracks, see the story on page 40. Shortly afterwards he was re-arrested and imprisoned in Mountjoy, Dublin for offences under the Defence of the Realm Regulations (DRR). The prison record gives his address as Bective, Navan. In 1921 he was arrested again and imprisoned in Mountjoy, Dublin on a charge of having documents in his possession. He also spent time in Pentonville Prison in London. He died at his home in Kiltale, Dunsany in February 1963 aged 65. The funeral took place from Kiltale Church to the adjoining Cemetery. Sources: RO 485. WS1696. MM9.1.1/KM79-5SZ. MM9.1.1/KM79-TXV. MM9.1.1/KMQR-5MF. The Meath Chronicle dated 26th February 1963, page 9.

Patrick McCabe, Bellewstown, Navan, Co. Meath was the 2nd Lieutenant in the Bective Company of Irish Volunteers in 1918. He held the role of Bective I.R.A. Company 2nd Lieutenant in 1920. At the end of September 1920 he was involved in the capture and burning of Trim R.I.C. Barracks, see page 40. He took the Anti-Treaty side and he was imprisoned in Dundalk Jail and the Curragh Internment

Camp during the Civil War. He died on 26th March 1974 and was buried in the Church of the Nativity Cemetery in Kilmessan, see page 286.

Sources: RO 485. The Meath Chronicle dated 13th April 1974, page 16. Headstone Inscription.

Henry (Harry) McGrane, Swainstown, Kilmessan, Co. Meath was Battalion Chief of Police, 2nd Battalion, Meath Brigade in May 1920. The records show that he continued as an active member of the I.R.A. throughout 1921 and 1922.

Sources: RO 485. WS1696.

Christopher Moran, Marshalstown, Kilmessan, Co. Meath was 1st Lieutenant in the Bective & Kilmessan I.R.A. Company in July 1921 and July 1922. He died on 15th August 1972 and was buried in the Church of the Nativity Cemetery in Kilmessan, see page 287. Source: RO 485. Headstone inscription.

Joseph Moran, Marshalstown, Kilmessan, Co. Meath was a Volunteer in the Bective & Kilmessan I.R.A. Company in July 1921. He died on 3rd April 1942 and was buried in the Church of the Nativity Cemetery in Kilmessan, see page 287.

Source: RO 485. Headstone Inscription.

William Moran, was born in 1903. He was the son of Eddie and Annie Moran who  lived in the cottage beside Rowley's Lock Bridge, see page 61. They were the Lock House Keepers for Boyne Navigation Company. William Moran served his time as a Wood Machinist and Chair Maker at Alysbury's Mill, Ramparts, Navan. He later lived at Marshalstown, Kilmessan, Co. Meath. In 1921 he was a Volunteer in the Bective & Kilmessan I.R.A. Company. He took the Pro-Treaty side and he joined the Free State Army in 1922. He was stationed in Co. Cork when Michael Collins was shot dead at Béal na Bláth on 22nd August 1922. He guarded the hospital in which Collins was taken to after the fatal ambush, see page 62. William was a member of the army detail who accompanied Michael Collins body back to Dublin. He moved to No 26 Academy St, Navan. He died on 19th October 1969 aged 65 and was buried in St. Mary's Cemetery, Navan, see page 341.

Source: RO 485. Personal interview with his son Liam Moran. Headstone Inscription.

Patrick Norris, Stamullen, Co. Meath was a Volunteer in the Bective & Kilmessan I.R.A. Company in July 1921. Source: RO 485

Jack O'Brien, Kilmessan, Co. Meath was elected the Bective I.R.A. Company Quartermaster in the summer of 1918. At the end of September 1920 he was involved in the attack on the heavily fortified Trim R.I.C. Barracks, see page 40.

Source: RO 485. WS1696. WS0858.

James Quinn, Kilmessan, Co Meath was a brother of below Patrick. In the summer of 1918 James was elected the Bective Irish Volunteers Company Adjutant. In September 1920 he was involved in an attack on the heavily fortified Trim R.I.C. Barracks, see the story on page 40. In March or April 1921 he was

appointed I.R.A. Battalion Adjutant, 1st Battalion, 2nd Brigade. In June 1921 he was involved in transporting arms, ammunition and explosives for a planned attack on a troop train near Celbridge, see the story on page 51. He was still Battalion Adjutant in July 1921. He died on 21st March 1926 aged 30 years and was buried in the Church of the Nativity Cemetery in Kilmessan, see page 287.
Source: RO 485 WS1696 WS0858. Headstone Inscription

Patrick Quinn, Bellinter, Kilcarne, Navan and also of Kilmessan, Co. Meath was born about 1900. He was a bricklayer by trade. He was a brother of above James. Patrick joined the Bective Section of the Trim Company of Irish Volunteers at its inception which was the latter end of 1917. When the Bective Company became separate from the Trim Company in the summer of 1918 he was elected the Bective Company 1st Lieutenant. When Frank Loughran was arrested in 1919 Patrick Quinn took over the position as the Bective I.R.A. Company Commanding Officer. At the end of September 1920 he was involved in the attack on the heavily fortified Trim R.I.C. Barracks, see the story on page 40. Following that attack he had to go "on the run". In October 1920 he was involved in an Active Service Unit (A.S.U.) while "on the run". In March or April 1921 he was appointed Battalion Commanding Officer, 1st Battalion, 2nd Brigade. In June 1921 he was involved in gathering arms, ammunition and explosives for a planned attack on a troop train near Celbridge, see the story on page 51. He later joined the Free State Army. In September 1936 he was appointed to the Brigade Committee for gathering information related to qualifying Volunteers for the Military Service Pensions. He died on 8th June 1968 and was buried in the Church of the Nativity Cemetery in Kilmessan, see page 287.
Sources: RO 485. WS1696. WS0858. Military Service Pension Collection, file reference No. 24SP1392. Headstone Inscription.

Christopher Reid, Kilmessan, Co. Meath was the Bective & Kilmessan I.R.A. Company Commanding Officer in October 1920. In 1920 he had to go "on the run" but he continued in an Active Service Unit (A.S.U.) during that period. He continued as the I.R.A. company Commanding Officer during 1921 and 1922.
Source: RO 485. WS1696.

Patrick Scully, Kilcarty, Kilmessan, Co. Meath was the Bective & Kilmessan I.R.A. Company Adjutant in July 1921. He died before 1936. Source: RO 485.

William Smith, Kilmessan, Co. Meath was a Volunteer in the Bective & Kilmessan I.R.A. Company in July 1922. Source: RO 485

James Twomey, Dunsany, Co. Meath was a Volunteer in the Bective & Kilmessan I.R.A. Company in July 1922. Source: RO 485

Christopher Wheelan, Creroge, Kilmessan, Co. Meath was the Bective & Kilmessan Company Quartermaster in July 1921 and 1922. He died on 15th April 1967 aged 70 years and was buried in the Church of the Nativity Cemetery in Kilmessan, see page 287. Source: RO 485. Headstone Inscription.

Edward Wheelan, Creroge, Kilmessan, Co. Meath was a Volunteer in the Bective & Kilmessan I.R.A. Company in July 1921. Source: RO 485

Boardsmill Company:

In 1921 the company strength was twelve men. In 1922 there were no men in the company so it ceased to exist. Source: RO 495

Matt Byrne was a Volunteer in the Boardsmill I.R.A. Company in July 1921. In 1936 his address was given as U.S.A. Source: RO 495

Michael Byrne, Boardsmill, Trim, Co. Meath was a Volunteer in the Boardsmill I.R.A. Company in July 1921. Source: RO 495

M. Collins, Boardsmill, Trim, Co. Meath was a Volunteer in the Boardsmill I.R.A. Company in July 1921. Source: RO 495

James Doyle, Boardsmill, Trim, Co. Meath was the Boardsmill I.R.A. Company Commanding Officer in July 1921. Source: RO 495

Peter Doyle, Boardsmill, Trim, Co. Meath was the Boardsmill I.R.A. Company Quartermaster in July 1921. Source: RO 495 Military Service Pension Collection, file reference No. 34-SP-42128

J. Egan, Boardsmill, Trim, Co. Meath was a Volunteer in the Boardsmill I.R.A. Company in July 1921. He was arrested and imprisoned around this time. Source: RO 495

B. Gogarty, Kilbride, Trim, Co. Meath was a Volunteer in the Boardsmill I.R.A. Company in July 1921. Source: RO 495

P. Heany, Longwood, Co. Meath was a Volunteer in the Boardsmill I.R.A. Company in July 1921. Source: RO 495

James Morgan, Boardsmill, Trim, Co. Meath was a Volunteer in the Boardsmill I.R.A. Company in July 1921. Source: RO 495

Robert Morgan, Boardsmill, Trim, Co. Meath was the Boardsmill I.R.A. Company 2nd Lieutenant in July 1921. In May 1966 he attended the 1916 Commemoration in Kildalkey. Source: RO 495. Meath Chronicle dated 7th May 1966, page 9.

James Rafferty, Killyon, Hill of Down, Enfield, Co. Meath was the Boardsmill Company 1st Lieutenant in July 1921. Source: RO 495

Luke Rickard, Boardsmill, Trim, Co. Meath was the Boardsmill Company Adjutant in July 1921. His name is engraved on a headstone in St. Loman's Cemetery, see page 384. Source: RO 495. Headstone inscription.

Bohermeen Company:

The earliest record that I can find showing the formation of a company of Volunteers in Bohermeen is in 1917. Willie Coogan, listed below, said that Bohermeen Company used to meet for drill at Gibney's shed just off the New Line. Patrick Loughran said in his Witness Statement that the Navan Company of Irish Volunteers helped to form and organise the Bohermeen Company of Irish

Volunteers at the latter end of 1918. Both of these accounts could be correct because the ranks of the Volunteers were decimated in 1918 by a nationwide split in the Volunteer movements when John Redmond called on the Volunteers to join the British Army during World War One. In January 1919 the Irish Volunteers became the I.R.A. and in 1919 the Bohermeen I.R.A. Company was part of the 6th Battalion. By Easter Sunday 4th April 1920 the R.I.C. had evacuated the Bohermeen Barracks due to attacks on neighbouring barracks and R.I.C. men had moved to the safety of bigger towns. The barracks were burnt down by local Volunteers to ensure the R.I.C. did not return. Patrick Loughran said an attack plan was being prepared but the R.I.C. abandoned it prior to attack. In 1921 the Bohermeen I.R.A. company strength was eighteen men. In 1922 its strength was reduced to two men. Sources: WS1624. WS1723.

John (Johnny) Bennett, Ardbraccan, Navan, Co. Meath was a brother of Patsy

Bennett, see Ardbraccan Company. Johnny worked in Tullamore learning his trade as a stonecutter from 1917 to 1919. During that period he joined the Irish Volunteers in Tullamore. On his return in 1919 he joined Bohermeen I.R.A. Company. In 1920 he moved to Belfast to work for 6 months. Later he moved to Martry I.R.A. Company where he became the company 2nd Lieutenant. In January 1921 he was Involved in the transportation of explosives from Martry to Moynalty. In 1925 he was a member of the Martry Football Team who were Feis Cup Winners that year. He died on 21st March 1985 aged 86 years and was buried in Bohermeen Cemetery, see page 317. Source: WS1650. RO 488. Politics and War in Meath 1913-23 by Oliver Coogan, P114. Royal and Loyal by Michael O'Brien page 93. Headstone Inscription. Photo kindly provided by Stephen Ball, Bohermeen.

Peter Bishop, Bohermeen, Navan, Co. Meath was a sub-Postmaster in Bohermeen

and he was the 2nd Lieutenant of Bohermeen I.R.A. Company in July 1921. Due to his ability to drive he later became attached to I.R.A. Divisional Headquarters as a driver. On the 2nd July 1921, about two weeks before the Truce, he was involved in a failed attack on a troop train near Celbridge, see the story on page 51. On 24th January 1922 he married Molly Brady, Cortown in Cortown Church. Joseph Gibbons, also from Bohermeen Company, was his best man. At this time he was Staff Captain of the 1st Eastern Division, I.R.A. In November 1936 he attended a meeting to appoint a Brigade Committee for gathering information related to qualifying Volunteers for the Military Service Pensions. He died on 21st September 1974 aged 76 years and was buried in Bohermeen Cemetery, see page 318. Sources: WS0932. RO 488. Meath Chronicle dated 28th January 1922 page 1. Headstone Inscription. Meath Chronicle dated 24th October 1931, page 1. Photo kindly provided by Stephen Ball, Bohermeen.

Michael Boylan, Ongenstown, Navan, Co. Meath was a Volunteer in the Bohermeen I.R.A. Company in July 1921. Source: RO 488

William (Willie) Coogan, Bohermeen, Navan, Co. Meath was working on the roads

for Meath Co. Council in 1917 when he joined the Bohermeen Company of Irish Volunteers. He later moved to the Martry I.R.A. Company where he became the company Quartermaster. In November 1936 he attended a meeting to appoint a Brigade Committee for gathering information related to qualifying Volunteers for the Military Service Pensions where he gave his address as Charlesfort, Kells, Co. Meath. He died on 24th August 1981 and was buried in Martry Cemetery, see page 302. Source: Politics and War in Meath 1913-23 by Oliver Coogan, page 113. Headstone Inscription. Photo kindly provided by Stephen Ball, Bohermeen.

Patrick Coyle, Neiltown, Bohermeen, Co. Meath was the Bohermeen Company Quartermaster in July 1921. In November 1936 he attended a meeting to appoint a Brigade Committee for gathering information related to qualifying Volunteers for Military Service Pensions. Source: RO 488. Photo kindly provided by Stephen Ball, Bohermeen.

Thomas Foley, Durhamstown, Bohermeen, Navan, Co. Meath was the I.R.A. Battalion Adjutant, 4th Battalion, 2nd Brigade, 1st Eastern Division in 1921 and 1922. In November 1936 he attended meeting to appoint a Brigade Committee for gathering information related to qualifying Volunteers for the Military Service Pensions. Sources: WS1622. RO 488. Photo kindly provided by Stephen Ball, Bohermeen.

Joseph Gibbons, Neilstown, Ardbraccan, Navan, Co. Meath was a native of

Bohermeen where he was a farmer. In July 1921 he was the Bohermeen I.R.A. Company Commanding Officer. On 24th January 1922 he was the best man at the wedding of his close friend Peter Bishop, listed above, and Molly Brady in Cortown Church. He spent some years in the U.S.A. before he moved to Drogheda. He was a Group Leader in the Local Defence Force in Dublin from 1940 to 1954. He died in Drogheda in January 1965 aged 65 and his funeral took place from Bohermeen Church to the local Cemetery, see page 319. Military Honours were provided at his funeral under the instructions of his good friend Peter Bishop. The firing party consisted of Richard McCabe, Arthur Rennicks, James Byrne, Patrick Matthews, and Michael Hyland. Sources: RO 488. The Meath Chronicle dated 28th January 1922 page 1. The Meath Chronicle dated 30th January 1965 page 9. Headstone Inscription. Photo kindly provided by Stephen Ball, Bohermeen.

Thomas Gibney, Bohermeen, Navan, Co. Meath was the I.R.A. Battalion Commanding Officer, 4th Battalion, 2nd Brigade, 1st Eastern Division in 1921 and 1922. He then joined the Free State Army. In 1936 he was appointed to the Brigade Committee for gathering information related to qualifying Volunteers for Military Service Pensions. He died on 6th April 1944 and was buried in Bohermeen Cemetery, see page 320. He is photographed here in his Free State Uniform. Sources: WS1622. Headstone Inscription. Photo kindly provided by Stephen Ball, Bohermeen.

Patrick Glennon was a Volunteer in the Bohermeen I.R.A. Company in July 1921. In 1935 he gave his address as Carrickmacross Co. Monaghan. Source: RO 488
Nicholas Harmon, Ardbraccan, Navan, Co. Meath was a Volunteer in the Bohermeen I.R.A. Company in July 1921. He died on 26th September 1939 aged 44 years and was buried in Bohermeen Cemetery, see page 320.
Source: RO 488. Headstone Inscription.
Edward (Ned) Harte was a blacksmith. In 1918 he made pikes from old springs of cars, traps and motors as weapons for the Bohermeen Company of Irish Volunteers. In 1920 or 1921 he was arrested and interned in Ballykinlar Internment Camp, Co. Down. He was held in Compound No 2. He died on 3rd December 1976 and was buried in Bohermeen Cemetery, see page 320.
Sources: WS0901. Prisoners of War by Liam O' Duibhir, page 315. Headstone Inscription.

Patrick Harte, Oldtown, Bohermeen, Navan, Co. Meath was the Bohermeen I.R.A. Company Adjutant in July 1921. His name is engraved on a headstone in Boyerstown Cemetery, see page 322. Source: RO 488. Headstone Inscription.

Pat Keane, Bohermeen, Navan, Co. Meath was a Volunteer in the Bohermeen

I.R.A. Company in 1921. John Newman's and Pat Keane's houses became main meeting places in Bohermeen. Sources: WS0857

James Loughran was born in Navan, Co. Meath about 1899. He was a Mechanic in the Leinster Motor Company in Kells, Co. Meath. In early 1921 he was a Volunteer in the Bohermeen I.R.A. Company when he and William Rooney (see Ardbraccan Company) were engaged by a party of R.I.C. William Rooney was a wanted man at the time. There was an exchange of fire and the two men were chased cross country from Irishtown to Ongenstown where they were captured. James Loughran was charged with endangering the safety of police and he received five years in Mountjoy, Dublin. He was released in December 1922 under the terms of the Treaty. He took the Anti-Treaty side and he contested Navan County Council elections as a Fianna Fail candidate. He died on 19th October 1931 following an accident in which he was thrown from his motorcycle. He was buried in Churchtown Cemetery Dunderry. There is a Loughran family plot in Churchtown and I presume he was buried there but his name is not engraved on a headstone, see page 329. Sources: RO 488. The Meath Chronicle dated 28th May 1921, page 1. The Meath Chronicle dated 4th June 1921, page 1. The Meath Chronicle dated 24th October 1931 page 1.

Edward Mallon, Ongenstown, Navan, Co. Meath was a Volunteer in the Bohermeen I.R.A. Company in July 1921. He died on 23rd June 1989 aged 88 years and was buried in Bohermeen Cemetery, see page 320. Source: RO 488. Headstone Inscription. Photo kindly provided by Stephen Ball, Bohermeen.

James Mallon, a native of Ongenstown, Navan, Co. Meath was a member of the Bohermeen G.A.A. Senior Football Team in 1910 and they became Champions that year. He later joined and played with the Martry Football Team. He was the 1st Lieutenant in the Bohermeen I.R.A. Company in July 1921. He was also a member of Sinn Fein and was elected to the Rural District Council in 1920. He was also elected to the Navan Board of Guardians. He was a Meath County Council Rate Collector for 25 years and he retired in 1955. He died in the Meath County Infirmary in Navan in June 1960. His funeral took place from Bohermeen Church to Martry Cemetery but I did not find his grave. Sources: Royal and Loyal by Michael O'Brien page 82. RO 488. Photo kindly provided by Stephen Ball, Bohermeen.

Patrick Mallon, Tankardstown, Donaghpatrick, Navan, Co. Meath was a Volunteer in the Bohermeen I.R.A. Company in July 1921. He died on 24th December 1965 and was buried in Martry Cemetery, see page 302. Source: RO 488. Headstone Inscription. Photo kindly provided by Stephen Ball, Bohermeen.

Thomas Mallon, Ongenstown, Navan, Co. Meath was born in Ongenstown about 1893. In July 1921 he was a Volunteer in the Bohermeen I.R.A. Company but he was arrested and imprisoned in Mountjoy, Dublin for offences under the Restoration of Order in Ireland Regulations (ROIR).

He died on 13th March 1960 aged 69 years and was buried in Martry Cemetery, see page 303. Sources: RO 488. MM9.1.1/KM79-BSZ. Headstone Inscription. Photo kindly provided by Stephen Ball, Bohermeen.

Joseph Martin was a Volunteer in the Bohermeen I.R.A. Company in July 1921 and July 1922. In 1935 his address was given as Geneve Bawn, Tyrellspass, Co. Westmeath. Source: RO 488

John Nally, Irishtown, Boyerstown, Navan, Co. Meath was a Volunteer in the Bohermeen I.R.A. Company in July 1921. His name is engraved on a headstone in Bohermeen Cemetery, see page 321. Source: RO 488. Headstone Inscription.

Thomas Nally, Irishtown, Boyerstown, Navan, Co. Meath was a Volunteer in the Bohermeen I.R.A. Company in July 1921. Source: RO 488

James Newman was a member of the Bohermeen G.A.A. Senior Football Team who became Champions in 1910. In July 1921 he was a Volunteer in the Bohermeen I.R.A. Company. In 1923 he was a member of the Meath G.A.A. Football Team who became Leinster Finalists that year. In 1935 his address was given as U.S.A. Sources: RO 488, Royal and Loyal by Michael O'Brien page 82 and page 120.

John Newman, Bohermeen, Navan, Co. Meath was a Volunteer in the Bohermeen Company of Irish Volunteers in 1916. After the failed Rising he got involved in mustering up disappointed Volunteers and trying to get them to regroup and reorganise. He was a Volunteer in the Bohermeen I.R.A. Company in 1921. John Newman's and Pat Keane's houses became main meeting places in Bohermeen. Sources: WS0857. Photo kindly provided by Stephen Ball, Bohermeen.

M. Gerald O'Reilly was born in 1903. He studied Agriculture in College in Cavan.

He became a Volunteer in the Bohermeen I.R.A. Company in July 1922. He became a member of a 30 man strong I.R.A. Active Service Unit who later became known as the Curraghtown A.S.U. On 5th July 1922 he was involved in the Battle of Curraghtown where he was arrested by the Free State Army, see the story on page 58. He was temporarily held in Trim and then interned in Dundalk, Co. Louth on 22nd July 1922. In 1923 he was imprisoned in Mountjoy. In 1926 he was arrested and jailed in Mountjoy again. On his release he emigrated to U.S.A. He worked for a short time in a carpet factory in Yonkers before getting a job as a conductor on the I.R.T. He transferred to the James Connolly Clan-na-Gael I.R.A. Club in New York. In 1935 his address was given as University Ave., New York, U.S.A. He became an organizer of the I.R.T. Conductor until he retired in 1970.

Source: RO 488. Dunderry A Folk History by Dunderry History Group & Johnny Keely. Unnamed section of a book provided by Stephen Ball, Bohermeen. Photo kindly provided by Stephen Ball, Bohermeen.

John Reilly, Grange, Bohermeen, Navan, Co. Meath was a Volunteer in the Bohermeen I.R.A. Company in July 1921. Source: RO 488

Arthur (Attie) Rennicks, Ardbraccan, Navan, Co. Meath was a Volunteer in the Bohermeen I.R.A. Company in July 1921. He died on 19th October 1993 and was buried in Ardbraccan Cemetery, see page 315. Photo kindly provided by his son Jim Rennicks, Ardbraccan and Stephen Ball, Bohermeen. Source: RO 488. Headstone Inscription.

Carnaross Company:

In 1913 an R.I.C. man named Paddy McGuinness, a native of Carnaross, was dismissed from the R.I.C. for playing a Gaelic football match while off duty. Later Paddy McGuinness, Sean Farrelly and some other local men formed a company of Irish Volunteers. Sean Farrelly subsequently claimed that this was the only company of Irish Volunteers in Co. Meath at the time, and it probably was. Volunteers paid six pence per week for the purchase of arms at a later date. The Carnaross Company had a strength of 26 men in 1913. In July 1914, at the outbreak of World War One, a huge split immerged in the Volunteer movement nationally. The Irish Parliamentary Party leader, John Redmond, called on the Irish Volunteers to join the National Volunteers and to fight in World War One under the command of the British Army. The Leaders of the Irish Volunteers and the Irish Republican Brotherhood (I.R.B.) rejected and condemned this call and the Carnaross Company voted in favour of staying loyal to the Irish Volunteers. In 1914 the Carnaross Company had raised enough money to buy some revolvers but not enough for everyone in the company to get a gun. Volunteers who could afford it paid for their own revolver. Philip Farrelly went to the Irish Volunteers General Head Quarters (G.H.Q.) with the money raised and came back with twenty brand new revolvers for the company. Meetings and target practice were held at Farrelly's old home. Training and drilling continued throughout 1915 and 1916. In early April 1916 the Carnaross Company, were visited by Senior Commanding Officers from the Irish Volunteers and from the I.R.B. This marked the start of the final preparations for the Easter Rising of 1916. The story of what happened is in Chapter 3. After the failed Rising the Carnaross Company regrouped. On 25th September 1917 many of the Carnaross Company attended the funeral of Thomas Ashe, see page 34. In 1918 Britain threatened to introduce Conscription in Ireland which would have seen young Irish men being conscripted into the British Army to fight in World War One. This became known as the Conscription Crisis and Anti-Conscription Campaigns began all over the country. Young Irish men flowed into the ranks of the Irish Volunteers and as a result the Carnaross Company strength rose to 60 men. In January 1919 the Irish Volunteers became the I.R.A. I.R.A. activities heightened over the next few years and by Easter Sunday 4th April 1920 the R.I.C. had evacuated the Carnaross Barracks due to attacks and R.I.C. men had moved to the safety of bigger towns. The Carnaross R.I.C. Barracks was burnt down by local Volunteers. The Carnaross I.R.A. Company took over Community Policing duties in the area and Sinn Fein set up a parish court in Carnaross. A man called Jimmy Roche was the Chairman of the Court. The Battalion Commanding Officer of the I.R.A. Police was Padraig (Paddy) McDonnell from Stonefield (see Ballinlough Company and his story on page 99). One of the Parish Justices was Larry Farnan, see listed below. In 1920 the Carnaross I.R.A. Company was attached to the 5th Battalion, Meath Brigade. In October 1920 a joint meeting of the 4th and 5th I.R.A. Battalions Officers was held in Carnaross to organise simultaneous attacks on enemy outposts and patrols. The extraordinary events of that meeting are mentioned on page 40. In December 1920 the whole Carnaross Company was involved in attack on Oldcastle R.I.C. Barracks. On 1st April 1921 the Carnaross Company was involved in an ambush of a military truck at Sylvan Park Kells, see the story on page 47. When I.R.A. structures were reorganised in April 1921 the Carnaross Company became attached to the 2nd Battalion, 3rd Brigade, 1st Eastern Division. In June 1921 the Carnaross Company was involved in an ambush of another military truck, this one in Drumbaragh, see the story on page 50. In July 1921 the company strength was 54 men. In July 1922 the strength of the company had reduced to fifteen men. Sources: WS01060. RO 489. WS1715. WS0172. WS1627. WS1648. WS1734.

Crooked Terry ?, Derver Lane, Carnaross, Kells, Co. Meath was a Volunteer in the Carnaross Company of Irish Volunteers in 1913. Source: WS1648

James Brady, Fegat, Carnaross, Kells, Co. Meath was a Volunteer in the Carnaross I.R.A. Company in July 1921. Source: RO 489

Edward Clarke, Fegat, Carnaross, Kells, Co. Meath was a Volunteer in the Carnaross I.R.A. Company In July 1921. In 1936 his address was given as England. Source: RO 489

Patrick Clarke, Fegat, Carnaross, Kells, Co. Meath was a Volunteer in the Carnaross I.R.A. Company in July 1921 and July 1922. Source: RO 489

Ned Connell, Curragh, Carnaross, Kells, Co. Meath was a Volunteer in the Carnaross I.R.A. Company in July 1921 and July 1922. Source: RO 489

Bryan Daly, became the Carnaross Company Quartermaster of the Irish Volunteers at the latter end of 1917. In April or May 1921 as part of a restructuring plan he was appointed I.R.A. Battalion Quartermaster, 2nd Battalion, 3rd Brigade, 1st Eastern Division. He was a wanted man and by the end of June 1921 he was "on the run" and camped out in the open on Mullagh Hill with about 30 other mainly Battalion and Brigade Officers attached to the 3rd Brigade. They formed and became involved in an I.R.A. Active Service Unit (A.S.U.). In July 1921 he was still the I.R.A. Battalion Quartermaster. In 1936 his address was given as Newark U.S.A. Sources: WS1627. WS1659. WS1734.

John Daly, Loughan, Kells, Co. Meath was a Volunteer in the Carnaross I.R.A. Company in July 1921 Source RO 489

Pat Daly, Loughan, Kells, Co. Meath was a Volunteer in the Carnaross I.R.A. Company in July 1921. Source: RO 489

Pádraig DeBurca from Kells was a school teacher. In July 1916 he was a Volunteer in the Carnaross Company of Irish Volunteers. After the failed Rising he got involved in reorganising the company in Kells and Carnaross. In April 1921 he became the Battalion Commanding Officer. He became a leading figure in Meath's Sinn Fein organisation. He later moved to Dublin and was replaced by Pat Farrelly of Moynalty. Source: WS0858. WS0901. Politics and War in Meath 1913-23 by Oliver Coogan. Page 100. WS0857. WS1659. Photograph kindly provided by MickO'Brien, Johnstown, author of Royal and Loyal.

Joseph Duffy, Dervor, Carnaross, Kells, Co. Meath was a Volunteer in the Carnaross I.R.A. Company in July 1921. Source: RO 489

Bernard (Bennie) Dunne, Cornasause, Carnaross, Kells, Co. Meath was born about 1895. He joined the Carnaross Company of Irish Volunteers in 1914 aged 19 years. In 1916 he was Carnaross Company 1st Lieutenant, Irish Volunteers. On 12th September 1919 he was arrested on a charge of being a member of the I.R.A. On 5th June 1920 while cycling home from Kells he was fired on by R.I.C. men from a passing car at Rathbracks, one mile from Kells. One bullet went through his chest under the heart and one bullet smashed his forearm. Left for dead in the ditch, he recovered but his arm was disabled for life. In April 1922 he received a pension of £40 per year. He remained 1st Lieutenant of the company until he was discharged in 1923. In July 1925 he was given a gratuity payment of £50 and his pension was stopped, he was 30 years of age. In 1933 his address was given as Keenogue, Julianstown, Co. Meath. In 1969, aged 74 he received a weekly pension of one pound six shillings and six pence. So it appears he received no payments from the state during a 44 year period. In September 1981 his Pension amounted to £256.30 per month and his address was given as No. 2 Little Strand St. Margaretta Villas, Skerries, Co. Dublin. On 21st January 1983 he died aged 88.
Sources: WS1734. RO 489. Military Service Pension Collection, file reference No. MSP IP22.

Christie Dunne, Cornasause, Carnaross, Kells, Co. Meath was a Volunteer in the Carnaross I.R.A. Company in July 1921. He died on 14th April 1974 aged 75 years and was buried in Carnaross Cemetery, see page 293.
Sources: RO 489. Military Service Pension Collection, file reference No. MD-49136. Headstone Inscription.

George Dunne, Cornasause, Carnaross, Kells, Co. Meath was a Volunteer in the Carnaross I.R.A. Company in July 1921. Source: RO 489

James Dunne, Cornasause, Carnaross, Co. Meath was a Volunteer in the Carnaross I.R.A. Company in 1921. On 1st April 1921 he was involved in an ambush of a military truck at Sylvan Park, Kells, see the story on page 47. Source: WS1060.

John Dunne, Cornasause, Carnaross, Co. Meath was a Volunteer in the Carnaross I.R.A. Company in July 1921. Source: RO 489

Michael (Mick) Dunne, Carnaross, Kells Co. Meath was a Volunteer in the Carnaross Company of Irish Volunteers in July 1913 and he continued as a Volunteer in July 1921. He was described by Sean Farrelly as a man with one eye closed all the time and always smiling behind his big beard. Sources: RO 489. WS1648.

Pat (Farmer) Dunne as he was known, Cornasause, Carnaross, Kells, Co. Meath was born in Kells about 1900. He became a Volunteer in the Carnaross Company of Irish Volunteers. On 1st April 1921 he was involved in an ambush of a military truck at Sylvan Park, Kells, see the story on page 47. He was arrested and imprisoned in Mountjoy, Dublin for offences under the Restoration of Order in Ireland Regulations (ROIR). He died on 11th November 1974 aged 74 years and was buried in Carnaross Cemetery, see page 293.

Peter Dunne, Cornasause, Carnaross, Kells, Co. Meath was a Volunteer in the Carnaross I.R.A. Company in July 1921. Source: RO 489

Thomas Dunne, Templemore, Co. Tipperary was a former Volunteer in the Carnaross Company of Irish Volunteers. He joined the Free State Army in July 1921. Source: RO 489

Bernard Farley, Fegat, Carnaross, Kells, Co. Meath was a Volunteer in the Carnaross I.R.A. Company in July 1921. Source: RO 489

Bernard Farley, Clonabraney, Crossakiel, Kells, Co. Meath was a Volunteer in the Carnaross I.R.A. Company in July 1921. Source: RO 489

Michael Farley, Clonagrowney, Carnaross, Kells, Co. Meath was a Volunteer in the Carnaross I.R.A. Company in July 1921 and July 1922. Source: RO 489

Philip Farley, Ballinapun, Carnaross, Kells, Co. Meath was a Volunteer in the Carnaross I.R.A. Company in July 1922. Source: RO 489

Laurence (Larry) Farnan, Kieran, Carnaross, Kells, Co. Meath was a Volunteer in the Carnaross Company of Irish Volunteers in April 1916 and he took part in the Easter Rising, see Chapter 3. In August 1920 Larry Farnan became one of three Parish Justices in the Carnaross Sinn Fein court. He was still a Volunteer in the Carnaross I.R.A. Company in July 1921. He died on 2nd October 1921 and was buried in Carnaross Cemetery, see page 293.

Bryan Farrelly, Carnaross, Kells, Co. Meath was a Volunteer in the Carnaross Company of Irish Volunteers in July 1913. He was a brother of the below Philip, Pat and Sean Farrelly. Source: WS1648.

Patrick (Pat) Farrelly, a native of Clonagrowney, Carnaross, Kells was a brother of above Bryan and below Sean and Philip. Pat was the 2nd Lieutenant of the Carnaross Company of Irish Volunteers at the latter end of 1917. In April 1920 he was appointed Battalion Commanding Officer, 4th Battalion (Kells), Meath Brigade, I.R.A. In 1920 and 1921 his address was given as Moynalty. In September 1920 he attended an I.R.A. Battalion meeting In Carnaross which resulted in charges of mutiny being made against participants at the meeting, see the story on page 40. In January 1921 he was involved in the rescue of arms and explosives which were seized by R.I.C. in Moynalty. On 28th March 1921 as part of an I.R.A. restructuring plan, he was appointed Brigade Commanding Officer, 3rd Brigade, 1st Eastern Division and he held that role until the end of 1922. He was a wanted man and by the end of June 1921 he was "on the run" and camped out in the open on Mullagh Hill with about 30 other mainly Battalion and Brigade Officers attached to the 3rd Brigade. They formed and became involved in an I.R.A. Active Service Unit (A.S.U.). He took the Anti-Treaty side and in October 1922 he was arrested by the Free State Army and held in Kells. He escaped from the Kells

Barracks and six days later he was recaptured in Oldcastle. Commandant Pat Farrelly died before 1936. Sources: WS0858. WS1734. WS1650. WS1659. WS1060. WS1625. RO 484. RO 489. RO 494. WS 1539. WS1625. WS1715. Faithful to Ireland by Tony Brady, page 80

Philip Farrelly, Carnaross, Kells, Co. Meath was a brother of below Sean and above Bryan and Pat. Philip was a Volunteer in the Carnaross Company of Irish Volunteers in 1913. In 1914 the Carnaross Company had raised enough money to buy some revolvers but not enough for everyone to get a gun. Volunteers who could afford it paid for their own revolver. Philip Farrelly went to the Irish Volunteers G.H.Q. with the money raised and came back with twenty brand new revolvers for the company. In November 1920 he was arrested and interned in Ballykinlar Internment Camp in Co. Down. He was held in Compound No 2. He died on 28th March 1964 aged 82 and was buried in Carnaross Cemetery, see page 294 Sources: WS1648. Prisoners of War by Liam O' Duibhir, page 315. WS1734. Headstone Inscription.

Sean Farrelly was a brother of above Bryan, Pat and Philip. A native of Carnaross, Kells, Co. Meath. He was born in 1890. He was a Volunteer in the Carnaross Company of Irish Volunteers in 1913. On 25th September 1917 he cycled to Dublin to attend the funeral of Thomas Ashe, see page 34. This was the first time Sean Farrelly was in Dublin. In April 1920 he was appointed 5th Battalion (Oldcastle) Vice Commanding Officer, Meath Brigade and he took charge of Special Services or Special Operations. He was arrested shortly afterwards and imprisoned in Mountjoy on a charge of having documents in his possession. His date of birth on his prison records conflict with those on his headstone so he gave the prison authorities the wrong information. In March 1921 as part of an I.R.A. restructuring plan he was appointed Brigade Vice Commanding Officer, 3rd Brigade, 1st Eastern Division. On 1st April 1921 he was involved in an ambush of a military truck at Sylvan Park, Kells, see the story on page 47. He was a wanted man and by the end of June 1921 he was "on the run" and camped out in the open on Mullagh Hill with about 30 other mainly Battalion and Brigade Officers attached to the 3rd Brigade. They formed and became involved in an I.R.A. Active Service Unit (A.S.U.). In September 1922 he was appointed Battalion Commanding Officer. In 1922 he took the Anti-Treaty side. In early 1923 he was wounded in a shootout at his home when the Free State Army tried to arrest him. He was interned in Gormanstown Prison Camp. In July 1957 his address was given as Scurlogstown, Trim, Co. Meath. He died in 1963 aged 73 years and was buried in the Church of the Nativity Cemetery in Kilmessan, see page 285.
Sources: WS1648. WS1734. WS1060. MM9.1.1/KMQR-PLJ. WS1625. WS1627. WS1659. WS1715. Faithful to Ireland by Tony Brady page 86. Headstone Inscription.

Thomas Farrelly, Oakley Park, Kells, Co. Meath was the 1st Lieutenant of the Carnaross I.R.A. Company in July 1921. He died on 6th May 1957 and was buried in Carnaross Cemetery, Kells, see page 294. Source: RO 489. Headstone Inscription.

? Feeney, Moyrath, was one of three drill instructors in the Carnaross Company In 1913. _{Source: WS1648.}

Thomas Hyland, Rahendrick, Carnaross, Kells, Co. Meath was a Volunteer in the Carnaross I.R.A. Company in July 1921. _{Source: RO 489}

Bryan Keelan, Loughan, Kells, Co. Meath was a Volunteer in the Carnaross I.R.A. Company in July 1921 and July 1922.
_{Sources: RO 489. Military Service Pension Collection, file reference No. MD-20416}

Bernard Leddy, Maperath, Kells, Co. Meath was a Volunteer in the Carnaross I.R.A. Company in July 1921. _{Source: RO 489}

John (Jack) Lynch, Loughan, Carnaross, Kells, Co. Meath was a postman in the area. In June 1921 he was a Volunteer in the Carnaross I.R.A. Company. Aged 19, he was the youngest Volunteer in the company when he was involved in an ambush of a military truck at Drumbaragh. He was wounded during the retreat, see the story on page 50. He survived his wounds and he died on 9th November 1982 aged 80 years at Our Lady's Hospital Navan. He was buried in Carnaross Cemetery, see page 294. _{Source: WS1659. Headstone Inscription. Irish Press dated 10th November 1982, page 2.}

James Lynch, Cornasause, Carnaross, Kells, Co. Meath was a Volunteer in the Carnaross I.R.A. Company in April 1921. On 1st April 1921 he was involved in an ambush of a military truck at Sylvan Park, Kells, see the story on page 47.
_{Sources: WS1060. RO 489.}

John Lynch, Cornasause, Carnaross, Kells, Co. Meath was a Volunteer in the Carnaross I.R.A. Company in July 1921. _{Source: RO 489}

Joseph Lynch, Cornasause, Carnaross, Kells, Co. Meath was a Volunteer in the Carnaross I.R.A. Company in July 1921. He died in May 1972 and was buried in Carnaross Cemetery, see page 294. _{Source: RO 489. Headstone Inscription.}

Laurence Lynch was a Volunteer in the Carnaross I.R.A. Company in July 1921. In 1936 his address was given as 20 Harcourt St, Dublin. _{Source: RO 489}

Michael Lynch, Leitrum, Mullagh, Kells, Co. Meath was a Volunteer in the Carnaross I.R.A. Company in July 1921. In July 1922 he was the Carnaross I.R.A. Company Commanding Officer. _{Source: RO 489}

Thomas Lynch, Cornasause, Carnaross, Kells was a Volunteer in the Carnaross I.R.A. Company in April 1921. On 1st April 1921 he was involved in an ambush of a military truck at Sylvan Park, Kells, see the story on page 47. He died in December 1958 and was buried in Carnaross Cemetery, see page 294 _{Sources: WS1060. RO 489. Headstone Inscription.}

Patrick Martin, Balrath, Kells, Co. Meath was a Volunteer in the Carnaross I.R.A. Company in July 1921 _{Source: RO 489}

Paddy McGuinnes, Carnaross, Kells, Co. Meath was an ex-R.I.C. man. He was dismissed from the R.I.C. for playing Gaelic football while off duty in 1913. He became a founder member of the Carnaross Irish Volunteers and was one of three drill instructors in the company. _{Source: WS1648.}

Matthew McInerney, Meenlagh, Carnaross, Kells, Co. Meath was a Volunteer in the Carnaross I.R.A. Company in July 1921 and July 1922. On 1st April 1921 he was involved in an ambush of a military truck at Sylvan Park, Kells, see the story on page 47. In June 1923 he was arrested by the Free State Army for destruction of Free State Army Captain Bond's house in Ballinlough.
Sources: WS1060. RO 489. Faithfull to Ireland by Tony Brady, page 84

Michael McInerney, Meenlagh, Carnaross, Kells, Co. Meath was a Volunteer in the Carnaross I.R.A. Company in April 1921. On 1st April 1921 he was involved in an ambush of a military truck at Sylvan Park, Kells, see the story on page 47. In June 1923 he was arrested by the Free State Army for destruction of Free State Army Captain Bond's house in Ballinlough. Sources: WS1060. RO 489. Faithfull to Ireland by Tony Brady, page 84

Robert McInerney, Meenlagh, Carnaross, Kells, Co. Meath was a Volunteer in the Carnaross I.R.A. Company in July 1921. Sources: RO 489

James McNamee, Pottlebane, Lisduff, Kells, Co. Meath was a Volunteer in the Carnaross I.R.A. Company in July 1922. He died on 4th October 1975 and was buried in Ballinlough cemetery, see page 291. Source: RO 489. Headstone Inscription.

Patrick, McNamee, Pottlebane, Lisduff, Kells, Co. Meath was a Volunteer in the Carnaross I.R.A. Company in July 1921 and July 1922. Source: RO 489.

William McNamee, Pottlebane, Lisduff, Kells, Co. Meath was a Volunteer in the Carnaross I.R.A. Company In July 1921. His name is engraved on a headstone in Ballinlough Cemetery, see page 292. Source: RO 489. Headstone inscription.

Thomas Mooney from Rosmeen Kells was a native of Dervor, Carnaross, Kells. In July 1921 he was a Volunteer in the Carnaross Company of Irish Volunteers. In 1922 he opposed the Treaty and he took up arms in the Civil War in Co. Kildare. He was captured and interned in the Curragh Internment Camp where he participated in a 35 day hunger strike which was called off before his death. He died on in May 1945 and he was buried in St. Colmcille's Cemetery, Kells. He was only about 45 years of age, see page 309.
Sources: RO 489. The Meath Chronicle dated 19th May 1945, page 5. Headstone Inscription.

Patrick (Pat) Mullally, Curragh, Carnaross, Kells, Co. Meath was a Volunteer in the Carnaross I.R.A. Company in July 1921. Source: RO 489

Thomas Mullally, Jonesboro, Carnaross, Kells, Co. Meath was a Volunteer in the Carnaross I.R.A. Company in July 1921. He died on 27th May 1962 and was buried in Carnaross Cemetery, see page 295. Source: RO 489. Headstone Inscription.

William Mullally was a Volunteer in the Carnaross I.R.A. Company in July 1921. In 1936 he was a member of An Garda Síochána and his address was given as Garda Barracks, Screen, Co. Sligo. Source: RO 489

Thomas Nevin, Loughan, Kells, Co. Meath was a Volunteer in the Carnaross I.R.A. Company in July 1921. He died before 1936. Source: RO 489

Edward (Ned) O'Connor, Woodpole, Carnaross, Kells, Co. Meath was a Volunteer in the Carnaross I.R.A. Company in April 1921. On 1st April 1921 he was involved in an ambush of a military truck at Sylvan Park, Kells, see the story on page 47. He moved to Mullagh. He died on 9th March 1970 and was buried in Carnaross Cemetery, see page 295. Source: WS1060. WS1627. RO 489. Headstone Inscription.

Barney Reilly, Carnaross, Kells, Co. Meath was a Volunteer in the Carnaross I.R.A. Company in 1915 and 1916. He took part in the Easter Rising, see the story in Chapter 3. Source: WS1648.

Bernard Reilly, Cornasause, Carnaross, Kells, Co. Meath was a Volunteer in the Carnaross I.R.A. Company in July 1921 and July 1922. He died on 24th January 1980 aged 89 years and was buried in Carnaross Cemetery. Source: RO 489. Headstone Inscription.

Charles Reilly, Balrath, Kells, Co. Meath was a Volunteer in the Carnaross I.R.A. Company in July 1921. Source: RO 489

Patrick Reilly, Cornasause, Carnaross, Kells, Co. Meath was a Volunteer in the Carnaross I.R.A. Company in July 1921. In 1936 his address was given as U.S.A. Source: RO 489

Oweny Rock, Carnaross, Kells, Co. Meath was a Volunteer in the Carnaross Company of Irish Volunteers in 1913. He was described by Sean Farrelly as an old man with one eye. He left the company within a short period when he realised that Volunteers did not get paid. Source: WS1648.

Luke Smith, Kieran, Carnaross, Kells, Co. Meath was a Volunteer in the Carnaross I.R.A. Company in July 1921 and July 1922. Source: RO 489

Matthew (Matt) Smith, Cloghanrush, Carnaross, Kells, Co. Meath was the Carnaross I.R.A. Company Commanding Officer in 1920 and 1921. On 23rd February 1920 he was involved in an ambush of an R.I.C. patrol at Dervor, Carnaross in which five members of the R.I.C. were wounded. On 1st April 1921 he was involved in an ambush of a military truck at Sylvan Park, Kells, see the story on page 47. In 1936 he was a member of An Garda Síochána and his address was given as Maryboro, Leixlip, Co. Kildare. Source: WS1659. RO 489. WS1060.

Michael Sweeney, Kells, Co. Meath was a Volunteer in the Carnaross Company of Irish Volunteers in July 1916. After the failed Rising he got involved in mustering up disappointed Volunteers and trying to get them to regroup and reorganise. Source: WS0857

John Tevlin, Kieran, Carnaross, Kells, Co. Meath was born in Kells, about 1889. On 12th September 1919 he was arrested and imprisoned in Mountjoy, Dublin for being a member of the I.R.A., an offence under the Defence of the Realm Regulations (DRR). He was sentenced to one year in jail. He went on hunger strike on 23rd October 1919 and he was released in November 1919. In July 1921 he was a Volunteer in the Carnaross Company of Irish Volunteers. He died on 11th June 1970 and was buried in Carnaross Cemetery, see page 295. Sources: RO 489. MM9.1.1/KM79-G8C. Faithful To Ireland by Tony Brady, page 32. Headstone Inscription.

Matthew (Matt) Tevlin, Carnaross, Kells, Co. Meath was appointed Battalion Engineer, 5th Battalion, Meath Brigade during restructuring of the Battalion Staff following a mutiny court-martial in September 1920, see the story on page 40. In April or May 1921 as part of another I.R.A. restructuring plan he was appointed Battalion Engineer, 2nd Battalion, 3rd Brigade, 1st Eastern Division. In 1921 his address was given as Rathbracks, Carnaross, Kells, Co. Meath. On 1st April 1921 he was involved in an ambush of a military truck at Sylvan Park, Kells, see the story on page 47. In June 1921 he led an ambush of a military truck at Drumbaragh, see the story on page 50. He was a wanted man and by the end of June 1921 he was "on the run" and camped out in the open on Mullagh Hill with about 30 other mainly Battalion and Brigade Officers attached to the 3rd Brigade. They formed and became involved in an I.R.A. Active Service Unit (A.S.U.).
Sources: WS1659. WS1060. WS1627. WS1715.

Philip (Phil) Tevlin was a Volunteer in the Carnaross Company of Irish Volunteers in July 1916. After the failed Rising he got involved in trying to bolster up disappointed Volunteers in an effort to get them to regroup and reorganise. In July 1916 he was a member of the I.R.B. At the latter end of 1917 he was appointed company Commanding Officer, Irish Volunteers. In early 1919 Phil Tevlin was appointed I.R.A. 5th Battalion Vice Commanding Officer and he became a representative of the Carnaross I.R.A. Company. Shortly afterwards Phil resigned his post as Battalion Vice Commanding Officer but continued as a member of the I.R.A. In December 1920 he was Battalion Quartermaster, 5th Battalion, Meath Brigade. He was arrested and imprisoned in 1921. The position of Battalion Commanding Officer was taken over by Matt Tevlin. The I.R.A. 5th Battalion Vice Commanding Officer post went to Sean Keogh in April 1921. On 1st April 1921 Phil was involved in an ambush of a military truck at Sylvan Park, Kells, see the story on page 47. Source: WS0857. WS0857. WS1615. WS1627. WS1060. WS1715. WS1734.

Michael Tully, Summerbank, Oldcastle, Co. Meath was a Volunteer in the Carnaross I.R.A. Company in July 1921. Source: RO 489

Jack Tyrell, Moynalty, Kells, Co. Meath was one of the three drill instructors in Carnaross Company of Irish Volunteers in 1913. Source: WS1648.

Patrick Waters, Balgree, Kells, Co. Meath was a Volunteer in the Carnaross I.R.A. Company in July 1921 Source: RO 489

Thomas Yore, Loughan, Kells, Co. Meath was a Volunteer in the Carnaross I.R.A. Company in July 1921. He died on 20th January 1970 aged 84 years and was buried in Carnaross Cemetery, see page 296 Source: RO 489. Headstone Inscription

Castletown Company:

The Castletown Company of Irish Volunteers was formed at the latter end of 1918. Patrick Loughran said in his Witness Statement that the Navan Company helped to form and organise the Castletown Company. In January 1919 the Irish Volunteers became the I.R.A. In 1919 the Castletown Company was part of the 6th Battalion. In 1921 the company strength was fifteen men. In 1922 there were no men in the company so it ceased to exist. Sources: RO 487. WS1624.

Terence Brady, Knightstown, Wilkinstown, Navan, Co. Meath was a Volunteer in the Castletown I.R.A. Company in July 1921. He took the pro-treaty side and joined the Free State Army in 1922. He had second thoughts and deserted the army and took the Anti-Treaty side. He lost his life because of that decision, see the story on page 65. Source: RO 487.

Thomas Carberry, Clynch, Castletown, Navan, Co. Meath was a Volunteer in the Castletown I.R.A. Company in July 1921. His name is inscribed on a headstone in Fletcherstown Cemetery, see page 350. Sources: RO 487. Headstone Inscription

Christopher Carolan, Castletown, Navan, Co. Meath was a member of the

Rathkenny G.A.A. Football Team who won the Feis Cup in 1920. In July 1921 he was a Volunteer in the Castletown I.R.A. Company. In 1922 he was a member of the Rathkenny G.A.A. Senior Football Team who became Champions that year. In 1923 he was a member of the Meath G.A.A. Football Team who became Leinster Finalists. Sources: RO 487. Royal and Loyal by Michael O'Brien page 93, 118 and 120.

G. Clarke, Clynch, Castletown, Navan, Co. Meath was a Volunteer in the Castletown I.R.A. Company in July 1921. Source: RO 487.

George Cudden was a member of the Rathkenny G.A.A. Football Team who won the Feis Cup in 1920. In July 1921 he was a Volunteer in the Castletown I.R.A. Company. In 1922 he was a member of the Rathkenny G.A.A. Senior Football Team who became Champions that year. He became a member of a 30 man strong I.R.A. Active Service Unit who later became known as the Curraghtown A.S.U. On 5th July 1922 he was involved in the Battle of Curraghtown where he was arrested by the Free State Army, see the story on page 58. He was temporarily held in Trim and then interned in Dundalk, Co. Louth on 22nd July 1922. He died before 1935. Source: RO 487. Dunderry A Folk History by Dunderry History Group & Johnny Keely.

J. Gogarty, Nobber, Co. Meath was a Volunteer in the Castletown I.R.A. Company in July 1922. Source: RO 487.

Patrick Hoey, Carnacop, Castletown, Navan, Co. Meath was a Volunteer in the Castletown I.R.A. Company in July 1921. He died on 19th February 1984 aged 82 and was buried in Castletown Kilpatrick Cemetery, see page 323. Source: RO 487. Headstone Inscription.

H. Kelly, Stephenstown, Castletown, Navan, Co. Meath was a Volunteer in the Castletown I.R.A. Company in July 1921. Source: RO 487.

G. Markey, Clynch, Castletown, Navan, Co. Meath was a Volunteer in the Castletown I.R.A. Company in July 1921. Source: RO 487.

H. Markey, Clynch, Castletown, Navan, Co. Meath was a Volunteer in the Castletown I.R.A. Company in July 1921. Source: RO 487.

Patrick Markey, Clynch, Castletown, Navan, Co. Meath was a Volunteer in the Castletown I.R.A. Company in July 1921. He was appointed Battalion Director of Signals. His name is engraved on a headstone in Castletown Kilpatrick Cemetery and it says that Patrick Markey died on 31st March 1980 aged 86 years, see page 323. Source: RO 487. Headstone Inscription.

Bernard Meade, Painstown, Castletown, Navan, Co. Meath was the Castletown I.R.A. Company Commanding Officer in July 1921. Source: RO 487.

G. Meade, Painstown, Castletown, Navan, Co. Meath was a Volunteer in the Castletown I.R.A. Company in July 1921. Source: RO 487.

P. Meade, Painstown, Castletown, Navan, Co. Meath was a Volunteer in the Castletown I.R.A. Company in July 1921. Source: RO 487.

Thomas (Tom) Meehan, Mountainstown, Wilkinstown, Navan, Co. Meath was a Volunteer in the Castletown I.R.A. Company in July 1921. He died in November 1986 and was buried in Fletcherstown Cemetery, see page 350. Source: RO 487. Headstone Inscription.

T. Price, Clynch, Castletown, Navan, Co. Meath was a Volunteer in the Castletown I.R.A. Company in July 1921. Source: RO 487.

T. Reilly, Klynch, Castletown, Navan, Co. Meath was a member of the Rathkenny G.A.A. Football Team who won the Feis Cup in 1920. In July 1922 he was a Volunteer in the Castletown I.R.A. Company. Sources: RO 487, Royal and Loyal by Michael O'Brien page 93

M. Sheridan, Bogtown, Castletown, Navan, Co. Meath was a Volunteer in the Castletown I.R.A. Company in July 1922. Source: RO 487.

Cloncurry Company:

Hugh Boylan, Kilbrook, Enfield, Co. Meath was a Volunteer in the Cloncurry I.R.A. Company in July 1921 and July 1922. Source: RO 483.

Christopher Brilly, Ardrunis, Summerhill, Co. Meath was the Cloncurry Company 1st Lieutenant in July 1921 and July 1922. Source: RO 483.

Patrick Butler, Cappagh, Kilcock, Co. Kildare was a Volunteer in the Cloncurry I.R.A. Company in July 1921 and July 1922. Source: RO 483.

Joseph Ennis, Cloncurry, Enfield, Co. Meath was the Cloncurry Company Adjutant in July 1921 and July 1922 but he was arrested and imprisoned during the 1921 - 1922 period. He died before 1936. Source: RO 483.

Patrick Ennis, Cloncurry, Enfield, Co. Meath was a Volunteer in the Cloncurry I.R.A. Company in July 1921 and July 1922. Source: RO 483.

John Feeney, Cloncurry, Enfield, Co. Meath was the Cloncurry I.R.A. Company 2nd Lieutenant at the beginning of 1921. When below Patrick Feeney was arrested John took over the role as company Commanding Officer. When Patrick was released in 1922 John moved to company Quartermaster. In 1936 his address was given as Scotland. Source: RO 483.

Lawrence Feeney, Cloncurry, Enfield, Co. Meath was a Volunteer in the Cloncurry I.R.A. Company in July 1921 and July 1922. Source: RO 483.

Patrick Feeney, Newtown, Enfield, Co. Meath was the Cloncurry I.R.A. Company Commanding Officer at the beginning of 1921. He was arrested and imprisoned for eleven months. During that time the above John Feeney took over as company Commanding Officer. When Patrick was released in 1922 he resumed his position as company Commanding Officer. Source: RO 483.

Thomas Feeney, Cloncurry, Enfield, Co. Meath was a Volunteer in the Cloncurry I.R.A. Company in July 1921 and July 1922. During that period he spent fourteen months in prison. Source: RO 483.

Edward Fitzsimons, Kilbrook, Enfield, Co. Meath was a Volunteer in the Cloncurry I.R.A. Company in July 1921 and July 1922. Source: RO 483. Military Service Pension Collection, file reference No. MB-5163 or MD-5163 or M5-5163

Thomas Fitzsimons, Kilbrook, Enfield, Co. Meath was a Volunteer in the Cloncurry I.R.A. Company in July 1921 and July 1922. Source: RO 483.

Ambrose Gannon, Newtown, Enfield, Co. Meath was a Volunteer in the Cloncurry I.R.A. Company in July 1921 and July 1922. Source: RO 483.

Andrew Gilligan, Cappagh, was a Volunteer in the Cloncurry I.R.A. Company in July 1921 and July 1922. Source: RO 483.

Peter Kelly, Kilbrook, Enfield, Co. Meath was a Volunteer in the Cloncurry I.R.A. Company in July 1921 and July 1922. Source: RO 483.

Andrew Ledwedge, Ballycarron, Enfield, Co. Meath was a Volunteer in the Cloncurry I.R.A. Company in July 1921 and July 1922. Source: RO 483.

Edward Ledwedge, Ballycarron, Enfield, Co. Meath was the Cloncurry I.R.A. Company Engineer in July 1921 and July 1922. Source: RO 483.

Michael Murray, Nicholastown, Kilcock, Co. Kildare was a Volunteer in the Cloncurry I.R.A. Company in July 1921 and July 1922. Source: RO 483.

Patrick Purcell, Cappagh, Enfield, Co. Meath was a Volunteer in the Cloncurry I.R.A. Company in July 1921 and July 1922. Source: RO 483.

Patrick Smyth, Coustown, Kilcock, Co. Kildare was a Volunteer in the Cloncurry I.R.A. Company in July 1921 and July 1922. Source: RO 483.

John Walsh, Cloncurry, Enfield, Co. Meath was a Volunteer in the Cloncurry I.R.A. Company in July 1921 and July 1922. Source: RO 483.

Clongill Company:

The Clongill I.R.A. Company was formed about early 1919 and became part of the 6th Battalion. The main local employer was Thomas Gerrard who owned Gibbstown House and surrounding lands. The Gerrards were good to their employees and the locals were loyal to the Gerrards with the result that many lads from the area would not join the I.R.A. By Easter Sunday 4th April 1920 the R.I.C. had evacuated the George's Cross R.I.C. Barracks at Mountainstown due to attacks on neighbouring barracks and R.I.C. men had moved to the safety of bigger towns. The barracks was burnt down by local Volunteers to ensure the R.I.C. did not return. Patrick Loughran of Navan Company said an attack plan was being prepared but the R.I.C. abandoned it prior to attack. In 1921 the Clongill I.R.A. Company had a strength of sixteen men and it was attached to the 3rd Battalion,

2nd Brigade, 1st Eastern Division. In 1922 the company strength was down to five men. Sources: RO 487. WS1723. WS1624. Personal Interview with Jimmy Dunphy, Gibbstown, 14/02/15.

Matthew (Mattie) Allen, The Shragh, Clongill, Donaghpatrick, Navan, Co. Meath was a Volunteer in the Clongill I.R.A. Company in July 1921. He died in June 1981 aged 81 years and was buried in Fletcherstown Cemetery, see page 349. Source: RO 487. Personal Interview with Jimmy Dunphy, Gibbstown, 14/02/15. Headstone Inscription.

J. Callaghan was a Volunteer in the Clongill I.R.A. Company at the latter end of 1921. In March 1935 his address was given as England. Source: RO 487.

Thomas Crahan, Demailstown, Wilkinstown, Navan, Co. Meath was the Quartermaster of the 3rd Battalion, 2nd Brigade, 1st Eastern Division I.R.A. in July 1921. He died on 19th October 1942 and was buried in Kilberry Cemetery, see page 331. Source: RO 487. Headstone Inscription

? Crahan, probably Paddy Crahan, Gibbstown, Navan, Co. Meath was a Volunteer in the Clongill I.R.A. Company in July 1921. Source: RO 487.

Philip Crahan was a Volunteer in the Clongill I.R.A. Company in July 1921. In March 1935 he was serving in the Free State Army. His name is engraved on a headstone in Donaghpatrick Churchyard Cemetery. It says that Philip Crahan died on 8th December 1946, see page 325. Source: RO 487. Headstone inscription.

P. Crosby was a Volunteer in the Clongill I.R.A. Company at the latter end of 1921. Source: RO 487.

Thomas Gilsenan, Gibbstown, Navan, Co. Meath was the Clongill Company Quartermaster in July 1921. Originally from An Rath Dubh in Teltown he was a blacksmith and he worked for Thomas Gerrard in Gibbstown House. He lived in what is now Connie McFadden's farm, previously Billy and Florrie Spillane's where he had a forge and he shod horses for the local farmers. Source: RO 487. Personal Interview with Jimmy Dunphy, Gibbstown, 14/02/15.

J. Halford, probably James (Jim) Halford, Clongill, Wilkinstown, Navan, Co. Meath was the Clongill Company 2nd Lieutenant in July 1921. Source RO: 487. Personal Interview Jimmy Dunphy, Gibbstown, 14/02/15

T. Halford, was a Volunteer in the Clongill I.R.A. Company in July 1921. In March 1935 he was serving in the Free State Army. Source: RO 487.

Frank Hand, The Shragh, Clongill, Donaghpatrick, Navan Co. Meath was a Volunteer in the Clongill I.R.A. Company at the latter end of 1921. He later became a member of An Garda Síochána. Source: RO 487. Personal Interview with Jimmy Dunphy, Gibbstown, 14/02/15.

James Hoey, Ladyrath, Wilkinstown, Navan, Co. Meath was born in Nobber, Co Meath about 1902. In July 1921 and July 1922 he was a Volunteer in the Clongill Company of Irish Volunteers. In 1922 he was a farm labourer. He became a member of a 30 man strong I.R.A. Active Service Unit who later became known as the Curraghtown A.S.U. On 5th July 1922 he was involved in the Battle of Curraghtown where he was arrested by the Free State Army, see the story on page 58. He was temporarily held in Trim and then interned in Dundalk, Co. Louth on 22nd July 1922. On 27th July 1922 he escaped from Dundalk Jail, see the story on page 59. On 28th July 1922 he was recaptured by Pro-Treaty I.R.A. and reinterned in Dundalk Jail. Sources: RO 487 MM9.1.1/KM3L-FYM. Louth County Archives http://www.louthcoco.ie/en/Services/Archives/Archive_Collections/ Dunderry A Folk History by Dunderry History Group & Johnny Keely.

M. Hoey, was a Volunteer in the Clongill I.R.A. Company in July 1921. Later his address was given as Dublin. Source: RO 487.

P. Lynch was a Volunteer in the Clongill I.R.A. Company at the latter end of 1921. He died before 1936. Source: RO 487.

J. McCabe was a Volunteer in the Clongill I.R.A. Company at the latter end of 1921. In 1936 his address was given as U.S.A. Source: RO 487.

T. McGuinness was a Volunteer in the Clongill I.R.A. Company in July 1921. Source: RO 487.

A. Murray, Gibbstown, Navan, Co. Meath was a Volunteer in the Clongill I.R.A. Company at the latter end of 1921. Source: RO 487.

J. Nugent, Oristown, Kells, Co. Meath was a Volunteer in the Clongill I.R.A. Company at the latter end of 1921. Source: RO 487.

Laurence Smyth, was a Volunteer in the Clongill I.R.A. Company in July 1921. He died on the 2nd November 1938 and was buried in St. Mary's Cemetery, Navan, see page 346. Source: RO 487. Headstone Inscription.

Michael Swan was born in Clongill, Navan, Co. Meath about 1903. In July 1921 he was the Battalion Director of first Aid. He became a member of a 30 man strong I.R.A. Active Service Unit who later became known as the Curraghtown A.S.U. On 5th July 1922 he was involved in the Battle of Curraghtown where he was arrested by the Free State Army, see the story on page 58. He was temporarily held in Trim and then interned in Dundalk, Co. Louth on 22nd July 1922. On 12th September 1922 he was recaptured at Kilberry, Navan and reinterned. In March 1935 his address was given as England and he was described as "At present in Religion" Sources: RO 487 MM9.1.1/KM3L-F23 Personal Interview with Jimmy Dunphy, Gibbstown, 14/02/15.

Seamus (Jim) Swan, Clongill, Navan, Co. Meath was a Volunteer in the Clongill I.R.A. Company in 1920, 1921 and 1922. He lived in what later became the family home of Maurice and Mary Spillane, Clongill. In April 1920 he was involved in the burning of George's Cross R.I.C. Barracks at Mountainstown, Kilshine. He said in a letter to the Military Pensions Board that he was involved in an aborted attack or ambush at Slane, that he was involved in the destruction of bridges, the trenching of roads to hinder troop movements and that between January and July 1921 one of the bridges he destroyed was on the main Navan Kells road. He goes on to say that in late 1920 he was involved in the shooting of a spy and the burning of his house shortly afterwards. He became a member of a 30 man strong I.R.A. Active Service Unit who later became known as the Curraghtown A.S.U. On 5th July 1922 he was involved in the Battle of Curraghtown where he was arrested by the Free State Army, see the story on page 58. He was temporarily held in Trim and then interned in Dundalk, Co. Louth on 22nd July 1922. He aldo said that he was involved in an attack on Belsaw Hill and an attack on Athboy Barracks. At the Annual Convention of the Navan and District Old I.R.A. Association in the CYMS Hall in Navan in February 1953 James Swan was appointed vice-chairman. He died in February 1965 aged 61 years and was buried in Fletcherstown Cemetery, see page 349. Source: Letter from James Swan to T.E. Duffy not dated but was around February 1936. RO 487. Headstone Inscription. Dunderry A Folk History by Dunderry History Group & Johnny Keely.

John Sweeney, Clongill, Wilkinstown, Navan, Co. Meath was the Clongill I.R.A. Company Commanding Officer in July 1921 and July 1922. He lived in the little house opposite Pat Brady's now Gerry Brady's in Clongill. Around 28th June 1922 he was arrested by the Free State Army in a roundup of anti-Treaty I.R.A. and he was taken to Kells Barracks. In March 1935 his address was given as Dublin. Source: RO 487. Personal Interview with Jimmy Dunphy, Gibbstown, 14/02/15. Faithful to Ireland by Tony Brady, page 73.

Patrick Sweeney was a Volunteer in the Clongill I.R.A. Company in July 1922. He lived in the little house opposite Pat Brady's or Gerry Brady's house in Clongill. In 1935 his address was given as Dublin. In July 1941 he was electrocuted at the Pigeon House Fort aged 41 years and was buried in Fletcherstown Cemetery, see page 351. Source: RO 487. Personal Interview with Jimmy Dunphy, Gibbstown, 14/02/15. Headstone Inscription

H. White, possibly Hugh White was a Volunteer in the Clongill I.R.A. Company in July 1921. He died before 1935. He was no relation to the Whites currently living in Clongill. Source: RO 487. Personal interview with Jimmy Dunphy, Gibbstown, 14/02/15.

J. White, Clongill, Wilkinstown, Navan, Co. Meath was the Clongill Company 1st Lieutenant in July 1921. Source: RO 487.

Patrick White, was born in Clongill, Wilkinstown, Navan, Co. Meath about 1904. In 1921 and 1922 he was the Battalion Vice Commanding Officer. In 1922 he was a labourer. He was arrested by Pro-Treaty I.R.A. and interned in Dundalk, Co. Louth on 22nd July. On 27th July 1922 he escaped from Dundalk Jail, see the story on page 59. In 1936 his address was given as Rathduff, Thomastown, Co. Kilkenny. He was no relation to the Whites currently living in Clongill. One of his brothers joined the Free State Army Soldier based in Navan. One of the many cases where brother opposed brother. Sources: RO 487. MM9.1.1/KM3L-F27. Louth County Archives http://www.louthcoco.ie/en/Services/Archives/Archive_Collections/ Faithful to Ireland by Tony Brady, page 73

R. White was a Volunteer in the Clongill I.R.A. Company in July 1921. He died before 1935. He was no relation to the Whites currently living in Clongill. Source: RO 487.

Commons Company:

In May 1920 the Commons Company guarded prisoners at an "unknown destination" in Bohermeen. The prisoners were involved with a British Army sniper who allegedly killed Mark Clinton, an I.R.A. Volunteer, see the story on page 70. For years the Commons area was in the Navan Company Area until around the end of 1920 when the Ardbraccan Company was formed and it included the Commons Area so Navan lost a few men from Commons to the Ardbraccan Company.

Patsy Bennett, see Ardbraccan Company

Patrick Boyle, see Ardbraccan Company.

James Byrne, see Ardbraccan Company.

Richard Byrne, see Ardbraccan Company.

Larry Collins, see Ardbraccan Company.

William McGuirk, see Ardbraccan Company.

Loughlin (Jack) O'Rourke, see Ardbraccan Company.

Michael Hyland, see Ardbraccan Company.

William Rooney, see Ardbraccan Company.

Patrick Stapleton, see Navan Company.

Valentine Stapleton, see Ardbraccan Company.

Thomas Walsh, see Ardbraccan Company.

Patrick Waters, see Ardbraccan Company.

Creewood Company:

John Cassidy, Creewood, Slane, Co. Meath was a Volunteer in the Creewood I.R.A. Company in July 1921 and July 1922. Source: RO 487.

Thomas Cassidy, Littlewood, Slane, Co. Meath was a Volunteer in the Creewood I.R.A. Company in July 1921 and July 1922. Sources: RO 487.

Andrew Clarke, Rathmaiden, Slane, Co. Meath was a Volunteer in the Creewood I.R.A. Company in July 1921 and July 1922 Source: RO 487.

Thomas Clarke, Rathmaiden, Slane, Co. Meath was a Volunteer in the Creewood I.R.A. Company in July 1921 and July 1922. Source: RO 487.

Joseph Commons, Balrenny, Slane, Co. Meath was a Volunteer in the Creewood I.R.A. Company in July 1921 and July 1922. In 1935 his address was given as England. Sources: RO 487.

Patrick Elliott, Grangegeeth, Slane, Co. Meath was a Volunteer in the Creewood I.R.A. Company in July 1921 and July 1922. Sources: RO 487.

Peter Fleming, Grangegeeth, Slane, Co. Meath was the Creewood Company Quartermaster in July 1921 and July 1922. Source: RO 487.

Patrick Kealy, GardrathIn, Grangegeeth, Slane, Co. Meath was a Volunteer in the Creewood I.R.A. Company July 1921 and July 1922. Sources: RO 487.

Michael (Mick) Keelan, Creewood, Slane, Co. Meath was the Creewood I.R.A. Company Commanding Officer In July 1921. In 1935 his address was given as U.S.A. Source: RO 487.

Michael Markey, Creewood, Slane, Co. Meath was a Volunteer in the Creewood I.R.A. Company in July 1921 and July 1922. In 1935 he was a member of An Garda Síochána. Source: RO 487.

William Markey, Creewood, Slane, Co. Meath was a Volunteer in the Creewood I.R.A. Company in July 1921 and July 1922. In 1935 he was a member of An Garda Síochána. Source: RO 487.

Matthew McCannon, Creewood, Slane, Co. Meath was a Volunteer in the Creewood I.R.A. Company in July 1921 and July 1922. Source: RO 487.

Joseph White, Creewood, Slane, Co. Meath was a Volunteer in the Creewood I.R.A. Company in July 1921 and July 1922. Source: RO 487.

Crossakiel Company:

Crossakiel Irish Volunteers Company of 200 men was formed in 1914 and was organised by a British Army officer called Captain Worship Booker. It only lasted six months. The Crossakiel area incorporated the Ballinlough Company area, so for further references to Crossakiel see Ballinlough Company.

Culmullin Company:

In August 1920 the Culmullin Company had a strength of thirteen men. In July 1920 Sinn Fein courts were set up, one in Dunshaughlin and one in a shed in a field in Culmullin. In 1921 Culmullin Company had a strength of fourteen men. The arms they had were twenty-five old Mauser rifles, two Winchester repeating rifles, two old pattern long Lee Enfield rifles, a good few revolvers of all types from point 22 to point 45 Webley and Colt, a couple of hundred shot guns of all types, sixty-three bombs or grenades, a couple of automatic pistols Peter-the-Painter type, three Thompson Sub-Machine Guns with twenty-nine pans of ammunition. In 1922 the strength of the company was down to seven men. Sources: RO 481. RO 482. WS1539.

Michael Bruton, Hayestown, Drumree, Co. Meath was a Volunteer in the Culmullin I.R.A. Company in 1920. In July 1921 and 1922 he was the Culmullin I.R.A. Company Commanding Officer. Sources: RO 481. WS1539.

James Colman, North Strand, Dublin was a Volunteer in the Culmullin I.R.A. Company in July 1921 and 1922. Source: RO 481

Patrick Duffy, Dunshaughlin, Co. Meath, was a Volunteer in the Culmullin I.R.A. Company in August 1920. He was involved in a raid on Parsonstown Manor where a small quantity of old handguns were seized as part of the general raid for arms as ordered by I.R.A. G.H.Q. Source: WS1539.

Michael Fox, Curraghtown, Drumree, Co. Meath was a Volunteer in the Culmullin I.R.A. Company in July 1921 and 1922. Source: RO 481

Thomas Gannon, The Rock, Laracor, Trim, Co. Meath was a Volunteer in the Culmullin I.R.A. Company in 1920, July 1921 and 1922. Sources: WS1539.

David Hall, Moyleggan, Batterstown, Navan, Co. Meath was born in Dublin City but reared in Culmullin. He became a Volunteer in the Kilmore Company of Irish

Volunteers in 1917. In 1919 the Kilmore Company of Irish Volunteers ceased to exist. In June 1920 he transferred to the Dunshaughlin I.R.A. Company where he served as a Volunteer. In July 1920 he was appointed President of the District Court when Sinn Fein set up their own parish courts. In August 1920 he transferred to Culmullin I.R.A. Company. He led a raid on Parsonstown Manor where a small quantity of old handguns were seized as part of the general raid for arms as ordered by I.R.A. G.H.Q. In December 1920 he was appointed I.R.A. 1st Battalion Adjutant (Dunboyne Battalion), Meath Brigade. On 28th March 1921 he was appointed I.R.A. 1st Brigade Commanding Officer. Later Commandant David Hall's address was given as Knutstown, Garristown, Co. Dublin. Sources: WS1060. WS1539. WS01715. RO 479. Photo from Dunshaughlin Board of Guardians 1922.

Joseph Kelly, Pelletstown, Dunshaughlin, Co. Meath was a Volunteer in the Culmullin I.R.A. Company in 1920, July 1921 and 1922.
Source: http://www.bureauofmilitaryhistory.ie/reels/bmh/BMH.WS1539.pdf

Joseph Lynch, Dunshaughlin, Co. Meath was a Volunteer in the Culmullin I.R.A. Company in August 1920. He was involved in a raid on Parsonstown Manor where a small quantity of old handguns were seized as part of the general raid for arms as ordered by I.R.A. G.H.Q. Source: WS1539.

James (Jim) McCormack, Pelletstown, Dunshaughlin, Co. Meath was a brother of below Nicholas. He was a Volunteer in the Culmullin I.R.A. Company in July 1921 and 1922. He died in 1965 and was buried in Knockmark Cemetery Drumree, see page 288. Source: RO 481. Headstone Inscription

John McCormack, Pelletstown, Dunshaughlin, Co. Meath was a Volunteer in the Culmullin I.R.A. Company in 1920, July 1921 and 1922. In 1920 he was arrested, court-martialed in Dublin Castle and interned in the Curragh. He died on 31st May 1946 and was buried in Knockmark Cemetery, Drumree, see page 289.
Source: RO 481. WS1539. Headstone Inscription.

Nicholas (Nick) McCormack, Pelletstown, Dunshaughlin, Co. Meath was a brother of above James. He was a Volunteer in the Culmullin I.R.A. Company in July 1922. He died in 1970 and was buried in Knockmark Cemetery Drumree, see page 288. Source: RO 481. Headstone Inscription

Michael Rattigan, Knockmark, Drumree, Co. Meath was a Volunteer in the Culmullin I.R.A. Company in July 1921 and 1922. He died on 25th April 1978 aged 86 years and was buried in Knockmark Cemetery, see page 289.
Source: RO 481. Headstone Inscription

Patrick Rooney, Curraghtown, Drumree, Co. Meath was the Culmullin Company Commanding Officer in August 1920. He remained with the company to the end of 1922 but I do not know what rank he held during that period. He died before 1936. Sources: WS1539.

R. Rooney was the Culmullin Company Commanding Officer in July 1921. He died before 1936. Source: RO 482

Richard Rooney, Curraghtown, Drumree, Co. Meath was a Volunteer in the Culmullin I.R.A. Company in July 1921 and 1922. Source: RO 481

John Smith, was a Volunteer in the Culmullin I.R.A. Company in 1920 Source: WS1539.

Edward Smyth was a farmer at Woodtown, Culmullin, Drumree. In July 1921 and 1922 he was a Volunteer in the Culmullin I.R.A. Company. He opposed the Treaty. He joined Fianna Fail when it was established in 1926. He died in the Meath Hospital, Dublin in October 1959 and his funeral took place to Culmullin Cemetery. Sources: RO 481. The Meath Chronicle dated 2nd November 1959 page 9

John Smyth, Rathregan, Batterstown, Co. Meath was the Adjutant of the 2nd Battalion, 1st Brigade, 1st Eastern Division in July 1921. Source: RO 481

William Smith, Cultromer, Drumree, Co. Meath was a Volunteer in the Kilmore Company in 1919. In June 1920 he transferred to the Dunshaughlin Company where he served as a Volunteer for two months. In August 1920 he transferred to Culmullin Company until the end of 1922.

James Wallace, Belshamstown, Batterstown, Co. Meath was a Volunteer in the Culmullin I.R.A. Company in July 1921 and 1922. He died before 1936. Source: RO 481

Matthew Wallace, Belshamstown, Batterstown, Co. Meath was born about 1904. He was a Volunteer in the Culmullin I.R.A. Company in 1920. He was arrested and court-martialed in Dublin Castle and interned in Sandhurst Prison in England aged 16. Source: WS1539.

Thomas Wallace was a Volunteer in the Culmullin I.R.A Company in August 1920. He was involved in a raid on Parsonstown Manor where a small quantity of old handguns were seized as part of the general raid for arms as ordered by I.R.A. G.H.Q. Source: WS1539.

James Wildridge, Drumree, Co. Meath was a Volunteer in the Culmullin I.R.A. Company in 1920. He was arrested, court-martialed in Dublin Castle and interned in the Curragh. He died on 22nd March 1959 and was buried in Knockmark Cemetery, Drumree, see page 289. Source: WS1539. Headstone Inscription.

Curragha Company:

In July 1921 the Curragha Company had a strength of seventeen men and in 1922 it continued to have a strength of seventeen men.

John Bissett, Curragha, Ashbourne, Co. Meath was the Curragha I.R.A. Company 1st Lieutenant in July 1921 and 1922. Source: RO 481

Christopher Caddell, Curragha, Dunboyne, Co. Meath was the Curragha I.R.A. Company Commanding Officer in July 1921 and 1922. In 1936 he was serving in the Free State Army and his address was given as Primatestown, Ashbourne, Co. Meath. Source: RO 481

William Carey, Ballyhack, Ashbourne, Co. Meath was a Volunteer in the Curragha I.R.A. Company in July 1921 and 1922. Source: RO 481

Joseph Clery, Curragha, Ashbourne, Co. Meath was a Volunteer in the Curragha I.R.A. Company in July 1921 and 1922. Source: RO 481

Peter Clery, Curragha, Ashbourne, Co. Meath was a Volunteer in the Curragha I.R.A. Company in July 1921 and 1922. Source: RO 481

Peter T. Clery, Curragha, Ashbourne, Co. Meath was a Volunteer in the Curragha I.R.A. Company in July 1921 and 1922. Source: RO 481

Patrick Collins, Primatestown, Ashbourne, Co. Meath was a Volunteer in the Curragha I.R.A. Company in July 1921 and 1922. Source: RO 481

Michael Gough, Primatestown, Ashbourne, Co. Meath was a Volunteer in the Curragha I.R.A. Company in July 1921 and 1922. Source: RO 481

Patrick Gough, Primatestown, Ashbourne, Co. Meath was the Curragha Company 2nd Lieutenant in July 1921. He continued to serve with the company in 1922 but I do not know at what rank. Source: RO 481

Fredrick Lillieropn, Rathfeigh, Tara, Co. Meath was a Volunteer in the Curragha I.R.A. Company in July 1921 and 1922. Source: RO 481

Peter McGrath, Kilbrew, Ashbourne, Co. Meath was a Volunteer in the Curragha I.R.A. Company in July 1921 and 1922. Source: RO 481

James Plunkett, Curragha, Ashbourne, Co. Meath was a Volunteer in the Curragha I.R.A. Company in July 1921 and 1922. Source: RO 481

Edward Rafferty, Cabin Hill, Ratoath, Co. Meath was a Volunteer in the Curragha I.R.A. Company in July 1921 and 1922. Source: RO 481

John Rafferty, Cabin Hill, Ratoath, Co. Meath was a Volunteer in the Curragha I.R.A. Company in July 1921 and 1922. Source: RO 481

John Smyth, Kilmoon, Ashbourne, Co. Meath was the Curragha Company Adjutant in July 1921 and 1922. Source: RO 481

Michael White, Painstown, Dunshaughlin, Co. Meath was a Volunteer in the Curragha I.R.A. Company in July 1922. Source: RO 481

Samuel White, Curragha, Ashbourne, Co. Meath was the Curragha I.R.A. Company Adjutant at least for a period in 1921. He continued to serve with the company in 1922 but I do not know at what rank. Source: RO 481

Drumbaragh Company:

The earliest record I can find in relation to the Drumbaragh Company of Irish Volunteers is that the company existed in May 1914 and had a strength of 35 men. The drill instructor was an ex-British Army Sergeant named Michael Dunphy. Parades, drills and route marches were held every Sunday with the parades being held in Kells. They had no weapons of any kind and drills and parades were done using wooden dummy rifles. Volunteers paid weekly subscription of three pence towards expenses and the purchase of arms and uniforms. Dunphy was also paid for instructing the company and he was the acting company Commanding Officer. After sometime the company purchased a point 22 Winchester rifle and each Volunteer paid for the ammunition he used during firing practice which cost a penny for three rounds. In July 1914, at the outbreak of World War One, a huge split immerged in the Volunteer movement nationally. John Redmond, who was the leader of the Irish Parliamentary Party, called on the Irish Volunteers to join the National Volunteers and to fight in World War One under the command of the British Army. The Leaders of the Irish Volunteers and the Irish Republican Brotherhood (I.R.B.) rejected and condemned this call and the Drumbaragh Company voted in favour of staying loyal to the Irish Volunteers. The drill instructor, Michael Dunphy, did not agree and he resigned from the company. At this time a young Volunteer named Sean Hayes took over command of the Drumbaragh Company beginning a long and interesting career in Irish military history, he is described below. In 1915 the strength of the company had reduced to 24 men, mainly due to the split in the organisation. In early April 1916 all companies in the area, including the Drumbaragh Company, were visited by Senior staff officers from Dublin. Among the visiting party was Gary Byrne, brother of Drumbaragh Company Commanding Officer, Willie Byrne. This marked the start of the final preparations for the Easter Rising of 1916. The only arms that the Drumbaragh Company could secure for the Easter Rising were about three ancient revolvers, a point 38 automatic pistol and the point 22 rifle that they had trained with and some ammunition. The story of what happened can be found in Chapter 3. Drills and training was done in a dis-used private house in Drumbaragh. In March 1917 the strength of the company was 40 men. In the spring of 1918 the strength of the company rose dramatically to 100 men. This sudden rise was due to the threat by the British Government to introduce

Conscription in Ireland forcing young men into the British Army to fight in World War One. When the threat of Conscription ceased the strength of the company dropped back to 45 men. In January 1919 the Irish Volunteers became the I.R.A. The Crossakiel R.I.C. Barracks was in the Drumbaragh Company Area and by Easter Sunday 4th April 1920 the R.I.C. had evacuated the Crossakiel Barracks due to attacks and R.I.C. men had moved to the safety of bigger towns. The barracks was burnt down by local Volunteers to ensure the R.I.C. did not return. In June 1921 the Drumbaragh Company was involved in an ambush of a military truck in Drumbaragh, see the story on page 50. Sources: WS1615. WS0172. WS1659.

Gerald (Gary) Byrne joined the I.R.B. in 1911. He was the 1st Lieutenant of "C" Company, 4th Battalion, Dublin Brigade, Irish Volunteers. He was temporarily drafted in from Dublin by Donal O'Hannigan to take charge of the Drumbaragh Company during the Easter Rising of 1916. Gary's brother, William listed below, who was the Drumbaragh Company Commanding Officer, moved aside to facilitate this. Gary organised and led the Drumbaragh and the Carnaross Companies of Irish Volunteers to the Hill of Tara for the Easter Rising of 1916, see the story in Chapter 3. Sources: WS0172. WS0143.

William Byrne, Kells, Co. Meath was born in 1890. He was also an I.R.B. man. He joined the Irish Volunteers in Rotunda in November 1913. He Joined the Kells Company of Irish Volunteers in 1914. July 1914 saw the outbreak of World War One and the split immerged in the Kells Volunteer movement and nationally. William Byrne was one of a handful of Volunteers who stayed loyal to the Irish Volunteers. However their company in Kells ceased to exist so he transferred to the Drumbaragh Company of Irish Volunteers. He moved from Dublin to Kells in winter 1915. In 1916 he was employed by the Meath Chronicle in Kells as a typesetter. He began organising Irish Volunteer units in the local area. He became the Drumbaragh Company Commanding Officer. On the 20th April 1916, the Thursday before the Rising, Donal O'Hannigan took over control of the whole Louth Meath area. He then appointed Gary Byrne, listed above, brother of William, to take over command of the Drumbaragh Company. William moved aside to facilitate this. All three of these key men were members of the I.R.B. On Easter Sunday, 23rd April, William Byrne met with other members of the company in Kells where they assembled for the Easter Rising of 1916, see the story in Chapter 3. On the Easter Monday he made his way to Dunboyne on his own and while there he was under the command of Donal O'Hannigan. Along with the Dunboyne Company and others he was part of the column of men who occupied Tyrrelstown House during the Easter Rising, see the story on page 23. Source: WS0143. Military Service Pension Collection, file reference No. MSP34REF54787. WS0172.

Sean Dardis was a Volunteer in the Drumbaragh Company of Irish Volunteers in April 1916. On Easter Sunday, 23rd April he mobilised for the Easter Rising of 1916, see the story in Chapter 3. Source: WS0172.

Sean Hayes was a native of Drumbaragh, Kells, Co. Meath. He was a member of the I.R.B. In May 1914 he joined Drumbaragh Company of Irish Volunteers. On Easter Sunday, 23rd April he mobilised for the Easter Rising of 1916, see the story in Chapter 3. After the failed Rising he got involved in mustering up disappointed Volunteers and trying to get them to regroup and reorganise. He became Drumbaragh Company Commanding Officer, Irish Volunteers. In 1919 he was arrested and interned in Ballykinlar Internment Camp, Co. Down. In April 1920 he was appointed Brigade Vice Commanding Officer, Meath Brigade, I.R.A. In May 1920 Sean Hayes was on the reporting staff of The Meath Chronicle. On Sunday 30th September 1920 he was involved in the attack on the heavily fortified Trim R.I.C. Barracks, see the story on page 40. He was appointed Brigade Commanding Officer, probably in 1921. He joined the Free State Army and was appointed to a post in Aer Lingus. He enjoyed singing and he played the bagpipes. He died in Dublin in December 1973. Sources: The Meath Chronicle dated 8th December 1973, page 11. WS0172. WS0857. WS0858. WS1715.

Sean Keogh, Smithstown, Crossakiel, Kells, Co. Meath joined the Crossakiel Company in 1914 but the company ceased that same year. In 1915 he joined the Irish Republican Brotherhood (I.R.B.). In 1916 he formed the Ballinlough Company of Irish Volunteers. In 1917 he became the Drumbaragh Company Commanding Officer and in July 1920 became Battalion Vice Commanding Officer when Seamus Cogan of the Stonefield Company was killed, see the story on page 72. Later in 1920 Sean became Battalion Commanding Officer but within a month he was arrested for illegal detention of one of his majesty's forces. Tom Manning (Ballinlough Company) took over his position as Battalion Vice Commanding Officer for a short time, see Tom Manning's profile on page 98. In February 1921 Sean was released from prison. In April 1921 he was involved in the ambush of a military truck at Sylvan Park Kells, see the story on page 47. He was arrested again and Interned in the Curragh. Charles Conaty took over as Battalion Commanding Officer. Sources: RO 489. WS0858. WS0857. WS01060. WS1615. WS1627

Frank O'Higgins was a keen player of the bagpipes. In 1914, 1915 and 1916 he was a Volunteer in the Drumbaragh Company of Irish Volunteers. He was a brother of Peter O'Higgins, see Ballinlough Company and a brother of Brian O'Higgins who fought in the 1916 Rising, was a founder member of Sinn Fein and a TD in Dail Eireann from 1921 to 1926. On Easter Sunday, 23rd April he mobilised for the Easter Rising of 1916, see the story in Chapter 3. In July 1916 he was a member of the I.R.B. Sources: WS1615. WS0172.

James (Jimmy) O'Neill was the Drumbaragh Irish Volunteers Company 2nd Lieutenant in March 1917. On 22nd July 1920 he was the Drumbaragh I.R.A. Company 2nd Lieutenant when he drove a car through a British Army checkpoint near Oldcastle. He was wounded in the resulting shoot out in which Seamus

Cogan was killed and two other occupants of the car were wounded, see the story on page 72. Source: WS1615.

Joseph Power was a Volunteer in the Drumbaragh Company of Irish Volunteers in 1916. On Easter Sunday, 23rd April he mobilised for the Easter Rising of 1916, see the story in Chapter 3. Source: WS0172.

Michael (Mick) Price was a Volunteer in the Drumbaragh Company of Irish Volunteers in 1916. He formed the Drumbaragh I.R.B. Circle in 1916. Source: WS1615.

Hugh Smith was owner and Editor of the Meath Chronicle which had its offices in Kells at the time. He also owned a motor cycle and in the run up to the Easter Rising he went to Dublin to secure arms for the Drumbaragh Company. He returned with about three ancient revolvers and one point 38 automatic and some ammunition. On Easter Sunday, 23rd April he mobilised for the Easter Rising of 1916, see the story in Chapter 3. After the failed Rising he got involved in trying to bolster up disappointed Volunteers in an effort to get them to regroup and reorganise. Source: WS0857. WS0172. WS0857.

Drumconrath Company:

In early 1918 the Drumconrath Company of Irish Volunteers were formed. In January 1919 the Irish Volunteers became the I.R.A. In early 1919 the I.R.A. reorganised their structures and Drumconrath I.R.A. Company became attached to the 4th Battalion, Meath Brigade. In May 1920 the R.I.C. evacuated the Drumconrath Barracks due to attacks and R.I.C. men moved to the safety of bigger towns. On 23rd May 1920 the Drumconrath R.I.C. Barracks was burnt down by I.R.A. Volunteers including Volunteers from Moynalty and Newcastle to ensure the R.I.C. did not return. The Drumconrath I.R.A. Company was still in existence in 1921 and in 1922. In 1922 the Drumconrath Company was part of the 3rd Battalion, (Ardee) 9th (Louth) Brigade, 1st Eastern Division.
Sources: RO489. RO528. WS1715. WS1625. WS1650.

Bernard Casey, Cookstown, Ardee, Co. Louth was a Volunteer in the Drumconrath I.R.A. Company in 1922. Source: RO 528

Michael Dunne, Ballyhoe, Drumconrath, Co. Meath was a Volunteer in the Drumconrath I.R.A. Company in 1922. Source: RO 528

James Englishby, Newtown, Drumconrath, Co. Meath was the 2nd Lieutenant in the Drumconrath I.R.A. Company in 1922. In 1936 his address was given as U.S.A.
Source: RO 528

John Fay, Rathtrasna, Drumconrath, Co. Meath was a Volunteer in the Drumconrath I.R.A. Company in 1922. There is a headstone in Drumconrath Cemetery which says that John Fay died on 10th November 1969 and was buried in U.S.A., see page 276. Source: RO 528. Headstone Inscription.

Patrick Foylen, Posseckstown Nobber, Co. Meath was a Volunteer in the Nobber I.R.A. Company in July 1921. In 1922 he was a Volunteer in the Drumconrath I.R.A. Company. Source: RO 489. RO 489

Christopher (Christy) Keelan, Ballyhoe, Drumconrath, Co. Meath was a Volunteer in the Drumconrath I.R.A. Company in 1922. He died on 28th February 1954 and was buried in Drumconrath Cemetery, see page 276. Source: RO 528. Headstone Inscription

Richard Keelan, Drumgill, Drumconrath, Co. Meath was a Volunteer in the Drumconrath I.R.A. Company in 1922. Source: RO 528

Patrick Martin, Edmondstown, Ardee, Co. Louth was a Volunteer in the Nobber I.R.A. Company in July 1921. For a period in 1922 he was the Drumconrath I.R.A. Company Commanding Officer. Source: RO 489. RO 528.

Patrick Meade, Breslinstown, Drumconrath, Co. Meath was a Volunteer in the Drumconrath I.R.A. Company in 1922. In 1936 his address was given as U.S.A. Source: RO 528

Barney Phillips, Newtown, Drumconrath, Co. Meath was a Volunteer in the Drumconrath I.R.A. Company in 1922. Source: RO 528

James Trainor, Balrath, Drumconrath, Co. Meath was a Volunteer in the Drumconrath I.R.A. Company in 1922. Source: RO 528

James Ward, Ballyhaise, Co. Cavan was a Volunteer in the Nobber I.R.A. Company in July 1921. In 1922 his address was given as Newstone, Drumconrath, Co. Meath and he was a Volunteer in the Drumconrath I.R.A. Company. In 1936 he was a member of An Garda Síochána. Source: RO 489. RO 528.

Matthew Ward, Newstone, Drumconrath, Co. Meath was a Volunteer in the Drumconrath I.R.A. Company in 1922. He died on 9th July 1978 and was buried in Drumconrath Cemetery, see page 277. Source: RO 528. Headstone Inscription

William Ward, Newtown, Drumconrath, Co. Meath was a Volunteer in the Drumconrath I.R.A. Company in 1922. Source: RO 528

Francis Watters, Drumconrath, Co. Meath was a Volunteer in the Nobber I.R.A. Company in July 1921. In 1922 he was the Battalion Quartermaster and he was also the Drumconrath Company Commanding Officer. His name is engraved on a headstone in Drumconrath Cemetery. It does not state when he died but it was before 1936, see page 277. Source: RO 489. RO 528. Headstone Inscription.

James Watters, Drumconrath, Co. Meath was the 1st Lieutenant in the Drumconrath I.R.A. Company in 1922. In 1936 his address was given as U.S.A. Source: RO 528

Duleek Company:

There does not appear to be any evidence of an Irish Volunteer Company in Duleek before 1921. In 1921 the company strength was 12. In 1922 there were none so the company ceased to exist.

Christopher Carolan, Roughgrange, Donore, Drogheda Co. Louth was a Volunteer in the Duleek I.R.A. Company in 1921. Source: RO 519

Richard Collier, Colgan Street, Duleek, Co. Meath was a Volunteer in the Duleek I.R.A. Company in 1921. Source: RO 519

John Collins, Downstown, Duleek, Co. Meath was a Volunteer in the Duleek I.R.A. Company in 1921. Source: RO 519

James Connell, Main Street, Duleek, Co. Meath was a Volunteer in the Duleek I.R.A. Company in 1921. Source: RO 519

Nicholas Connell, Longford, Duleek, Co. Meath was the Duleek I.R.A. Company Commanding Officer in 1921. Source: RO 519

Patrick Connell, Main Street, Duleek, Co. Meath was a Volunteer in the Duleek I.R.A. Company in 1921. Source: RO 519

Patrick Downes, Curragha, Ratoath, Co. Meath was a Volunteer in the Duleek I.R.A. Company in 1921. Source: RO 519

John Dunne, Main Street, Duleek, Co. Meath was a Volunteer in the Duleek I.R.A. Company in 1921. Source: RO 519

Peter Keelan, Corbollis, Donore, Drogheda, Co. Louth was a Volunteer in the Duleek I.R.A. Company in 1921. Source: RO 519

John Lee, Larrix Street, Duleek, Co. Meath was a Lieutenant in the Duleek I.R.A. Company in 1921. Source: RO 519

Patrick Lee, Larrix Street, Duleek, Co. Meath was a Volunteer in the Duleek I.R.A. Company in 1921. Source: RO 519

Francis McCourt, Woodmill, Slane, Co. Meath was a Volunteer in the Duleek I.R.A. Company in 1921. Source: RO 519

Dunboyne Company:

In 1914 there were two Irish Volunteer companies established in Dunboyne. In July, at the outbreak of World War One, a huge split immerged in the Volunteer movement nationally. John Redmond, leader of the Irish Parliamentary Party, called on the Irish Volunteers to join the National Volunteers and to fight in World War One under the command of the British Army. The majority of one of the Dunboyne Company voted in favour of Redmond's call and the other company voted against. The majority of Dunboyne Volunteers went to fight in the Great War, as it was called. The remaining company of Irish Volunteers forged ahead with a strength of 32 men one of which was a young man called Sean Boylan who later became a leading figure in the Irish Volunteers, the I.R.A. and the I.R.B. See Sean Boylan's details below. The Dunboyne Company Instructor was a man called Captain Larry Murtagh from Chapelizod. The company had no weapons of any kind at that time. They performed drills with wooden dummy rifles sometimes with the Chapelizod Company in their area. After sometime the company purchased a point 22 rifle and each Volunteer paid for the ammunition he used during firing practice which cost about a penny for three rounds. On 24th April 1916 the Dunboyne Company mobilised for the Easter Rising, see the story in Chapter 3. It was about December 1916 before Sean Boylan was released from jail after the Rising and he immediately started rounding up and reorganising Irish Volunteers again. In 1917 the Dunboyne Company of Irish Volunteers had a strength of twelve men, nine of whom were members of the I.R.B. In 1918 the Dunboyne Company strength rose to 40 men mainly due to the threat of Conscription of young men to the British Army. When the threat of Conscription passed the Dunboyne Company strength reduced to 24 men. In January 1919 the Irish Volunteers became the I.R.A. In April 1920 the Dunboyne I.R.A. Company became attached to the 1st Battalion, Meath Brigade. In 1920 the leaders of the I.R.A. and the Irish Republican Brotherhood (I.R.B.) recognised that Dunboyne was an important gateway to and from Dublin for messages, arms and ammunition. For that reason ambushes, attacks and anything that could draw attention to the Dunboyne area were rarely sanctioned by I.R.A. G.H.Q. Dunboyne Company fulfilled its role to make it possible for Dublin I.R.A. G.H.Q. to communicate and transit goods to and from North and North West of Ireland. The Dunboyne Volunteers were always out on their bicycles performing this task. By now Dunboyne Company was regarded as the best armed unit in the area, having about seven Mauser rifles and thirty revolvers and two automatic pistols. In July 1921 the company had a strength of 27 men and they had the same strength in 1922. Sources: WS0212. RO 480. WS0172. WS0212. WS0269. WS1539. WS1715.

Joseph Battersby, Sterling, Dunboyne, Co. Meath was a Volunteer in the Dunboyne Company of Irish Volunteers in July 1921 and July 1922. Source: RO 480

Edward (Ned) Boylan, Dunboyne, Co. Meath was a brother of below Peter, Joseph and Sean Boylan. He was a member of the I.R.B. and a Volunteer in the Dunboyne Company of Irish Volunteers in 1914. In May 1966 he attended the 1916 Commemoration in Dunboyne. He died on 14th March 1968 and was buried in the family plot in Loughsallagh Cemetery Dunboyne along with his brothers, see page 278. Sources: WS0212. Meath Chronicle dated 7th May 1966, page 9. Headstone Inscription.

Peter Boylan, Dunboyne, Co. Meath was a brother of below Sean, Joseph and above Ned Boylan. From 1914 to 1916 Peter was a Volunteer in the Dunboyne Company of Irish Volunteers. During the 1916 Rising he served under the command of Donal O'Hannigan at Dunboyne. Along with the Dunboyne Company and others he was part of the column of men who occupied Tyrrelstown House during the Easter Rising, see the story on page 23. He is listed on the Roll of Honour which is on Public Display in the National Museum. On 2nd May 1916 he was arrested on charges related to the Easter Rising. In 1917 he became a member of the I.R.B. In 1938 his address was given as 7 Upper Beechwood Avenue, Rathmines, Dublin. He died in March 1965 and was buried in the family plot in Loughsallagh Cemetery Dunboyme alongside his brothers, see page 278. Sources: RO 480. WS0212. WS 0269. Headstone Inscription.

Sean Boylan, Edenmore, Dunboyne, Co. Meath was involved in the 1916 Rising.

Sean Boylan, photo kindly provided by Mick O'Brien, Johnstown

His name appears in the Irish Military Archives Alphabetical List of 1916 Veterans. Born in 1884, Sean Boylan was the Grandfather of the former G.A.A. Meath Football Team Manager and he too was involved in G.A.A., he was Chairman of the County Board from 1920 to 1922. He was a member of the Irish Republican Brotherhood (I.R.B.). In 1914 he became a Volunteer in the Dunboyne Company of the Irish Volunteers. Padraig Pearse appointed Sean Boylan to look after the whole Meath Area on the General Council of Irish Volunteers. Although Sean lived in Dunboyne he cycled day and night, to meetings, organising, leading and controlling all of the Irish Volunteer companies in the County for a number of years. He was at the forefront of all training, and preparation of companies for the Easter Rising throughout Meath up to the Easter Rising of 1916. He travelled by bicycle from area to area usually in the dark of night and in all kinds of weather. He became one of Michael Collins right hand men. During the Rising he seved under the command of Donal O'Hannigan at Dunboyne. Along with the Dunboyne Company and others he was part of the column of men who occupied Tyrrelstown House during the Easter Rising, see the story on page 23. On 2nd May 1916, immediately after the Rising, he was arrested along with his brothers Ned, Peter and Joe, listed above. Joe was not involved in the Irish Volunteers or in the Easter Rising. Sean Boylan was imprisoned in Wandsworth Prison, Woking Prison on Salisbury Plain, Frongoch Internment Camp in Wales and other Internment Camps in England and Wales. He was released about December 1916. For the next two years he regrouped the Irish Volunteers, he trained them, he reorganised them, he started a recruitment campaign, formed new companies all over Co. Meath and he put military structures in place. On 25th September 1917 he attended the funeral of Thomas Ashe, see page 34. In April 1920 he was appointed Brigade Commanding Officer of the Meath Brigade, I.R.A. During May - June period of 1920 he was involved in the arrest, imprisonment and trial of a criminal gang who were operating in North Meath and who allegedly killed Mark Clinton, an I.R.A. Volunteer, see the story on page 70. In September 1920 he attended a meeting in Carnaross in which he found it necessary to charge the Battalion Commanding Officer with Mutiny, see the story on page 40. On Sunday 30th September 1920 he was involved in the attack on the heavily fortified Trim R.I.C. Barracks, see the story on page 40. In April 1921 he was Involved in an ambush of a military truck at Sylvan Park Kells, see the story on page 47. About May 1921 he was appointed Divisional Commanding Officer and became Commandant General. About 21st June 1921 he was involved in the trial of a prototype trench mortar gun which exploded killing Captain Matty Furlong of Dublin, see the story on page 50. On 2nd July 1921, days before the Truce he was Involved in the planning of a failed attack of a troop train at Celbridge, see the story on page 51. He was a member of Meath County Council in 1921. In April 1922 he was arrested. His address at the time was given as Athboy. In the aftermath of the Irish Civil War he was unhappy with the way the Free State Army was being downsized. On 1st April 1925 he resigned from the Free State Army on health grounds aged 41 and with pension of £230 per year. In May 1966 he attended the 1916 Commemoration in Dunboyne. On 10th May 1970 he died aged 86 and was buried in the family plot in Loughsallagh Cemetery Dunboyne alongside his brothers, see page 278. Sources: RO 480. Military Service Pension Collection, file reference No. 24SP11477. WS0212. Royal and Loyal by Michael O'Brien page 78 & 110. WS1060. WS1539. Headstone Inscription. Meath Chronicle dated 7th May 1966, page 9.

John Brady, Dunboyne, Co. Meath was a Volunteer in the Dunboyne I.R.A. Company in July 1921 and July 1922. In 1936 he was serving in the Free State Army. Source RO 480

Peter Byrne, a member of the I.R.B., was a Volunteer in the Dunboyne Company of Irish Volunteers in 1914. During the 1916 Rising he served under the command of Donal O'Hannigan at Dunboyne. Along with the Dunboyne Company and others he was part of the column of men who occupied Tyrrelstown House during the Easter Rising, see the story on page 23. He died on 26th December 1926 and was buried in Loughsallagh Cemetery, see page 278. Source: WS0212. Headstone Inscription.

Frank Carolan was born in Kilcloon, Co. Meath about 1897. In April 1921 he was the appointed Vice Commanding Officer of the 1st Battalion (Dunboyne), Meath Brigade, I.R.A. In September 1920 he was involved in an attack on the heavily fortified Trim R.I.C. Barracks, see the story on page 40. In July 1922 he was a farmer and Commanding Officer of the 1st Battalion, 1st Brigade, 1st Eastern Division. He was arrested by Pro-Treaty I.R.A. and interned in Dundalk, Co. Louth on 3rd August 1922. On 14th August 1922 he was rescued from jail along with about 200 other internees by a group of Anti-Treaty I.R.A. who forcibly took Dundalk Military Barracks before taking control of the Dundalk Jail and releasing all of their Comrades. In 1936 his address was given as U.S.A. Sources: WS1715. RO 479. RO 480. WS01060. MM9.1.1/KM3L-NW7. Louth County Archives http://www.louthcoco.ie/en/Services/Archives/Archive_Collections/WS0858

James Carroll, Dunboyne, Co. Meath was a Volunteer in the Dunboyne I.R.A. Company in July 1921 and July 1922. In 1936 he was serving in the Free State Army. Source: RO 480

Patrick Clinton was the I.R.A. Battalion Intelligence Officer, 1st Battalion (Dunboyne), Meath Brigade, 1st Eastern Division around 1918. In September 1920 he attended a meeting in Carnaross in which officers were accused of mutiny, see the story on page 40. At the end of 1920 he was the Brigade Intelligence Officer. On the 2nd July 1921, about two weeks before the Truce, he led men to a failed attack on a troop train near Celbridge, see the story on page 51. In July 1921 he was the I.R.A. Colonel Commandant and the Divisional Adjutant and Acting Director of Intelligence. Sources: WS1723. WS1696. WS1627. WS1060. WS0932.

Aidan Crean, Bennettstown, Dunboyne, Co. Meath was a Volunteer in the Dunboyne Company of Irish Volunteers in 1914, 1915 and 1916. During the 1916 Easter Rising he served under the command of Donal O'Hannigan at Dunboyne. Along with the Dunboyne Company and others he was part of the column of men who occupied Tyrrelstown House during the Easter Rising, see the story on page 23. He is listed on the Roll of Honour which is on Public Display in the National Museum. Sources: WS0212. Politics and War in Meath 1913-23 by Oliver Coogan. WS0212.

Bernard (Barney) Dunne was appointed Battalion Commanding Officer in April 1920, 1st Battalion (Dunboyne) Meath Brigade, I.R.A. In September 1920 he was involved in an attack on the heavily fortified Trim R.I.C. Barracks, see the story on page 40. In March 1921 he was the 1st Eastern Division Medical Officer Captain. In April 1921 he was a Brigade Adjutant. He took the Pro-Treaty side. On 25th April 1922, An Toglac Newspaper reports of an attack by anti-Treaty I.R.A. on Brigadier-Adjutant Dunne, 1st Eastern Division as he left a shop in Dunshaughlin. Dunne refused to raise his hands and was shot and wounded in the chest. In 1936 he was serving in the Free State Army and his address was given as The Curragh Camp, Co. Kildare. Sources: WS1539. RO 479. WS1715. An Toglac dated 25th April 1922, page 13.

Christopher Ennis, Dunboyne, Co. Meath was a Volunteer in the Dunboyne I.R.A. Company in July 1921 and July 1922. Source: RO 480

Thomas Ennis, Quarryland, Dunboyne, Co. Meath was the Intelligence Officer of the 1st Battalion, 1st Brigade, 1st Eastern Division, I.R.A. in July 1921. Source: RO 479

F. Farrell, Dunboyne, Co. Meath was the Dunboyne I.R.A. Company Quartermaster in 1921. Source: RO 480

Francis (Frank) Farrell, Naulswood, Dunboyne, Co. Meath was a Volunteer in the Dunboyne Company of Irish Volunteers in 1916. During the 1916 Rising he seved under the command of Donal O'Hannigan at Dunboyne. Along with the Dunboyne Company and others he was part of the column of men who occupied Tyrrelstown House during the Easter Rising, see the story on page 23. In July 1921 and July 1922 he was the Dunboyne I.R.A. Company Adjutant. Source: RO 480

Hugh Farrell, was a Volunteer in the Dunboyne Company of Irish Volunteers in 1916. On 24th April 1916 he was mobilised in Dunboyne for the Easter Rising. He served under the command of Donal O'Hannigan at Dunboyne. Along with the Dunboyne Company and others he was part of the column of men who occupied Tyrrelstown House during the Easter Rising, see the story on page 23. In August 1938 his address was given as 120 Leix Road, Cabra, Dublin. Source: RO 480. WS0269.

James Farrell, Folistown, Dunboyne, Co. Meath was the Dunboyne I.R.A. Company Quartermaster In 1921 and July 1922. Source: RO 480

Thomas Farrell, Folistown, Dunboyne, Co. Meath was a Volunteer in the Dunboyne I.R.A. Company in July 1921 and July 1922. Source: RO 480

Joseph Gaynor, Vesingstown, Dunboyne, Co. Meath was a Volunteer in the Dunboyne I.R.A. Company in July 1921 and July 1922. In 1936 he was serving in the Free State Army. Source: RO 480

Matthew Hollywood, Rathleek, Dunboyne, Co. Meath was a Volunteer in the Dunboyne I.R.A. Company in July 1921 and July 1922. In 1966 he was serving in the Free State Army. Source: RO 480

Nicholas Horan, Cushinstown, Dunboyne, Co. Meath was the Dunboyne I.R.A. Company Commanding Officer in July 1921. Source: RO 479

Peter James was a Volunteer in the Dunboyne Company of Irish Volunteers in 1914. Source: WS0212.

Christopher Keating, was a member of the I.R.B. He was also a Volunteer in the Dunboyne Company of Irish Volunteers and I.R.A. from 1914 to 1922. On 24th April 1916 he was mobilised in Dunboyne for the Easter Rising. He served under the command of Donal O'Hannigan at Dunboyne. Along with the Dunboyne Company and others he was part of the column of men who occupied Tyrrelstown House during the Easter Rising, see the story on page 23. Later his address was given as Scunthorpe, England. His name is engraved on a headstone in Rooske Cemetery. It says that Christopher Keating died on 2nd May 1970 aged 74 years, see page 281. Sources: RO 480. WS0212. WS0269. Headstone Inscription.

James Keating was a Volunteer in the Dunboyne Company of Irish Volunteers in 1916. During the Rising he served under the command of Donal O'Hannigan at Dunboyne. Along with the Dunboyne Company and others he was part of the column of men who occupied Tyrrelstown House during the Easter Rising, see the story on page 23. He is listed on the Roll of Honour which is on Public Display in the National Museum. In August 1938 his address was given as Iowa, U.S.A.
Sources: RO 480. Politics and War in Meath 1913-23 by Oliver Coogan. WS0212. WS0269.

Peter Keating was a member of the I.R.B. He was a Volunteer in the Dunboyne Company of Irish Volunteers from 1914 to 1916. On 24th April 1916 he was mobilised in Dunboyne for the Easter Rising. He served under command of Donal O'Hannigan at Dunboyne. Along with the Dunboyne Company and others he was part of the column of men who occupied Tyrrelstown House during the Easter Rising, see the story on page 23. He is listed on the Roll of Honour which is on Public Display in the National Museum. In August 1938 his address was given as Iowa, U.S.A. Sources: RO 480. Politics and War in Meath 1913-23 by Oliver Coogan. WS0212. WS0269.

John Kelly, Dunboyne, Co. Meath was a Volunteer in the Dunboyne Company of Irish Volunteers from 1914 to 1916. In early 1920 he was the I.R.A. Brigade Chief of Police, 1st Brigade. He was also a member of the I.R.B. During May - June period of 1920 he was involved in the arrest and imprisonment of a criminal gang who were operating in North Meath and who allegedly killed Mark Clinton, an I.R.A. Volunteer, see the story on page 70. In July 1921 he continued as the Brigade Chief of Police. In May 1966 he attended the 1916 Commemoration in Dunboyne. He died in December 1937 and was buried in Loughsallagh Cemetery, see page 279. Sources: RO 479. WS0212. WS0212. WS1715. Meath Chronicle dated 7th May 1966, page 9.

Michael Kelly, Dunboyne, Co. Meath was a member of the I.R.B. and a Volunteer in the Dunboyne Company of Irish Volunteers and the I.R.A. from 1914 to 1922. In May 1966 he attended the 1916 Commemoration in Dunboyne. His name is inscribed on a headstone in Loughsallagh Cemetery, see page 279.
Sources: RO 480. WS0212. WS0212. Headstone Inscription. Meath Chronicle dated 7th May 1966, page 9.

John King, Dunboyne, Co. Meath was a Volunteer in the Dunboyne I.R.A. Company in July 1921 and July 1922. In 1936 he was serving in the Free State Army.
Source: RO 480

Owen King, Pace, Dunboyne, Co. Meath was a Volunteer in the Dunboyne Company of Irish Volunteers from 1914 to 1916. On 24th April 1916 he was mobilised in Dunboyne for the Easter Rising. He served under the command of Donal O'Hannigan at Dunboyne. Along with the Dunboyne Company and others he was part of the column of men who occupied Tyrrelstown House during the Easter Rising, see the story on page 23. He is listed on the Roll of Honour which is on Public Display in the National Museum. His name is inscribed on a headstone in Loughsallagh Cemetery, see page 279.

Sources: RO 480. WS0212. Politics and War in Meath 1913-23 by Oliver Coogan. WS0212. WS0269. Headstone Inscription.

Michael Larkin, Dunboyne, Co. Meath was a Volunteer in the Dunboyne I.R.A. Company in July 1921 and July 1922. Source: RO 480

Peter Lee left Dunboyne in a group of 10 or 12 men from the area to Powerstown House in Mulhuddart on Easter Monday to become involved in the Easter Rising.

Source: Politics and War in Meath 1913-23 by Oliver Coogan page 109

John Leonard, Dunboyne, Co. Meath was a Volunteer in the Dunboyne I.R.A. Company in July 1921 and July 1922. His name is engraved on a headstone in Rooske Cemetery. It says that John Leonard died on 9th July 1975 aged 77 years, see page 282. Source: RO 480. Headstone Inscription

Thomas Leonard, Lustown, Dunboyne, Co. Meath was a Volunteer in the Dunboyne I.R.A. Company in July 1921. In 1922 he was a Battalion Officer.

Source: RO 480

Francis Lowndes, Hamwood, Dunboyne was a Volunteer in the Dunboyne Company of Irish Volunteers in 1916. On 24th April 1916 he was mobilised in Dunboyne for the Easter Rising. He served under the command of Donal O'Hannigan at Dunboyne. Along with the Dunboyne Company and others he was part of the column of men who occupied Tyrrelstown House during the Easter Rising, see the story on page 23. He is listed on the Roll of Honour which is on Public Display in the National Museum.

Source RO 480. Politics and War in Meath 1913-23 by Oliver Coogan. WS0212.

Christopher (Kit) Lynam was a Volunteer in the Dunboyne Company of Irish Volunteers from 1914 to 1916. On 24th April 1916 he was mobilised in Dunboyne for the Easter Rising. He served under the command of Donal O'Hannigan at Dunboyne. Along with the Dunboyne Company and others he was part of the column of men who occupied Tyrrelstown House during the Easter Rising, see the story on page 23. On 2nd May 1916 he was arrested along with the Boylan brothers for offences related to the Easter Rising. In 1920 he was the Dunboyne I.R.A. Company Commanding Officer. In April 1921 he was a Battalion Commanding Officer. Kit Lynam was later replaced by Bernard Dunne. Commandant Christopher (Kit) Lynam died before 1938.

Sources: WS0858. WS0901. WS0857. WS0212. RO 480 WS0269. WS0212.

Daniel Madden was mobilised in Dunboyne for the Easter Rising on 24th April 1916. He served under the command of Donal O'Hannigan at Dunboyne. Along with the Dunboyne Company and others he was part of the column of men who occupied Tyrrelstown House during the Easter Rising, see the story on page 23. He is listed on the Roll of Honour which is on Public Display in the National Museum. In July 1921 he was still an active Volunteer of the Dunboyne Company. In 1938 his address was given as Barrenhill, Clonsilla, Dublin.

Sources: RO 480. Politics and War in Meath 1913-23 by Oliver Coogan. WS0269.

James Maguire, Beggstown, Dunboyne, Co. Meath was a brother of below William. He lived at Newtown, Dunboyne before he moved to Beggistown. He was a Volunteer in the Dunboyne Company of Irish Volunteers from 1914 to 1916. He was involved in the 1916 Easter Rising at Dunboyne and at Tyrellstown House and he is listed on the Roll of Honour which is on Public Display in the National Museum. During 1916 he was appointed Brigade Quartermaster. In April 1920 he became Battalion Transport Officer, 1st Battalion, Meath Brigade, I.R.A. In September 1920 he was involved in the attack on the heavily fortified Trim R.I.C. Barracks, see the story on page 40. In April 1921 he was appointed Brigade Quartermaster. In 1936 his address was given as Beggstown, Dunboyne. He died on 26th February 1958 aged 64 and was buried in Rooske, see page 282.

Source: RO 480. RO 479. WS0212. Politics and War in Meath 1913-23 by Oliver Coogan. WS0858. WS1715. Personal Interview with his son John in Rooske Cemetery on 14th March 2015. Headstone Inscription.

William Maguire, Castlefarm, Dunboyne, Co. Meath was a brother of above James. He was the Dunboyne I.R.A. Company 1st Lieutenant in 1921 and July 1922. He died on 21st October 1959 and was buried in Rooske, see page 282. Source: RO 480. Personal Interview with his nephew John Maguire in Rooske Cemetery on 14th March 2015. Headstone Inscription.

Philip McGovern, Slane, Co. Meath was a Volunteer in the Dunboyne Company of Irish Volunteers in July 1921. In 1936 he was serving in the Free State Army.

Source: RO 480

Sean McGurl see Athboy Company. Sources: RO 480, Politics and War in Meath 1913-23 by Oliver Coogan.

Nicholas Moran, Cushinstown, Dunboyne, Co. Meath was involved in an attack on the heavily fortified Trim R.I.C. Barracks in September 1920, see the story on page 40. In July 1921 and July 1922 he was the Dunboyne I.R.A. Company Commanding Officer. He was instrumental in ensuring that the Dunboyne Company fulfilled its role to make it possible for Dublin I.R.A. G.H.Q. to communicate and transit goods to the North and North West of Ireland. In 1936 he was serving in National Army.

Sources: RO 480. WS1539.

Nicholas Moran, Mill Farm, Dunboyne, Co. Meath was a Volunteer in the Dunboyne Company of Irish Volunteers. In 1936 he was serving in the Free State Army. Sources: RO 480.

Peter Moran, Jarretstown, Dunboyne, Co. Meath was a Volunteer in the Dunboyne I.R.A. Company

Charles Muldoon, Mulhuddart, Co. Dublin was a Volunteer in the Dunboyne I.R.A. Company in July 1921 and July 1922. Source: RO 480

James Mullaly, Woodpark, Dunboyne, Co. Meath joined the Dunboyne Company of Irish Volunteers in 1915. He was one of the few Meath Volunteers who were involved in the 1916 Easter Rising. His name appears in the Irish Military Archives Alphabetical List of 1916 Veterans. During the Rising he served under the command of Donal O'Hannigan at Dunboyne. Along with the Dunboyne Company and others he was part of the column of men who occupied Tyrrelstown House during the Easter Rising, see the story on page 23. After the surrender in Dublin he evaded arrest by travelling cross country. His name is also listed on the Roll of Honour which is on Public Display in the National Museum.

Source: RO 480. Politics and War in Meath 1913-23 by Oliver Coogan.
http://www.militaryarchives.ie/fileadmin/user_upload/MSPC/WENTIRELISTRELEASE1.pdf MSP34REF54393

Patrick Mullaly was a Volunteer in the Dunboyne Company of Irish Volunteers in 1916. During the 1916 Rising he served under the command of Donal O'Hannigan at Dunboyne. Along with the Dunboyne Company and others he was part of the column of men who occupied Tyrrelstown House during the Easter Rising, see the story on page 23. He is listed on the Roll of Honour which is on Public Display in the National Museum. In 1938 his address was given as Tallaght, Dublin.

Source: RO 480. Politics and War in Meath 1913-23 by Oliver Coogan.

Alex Murray, Hill View, Dunboyne, Co. Meath was a Volunteer in the Dunboyne Company of Irish Volunteers in July 1921 and July 1922. Source: RO 480

James Murtagh, Newtown, Dunboyne, Co. Meath was the Chemist in the 1st Brigade, 1st Eastern Division, I.R.A. in July 1921. Source: RO 479

Larry Murtagh, Chapelizod, Co. Dublin was the Dunboyne Company of Irish Volunteers Commanding Officer in 1914. Source: WS0212.

Peter Newman was a Volunteer in the Dunboyne Company of Irish Volunteers in 1916. During the 1916 Rising he served under the command of Donal O'Hannigan at Dunboyne. Along with the Dunboyne Company and others he was part of the column of men who occupied Tyrrelstown House during the Easter Rising, see the story on page 23. In 1938 his address was given as 31 Portland Place, Drumcondra, Dublin. Source: RO 480

Gearoid O'Broin was a Volunteer in the Dunboyne Company of Irish Volunteers in 1916. He was involved in the 1916 Easter Rising and he is listed on the Roll of Honour which is on Public Display in the National Museum. Source: Politics and War in Meath 1913-23 by Oliver Coogan

Giolla Criost O'Broin was born in 1879. He was a Volunteer in the Dunboyne Company of Irish Volunteers in 1916. He was involved in the 1916 Easter Rising and he is listed on the Roll of Honour which is on Public Display in the National Museum. He died in 1972 aged 93 years and was buried in Loughsallagh Cemetery, see page 279. Source: Politics and War in Meath 1913-23 by Oliver Coogan page 58

Liam O'Broin was a Volunteer in the Dunboyne Company of Irish Volunteers in 1916. He was involved in the 1916 Easter Rising and he is listed on the Roll of Honour which is on Public Display in the National Museum.

Source: Politics and War in Meath 1913-23 by Oliver Coogan

Christopher O'Byrne was a Volunteer in the Dunboyne Company of Irish Volunteers in 1916. In August 1938 his address was given as 21 Parnell Square, Dublin. Source: RO 480

Peter O'Byrne was a Volunteer in the Dunboyne Company of Irish Volunteers in 1916. Source: RO 480

Thomas O'Neill, Lower Gardiner Street, Dublin was a Volunteer in the Dunboyne I.R.A. Company in July 1921 and July 1922. In 1922 his address was given as Camden Street. Source: RO 480

Bernard O'Reilly was the Intelligence Officer of the 1st Battalion (Dunboyne), Meath Brigade, I.R.A. in April 1920. Source: WS1715.

Christopher Pollin, Dunboyne, Co. Meath was a Volunteer in the Dunboyne I.R.A. Company in July 1921 and July 1922. In 1936 he was serving in the Free State Army. Source: RO 480

Bernard (Barney) Reilly, Dunboyne, Co. Meath was a Lieutenant in the Dunboyne I.R.A. Company in 1920. On 9th December 1920 he was shot and killed by "friendly fire". He was buried in Dunboyne. Sources: Politics and war in Meath by Oliver Coogan, page 152. WS1060. WS1539. Meath Chronicle dated 27th April 1935. Meath Chronicle dated 7th May 1966.

James Reilly, Dunboyne, Co. Meath was a Volunteer in the Dunboyne I.R.A. Company in July 1921. In July 1922 he was a Battalion Officer. Sources: RO 479. RO 480.

William Reilly, Dunboyne, Co. Meath was the Dunboyne I.R.A. Company 2nd Lieutenant in 1921 and July 1922. In 1918 the Reilly's of Dunboyne were blacksmiths and they made pikes from old springs of cars, traps and motors for use as weapons. His name in inscribed on a headstone in Loughsallagh Cemetery, see page 280. Source: WS0901. RO 480. Headstone Inscription.

John Smyth, Rathleek, Dunboyne, Co. Meath was a Volunteer in the Dunboyne I.R.A. Company in July 1921 and July 1922. Source: RO 480

Patrick Woods, Clonee, Co. Meath was a Volunteer in the Dunboyne I.R.A. Company in July 1921. He was arrested and interned in Ballykinlar Internment Camp, Co. Down. He was held in Compound No 2. He continued his involvement with the Dunboyne Company throughout 1922. His name is engraved on a headstone in Rooske Cemetery, Dunboyne. It says that Patrick died on 24th March 1982 aged 84 years. Sources: RO 480. Prisoners of War by Liam O' Duibhir, page 315. Headstone Inscription.

Dunderry Company:

The Dunderry Company of Irish Volunteers was formed at the latter end of 1917. It was organised by Paddy Mooney and Seamus O'Higgins of Trim Company. On Sunday 12th August 1917 the Irish Volunteers County Convention was held at Philpotstown, Dunderry. Around 1918 a meeting to appoint the Meath Brigade staff was held in Dunderry. In January 1919 the Irish Volunteers became the I.R.A. On 2nd November 1919 the Dunderry I.R.A. Company blocked all the roads in their area as part of the co-ordinated attack on Lismullen R.I.C. Barracks also known as Dillon's Bridge, see the story on page 37. In the summer of 1920 the Dunderry I.R.A. Company was attached to the 2nd Battalion, Meath Brigade. In 1921 the Dunderry Company had a strength of 21 men. In 1922 the Dunderry Company had a strength of thirteen men. Sources: RO 485. WS0857. WS1696.

John Caffrey, Yellow Walls, Robinstown, Co. Meath was a Volunteer in the Dunderry I.R.A. Company in July 1921. Source: RO 485

Christopher Coffey, Tullaghanstown, Navan, Co. Meath was a Volunteer in the Dunderry I.R.A. Company in July 1921. In early 1921 he was "on the run" and involved in an A.S.U. that took part in an ambush of a military foot patrol at Haggard Street, Trim, see the story on page 43. Sources: WS1060.

William Connor, Logantown, Trim, Co. Meath was a Volunteer in the Dunderry I.R.A. Company in July 1921. Source: RO 485

John Conway, Halltown, Navan, Co. Meath was a Volunteer in the Dunderry I.R.A. Company in July 1921. He died on 31st December 1978 aged 81 years and was buried in Churchtown Cemetery, Dunderry, see page 329. Source: RO 485

Patrick Farrelly was the Dunderry I.R.A. Company 2nd Lieutenant In July 1921 and July 1922. He died before 1936. Source: RO 485

James Fitzsimons, Tullaghanstown, Navan, Co. Meath and also of 18 Imaal Road, Cabra, Co. Dublin was born about 1899. He described himself as a farm labourer. He joined the Dunderry Company of Irish Volunteers in 1918. He became an I.R.A. policeman. He joined the Free State Army on 7th February 1922. He was the only member of the Dunderry Irish Volunteers who joined the Free State Army. He was discharged from the Free State Army on 2nd September 1922 due to poor health.
Source: Military Service Pension Collection, file reference No 24SP1392

Thomas Gill, Jamestown, Bohermeen, Co. Meath was a Volunteer in the Dunderry I.R.A. Company in July 1922. Source: RO 485

James Hyland, Kilcooley, Trim, Co. Meath was a Volunteer in the Dunderry I.R.A. Company in July 1921. His name is inscribed on a headstone in Dunderry Cemetery but I am not 100% sure if it is the same James Hyland. The inscription says James Hyland Dunganney, Trim died 25th July 1980 aged 80 years, see page 327. Source: RO 485. Headstone Inscription.

Peter Kane, Tullaghanstown, Navan, Co. Meath was a Volunteer in the Dunderry I.R.A. Company in July 1921. Source: RO 485

Michael Kiernan, Fordstown, Kells, Co Meath was "on the run" and involved in an A.S.U. that, in early 1921, took part in an ambush of a military foot patrol at Haggard Street, Trim, see the story on page 43. In 1921 he was the Dunderry I.R.A. Company Engineer. He then became the Battalion Engineer. Sources: RO 485. WS1060.

Bernard Loughran was a Volunteer in the Dunderry I.R.A. Company in July 1921 and July 1922. In 1936 his address was given as Tourmakeady, Co. Mayo. His name is inscribed on a headstone in Churchtown Cemetery Dunderry but I am not sure if it is the same Bernard Loughran. The inscription says that Bernard Loughran died on 31st January 1980 and it is inscribed on a headstone belonging to Loughran from Shambo. Source: RO 485. Headstone inscription

Edward Lynch, Rathmore, Athboy, Co. Meath was the Dunderry I.R.A. Company Adjutant in July 1921 and for a period in 1922. Source: RO 485

Laurence Lynch was a Volunteer in the Dunderry I.R.A. Company in July 1921. In 1936 he was a member of An Garda Síochána. Source: RO 485

Michael Lynch, Rathmore, Athboy, Co. Meath was the Dunderry I.R.A. Company Adjutant for a period in 1922. Source: RO 485

Patrick Lynch was the Dunderry I.R.A. Company 1st Lieutenant in July 1921 and July 1922. He died before 1936. Source: RO 485

John Masterson, Ballardin, Dunderry, Co. Meath was a Volunteer in the Dunderry I.R.A. Company in July 1921 and July 1922. He spent most of this period in jail. Source: RO 485

Thomas Morris, Rathnally, Trim, Co. Meath was a Volunteer in the Dunderry I.R.A. Company in July 1921. Source: RO 485

Patrick Mulligan, Dunderry, Navan, Co. Meath was a Volunteer in the Dunderry I.R.A. Company in July 1921 and July 1922. He died on 4th February 1971 aged 68 years and was buried in Dunderry Cemetery, see page 327. Source: RO 485. Headstone Inscription.

Bernard Nugent was a Volunteer in the Dunderry I.R.A. Company in July 1921. Source: RO 485

Thomas Nulty was a Volunteer in the Dunderry I.R.A. Company in July 1921. In 1936 his address was given as U.S.A. He died on 13th January 1978 and was buried in St. Mary's Cemetery, Navan, see page 341. Source: RO 485. Headstone Inscription.

Stephen Sherry was a native of Eskaroon, Dunderry, Co. Meath. In July 1921 he had an address at Yellow Walls, Robinstown, Co. Meath and he was a Volunteer in the Dunderry I.R.A. Company. Source: RO 485. Dunderry A Folk History by Dunderry History Group & Johnny Keely.

William Sherry, was the Dunderry I.R.A. Company 2nd Lieutenant in 1919. He was a member of An Garda Síochána and was stationed in Monaghan in March 1925. There was a William Sherry in Trim I.R.A. Company in 1921 and 1922. I don't know if it is the same William Sherry, see Trim Company. Source: Military Service Pension Collection, file reference No 24SP1392

James Slevin, Ballardin, Dunderry, Co. Meath was appointed to the Brigade Committee for gathering information related to qualifying Volunteers for the Military Service Pensions in 1936. Source: RO 485

Joseph Slevin, Philpotstown, Dunderry, Co. Meath was the Dunderry I.R.A. Company Commanding Officer in July 1921 and July 1922. Source: RO 485

Owen Smith, Yellow Walls, Dunderry, Co. Meath was a Volunteer in the Dunderry I.R.A. Company in July 1921 and July 1922. Source: RO 485

Patrick Smith was the Dunderry I.R.A. Company Quartermaster in July 1921 and July 1922. In 1936 his address was given as U.S.A. Source: RO 485

Thomas Smith, Rathmore, Athboy, Co. Meath was the Dunderry I.R.A. Company Adjutant for a period in 1922. On 11th May 1923 he was taken into custody by the Free State Army. Source: RO 485. Dunderry A Folk History by Dunderry History Group & Johnny Keely.

Richard Yore, Ballardin, Dunderry, Co. Meath started of as a young Bicycle Dispatch Rider for the Volunteers. He was a Volunteer in the Dunderry I.R.A. Company in July 1921 and July 1922. He died on 7th April 1979 and was buried in Dunderry Cemetery, see page 328. Source: RO 485. Dunderry A Folk History by Dunderry History Group & Johnny Keely. Headstone Inscription.

Dunmoe Company:

In 1921 the Dunmoe Company had a strength of seventeen men. In 1922 there were no members so the company ceased to exist. Source: RO 486

John Bennett was a Volunteer in the Dunmoe I.R.A. Company in July 1921. In 1936 his address was given as Dublin. Source: RO 486

Laurence Brady, Simonstown, Navan, Co. Meath was a Volunteer in the Dunmoe I.R.A. Company in July 1921. Source: RO 486

Christopher Carolan, Batterstown, Navan, Co. Meath was a Volunteer in the Dunmoe I.R.A. Company in July 1921. He died on 9th December 1969 and was buried in Donaghmore Cemetery in Navan, see page 324. Source: RO 486 Military Service Pension Collection, file reference No. 14-SP-2960. Headstone Inscription.

Michael Delany, Flower Hill, Navan, Co. Meath was the Dunmoe Company 1st Lieutenant in July 1921. Source: RO 486

Patrick Fitzsimons, Kilberry, Navan, Co. Meath was a Volunteer in the Dunmoe I.R.A. Company in July 1921. His name is engraved on a headstone in Kilberry Cemetery, Navan, see page 332. It says that he died on 17th January 1979. Source: RO 486. Headstone Inscription.

Thomas Foran, Antylstown, Navan, Co. Meath was a Volunteer in the Dunmoe I.R.A. Company in July 1921. Source: RO 486

James Kavanagh, Dunmoe, Navan, Co. Meath was a Volunteer in the Dunmoe I.R.A. Company in July 1921. He died on 23rd February 1976 and was buried in St. Mary's Cemetery, Navan, see page 338. Sources: RO 486. Headstone Inscription.

Michael Kavanagh, Dunmoe, Navan, Co. Meath was the Adjutant of the 2nd Battalion, 2nd Brigade, 1st Eastern Division in July 1921.
In 1936 he was appointed to the Brigade Committee for gathering information related to qualifying Volunteers for the Military Service Pensions. He died on 26th November 1992 aged 95 years and was buried in St. Mary's Cemetery, Navan, see page 338. Sources: RO 486. Headstone Inscription.

Thomas Kavanagh was a Volunteer in the Dunmoe I.R.A. Company in July 1921. In 1937 he was serving in the Free State Army. Source: RO 486

Kevin Kennedy was the Dunmoe I.R.A. Company 2nd Lieutenant in July 1921. In 1936 his address was given as Australia. Source: RO 486

Laurence Matthews, Graigs, Navan, Co. Meath was a Volunteer in the Dunmoe I.R.A. Company in July 1921. Source: RO 486

William Matthews was the Dunmoe I.R.A. Company Commanding Officer in July 1921. In 1936 his address was given as U.S.A. Source: RO 486

Bernard McCabe, Dunmoe, Navan, Co. Meath was a Volunteer in the Dunmoe I.R.A. Company in July 1921. Source: RO 486

James McCabe, Dunmoe, Navan, Co. Meath was a Volunteer in the Dunmoe I.R.A. Company in July 1921. Source: RO 486

Francis (Frank) Melady was a native of Donaghmore Navan. In July 1921 he was a Volunteer in the Dunmoe I.R.A. Company and his address was given as Emmet Terrace, Navan. He served with the Free State Army for a number of years before moving to England. He returned home to Navan in about 1970 and his address was given as 46 Parnell Park, Navan. He died in Peamount Hospital in February 1974 aged 72 years. His funeral took place from St. Mary's Church to St. Mary's Cemetery Navan. Sources: RO 486. The Meath Chronicle dated 9th February 1974, page 7

Thomas Newman was a Volunteer in the Dunmoe I.R.A. Company in July 1921. In 1937 his address was given as England. Source: RO 486

James Pierce, Proudstown, Navan, Co. Meath was a Volunteer in the Dunmoe I.R.A. Company in July 1921. Source: RO 486

Thomas Walsh, Mullingar, Co. Westmeath was a Volunteer in the Dunmoe I.R.A. Company in July 1921. His name is engraved on a headstone in St. Mary's Cemetery, Navan, see page 346. If it is the same person he lived on Flower Hill and his parents may have owned Beechmount House. This would need more research to confirm. Source: RO 486. Headstone Inscription.

Dunshaughlin Company:

In 1919 Kilmore I.R.A. Company ceased to exist. Some Volunteers were transferred to Dunshaughlin and others went to Kiltale and Kilcloon companies. In 1920 Dunshaughlin I.R.A. Company had a strength of 28 men and they trained in fields in Gerrardstown. In July 1920 Sinn Fein parish courts were set up, one in Dunshaughlin and one in a shed in a field. The old Workhouse outside Dunshaughlin was taken over by about 180 British Military personnel. In July 1921 the strength of the Dunshaughlin I.R.A. Company was down to eighteen men. There was a Constable Malone and a Constable Crean serving in the R.I.C. barracks in Dunshaughlin. They provided the I.R.A. with names of informants in the Dunshaughlin area, when R.I.C. raids were planned and little bits of useful information. In 1922 the Dunshaughlin I.R.A. Company had a strength of 21 men.
Sources: WS1539. RO 481.

Christopher Baker, Ratoath, Co. Meath was the Battalion Adjutant, 1st Battalion, 1st Brigade, 1st Eastern Division, I.R.A. in 1921. In October 1936 he was serving in the Free State Army. Sources: RO 479. RO 480

Michael Blake, Painstown, Dunshaughlin, Co. Meath was the Dunshaughlin I.R.A. Company Commanding Officer in July 1921. In July 1922 he was the Dunshaughlin I.R.A. Company Intelligence Officer. Source: RO 481

Patrick Blake, was the Dunshaughlin I.R.A. Company Commanding Officer in June 1920 and July 1922. Sources: RO 481. WS1539.

John Dalton was a Volunteer in the Dunshaughlin Company of Irish Volunteers in July 1921 and July 1922. In 1936 his address was given as Goresbridge, Co. Kilkenny. Source: RO 481

Robert Daly, Dunshaughlin, Co. Meath. I do not have a date when he joined the Dunshaughlin I.R.A. Company. He transferred to the Kilbride I.R.A. Company where he was a Volunteer on 1921 and 1922. In 1922 he was a Battalion Officer. Source: RO 480

Patrick Duffy, Dunshaughlin, Co. Meath was a Volunteer in the Dunshaughlin I.R.A. Company in July 1921 and July 1922. Source: RO 481

Thomas Dungan, Killeen, Dunshaughlin, Co. Meath was the Intelligence Officer of the 2nd Battalion, 4th Brigade, 1st Eastern Division in July 1921 and July 1922. Sources: RO 479. RO 481.

Augustine Gillic, Dunshaughlin, Co. Meath was the Commanding Officer of the 2nd Battalion, 1st Brigade, 1st Eastern Division, I.R.A. in 1921 and 1922. Sources: WS1539. RO 479. RO 481.

David Hall, see Culmullin Company.

Daniel Kenny, Dunshaughlin, Co. Meath was a Volunteer in the Dunshaughlin I.R.A. Company in July 1921 and July 1922. Source: RO 481

James Kenny, Dunshaughlin, Co. Meath was a Volunteer in the Dunshaughlin I.R.A. Company in July 1921 and July 1922. Source: RO 481

Patrick Kenny, Dunshaughlin, Co. Meath was an I.R.A. Battalion Adjutant in 1919. A box of mills bombs or hand grenades were sent by train from I.R.A. G.H.Q. addressed to P.J. Murray's Hardware Store in Dunshaughlin and described as nails. Patrick Kenny was instructed to intercept the box at Drumree Railway Station and deliver it to the Battalion Quartermaster but he failed and the box was delivered to the hardware store. When the box was opened the R.I.C. were alerted and they took the box away. Patrick Kenny had to appear before the I.R.B. and he was suspended. In July 1921 and 1922 he continued his participation in the Dunshaughlin I.R.A. Sources: RO 481. WS1539.

James Keogh, Greenpark, Dunshaughlin, Co. Meath was a Volunteer in the Dunshaughlin I.R.A. Company in July 1921 and July 1922. Source: RO 481

Matthew Keogh, Greenpark, Dunshaughlin, Co. Meath was a Volunteer in the Dunshaughlin I.R.A. Company in July 1921 and July 1922. Source: RO 481

Patrick Keogh was a Volunteer in the Dunshaughlin I.R.A. Company in July 1921 and July 1922. Source: RO 481

John King, Dunshaughlin, Co. Meath was a Volunteer in the Dunshaughlin I.R.A. Company in July 1921 and July 1922. Source: RO 481

John Lynch, Dunshaughlin, Co. Meath was a Volunteer in the Dunshaughlin I.R.A. Company in July 1921 and July 1922. Source: RO 481

Joseph Lynch, Dunshaughlin, Co. Meath was a Volunteer in the Dunshaughlin I.R.A. Company in July 1921 and July 1922. Source: RO 481

Patrick Lynch, Dunshaughlin, Co. Meath was a Volunteer in the Dunshaughlin I.R.A. Company in July 1922. Source: RO 481

Patrick Lynch, Dunshaughlin, Co. Meath was the Quartermaster of the 2nd Battalion, 1st Brigade, 1st Eastern Division in July 1921 and July 1922. Source: RO 479. RO 481

Michael Manning, Caulstown, Dunboyne, Co. Meath was the Vice Commanding Officer of the 1st Battalion, 1st Brigade, 1st Eastern Division, I.R.A. in July 1921. He died on 2nd March 1932 aged 33 years and was buried in Rooske Cemetery, Dunboyne, see page 282. Source: RO 479. RO 480. Headstone Inscription & personal Interview with John Maguire (son of James Maguire, Dunboyne Company) in Rooske Cemetery on 14th March 2015.

Thomas McClorey, Dunshaughlin, Co. Meath was the Dunshaughlin I.R.A. Company Quartermaster in July 1921 and July 1922. Source: RO 481

Patrick McLoughlin, Dunshaughlin, Co. Meath was a Volunteer in the Dunshaughlin I.R.A. Company in July 1921 and July 1922. Source: RO 481

Anthony Murphy was a Volunteer in the Dunshaughlin I.R.A. Company in July 1921 and July 1922. In 1936 his address was given as Kilcock, Co. Meath Source: RO 481

James Plunkett, Dunshaughlin, Co. Meath was a Volunteer in the Dunshaughlin I.R.A. Company in July 1921 and July 1922. Source: RO 481

William Rafferty was a Volunteer in the Dunshaughlin I.R.A. Company in July 1921 and July 1922. He died before 1936. Source: RO 481

Andrew Reilly, Dunshaughlin, Co. Meath was the Battalion Intelligence Officer in July 1921. Source: RO 481

John Smith, Dunshaughlin, Co. Meath was the Adjutant of the 2nd Battalion, 1st Brigade, 1st Eastern Division in July 1921. Source: RO 479

William Smith, see Culmullin Company.

Enfield Company:

In July 1921 the Enfield Company had a strength of twelve men and in July 1922 it continued to have a strength of twelve men. Source: RO 483.

The hand written records for Enfield Company are very difficult to read. I have recorded them here as best I can.

Denis Duggan Posseckstown, Enfield, Co. Meath was a Volunteer in the Enfield Company of Irish Volunteers in 1917. Source: RO 483

Thomas Dunne, Enfield, Co. Meath was a Volunteer in the Enfield Company of Irish Volunteers in 1917. In July 1921 and 1922 he was the Enfield I.R.A. Company Intelligence Officer. Source: RO 483

Jack Ennis, Cloncurry, Enfield, Co. Meath was a Volunteer in the Enfield Company of Irish Volunteers in 1917. He died before 1936. Source: RO 483

William Ennis, Rathrone, Enfield, Co. Meath was a Volunteer in the Enfield Company of Irish Volunteers In 1917. In July 1921 and 1922 he was a Volunteer in the Enfield I.R.A. Company. Source: RO 483

Christopher Geeicle?, Rynd??lle, Enfield, Co Meath was a Volunteer in the Enfield Company of Irish Volunteers in 1917. Sorry, but the hand written records are very difficult to read. Source: RO 483

Terrence Geeicle?, Johnstown Bridge, Enfield, Co. Meath was a Volunteer in the Enfield Company of Irish Volunteers in 1917. Sorry, but the hand written records are very difficult to read. Source: RO 483

Albert Greville, Enfield, Co. Meath was a Volunteer in the Enfield I.R.A. Company in July 1921 and 1922. Source: RO 483

Patrick Grogan, Newcastle, Enfield, Co. Meath was a Volunteer in the Enfield Company of Irish Volunteers in 1917. In July 1921 he took over the position of Enfield I.R.A. Company Commanding Officer when Patrick Ledwidge was arrested and interned. In 1922 he continued as the Enfield I.R.A. Company Commanding Officer. Source: RO 483

James Halpin, Rathene, Enfield, Co. Meath was a Volunteer in the Enfield Company of Irish Volunteers in 1917. He died before 1936. Source: RO 483

David Hamilton, Rathcall, Enfield, Co. Meath was a Volunteer in the Enfield Company of Irish Volunteers In 1917. Source: RO 483

James Hamilton, Rathcall, Enfield, Co. Meath was a Volunteer in the Enfield Company of Irish Volunteers in 1917. Source: RO 483. Military Service Pension Collection, file reference No. 24-SP-5160

Michael Hanly, Rathcall, Enfield, Co. Meath was a Volunteer in the Enfield Company of Irish Volunteers 1917. Source: RO 483. Photo kindly provided by Seamus Brennan, Trim co-author of Wielding the Ash, Kicking the Leather.

Thomas Healy, Hotwell, Enfield, Co. Meath was a Volunteer in the Enfield Company of Irish Volunteers in 1917. In July 1921 and 1922 he was a Volunteer in the Enfield I.R.A. Company. Source: RO 483

Dominick Hudson, Rosestown, Enfield, Co. Meath was a Volunteer in the Enfield Company of Irish Volunteers In 1917. In July 1921 and 1922 he was a Volunteer in the Enfield I.R.A. Company. In 1936 his address was given as Dublin. Source: RO 483

Edward Kearney, Enfield, Co. Meath was the Enfield Company of Irish Volunteers 2nd Lieutenant in 1917. In July 1921 and 1922 he was the Enfield I.R.A. Company Quartermaster. He died before 1936. Source: RO 483

Patrick Ledwidge, Rosetown, Enfield, Co. Meath was the Enfield Company of Irish Volunteers Commanding Officer in 1917. He continued in that role but he was arrested and interned in July 1921. The role of Enfield I.R.A. Company Commanding Officer was taken over then by Patrick Grogan. Patrick Ledwidge was still being held in prison in 1922. Source: RO 483

James Lynam, Rosetown, Enfield, Co. Meath was the Enfield Company of Irish Volunteers 1st Lieutenant in 1917. He continued to serve with the company In 1921 and 1922 but I do not know at what rank. Source: RO 483

John Lynam, Rossestown, Enfield, Co. Meath was a Volunteer in the Enfield Company of Irish Volunteers in 1917. In July 1921 and 1922 he was a Volunteer in the Enfield I.R.A. Company. In 1936 his address was given as Dublin.
Source: RO 483. Military Service Pension Collection, file reference No. 34-SP-47119

John Manning, Bainstown, Enfield, Co. Meath was a Volunteer in the Enfield Company of Irish Volunteers in 1917. In July 1921 and 1922 he was a Volunteer in the Enfield I.R.A. Company. In 1936 his address was given as Dublin. Source: RO 483

William Parke, Balnakill, Enfield, Co. Meath was a Volunteer in the Enfield Company of Irish Volunteers in 1917. Source: RO 483

Hugh Reilly, Rathene, Enfield, Co. Meath was a Volunteer in the Enfield Company of Irish Volunteers in 1917. In July 1921 and 1922 he was a Volunteer in the Enfield I.R.A. Company. In 1936 his address was given as Dublin. Source: RO 483

Barney Tormey, Enfield, Co. Meath was a Volunteer in the Enfield Company of Irish Volunteers in 1917. Source: RO 483

Fennor Company:

When I.R.A. structures were reorganised in April 1921 the Fennor Company became attached to the 2nd Battalion, 3rd Brigade, 1st Eastern Division. In July 1921 the Fennor I.R.A. Company had a strength of fifteen men. In July 1922 there were no Volunteers so the Fennor I.R.A. Company ceased to exist.
Sources: RO 489. WS1627

Thomas Conaty was a Volunteer in the Fennor I.R.A. Company in July 1921. He died before 1936. Source: RO 489

Owen Daly, Lugganboy, Eighter, Virginia, Co. Cavan was a Volunteer in the Fennor I.R.A. Company in July 1921. He was also the Fennor Company Representative.
Source: RO 489

Patrick Daly was a Volunteer in the Fennor I.R.A. Company in July 1921. He died before 1936. Source: RO 489

Owen Garry, Newcastle, Oldcastle, Co. Meath was a Volunteer in the Fennor I.R.A. Company in July 1921. Source: RO 489

Brian Halpin, Newcastle, Oldcastle, Co. Meath was a Volunteer in the Fennor I.R.A. Company in July 1921. Source: RO 489

Peter Kavanagh, Newcastle, Oldcastle, Co. Meath was a Volunteer in the Fennor I.R.A. Company in July 1921. Source: RO 489

Terry Kiernan, Fennor, Oldcastle, Co. Meath was a Volunteer in the Fennor I.R.A. Company in July 1921. Source: RO 489

Jack McEnroe, Lugganboy, Eighter, Virginia, Co. Cavan was a Volunteer in the Fennor I.R.A. Company in July 1921. Source: RO 489

Thomas Mulvaney, Lugganboy, Eighter, Virginia, Co. Cavan was a Volunteer in the Fennor I.R.A. Company in 1921. In April 1921 he was involved in an ambush of a military truck at Sylvan Park Kells, see the story on page 47. I don't understand why he was in that area at that time. Source: WS01060

Patrick Reilly, Fennor, Oldcastle, Co. Meath was a Volunteer in the Fennor I.R.A. Company in July 1921. Source: RO 489

John Smith was a Volunteer in the Fennor I.R.A. Company in July 1921. In 1936 his address was given as Cheshire, England. Source: RO 489

Peter Smith, Fennor, Oldcastle, Co. Meath was the Fennor Company Commanding Officer in July 1921. In 1936 his address was given as Hillside Ave., New York, U.S.A. Source: RO 489

Mick Tuite, Ardfrail, Oldcastle, Co. Meath was a Volunteer in the Fennor I.R.A. Company in July 1921. Source: RO 489

Benny Tully, Fennor, Oldcastle, Co. Meath was a Volunteer in the Fennor I.R.A. Company in July 1921. Source: RO 489

Thomas Tully, Ardfrail, Oldcastle, Co. Meath was a Volunteer in the Fennor I.R.A. Company in July 1921. Source: RO 489

Fordstown Company:

Baile Forda
FORDSTOWN

In 1918 the Fordstown Company of Irish Volunteers was formed with the help of Luke Bradley. The company was attached to the Irish Volunteers 3rd Battalion, Meath Brigade. In January 1919 the Irish Volunteers became the I.R.A. In April 1921 the Fordstown I.R.A. Company became attached to the 2nd Battalion, 4th Brigade and in July 1921 the company had a strength of fifteen men. The company was attached to the 2nd Battalion, 4th Brigade, 1st Eastern Division. In July 1922 there were no Volunteers so the Fordstown I.R.A. Company ceased to exist. Luke Bradley said in his witness statement that the reason that they never had any more than 14 or 15 Volunteers was because Fordstown's small farmers were mainly loyal British subjects. Sources: RO 496. WS1723. WS1623.

Thomas Boland, Fordstown, Kells, Co. Meath was a Volunteer in the Fordstown I.R.A. Company in July 1921. Source: RO 496

Luke Bradley was born in Fordstown, Kells, Co Meath in 1894. He was working in Dublin from 1914 to 1916 where he joined the Irish Citizen Army. He was one of the few Meath men who were actually involved in the 1916 Rising in Dublin. His name appears in the Irish Military Archives Alphabetical List of 1916 Veterans. He was a farm labourer for 28 years. In January 1918 he helped to form the Fordstown Irish Volunteers Company and he became the Fordstown Company Commanding Officer, 3rd Battalion, Meath Brigade. At end of spring 1921 he was appointed I.R.A. Battalion Vice Commanding Officer, 2nd Battalion, 4th Brigade, 1st Eastern Division. In July 1921 it was recorded that he still held that role. He died on 3rd November 1976 aged 83 years and was buried in Girley Graveyard, see page 299. See more about Luke Bradley's involvement in the 1916 Rising in Chapter 3. Sources: RO 496. WS1660. WS1623. WS1723.

Patrick Crosby, Nobber, Co. Meath was a Volunteer in the Fordstown I.R.A. Company in July 1921. Source: RO 496

Patrick Curren, Fordstown, Kells, Co. Meath was a Volunteer in the Fordstown I.R.A. Company in July 1921. Source: RO 496

John Finnegan, Fordstown, Kells, Co. Meath was the Fordstown I.R.A. Company 2nd Lieutenant in July 1921. He died before 1936. Source: RO 496

Edward (Ned) Lenehan, Fordstown, Kells, Co. Meath was appointed company 1st Lieutenant, 3rd Battalion, Meath Brigade when the Fordstown Company of Irish Volunteers was formed in 1918. In July 1921 he was the Fordstown I.R.A. Company Commanding Officer. Source: WS1623. RO 496.

Daniel Lynch, Fordstown, Kells, Co. Meath was a Volunteer in the Fordstown I.R.A. Company in July 1921. Source: RO 496

John McGuinness was a Volunteer in the Fordstown I.R.A. Company in July 1921. In 1936 his address was given as Clane Co. Kildare. Source: RO 496

John Nulty, Fordstown, Kells, Co. Meath was a Volunteer in the Fordstown I.R.A. Company in July 1921. Source: RO 496

Joseph (Joe) Reynolds, Fordstown, Kells, Co. Meath was appointed the Fordstown Company Adjutant, 3rd Battalion, Meath Brigade when the Fordstown Company of Irish Volunteers was formed in 1918. In July 1921 he continued to hold the rank of Fordstown I.R.A. Company Adjutant. Sources: WS1623. RO 496

Nicholas Sheridan, Fordstown, Kells, Co. Meath was a Volunteer in the Fordstown I.R.A. Company in July 1921. He died before 1936. Source: RO 496

Patrick Sheridan, Fordstown, Kells, Co. Meath was a Volunteer in the Fordstown I.R.A. Company in July 1921. Source: RO 496

Peter Smyth was appointed the Fordstown Company 2nd Lieutenant, 3rd Battalion, Meath Brigade when the Fordstown Company of Irish Volunteers was formed in 1918. In July 1921 he was the Fordstown I.R.A. Company 1st Lieutenant. In 1936 his address was given as India. Sources: WS1623. RO 496.

Patrick (Pat) Timmons, Fordstown, Kells, Co. Meath was a member of the Bohermeen G.A.A. Senior Football Team who became Champions in 1910. In 1918 he was appointed the Fordstown Company of Irish Volunteers Quartermaster, 3rd Battalion, Meath Brigade. In July 1921 he continued to hold the rank of Fordstown I.R.A. Company Quartermaster. Sources: Royal and Loyal by Michael O'Brien page 82. WS1623. RO 496

Edward Woods, Drewstown, Kells, Co. Meath was a Volunteer in the Fordstown I.R.A. Company in July 1921. Source: RO 496

Robert Woods, Fordstown, Kells, Co. Meath was a Volunteer in the Fordstown I.R.A. Company in July 1921. Source: RO 496

Johnstown Company:

The Johnstown Company of Irish Volunteers was formed at the latter end of 1918. Patrick Loughran said in his Witness Statement that the Navan Company helped to form and organise the Johnstown Company. In January 1919 the Irish Volunteers became the I.R.A. In 1919 the Johnstown I.R.A. Company was part of the 6th Battalion, Meath Brigade. In November 1919 Johnstown I.R.A. Company along with other Volunteers from the Navan I.R.A. Battalion area attacked Lismullen R.I.C. Barracks, see the story on page 37. In September 1920 the Johnstown I.R.A. Company played a fairly small but important role in the attack on the heavily fortified Trim R.I.C. Barracks, see the story on page 40. This was followed by a large scale round-up of Volunteers by military, police and Black and Tans. In 1921 the Johnstown Company had a strength of 39 men. In July 1922 there were no Volunteers so the Johnstown Company ceased to exist. Sources: RO 486. WS01060. WS1624.

Matthew Barry was the Johnstown I.R.A. Company Commanding Officer. On the 2nd July 1921, about two weeks before the Truce, he was involved in a failed attack on a troop train near Celbridge, see the story on page 51. In 1936 he was serving in the Free State Army. In March 1954 his address was given as Kilsallaghan. Source: WS0932. RO 486.

James Boylan, Johnstown, Navan, Co. Meath was involved in an attack on Lismullen R.I.C. Barracks on 2nd November 1919, see the story on page 37. He became a member of a 30 man strong I.R.A. Active Service Unit who later became known as the Curraghtown A.S.U. On 5th July 1922 he was involved in the Battle of Curraghtown where he was arrested by the Free State Army, see the story on page 58. He was temporarily held in Trim and then interned in Dundalk, Co. Louth on 22nd July 1922. Sources: Interview with Mick O'Brien, Johnstown. Politics and war in Meath 1913-23 by Oliver Coogan. Meath Chronicle. Dunderry A Folk History by Dunderry History Group & Johnny Keely.

John Boyle, Walterstown, Navan, Co. Meath was a Volunteer in the Johnstown I.R.A. Company in July 1921. Source: RO 486.

Patrick Boyle was the Johnstown I.R.A. Company 2nd Lieutenant in July 1921. In 1936 his address was given as Drogheda, Co. Louth. Source: RO 486.

James Brien, Castletown, Navan, Co. Meath was a Volunteer in the Johnstown I.R.A. Company in July 1921. Source: RO 486

John Brien, Johnstown, Navan, Co. Meath enlisted in the National Volunteers in January 1916 and he fought with the British Army in the First World War. He survived the war and returned home in 1918 and joined the Irish Volunteers. He was a Volunteer in the Johnstown I.R.A. Company in July 1921. He died on 25th October 1944 aged 71 years and was buried in Kilcarne Cemetery, Navan, see page 334. He is pictured here in his Irish Volunteer's Uniform. Photograph kindly provided by his son Mick O'Brien, author of Royal and Loyal, Meath's G.A.A. history. Source: RO 486. Personel Interview with Mick O'Brien, Johnstown.

Peter Brien, Dunshaughlin, Co. Meath was a Volunteer in the Johnstown I.R.A. Company in July 1921. Source: RO 486

See also O'Brien

Vincent Callen, Dowdstown, Navan, Co. Meath was a Volunteer in the Johnstown I.R.A. Company in July 1921. Source: RO 486

Patrick Carroll, Athlumney, Navan, Co. Meath was a Volunteer in the Johnstown I.R.A. Company in July 1921. Source: RO 486

Thomas Carroll, Athlumney, Navan, Co. Meath was a Volunteer in the Johnstown I.R.A. Company in July 1921. Source: RO 486

Thomas Coyle, Oldtown, Johnstown, Navan Co. Meath was appointed the I.R.A. Brigade Adjutant, 2nd Brigade, 1st Eastern Division in March / April 1921. On 25th May 1926 he was found shot dead at his home. Due to apparent suicide the

Catholic Church would not allow him to be buried in consecrated ground so he had to be buried outside the walls of Kilcarne Cemetery. The grave is unmarked so no one knows exactly where it is but thought to be just to the left hand side outside the entrance to Kilcarne Cemetery, see page 333.
Sources: WS1715. WS1622. RO 484. WS1696. Interview with Mick O'Brien, Johnstown.

John Drumm, Skryne, Tara Co. Meath was a Volunteer in the Johnstown I.R.A. Company in July 1921. Source: RO 486

Michael Dungan, Dowdstown, Navan, Co. Meath was a Volunteer in the Johnstown I.R.A. Company in July 1921. Source: RO 486

John Dunly, Walterstown, Navan, Co. Meath was a Volunteer in the Johnstown I.R.A. Company in July 1921. Source: RO 486

Nicholas Dunly was a Volunteer in the Johnstown I.R.A. Company in July 1921. He died before 1937. Source: RO 486

Laurence Englishby was a Volunteer in the Johnstown I.R.A. Company in July 1921. He died before 1937. Source: RO 486

William Fay, Oldtown, Navan, Co. Meath was a Volunteer in the Johnstown I.R.A. Company in July 1921. Source: RO 486

Bartley Fitzpatrick, Kilcarne, Navan, Co. Meath was a Volunteer in the Johnstown I.R.A. Company in July 1921. Source: RO 486

Michael Gordan, Oldtown, Navan, Co. Meath was a Volunteer in the Johnstown I.R.A. Company in July 1921. Source: RO 486

Anthony Holten, Oldtown, Navan, Co. Meath was a Volunteer in the Johnstown I.R.A. Company in July 1921. Source: RO 486

Bartley Holten was a Volunteer in the Johnstown I.R.A. Company in July 1921. He died before 1937. Source: RO 486

Patrick (Pat) Kelly fought in the Boer War and World War One with the British Army. He later joined the Irish Volunteers. His experience would have been very valuable. During May - June period of 1920 he was involved in the arrest and imprisonment of a criminal gang who were operating in North Meath and who allegedly killed Mark Clinton, an I.R.A. Volunteer, see the story on page 70. On 28th March 1921 he was appointed Commanding Officer of the 2nd Brigade, 1st Eastern Division, I.R.A. He took over the role from Pat Fitzsimons, see Navan Company. On the 2nd July 1921, about two weeks before the Truce, Pat Kelly was involved in a failed attack on a troop train near Celbridge, see the story on page 51. In November 1936 at a meeting related to qualifying Volunteers for the Military Service Pensions he was appointed to the Brigade Committee for gathering information. On 24th November 1951 he was reported missing. It is thought that he jumped of Kilcarne Bridge into the river Boyne. His body was not found for six weeks. Mick O'Brien, Johnstown and author of Royal and Loyal said he served at Pat Kelly's funeral mass. Patrick Kelly was buried on 8th January 1952 in Kilcarne Cemetery. He was the last member of his family so there was no

one left to write his name on the headstone and that is the way it remains today, see his grave on page 334. I hope this entry ensures that his grave is not lost and perhaps it could be properly identified for the 2016 Centenary.
Sources: WS1715. RO 482. RO 484. WS0932. WS1060. WS1622. WS1696. Personal Interview with Mick O'Brien, Johnstown.

Thomas Kelly was a Volunteer in the Johnstown I.R.A. Company in July 1921. In 1924 he was a member of the Navan Gaels G.A.A. Football Team. Sources: RO 486. Royal and Loyal by Michael O'Brien page 127

Joseph Lynch was the Johnstown I.R.A. Company 1st Lieutenant in July 1921. In 1936 his address was given as Co. Kildare. Source: RO 486

Patrick Lynch, Johnstown, Navan, Co. Meath was a Volunteer in the Johnstown I.R.A. Company in July 1921. Source: RO 486

Patrick Maguire, Brownstown, Navan, Co. Meath was a Volunteer in the Johnstown I.R.A. Company in July 1921. In 1923 he was Captain of the Walterstown G.A.A. Football Team. Source: RO 486. Royal and Loyal by Mick O'Brien, Johnstown.

Patrick McDonald, Johnstown, Navan, Co. Meath was a Volunteer in the Johnstown I.R.A. Company in July 1921. Source: RO 486

Michael Monaghan, Walterstown, Navan, Co. Meath was a Volunteer in the Johnstown I.R.A. Company in July 1921. Source: RO 486

Thomas Moran was a Volunteer in the Johnstown I.R.A. Company in July 1921. In 1937 his address was given as U.S.A. Source: RO 486

Samuel Murray, Kilcarne, Navan, Co. Meath was a Volunteer in the Johnstown I.R.A. Company in July 1921. Source: RO 486

Patrick Neill was a Volunteer in the Johnstown I.R.A. Company in July 1921. In 1937 his address was given as U.S.A. Source: RO 486

John (Jack) O'Brien, Assey, Kilcarne, Navan, Co. Meath. In March or April 1921 he was appointed Battalion Quartermaster, 1st Battalion, 2nd Brigade. On the 2nd July 1921, about two weeks before the Truce, he was involved in a failed attack on a troop train near Celbridge, see the story on page 51. In January 1925 he was a member of An Garda Síochána and he was stationed in Delvin, Co. Westmeath.
Sources: RO 485. WS1696. WS1696. WS0932. Military Service Pension Collection, file reference No 24SP1392.

See also Brien

William O'Neill, Brownstown, Navan, Co. Meath was a Volunteer in the Johnstown I.R.A. Company. In July 1921 he was the Engineer of the 1st Brigade, 1st Eastern Division. In July 1922 he was the Vice Commanding Officer of the 1st Battalion, 1st Eastern Division. In 1937 his address was given as Dunboyne. He died on 15th June 1978 and was buried in Kilcarne cemetery, see page 334. Source: RO 486. WS1715. Interview with Mick O'Brien, Johnstown. Headstone Inscription.

William O'Neill.

John Pickett, Johnstown, Navan, Co. Meath was a Volunteer in the Johnstown I.R.A. Company in July 1921. Source: RO 486

Christopher Sherry was a Volunteer in the Johnstown I.R.A. Company in July 1921. In 1937 his address was given as England. Source: RO 486

William Shiels, Johnstown, Navan, Co. Meath was a Volunteer in the Johnstown I.R.A. Company in July 1921. Source: RO 486. Military Service Pension Collection, file reference No. MD-49433

James Smith, Johnstown, Navan, Co. Meath was a Volunteer in the Johnstown I.R.A. Company in July 1921. In 1932 he played G.A.A. Football with Johnstown. He died on 9th June 1955 and was buried in Kilcarne Cemetery, Navan, see page 334. Source: RO 486. Royal and Loyal by Mick O'Brien. Headstone Inscription and personal interview with Mick O'Brien, Johnstown.

James Smith,

Peter Smith, Johnstown, Navan, Co. Meath was a Volunteer in the Johnstown I.R.A. Company in July 1921. In 1962 he was Chairman of the Walterstown G.F.C. Source: RO 486. Royal and Loyal by Mick O'Brien. Military Service Pension Collection, file reference No. 34-SP-53157

Peter Smyth.

John Smyth, Athlumney, Navan, Co. Meath was a Volunteer in the Johnstown I.R.A. Company in July 1921. Source: RO 486

Julianstown & Laytown Company:

In July 1921 the Julianstown & Laytown Company had a strength of 18 men. In July 1922 there were no Volunteers so the company ceased to exist. Source: RO 519

Patrick Boyd, Lawless Tce. Balbriggan was the Julianstown & Laytown I.R.A. Company Commanding Officer in 1921. Source: RO 519

John Clinton, Piltown, Drogheda, Co. Louth was a Volunteer in the Julianstown & Laytown I.R.A. Company in 1921. Source: RO 519

John Doherty, Drogheda, Co. Louth was a Volunteer in the Julianstown & Laytown I.R.A. Company in 1921. Source: RO 519

William Farrell, Piltown, Drogheda, Co. Louth was a Volunteer in the Julianstown & Laytown I.R.A. Company in 1921. Source: RO 519

John Gough, Julianstown, Co. Meath was a Volunteer in the Julianstown & Laytown I.R.A. Company in 1921. Source: RO 519

John Harmon, Drogheda, Co. Louth was a Volunteer in the Julianstown & Laytown I.R.A. Company in 1921. Source: RO 519

James Kelly, Claristown, Julianstown, Co. Meath was a Volunteer in the Julianstown & Laytown I.R.A. Company in 1921. Source: RO 519

James Kennedy, Julianstown, Co. Meath was a Volunteer in the Julianstown & Laytown I.R.A. Company in 1921. Source: RO 519

George King, Julianstown, Co. Meath was the Julianstown & Laytown I.R.A. Company Lieutenant in 1921. Source: RO 519

Michael Levins, Laytown, Co. Meath was a Volunteer in the Julianstown & Laytown I.R.A. Company in 1921. Source: RO 519

Peter Levins, Laytown, Co. Meath was a Volunteer in the Julianstown & Laytown I.R.A. Company in 1921. Source: RO 519

William Lyons, Ninch, Laytown, Co. Meath was a Volunteer in the Julianstown & Laytown I.R.A. Company in 1921. Source: RO 519

John McGrane, Julianstown, Co. Meath was a Volunteer in the Julianstown & Laytown I.R.A. Company in 1921. Source: RO 519

Robert McGrane, Julianstown, Co. Meath was a Volunteer in the Julianstown & Laytown I.R.A. Company in 1921. Source: RO 519

James Monaghan, Moorchurch, Julianstown, Co. Meath was a Volunteer in the Julianstown & Laytown I.R.A. Company in 1921. Source: RO 519

Henry O'Neill, Laytown, Co. Meath was a Volunteer in the Julianstown & Laytown I.R.A. Company in 1921. Source: RO 519

John Russell, Dardistown, Co. Meath was a Volunteer in the Julianstown & Laytown I.R.A. Company in 1921. Source: RO 519

Patrick Wiseman, Claristown, Julianstown, Co. Meath was a Volunteer in the Julianstown & Laytown I.R.A. Company in 1921. Source: RO 519

Kells Company:

The earliest record I can find in relation to the Kells Company of Irish Volunteers is

that the company existed in 1914. Parades, drills and route marches were held regularly. Route marches were always accompanied by R.I.C. officers to keep an eye on what was going on. In July 1914, at the outbreak of World War One, a huge split immerged in the Volunteer movement nationally. John Redmond, who was the leader of the Irish Parliamentary Party, called on the Irish Volunteers to join the National Volunteers and to fight in World War One under the command of the British Army. The Leaders of the Irish Volunteers and the Irish Republican Brotherhood (I.R.B.) rejected and condemned this call but the majority of the Kells Company voted in favour of Redmond's call. This split the Kells Irish Volunteers, the majority of whom became known as National Volunteers and went to fight in World war One or the Great War, as it was called. A handful of Kells Volunteers stayed loyal to the Irish Volunteers but their number was so small that the Kells Company of Irish Volunteers ceased to exist. The few remaining Kells Volunteers had to join either Drumbaragh or Carnaross companies who were the only companies of Irish Volunteers left in the Kells area after the split. The Meath Chronicle Office was located in Kells at the time and the owner and editor, Hugh Smith, who was a Volunteer in the Drumbaragh Company, allowed the Irish Volunteers to hold meetings at his offices. For that reason, the few Kells men that did engage in the 1916 Rising did so as members of the Carnaross and Drumbaragh companies. Around 1917 or 1918 the Kells Company of Irish Volunteers was reformed. On St. Patricks Day 1918 there was a Rally of Irish Volunteers in Kells and ten companies of Volunteers attended. In January 1919 the Irish Volunteers became the I.R.A. In April 1920 the I.R.A. reorganised their structures and the Kells I.R.A. Company became attached to the 4th Battalion, Meath Brigade. On 16th July 1920 a detachment of 150 British Troops were drafted into Kells where they occupied the Fever Hospital. They were known as the South Wales Borderers. Local girls were warned not to associate with them but at least two girls received hair chopping for ignoring the warnings. The Irish Volunteers built up their companies and ranks again and the records show that in July 1921 the Kells Company had a strength of 35 men. In 1921 the Kells Company was involved in the destruction of Carlanstown Bridge and Ballinamona Bridge in an effort to restrict British Troop movements in the area. In July 1922 the Kells I.R.A. Company strength was 24 men and the Kells Company was involved in attack on Free State Forces in the Kells Barracks. In 1923 they were involved in an attack on the Athboy Barracks and a 2nd attack on Kells Barracks. Source: RO 489. WS1060. WS0172. WS1650. Dunderry A Folk History by Dunderry History Group & Johnny Keely.

Joseph Berrill was a Volunteer in the Kells I.R.A. Company in July 1921. In 1936 his address was given as Dundalk, Co. Louth. Source: RO 489

William (Willie) Black, Church View, Kells, Co. Meath was a Volunteer in the Kells I.R.A. Company in July 1921. He was later employed as a Greenkeeper in Headfort Golf Club. According to a headstone in St. Colmcille's Cemetery Kells he was buried in St. Columba's Cemetery Kells but I did not find his grave. Source: RO 489. Meath Chronicle dated 11th June 1938 page 1. Military Service Pension Collection, file reference No. MD-48948. Headstone Inscription

James Boylan, Dulane, Kells, Co. Meath was a Volunteer in the Kells I.R.A. Company in July 1921. He died on 10th June 1965 and was buried in Dulane Cemetery, Kells, see page 297. Source: RO 489. Headstone Inscription.

John Brady, Carrick Street, Kells, Co. Meath was a Volunteer in the Kells I.R.A. Company in July 1921. He was arrested and imprisoned. Source RO 489

Leo Brady, was a Volunteer in the Kells I.R.A. Company In July 1921. He was arrested and imprisoned. In 1936 his address was given as Dublin. Source: RO 489

Patrick Brady was born in Clonmellon, Co. Westmeath about 1903. In July 1921 he lived in Kells and he was a Volunteer in the Kells I.R.A. Company. In February 1921 he was involved in a raid on Kells Post Office to remove a Telegraph Machine that was being used by the R.I.C., see the story on page 46. He was arrested and imprisoned in Mountjoy, Dublin for offences under the Restoration of Order in Ireland Regulations (ROIR). He was aged eighteen years. Source: WS1060. RO 489.

Thomas Brady, Fair Green, Kells, Co. Meath was born about 1901. He was a Volunteer in the Kells I.R.A. Company in July 1921. In February 1921 he was involved in a raid on Kells Post Office to remove a Telegraph Machine that was being used by the R.I.C., see the story on page 46. He died in August 1981 aged 82 years and was buried in St. Colmcille's Cemetery Kells, see page 306. Source: WS1060. RO 489. Headstone Inscription

Christopher Caffrey, Rockfield, Kells, Co. Meath was a Volunteer in the Kells I.R.A. Company in July 1921. Source: RO 489

L. Caffrey, Cookstown, Kells, Co. Meath was a Volunteer in the Kells I.R.A. Company in July 1921. Source RO 489

William Caffrey, Rockfield, Kells, Co. Meath was a Volunteer in the Kells I.R.A. Company in July 1921. He died in July 1967 and was buried in St Colmcille's Cemetery, Kells, see page 307. Source: RO 489. Headstone Inscription.

Bernard (Benny) Carolan, Farrell Street, Kells, Co. Meath was born in Kells around  1895. In December 1920 he became the Kells I.R.A. Company Commanding Officer. He took over the role from Robert (Bob) Mullen. In February 1921 he was involved in a raid on Kells Post Office to remove a Telegraph Machine that was being used by the R.I.C., see the story on page 46. He was arrested and imprisoned in Mountjoy, Dublin for offences under the Restoration of Order in Ireland Regulations (ROIR) in June 1921. Michael Donagh took over the role as company Commanding Officer. Bernard Carolan died in September 1984 aged 90 years and was buried in St. Colmcille's Cemetery, Kells, see page 307. Sources: RO 489. WS1060. MM9.1.1/KM79-BSV. Headstone Inscription. Photo kindly provided by Tony Brady, author of Faithful to Ireland. Thanks to Bernard Carolan's family for their permission to use the photograph here.

Patrick Carry, Loyd, Kells, Co. Meath was born in 1864. In July 1921 and July 1922 he was a Volunteer in the Kells I.R.A. Company. He died in 1942 aged 78 years and was buried in St. Johns Cemetery, Kells, see page 312. Source: RO 489. Headstone Inscription

Patrick Clarke, Carrick Street, Kells, Co. Meath was a Volunteer in the Kells I.R.A. Company in July 1921. In 1921 he was arrested and interned in Ballykinlar Internment Camp, Co. Down. He was held in Compound No 2. On his release he continued his role with the Kells I.R.A. Company throughout 1922.
Sources: RO 489. Prisoners of War by Liam O' Duibhir, page 315

Anthony Conlon was born in Cookstown about 1904. He was the owner of some shops in Kells including a menswear shop. In July 1921 he was a Volunteer in the Kells I.R.A. Company. Married twice and lived in what was locally known as Coyne's at the top of Carrick St. He then moved to Kenlis Place before building a house on the Navan Road. Source: RO 489. Local interviews by Carol Owens, Kells.

Bill Connell, Kells, Co. Meath was a Volunteer in the Kells I.R.A. Company in July 1921. In February 1921 he was involved in a raid on Kells Post Office to remove a Telegraph Machine that was being used by the R.I.C., see the story on page 46.
Sources: WS1060. RO 489.

James Connell, Calliagstown, Kells, Co. Meath was born in Kells about 1901. In July 1921 and July 1922 he was a Volunteer in the Kells I.R.A. Company. In 1921, he was arrested and imprisoned in Mountjoy, Dublin for offences under the Restoration of Order in Ireland Regulations (ROIR). He took the Anti-Treaty side and in early 1923 he was arrested in Kells by the Free State Army and interned. He died in September 1969 and was buried in St. Colmcille's Cemetery, Kells, see page 307. Sources: RO 489. MM9.1.1/KM79-BS5. Faithful to Ireland by Tony Brady, page 83.

Leo Connell was a Volunteer in the Kells I.R.A. Company in July 1921. He died before 1936. Source: RO 489

James Cumiskey, Fair Green, Kells, Co. Meath was a Volunteer in the Kells I.R.A. Company in July 1921. Source: RO 489

Michael Cumiskey, Columba Terrace, Kells, Co. Meath was a Volunteer in the Kells I.R.A. Company in July 1921 and July 1922. In February 1921 he was involved in a raid on Kells Post Office to remove a Telegraph Machine that was being used by the R.I.C., see the story on page 46. In 1922 his address was given as Fair Green, Kells. Source: WS1060. RO 489.

Patrick Dolan, Columba Terrace, Kells, Co. Meath was a Volunteer in the Kells I.R.A. Company in July 1921 and July 1922. In February 1921 he was involved in a raid on Kells Post Office to remove a Telegraph Machine that was being used by the R.I.C., see the story on page 46. Source: WS1060. RO 489.

Michael Donagh, Bective Street, Kells, Co. Meath was the Kells I.R.A. Company Commanding Officer in July 1921. He took over the role from Bernard Carolan. In 1936 his address was given as Mercantile Marine, Dublin. He died in December 1936 and he was interred in Glasnevin Cemetery, Dublin. His name is inscribed on the family plot headstone in St. Colmcille's Cemetery, Kells, see page 307. Source: RO 489. Headstone Inscription

William Donegan, Carrick Street, Kells, Co. Meath was the Kells I.R.A. Company Quartermaster in July 1921 and July 1922. In February 1921 he was involved in a raid on Kells Post Office to remove a Telegraph Machine that was being used by the R.I.C., see the story on page 46. Source: WS1060. RO 489.

Edward Duignan, Kells, Co. Meath was a Volunteer in the Kells I.R.A. Company in July 1921. He was arrested and imprisoned also in that year. Source: RO 489

Michael Flanagan, Suffolk Street, Kells, Co. Meath was the Kells I.R.A. Company 1st Lieutenant in July 1921. Source: RO 489

Bernard Flynn, Fair Green, Kells, Co. Meath was a Volunteer in the Kells I.R.A. Company in July 1921. In February 1921 he was involved in a raid on Kells Post Office to remove a Telegraph Machine that was being used by the R.I.C., see the story on page 46. In 1922 he was the Kells I.R.A. Company 1st Lieutenant. He died in July 1959 and was buried in St. Colmcille's Cemetery, Kells, see page 308. Source: WS1060. RO 489. Headstone Inscription.

Patrick (Pat) Flynn, Carrick Street, Kells, Co. Meath was a Volunteer in the Kells I.R.A. Company in July 1921. He was arrested and interned in Ballykinlar Internment Camp, Co. Down. He was held in Compound No 2.
He died before 1936. The same name is inscribed on a headstone in St. Colmcille's Cemetery which says that he died in January 1926 aged 25 years, see page 308. Sources: RO 489. Prisoners of War by Liam O' Duibhir, page 315. Headstone Inscription.

Michael Fox, St. Patrick's Terrace, Kells, Co. Meath was a Volunteer in the Kells I.R.A. Company in July 1921. In February 1921 he was involved in a raid on Kells Post Office to remove a Telegraph Machine that was being used by the R.I.C., see the story on page 46. He also gave his address as Maudlin Road, Kells. Source: WS1060. RO 489.

James Grace, No 4, Maudlin Road, Kells, Co. Meath was born in 1894. In July 1921 he was a Volunteer in the Kells I.R.A. Company. He died on 17th March 1970 aged 76 years and was buried in St. Johns Cemetery, Kells, see page 312.
Source: RO 489. Headstone Inscription.

John (Jack) Heraghty, Cannon Street, Kells, Co. Meath was a Volunteer in the Kells I.R.A. Company in July 1921. In February 1921 he was involved in a raid on Kells Post Office to remove a Telegraph Machine that was being used by the R.I.C., see the story on page 46. He was arrested and jailed and according to the prison records he was born in Westport, Co. Mayo about 1899. In 1921 he was arrested again and imprisoned in Mountjoy, Dublin for offences under the Restoration of Order in Ireland Regulations (ROIR). He died in March 1928 and was buried in St. Colmcille's Cemetery, see page 308. Source: RO 489. MM9.1.1/KM79-BSR. WS1060. RO 489.

Patrick Keelan, Kells, Co. Meath was a Volunteer in the Kells I.R.A. Company in July 1921 and July 1922. In 1921 He was arrested and interned in Ballykinlar Internment Camp, Co. Down. He was held in Compound No 2. In 1936 his address was given as U.S.A. Sources: RO 489. Prisoners of War by Liam O' Duibhir, page 315

Robert Lear, Farrell Street, Kells, Co. Meath was born in Kells about 1899. In July 1921 he was a Volunteer in the Kells I.R.A. Company but he was arrested and imprisoned in Mountjoy, Dublin for offences under the Restoration of Order in Ireland Regulations (ROIR). Source: RO 489. MM9.1.1/KM79-BSG

John Leddy, Loyd, Kells, Co. Meath was a Volunteer in the Kells I.R.A. Company In July 1921 and July 1922. Source: RO 489

Joseph Lynch, was a Volunteer in the Kells I.R.A. Company in July 1921. He died before 1936. Source: RO 489

Patrick Maguire, Maudlin Road, Kells, Co. Meath was a Volunteer in the Kells I.R.A. Company in 1921. In February 1921 he was involved in a raid on Kells Post Office to remove a Telegraph Machine that was being used by the R.I.C., see the story on page 46. He died in March 1970 and was buried in St. Colmcille's Cemetery, Kells, see page 308. He was survived by his children Patsy Maguire, Anna Chadwick, Kathleen Collins and Betty McCabe. Source: WS1060 RO 489.

James McDonnell, Kells, Co. Meath was born in Trim, Co. Meath about 1898. In July 1921 he was a Volunteer in the Kells I.R.A. Company. In February 1921 he was involved in a raid on Kells Post Office to remove a Telegraph Machine that was being used by the R.I.C., see the story on page 46. He was arrested and imprisoned in Mountjoy, Dublin for offences under the Restoration of Order in Ireland Regulations (ROIR). Sources: WS1060. RO 489. MM9.1.1/KM79-BS2.

John McGillic, Farrell Street, Kells, Co. Meath was a Volunteer in the Kells I.R.A. Company in July 1921 and July 1922. In February 1921 he was involved in a raid on Kells Post Office to remove a Telegraph Machine that was being used by the R.I.C., see the story on page 46. Source: WS1060. RO 489.

Owen McGillic, Farrell Street, Kells, Co. Meath was a Volunteer in the Kells I.R.A. Company in July 1921. Source: RO 489

John McGuire, The Workhouse, Kells, Co. Meath was a Volunteer in the Kells I.R.A. Company in July 1921 and July 1922. He was imprisoned in 1921. Source: RO 489

Patrick Monaghan, Mullaghea, Kells, Co. Meath was the Kells I.R.A. Company 2nd Lieutenant for a period in 1921 and In July 1922. He took the Anti-Treaty side in 1922 and in early 1923 he was arrested in Kells by the Free State Army and interned. In 1937 his address was given as Cakestown Kells.
Source: RO 489. Faithful to Ireland by Tony Brady, page 83.

Thomas Monaghan, Mullaghea, Kells, Co. Meath was the Kells I.R.A. Company 2nd Lieutenant for a period in 1921. Source: RO 489

John Morris, was a Volunteer in the Kells I.R.A. Company in July 1921 but he was arrested and interned in Ballykinlar Internment Camp, Co. Down. He was held in Compound No 2. In 1936 his address was given as Co. Cavan.
Sources: RO 489. Prisoners of War by Liam O' Duibhir, page 315

Joseph Morris, Cannon Street, Kells, Co. Meath was arrested and interned in Ballykinlar Internment Camp, Co. Down, probably in 1921. He was held in Compound No 2 where he developed bad health. In July 1922 he was the Kells Company Commanding Officer. On 12th October 1923 he died aged 23 years.
Sources: RO 489. Faithful to Ireland by Tony Brady, page 86.

Thomas Morris, Church View, Kells, Co. Meath was a Volunteer in the Kells I.R.A. Company in July 1922. Source: RO 489

Robert (Bob) Mullen, Bective Street, Kells was appointed the Kells I.R.A. Company Commanding Officer in October 1919. In August 1920 he was involved in armed raid on the Northern Bank in Kells to seize two revolvers from the Bank.
In September 1920 he led the Kells I.R.A. Company in blocking roads to Trim with fallen trees as part of a co-ordinated attack on the heavily fortified Trim R.I.C. Barracks, see the story on page 40. In December 1920 he was arrested and jailed. Bernard Carolan took over the role as Kells I.R.A. Company Commanding Officer. In 1921 Bob was arrested again and interned in Ballykinlar Internment Camp, Co. Down. He was held in Compound No 2. In 1922 he was an active member of the Kells I.R.A. Company again.
Source: WS0858. WS1650. RO 489. WS1060. Prisoners of War by Liam O' Duibhir, page 315

P. Murray, Cookstown, Kells was a Volunteer in the Kells I.R.A. Company in July 1921. Source RO 489

Thomas Murray, Newrath, Kells was the Kells I.R.A. Company 2nd Lieutenant for a period in 1921. He died in October 1962 aged 68 and was buried in St. Colmcille's Cemetery, see page 309. Source: RO 489. Headstone Inscription.

Thomas Reilly, Bective Street, Kells was the Kells I.R.A. Company 2nd Lieutenant for a period in 1921 and during 1922. See headstone in St. Colmcille's Cemetery, Kells on page 309. Source: RO 489. Headstone Inscription.

Peter Reynolds, Climber Hall, Kells was a Volunteer in the Kells I.R.A. Company in July 1921. Source RO 489

Michael Sheridan, Maudlin Road, Kells, Co. Meath was a Volunteer in the Kells I.R.A. Company in July 1921 and July 1922. In 1937 he gave his address as St. Patrick's Terrace Kells. Source: RO 489

Michael Skelly, Climber Hall, Kells, Co. Meath was a Volunteer in the Kells I.R.A. Company in July 1921. He was arrested and interned in Ballykinlar Internment Camp, Co. Down. He was held in Compound No 2.
Sources: RO 489. Prisoners of War by Liam O' Duibhir, page 315

Patrick Smith, Maudlin Street, Kells, Co. Meath was a Volunteer in the Kells I.R.A. Company in July 1921. He was arrested and interned in Ballykinlar Internment Camp, Co. Down that year. He was held in Compound No 2.
Sources: RO 489. Prisoners of War by Liam O' Duibhir, page 315

Daniel (Dan) Sullivan was a Volunteer in the Kells I.R.A. Company in July 1921. He was arrested and interned in Ballykinlar Internment Camp, Co. Down that year. He was held in Compound No 2. He became a member of a 30 man strong I.R.A. Active Service Unit who later became known as the Curraghtown A.S.U. On 5th July 1922 he was involved in the Battle of Curraghtown where he was arrested by the Free State Army, see the story on page 58. He was temporarily held in Trim and then interned in Dundalk, Co. Louth on 22nd July 1922.
Sources: RO 489 Prisoners of War by Liam O' Duibhir, page 315. Dunderry A Folk History by Dunderry History Group & Johnny Keely.

James (Jim) Sweeney, Maudlin Road, Kells, Co. Meath joined the Volunteers in 1917. He was a Volunteer in the Kells I.R.A. Company in July 1921. He also had an address at Fyanstown, Kells. He was a member of Kells Urban District Council for 50 years. He was elected to Sinn Fein Urban Council in 1920. He was Chairman of the Council for several years and Vice-chairman for many more. He died on 31st March 1970. Source: RO 489. Meath Chronicle: 4th April 1970, Page 1

Farrell Tully, Maudlin Road, Kells, Co. Meath was born in Kells about 1892. In July 1921 and July 1922 he was a Volunteer in the Kells I.R.A. Company. In February 1921 he was involved in a raid on Kells Post Office to remove a Telegraph Machine that was being used by the R.I.C. He was injured in the melee with R.I.C. men and was captured during the operation, see the story on page 46. He was imprisoned in Mountjoy, Dublin for offences under the Restoration of Order in Ireland Regulations (ROIR). He died in March 1961 and was buried in St. Colmcille's Cemetery, see page 311. Sources: WS1060. RO 489. MM9.1.1/KMQR-T1W Photo kindly provided by Tony Brady, author of Faithful to Ireland.

Nicholas Tully, Farrell Street, Kells, Co. Meath was born in Kells about 1900. In July 1921 he was a Volunteer in the Kells I.R.A. Company. In February 1921 he was involved in a raid on Kells Post Office to remove a Telegraph Machine that was being used by the R.I.C., see the story on page 46. He was arrested and imprisoned in Mountjoy, Dublin for offences under the Restoration of Order in Ireland Regulations (ROIR).
Sources: RO 489. WS1060. MM9.1.1/KM79-BSF.

Patrick Tully, Maudlin Road, Kells, Co. Meath was a Volunteer in the Kells I.R.A. Company in July 1921. He died in January 1975 and was buried in St. Colmcille's Cemetery, see 310. Source RO 489 Headstone Inscription.

Kentstown Company:

In July 1921 the Kentstown Company had a strength of twelve men. In July 1922 there were no Volunteers so the Kentstown Company ceased to exist.
Source: RO 486

Patrick Byrne, Summerville, Navan, Co. Meath was the Kentstown I.R.A. Company Quartermaster in July 1921. Source: RO 486

James Green, Whitecross, Duleek, Co. Meath was a Volunteer in the Kentstown I.R.A. Company in July 1921. Source: RO 486

Arthur Kelly, Rathanna, Beauparc, Navan, Co. Meath was a Volunteer in the Kentstown I.R.A. Company in July 1921. Source: RO 486

James Lenehan, Giltown, Slane, Co. Meath was a Volunteer in the Kentstown I.R.A. Company in July 1921. Source: RO 486

Patrick Lenehan Giltown, Slane, Co. Meath was the Kentstown I.R.A. Company 1st Lieutenant in July 1921. Source: RO 486.

John Matthews, Kentstown, Navan, Co. Meath was the Kentstown Company Adjutant in July 1921. His name is engraved on a headstone in St. Mary's Cemetery, Navan, see page 340. Source: RO 486. Headstone Inscription.

Patrick O'Hare, Skryne, Tara, Co. Meath was a Volunteer in the Kentstown I.R.A. Company in July 1921. He died on 18th March 1981 aged 80 years and was buried in Saint Colmcille's Churchyard, Skryne, Tara, see page 335.
Sources: RO 486. Headstone Inscription.

Laurence Ruddy, Rathanna, Beauparc, Navan, Co. Meath was a Volunteer in the Kentstown I.R.A. Company in July 1921. He died before 1936. Source: RO 486

John Shiels was the Kentstown I.R.A. Company Commanding Officer in July 1921. In 1937 his address was given as Sicly, Duleek, Co. Meath. Source: RO 486

Joseph Shiels was a Volunteer in the Kentstown I.R.A. Company in July 1921. In 1937 his address was given as Sicly, Duleek, Co. Meath. Source: RO 486
Nicholas Traynor was a Volunteer in the Kentstown I.R.A. Company in July 1921. In 1937 his address was given as Bettystown, Co. Meath. He died on 30th November 1969 aged 64 years and was buried in Kentstown Churchyard Cemetery. Source: RO 486. Headstone Inscription.
Peter Warters, Beauparc, Navan, Co. Meath was the Kentstown I.R.A. Company Intelligence Officer in July 1921. Source: RO 486

Kilbeg Company:

In early 1918 the Kilbeg Company of Irish Volunteers was formed. In January 1919 the Irish Volunteers became the I.R.A. In July 1921 the Kilbeg Company had a strength of fifteen men. In July 1922 the company strength was ten men. Generally the Kilbeg Company worked closely with the Moynalty and Newcastle companies. They supported each other in joint operations. In February 1921 the Kilbeg Company was involved in a raid on Kells Post Office to destroy a Telegraph Machine that was being used by the R.I.C. and British Forces, see page 46. The Captain and officers of the Kilbeg Company were all arrested prior to the treaty in 1921. Sources: RO 489. WS1625. WS1650.

John Bennett, Kilmainham, Kells was the Kilbeg Company Commanding Officer in July 1921. He was imprisoned during that year. Source: RO 489
Patrick Clarke, Kilbeg, Carlanstown, Co. Meath was a Volunteer in the Kilbeg I.R.A. Company in July 1922. Source: RO 489
James Cluskey, Carlanstown, Co. Meath was a Volunteer in the Kilbeg I.R.A. Company in July 1921. Source: RO 489
Thomas Connor, Kells, Co. Meath was the Kilbeg Company 1st Lieutenant in July 1921. In 1936 his address was given as Dublin. Source: RO 489
Hugh Farrelly, Kilbeg, Carlanstown, Co. Meath was a Volunteer in the Kilbeg I.R.A. Company in July 1922. Source: RO 489
Patrick Flanagan, Castletown Moor, Kells, Co. Meath was a Volunteer in the Kilbeg I.R.A. Company in July 1921 and July 1922. On 29th January 1921 he was involved in an ambush of an R.I.C. patrol at Mullagh Lake. Source: RO 489
Patrick Gibney, Carlanstown, Co. Meath was a Volunteer in the Kilbeg I.R.A. Company in July 1921. Source: RO 489. Military Service Pension Collection, file reference No. MD-20250
Brian Hamill, Castletown Moor, Carlanstown, Co. Meath was a Volunteer in the Kilbeg I.R.A. Company in July 1921 and July 1922. Source: RO 489
James McGillick, Newtown, Moynalty, Co. Meath was a Volunteer in the Kilbeg I.R.A. Company in July 1921 and July 1922. Source: RO 489
Patrick McGillick, Newtown, Moynalty, Co. Meath was a Volunteer in the Kilbeg I.R.A. Company in July 1921 and July 1922. Source: RO 489

Patrick Mooney, Stahalmog, Kilbeg, Carlanstown, Co. Meath was the Kilbeg I.R.A. Company Adjutant in July 1921. In 1922 he took the pro-Treaty side and he joined the Free State Army as a Private. On 17th June 1922 he was part of a group of Free State soldiers who distributed Ballot Boxes in Drogheda for the General Election the next Day. On their return journey from Drogheda in a Free State Army Crossley Tender the vehicle crashed into a wall near the gates of Slane Castle. He was taken to the Infirmary in Navan where he died. He was buried in Stahalmog Old Cemetery see page 313.
Source: RO 489. Faithful to Ireland by Tony Brady, page 73. Headstone Inscription.

Eddie Murtagh, Carlanstown, Co. Meath was a Volunteer in the Kilbeg I.R.A. Company in July 1921. Source: RO 489

Bartle Reilly, Kilbeg, Carlanstown, Co. Meath was the Kilbeg Company of Irish Volunteers Commanding Officer in 1918. In January 1921 he was being held prisoner. In 1922 he was actively involved with the Kilbeg I.R.A. Company but I do not know at what rank. Source: WS1650. RO 489.

Edward Reilly, Kilbeg, Carlanstown, Co. Meath was a Volunteer in the Kilbeg I.R.A. Company in July 1922. Source: RO 489

James Reilly, Gravelstown, Carlanstown, Co. Meath was a Volunteer in the Kilbeg I.R.A. Company in July 1921. Source: RO 489

John Smyth, Robinstown, Kilbeg, Carlanstown, Co. Meath was the Kilbeg I.R.A. Company Commanding Officer in July 1921 and July 1922. Source: RO 489

Thomas Timmons was a Volunteer in the Kilbeg I.R.A. Company in July 1921 and July 1922. Source: RO 489

John Tully, Derrypark, Carlanstown, Co. Meath was the Kilbeg I.R.A. Company Commanding Officer in July 1921. He was imprisoned during that year. Source: RO 489

Kilberry Company:

The Kilberry I.R.A. Company was formed about early 1919 and became part of the 6th Battalion. In July 1921 the Kilberry I.R.A. Company was attached to the 3rd Battalion, 2nd brigade and it had a strength of 23 men. In July 1922 it had a strength of 22 men. Sources: RO 487. WS1624.

Christopher Allen, Kilberry, Navan, Co. Meath was the Kilberry I.R.A. Company 1st Lieutenant in July 1921 and July 1922. Later his address was given as Killeen, Dunsany, Co. Meath. He died before 1935. Source: RO 487. Photo kindly provided by Lorraine Lynch, Scanlon's of Kilberry.

Nicholas Bray, Kilberry, Navan, Co. Meath was a Volunteer in the Kilberry I.R.A. Company In July 1921 and July 1922. In 1935 his address was given as Balbriggan, Co. Dublin. His name is engraved on a headstone in Kilberry Cemetery. It says Nicholas Bray died 10th May 1945, see page 331. Source: RO 487. Headstone Inscription. Photo kindly provided by Lorraine Lynch, Scanlon's of Kilberry.

James Clarke, Sillogue, Donaghpatrick, Navan, Co. Meath was a Volunteer in the Kilberry I.R.A. Company in July 1921 and July 1922. Source: RO 487 and
John Clarke, Sillogue, Donaghpatrick, Navan, Co. Meath was a Volunteer in the Kilberry I.R.A. Company in July 1921 and July 1922. He died before 1935. Source: RO 487. Photo kindly provided by Lorraine Lynch, Scanlon's of Kilberry.

John Doggett, Rushwee, Navan, Co. Meath was born in Stackallan, Navan about 1892. In July 1921 and July 1922 he was a Volunteer in the Kilberry I.R.A. Company. In 1922 he was a shop keeper. He was arrested by Pro-Treaty I.R.A. and interned in Dundalk, Co. Louth on 22nd July 1922. On 27th July 1922 he escaped from Dundalk Jail, see the story on page 59. He died at his home in Rushwee on 16th November 1953. His funeral took place from Rushwee Church to Gernonstown. In 2015 I did not find his headstone in Gernonstown Cemetery but the cemetery is heavily overgrown. I did find a family plot in Gernonstown Cemetery for Doggett's of Rushwee, see page 363, but his name is not engraved on it. Sources: RO 487. MM9.1.1/KM3L-FPZ. Louth County Archives http://www.louthcoco.ie/en/Services/Archives/Archive_Collections/ The Meath Chronicle dated 21st November 1953, page 1. Headstone Inscription.

Patrick Doran from Kilberry, Navan, Co. Meath was born in Kilberry about 1897. His younger brothers were James and below Thomas. In July 1920 Patrick was a Volunteer in the Kilberry I.R.A. Company. The eldest son of widow Mrs. Mary Doran, the proprietor of what is now known as Scanlon's of Kilberry. Patrick managed the pub which was frequently raided by R.I.C. and British Forces, causing severe damage and loss of trade. Patrick became an I.R.A. Police Officer and on 6th December 1920 he and his brother Thomas were arrested at their home in Kilberry. On 4th January 1921 they were jailed for 6 or 9 months in Mountjoy on a charge of having two handbooks (possibly military training handbooks). Patrick contracted Tuberculosis, Typhoid or Enteric Fever in prison. He was transferred to Navan Infirmary where he died on 5th February 1921 aged 25 years. Raids on the pub continued. Mary Doran sold the pub and moved to Dublin in June 1923. I have found no evidence that she received any compensation from the state for her loss. Sources: RO 487. MM9.1.1/KMQR-5S8. Meath Chronicle dated 18th February 1922, page 1.

Thomas Doran, Kilberry, Navan, Co. Meath was a Volunteer in the Kilberry I.R.A. Company in 1920. He was the second son of widow Mrs. Mary Doran, the proprietor of what is now known as Scanlon's of Kilberry. Thomas and his brother Patrick (see above) were arrested by British Forces on 6th December 1920. They were jailed for 6 or 9 months in Mountjoy from 4th January 1921. Thomas survived his sentence barely alive and spent two months in Navan Hospital as a result. The pub was frequently raided by British forces, causing severe damage and loss of trade. His Mother Mary Doran sold the pub and moved to Dublin in June 1923. I have found no evidence that she received any compensation from the state. In 1935 Thomas's address was given as Montpelier Hill, Dublin. He died on 21st December 1969 and was buried in Kilberry Cemetery, see page 332. Sources: RO 487. Military Service Pension Collection, file reference No. 1D23. Headstone Inscription

Francis (Frank) Gartland was the Kilberry Company Commanding Officer in July 1921 and July 1922. Source: RO 487

James Gilsenan, Kilberry, Navan, Co. Meath was a Volunteer in the Kilberry I.R.A. Company in July 1921 and July 1922. In 1922 he was arrested and jailed. He died on 19th September 1980 and was buried in Kilberry Cemetery, see page 332. Source: RO 487. Headstone Inscription.

Patrick Gilsenan, Kilberry, Navan, Co. Meath was the Kilberry I.R.A. Company Adjutant in July 1921 and July 1922. In 1922 he was arrested and jailed. He died on 16th July 1974 and was buried in Kilberry Cemetery, see page 332. Source: RO 487. Military Service Pension Collection, file reference No. MD-202539. Headstone Inscription.

B. Heaney, Kilberry, Navan, Co. Meath was a Volunteer in the Kilberry I.R.A. Company in July 1921. Source: RO 487.

James Heaney, Corballis, Kilberry, Navan, Co. Meath was born in Kilberry about 1904. In July 1921 and July 1922 he was the Kilberry I.R.A. Company 2nd Lieutenant. In 1922 he described himself as a Farmer. He became a member of a 30 man strong I.R.A. Active Service Unit who later became known as the Curraghtown A.S.U. On 5th July 1922 he was involved in the Battle of Curraghtown where he was arrested by the Free State Army, see the story on page 58. He was temporarily held in Trim and then interned in Dundalk, Co. Louth on 22nd July 1922. On 27th July 1922 he escaped from Dundalk Jail, see the story on page 59. Sources: RO 487. MM9.1.1/KM3L-FKS. Louth County Archives http://www.louthcoco.ie/en/Services/Archives/Archive_Collections/ Dunderry A Folk History by Dunderry History Group & Johnny Keely.

Owen Heaney, Balsaw Hill, Wilkinstown, Navan, Co. Meath was born in Kilberry in 1902. In July 1921 he was the Battalion Intelligence Officer, 3rd Battalion, 2nd Brigade. In 1922 he described himself as a farmer. He became a member of a 30 man strong I.R.A. Active Service Unit who later became known as the Curraghtown A.S.U. On 5th July 1922 he was involved in the Battle of Curraghtown where he was arrested by the Free State Army, see the story on page 58. He was temporarily held in Navan R.I.C. Barracks from which he escaped. He was recaptured and interned in Dundalk, Co. Louth on 22nd July 1922. On 27th July 1922 he escaped from Dundalk Jail, see the story on page 59. On 7th September 1922 he was involved in an attack on Athboy Barracks in which Official Forces I.R.A. Volunteer Joseph Smyth of Ethelstown, Kells was shot dead, see page 62. Owen Heaney later became a prominent member of Fianna Fail in the Kilberry area. He provided a farm contracting service to local farmers ploughing and tilling land. He was involved in Wilkinstown Gun Club and he enjoyed his sport and his days out shooting. He was a very fit and able bodied man for his age. In October 1993 Owen died aged 91 and was buried in Kilberry Cemetery, see page 332. Sources: RO 487. Meath Chronicle, 02/01/2013, Obituary of Mrs Rose Heaney nee Blaney wife of Owen Heaney, inscription on his Gravestone. MM9.1.1/KM3L-FK9. Louth County Archives http://www.louthcoco.ie/en/Services/Archives/Archive_Collections/ Dunderry A Folk History by Dunderry History Group & Johnny Keely.

Faithful to Ireland by Tony Brady, page 76. Personal interview with his son Owen Heaney and his family who kindly provided the photograph.

Thomas Hetherton, Kilberry, Navan, Co. Meath was a Volunteer in the Kilberry I.R.A. Company in July 1921 and July 1922. Source: RO 487

Christopher Heffernan was a Volunteer in the Kilberry I.R.A. Company in July 1921 and July 1922. In 1935 his address was given as Ashbourne Road, Finglas, Dublin. Source: RO 487

James Lynch, Navan, Co. Meath was the Kilberry I.R.A. Company Quartermaster in July 1921 and July 1922. Source: RO 487

Patrick Lynch, Kilberry, Navan, Co. Meath was a Volunteer in the Kilberry I.R.A. Company in July 1921 and July 1922. Source: RO 487

John McCaffrey, Rathcoon, Kilberry, Navan, Co. Meath was the Battalion Adjutant in July 1921 and July 1922. Source: RO 487

James McHugh was a Volunteer in the Kilberry I.R.A. Company in July 1921 and July 1922. In 1935 he was a member of An Garda Síochána and he was guarding Shannon Power Station, Limerick. Source: RO 487

Thomas Mchugh, was a Volunteer in the Kilberry I.R.A. Company in July 1921 and July 1922. In 1935 his address was given as Dublin. Source: RO 487

John McKeown was born in Clifden, Co. Galway about 1904. In July 1921 and July 1922 he was a Volunteer in the Kilberry I.R.A. Company. In 1922 he was a labourer when he was arrested by Pro-Treaty I.R.A. and interned in Dundalk, Co. Louth on 22nd July 1922. On 27th July 1922 he escaped from Dundalk, see the story on page 59. In 1935 his address was given as Finglas, Dublin. Sources: RO 487. MM9.1.1/KM3L-FK9. Louth County Archives http://www.louthcoco.ie/en/Services/Archives/Archive_Collections/ and Louth County Archives

James Mongey was a Volunteer in the Kilberry I.R.A. Company in July 1921 and July 1922. In 1935 his address was given as Dublin. Source: RO 487

Joseph Ryan was a farmer in Gormanlough, Stackallen, Navan. In 1920 and July 1921 he was a Volunteer in the Kilberry I.R.A. Company. At Christmas 1920 he was being held prisoner under the Restoration of Order Act. His house was repeatedly raided by Crown Forces. On 25th December 1920 the Meath Chronicle published a list of the Meath men being held under the act and he was listed. He was opposed to the Treaty but took little interest in party politics. He died at his home on 13th November 1959. His funeral took place from Rushwee Church to St. Mary's Cemetery Navan. Sources: RO 487. Politics and War in Meath 1913-23 by Oliver Coogan, page 149. The Meath Chronicle dated 21st November 1959, page 1

Peter Sheilds, was a Volunteer in the Kilberry I.R.A. Company in July 1921 and July 1922. He became a member of a 30 man strong I.R.A. Active Service Unit who later became known as the Curraghtown A.S.U. On 5th July 1922 he was involved in the Battle of Curraghtown where he was arrested by the Free State Army, see the story on page 58. He was temporarily held in Trim and then interned in Dundalk, Co. Louth on 22nd July 1922. In 1935 his company comrades said his address was unknown. Source: RO 487. Dunderry A Folk History by Dunderry History Group & Johnny Keely.

C. Sherry was a Volunteer in the Kilberry I.R.A. Company in July 1921. In 1935 his company comrades said his address was unknown. Source: RO 487

Kilbride Company (Mulhuddart):

In 1918 the Kilbride Company had a strength of 32 men. In January 1919 the Irish Volunteers became the I.R.A. In July 1921 the company had a strength of 22 men. In July 1922 the company continued to have a strength of 22 men.
Source: RO 480

Christopher Beehan was a Volunteer in the Kilbride I.R.A. Company in July 1921 and July 1922. In 1936 his address was given as Hill View, Mulhuddart, Co. Dublin.
Source: RO 480

Michael Bruton was a Volunteer in the Kilbride I.R.A. Company in July 1921 and July 1922. In 1936 his address was given as The Ward, Co. Dublin. His name is engraved on a headstone in Kilbride Cemetery, see page 268.
Source: RO 480. Headstone Inscription.

Robert Daly was a native of Dunshaughlin but I do not have a date when he joined the Dunshaughlin I.R.A. Company. He transferred to the Kilbride Company where he was a Volunteer in 1921 and 1922. In 1922 he was a Battalion Officer. Robert Daly died at the residence of his daughter Mrs. W. Swan, Ringlestown, Kilmessan on 9th February 1969. His funeral took place from Kilmessan Church to Ballymaglassan Cemetery.
Sources: RO 480 The Meath Chronicle dated 22 February 1969, page 11. Headstone inscription.

John Gregan was a Volunteer in the Kilbride I.R.A. Company in July 1921 and July 1922. In 1936 he was a member of the Garda Siochana. Source: RO 480

William Gregan was a Volunteer in the Kilbride I.R.A. Company in July 1921 and July 1922. In 1936 his address was given as Hollywoodrath, Mullhuddart, Co. Dublin. Source: RO 480

James Hickey was a Volunteer in the Kilbride I.R.A. Company in July 1921 and July 1922. In 1936 his address was given as Hill View, Mullhuddart, Co. Dublin
Source: RO 480

John (Jack) Horan, a native of Birr, Co. Offaly was nominated District Justice to the Sinn Fein parish court in the Battalion Area of Trim, Kiltale, Bective and Dunderry in May 1920. In July 1921 and July 1922 he continued as a Volunteer in the Kilbride I.R.A. Company. Sources: RO 480. WS1696.

James Isdale was a Volunteer in the Kilbride I.R.A. Company in July 1921 and July 1922. In 1936 his address was given as Hill View, Mullhuddart, Co. Dublin. Source: RO 480

Christopher Manning was a Volunteer in the Kilbride I.R.A. Company in July 1921 and July 1922. In 1936 his address was given as Pace, Dunboyne, Co. Meath.
Source: RO 480

John (Jack) Manning was the Kilbride Company Commanding Officer in July 1921 and July 1922. He was a brother of below Thomas (Tom). On the 2nd July 1921, about two weeks before the Truce, he assisted in the mobilisation of Volunteers in a failed attack on a troop train near Celbridge, see the story on page 51. In 1936 he was serving with the Free State Army and his address was given as Sandpits, Castleknock, Co. Dublin. Source: RO 480. Bureau of Military History Military Service Pension Collection, file reference No MSP34REF38375 of Mary Connell, Lustown, Batterstown, Co Meath

Michael Manning was a Volunteer in the Kilbride I.R.A. Company in July 1921 and July 1922. In 1936 his address was given as Priestown, Mullhuddart, Co. Dublin. Source: RO 480

Richard Manning was a Volunteer in the Kilbride I.R.A. Company in July 1921 and July 1922. In 1936 his address was given as Caulstown, Dunboyne Source: RO 480

Thomas (Tom) Manning was born in 1899. He was a brother of above John (Jack). In September 1918 he joined the Kilbride Company of Irish Volunteers. He was a Volunteer until 1921. In July 1921 he was the Kilbride I.R.A. Company Adjutant. He claimed that he had to get into a fox covet to avoid being shot by British Military at a place called Lagore, between Ratoath and Dunshaughlin Co. Meath. Sources: Oliver Coogan's Politics and war in Meath 1913-23 Page 112. RO 480.

Joseph McGovern was a Volunteer in the Kilbride I.R.A. Company in July 1921 and July 1922. In 1936 his address was given as Caulstown, Dunboyne Co. Meath. Source: RO 480

Patrick Govern was a Volunteer in the Kilbride I.R.A. Company in July 1921 and July 1922. In 1936 his address was given as Caulstown, Dunboyne, Co. Meath. Source: RO 480

Thomas McMahon was a Volunteer in the Kilbride I.R.A. Company in July 1921 and July 1922. In 1936 his address was given as Hill View, Mullhuddart, Co. Dublin. Source: RO 480

Matthew McNulty was a Volunteer in the Kilbride I.R.A. Company in July 1921 and July 1922. Source: RO 480

John Quinn was the Kilbride I.R.A. Company Quartermaster In July 1921 and July 1922. In 1936 his address was given as Priestown, Mullhuddart, Co. Dublin. Source: RO 480

Francis Smyth was a Volunteer in the Kilbride I.R.A. Company in July 1921 and July 1922. In 1936 he was serving with the Free State Army and his address was given as Balfstown, Mullhuddart, Co. Dublin. His name in engraved on a headstone in Kilbride Cemetery, see page 268. Source: RO 480. Headstone Inscription

Peter Smyth was a Volunteer in the Kilbride I.R.A. Company in July 1921 and July 1922. In 1936 his address was given as Celbridge, Co. Kildare. Source: RO 480

Peter Smyth was a Volunteer in the Kilbride I.R.A. Company in July 1921 and July 1922. In 1936 his address was given as Celbridge, Co. Kildare. Source: RO 480

Patrick Walsh, Hollywoodrath, Co. Dublin was a Volunteer in the Kilbride I.R.A. Company in July 1921 and July 1922. Source: RO 480

John White, Hill View, Mulhuddart, Co. Dublin was a Volunteer in the Kilbride I.R.A. Company in July 1921 and July 1922. Source: RO 480. Military Service Pension Collection, file reference No. MD 48323 7/6/72

Kilcloon Company:

In 1919 Kilmore Company ceased to exist. The Volunteers were transferred to Kiltale, Kilcloon and Dunshaughlin. Likewise in 1921 the Summerhill Company ceased to exist and the Volunteers transferred to the Kilcloon Company. In July 1921 the Kilcloon Company had a strength of 32 men. In July 1922 the company had a strength of eighteen men.
Sources: RO 480

James Barry, Arodstown, Summerhill, Co. Meath was a Volunteer in the Kilcloon I.R.A. Company in 1921. He transferred from the Summerhill Company in July 1921 when the Summerhill Company ceased to exist. Source: RO 480

John Barry, College Park, Summerhill, Co. Meath was a Volunteer in the Kilcloon I.R.A. Company in 1921. He transferred from the Summerhill Company in July 1921 when the Summerhill Company ceased to exist. Source: RO 480

Patrick Boylan, Kilmore, Kilcock, Co. Meath was a Volunteer in the Kilcloon I.R.A. Company in July 1921 and July 1922. Source: RO 480

Patrick Callaghan, Ravensdale, Leixlip, Co. Kildare was a Volunteer in the Kilcloon I.R.A. Company in July 1921 and July 1922. Source: RO 480

Peter Callaghan, Kilcloone, Dunboyne, Co. Meath was the Commanding Officer of the 1st Battalion, 1st Brigade, 1st Eastern Division in 1921. He died before 1936.
Source: WS1539. RO 479. 480.

Francis Carolan, Ballynare, Dunboyne, Co. Meath was born in Ballynare about 1896. In July 1921 and July 1922 he was a Volunteer in the Kilcloon I.R.A. Company. In 1921 he was arrested and imprisoned in Mountjoy, Dublin on a charge of having arms. In 1936 his address was given as 1100 East St., Wheeling W, Virginia, U.S.A. Sources: RO 480. MM9.1.1/KMQR-RK9.

Joseph Cols, Arodstown, Summerhill, Co. Meath was a Volunteer in the Kilcloon I.R.A. Company in 1921. He transferred from the Summerhill Company in July 1921 when the Summerhill Company ceased to exist. Source: RO 480

Patrick Cols, Mullagh, Kilcock, Co. Meath was a Volunteer in the Kilcloon I.R.A. Company in 1921. He transferred from the Summerhill Company in July 1921 when the Summerhill Company ceased to exist. Source: RO 480

Stephen Darcy, Kilcloon, Dunboyle, Co. Meath was the Kilcloon I.R.A. Company Quartermaster in July 1921 and July 1922. Source: RO 480

Joseph Farrell, see Summerhill Company.

Page 185

Patrick Fay, Cloneymeath, Summerhill, Co. Meath, was a Volunteer in the Kilcloon I.R.A. Company in 1921. He transferred from the Summerhill Company in July 1921 when the Summerhill Company ceased to exist. Source: RO 480

Joseph Fitzsimons, Moynalvy, Summerhill, Co. Meath was a Volunteer in the Kilcloon I.R.A. Company in 1921. He transferred from the Summerhill Company in July 1921 when the Summerhill Company ceased to exist. Source: RO 480

James Gannon, Galtrim, Summerhill, Co. Meath was a Volunteer in the Kilcloon I.R.A. Company in 1921. He transferred from the Summerhill Company in July 1921 when the Summerhill Company ceased to exist. Source: RO 480

Richard Garry, Kilcloon, Dunboyle, Co. Meath was a Volunteer in the Kilcloon I.R.A. Company in July 1921 and July 1922. Source: RO 480

Edward Gill, Derrypatrick, Drumree, Co. Meath was a Volunteer in the Kilcloon I.R.A. Company in 1921. He transferred from the Summerhill Company in July 1921 when the Summerhill Company ceased to exist. Source: RO 480

Thomas Goodwin, Baltrasna, Drumree, Co. Meath was a Volunteer in the Kilcloon I.R.A. Company In July 1922. Source: RO 480

William Goodwin, Baltrasna, Drumree, Co. Meath was a Volunteer in the Kilcloon I.R.A. Company in July 1921 and July 1922. On the 2nd July 1921, about two weeks before the Truce, he was involved in a failed attack on a troop train near Celbridge. He was wounded during the operation but managed to hide himself. He was rescued by Cumann na mBan and moved to safety, see the story on page 51. Source: RO 480

Michael Hiney, Drumlargan, Kilcock, Co. Kildare was appointed Brigade Commanding Officer, 4th Brigade, 1st Eastern Division on 28th March 1921. Sources: WS1715. WS1060. WS1623. WS1723. RO 494. RO 495. WS1660.

James Malone, Moynalvy, Summerhill, Co. Meath was a Volunteer in the Kilcloon I.R.A. Company in 1921. He transferred from the Summerhill Company in July 1921 when the Summerhill Company ceased to exist. Source: RO 480

James Monaghan, Clarkstown, Kilcock, Co. Meath was a Volunteer in the Kilcloon I.R.A. Company in July 1921 and July 1922. Source: RO 480

William Nixon, Kilmore, Kilcock, Co. Meath was a Volunteer in the Kilcloon I.R.A. Company in July 1922. Source: RO 480

Christopher Norris, Kilcloon, Dunboyne, Co. Meath was the Kilcloon I.R.A. Company Adjutant in July 1921 and July 1922. Source: RO 480

James Phoenix, Phepotstown, Kilcock, Co. Meath was a Volunteer in the Kilcloon I.R.A. Company in July 1921 and July 1922. Source: RO 480

Michael Phoenix, Kilcloon, Dunboyne, Co. Meath was the Kilcloon I.R.A. Company Commanding Officer In 1920, July 1921 and July 1922. In September 1920 he was involved in the attack on the heavily fortified Trim R.I.C. Barracks, see the story on page 40. Sources: WS0858. RO 480.

Richard Phoenix, Kilcloon, Dunboyne, Co. Meath was a Volunteer in the Kilcloon I.R.A. Company in July 1921 and July 1922. Source: RO 480

James Powderly, Deerpark, Garlow Cross, Navan, Co. Meath was a Volunteer in the Kilcloon I.R.A. Company in 1921. He transferred from the Summerhill Company in July 1921 when the Summerhill Company ceased to exist. Source: RO 480

John Richardson, Tarnadrum, Kilcock, Co. Meath was a Volunteer in the Kilcloon I.R.A. Company in July 1921 and July 1922. Source: RO 480

Matthew Russell, Ballymacoll, Dunboyne, Co. Meath was a Volunteer in the Kilcloon I.R.A. Company in July 1921 and July 1922. Source: RO 480

William Russell, Ballymacoll, Dunboyne, Co. Meath was the Kilcloon I.R.A. Company Intelligence Officer in July 1921. Source RO 480

Christopher Sheridan, Cloneymeath, Summerhill Co. Meath was a Volunteer in the Kilcloon I.R.A. Company in 1921. He transferred from the Summerhill Company in July 1921 when the Summerhill Company ceased to exist. Source: RO 480

Matthew Sheridan, Maudlins, Trim, Co. Meath was a Volunteer in the Kilcloon I.R.A. Company in 1921. He transferred from the Summerhill Company in July 1921 when the Summerhill Company ceased to exist. Source: RO 480

Patrick Thomson, Kilmore, Kilcock, Co. Meath was a Volunteer in the Kilcloon I.R.A. Company in 1921. He transferred from the Summerhill Company in July 1921 when the Summerhill Company ceased to exist. Source: RO 480

James Walsh, Arodstown, Moynalvy, Summerhill, Co. Meath was a Volunteer in the Kilcloon I.R.A. Company in July 1921 and July 1922. Source: RO 480

Richard Walsh, Arodstown, Moynalvy, Summerhill, Co. Meath was a Volunteer in the Kilcloon I.R.A. Company in July 1921 and July 1922. Source: RO 480

Kildalkey Company:

According to Luke Bradley's Witness Statement a Kildalkey Company of Irish Volunteers was formed in 1914. In July 1914, at the outbreak of World War One, a huge split immerged in the Volunteer movement nationally. John Redmond, who was the leader of the Irish Parliamentary Party, called on the Irish Volunteers to join the National Volunteers and to fight in World War One under the command of the British Army. This decimated the Kildalkey Company and it ceased to exist. In 1917 the Kildalkey Company of Irish Volunteers was reformed with assistance from Athboy Company's Seamus Finn and Joseph Martin. The company had a strength of 29 or 30 men. In 1918 the strength of the Kildalkey Company increased to 60 due to the threat of conscription into the British Army. The company was attached to the Irish Volunteers 3rd Battalion Meath Brigade. In January 1919 the Irish Volunteers became the I.R.A. In 1919 the Kildalkey I.R.A. Company went back to a strength of about 30 men. In April 1920 under directions from Dail Eireann the I.R.A. took over Community Policing and Sinn Fein set up a parish court in Kildalkey. Pat Potterton and Pat Corrigan became Court Justices. In April 1921 the Kildalkey Company became attached to the 2nd Battalion, 4th Brigade. In July 1921 the Kildalkey Company had a strength of 32 men. In July 1922 the company had no Volunteers so it ceased to exist. Sources: WS1723. WS1660. RO 496.

Matthew Browne was a Volunteer in the Kildalkey I.R.A. Company in July 1921. In 1936 he was a member of An Garda Síochána and his address was given as Dunmanway, Co. Cork. Source: RO 496

Joseph Clarke, Clontannon, Athboy, Co. Meath was a Volunteer in the Kildalkey I.R.A. Company in July 1921. Source: RO 496.

John Corrigan, Kildalkey, Co. Meath was the Kildalkey Company of Irish Volunteers 1st Lieutenant in December 1917. In 1921 he was the Kildalkey I.R.A. Company Commanding Officer. At the end of Spring 1921 he was appointed I.R.A. Battalion Commanding Officer, 2nd Battalion, 4th Brigade, 1st Eastern Division. He sometimes stayed at the Temperance Hotel in Kells when travelling to meetings in that area. Sources: WS1660. WS1623. WS1623. RO 496. WS1723.

Thomas Corrigan was a Volunteer in the Kildalkey I.R.A. Company in July 1921. In 1936 his address was given as 68 Ranelagh, Dublin. Source: RO 496.

Patrick (Pat) Corrigan, Kildalkey Co. Meath was Battalion Vice Commanding Officer, 3rd Battalion (Delvin) Meath Brigade, 1st Eastern Division, Irish Volunteers around 1918. In December 1920 he was Brigade Vice Commanding Officer, 4th Brigade, 1st Eastern Division, I.R.A. In 1936 he was serving with the Free State Army and his address was given as Collins Barracks, Co. Cork. Sources: WS1623. WS1060. WS1723. WS1715. RO 494

James Davis, Kildalkey, Co. Meath was the Kildalkey Company Adjutant in July 1921. He died before 1936. Source: RO 496.

Christopher Fagan was a Volunteer in the Kildalkey I.R.A. Company in July 1921. He became a member of a 30 man strong I.R.A. Active Service Unit who later became known as the Curraghtown A.S.U. On 5th July 1922 he was involved in the Battle of Curraghtown where he was arrested by the Free State Army, see the story on page 58. He was temporarily held in Trim and then interned in Dundalk, Co. Louth on 22nd July 1922. In 1936 his address was given as U.S.A. Source: RO 496. Dunderry A Folk History by Dunderry History Group & Johnny Keely.

James Farrelly, Clonmore, Athboy, Co. Meath was a Volunteer in the Kildalkey I.R.A. Company in July 1921. In May 1966 he attended the 1916 Commemoration in Kildalkey. Source: RO 496. Meath Chronicle dated 7th May 1966, page 9.

Michael Farrelly, Clonmore, Athboy, Co. Meath was a Volunteer in the Kildalkey I.R.A. Company in July 1921. Source: RO 496.

Philip Farrelly, Clonylogan, Kildalkey, Co. Meath was a Volunteer in the Kildalkey I.R.A. Company in July 1921. Source: RO 496.

James Gaffney, Addinstown, Athboy, Co. Meath was a Volunteer in the Kildalkey I.R.A. Company in July 1921. In May 1966 he attended the 1916 Commemoration in Kildalkey. Source: RO 496. Meath Chronicle dated 7th May 1966, page 9.

Peter Gaffney was a Volunteer in the Kildalkey I.R.A. Company in July 1921. He died before 1936. Source: RO 496.

Peter Gilleran, was appointed I.R.A. Battalion Intelligence Officer, 2nd Battalion, 4th Brigade, 1st Eastern Division at end of spring 1921. Source: WS1623.

James Gilligan was appointed I.R.A. Battalion Engineer, 2nd Battalion, 4th Brigade, 1st Eastern Division at end of spring 1921. Source: WS1623.

Michael Halligan, Moatstown, Kildalkey, Co. Meath was the Kildalkey Company Quartermaster in July 1921. In May 1966 he attended the 1916 Commemoration in Kildalkey. Source: RO 496. Meath Chronicle dated 7th May 1966, page 9.

Michael Hesnan, The Wood, Kildalkey, Co. Meath was a Volunteer in the Kildalkey I.R.A. Company in July 1921. Source: RO 496.

Patrick Kearney, The Wood, Kildalkey, Co. Meath was a Volunteer in the Kildalkey I.R.A. Company in July 1921. Source: RO 496.

Samuel Kelly, The Wood, Kildalkey, Co. Meath was a Volunteer in the Kildalkey I.R.A. Company in July 1921. In May 1966 he attended the 1916 Commemoration in Kildalkey. Source: RO 496. Meath Chronicle dated 7th May 1966, page 9.

Joseph (Joe) Ledwith was the Kildalkey Company of Irish Volunteers 2nd Lieutenant in December 1917. In July 1921 he was the Kildalkey I.R.A. Company Commanding Officer. In May 1966 he attended the 1916 Commemoration in Kildalkey. Sources: WS1660. RO 496. Meath Chronicle dated 7th May 1966, page 9.

Matt Ledwith was appointed I.R.A. Battalion Quartermaster, 2nd Battalion, 4th Brigade, 1st Eastern Division at the end of spring 1921. In July 1921 he was recorded as still holding that role. In 1936 he was serving with the Free State Army.
Sources: RO 496. WS1660. WS1723.

John Lynch, Frayne, Athboy, Co. Meath was a Volunteer in the Kildalkey I.R.A. Company in July 1921. Source: RO 496.

James McDonnell, Clonmore, Athboy, Co. Meath was a Volunteer in the Kildalkey I.R.A. Company in July 1921. In May 1966 he attended the 1916 Commemoration in Kildalkey. Source: RO 496. Meath Chronicle dated 7th May 1966, page 9.

Patrick McGurl: See Athboy Company.

Thomas Miggan, was a Volunteer in the Kildalkey I.R.A. Company in July 1921. He died before 1936. Source: RO 496.

James Mulvaney was a Volunteer in the Kildalkey I.R.A. Company in July 1921. In early September 1922 he was arrested following an attack on Athboy Barracks in which one of the Official Forces I.R.A. was killed, see page 62. In 1936 his address was given as U.S.A. Source: RO 496. Faithful to Ireland by Tony Brady, page 78.

William Mulvaney, The Wood, Kildalkey, Co. Meath was a Volunteer in the Kildalkey I.R.A. Company in July 1921. Source: RO 496.

John Murray, Clonycairn, Ballivor, Co. Meath was a Volunteer in the Kildalkey I.R.A. Company in July 1921. Source: RO 496.

William Murray, Clonmore, Athboy, Co. Meath was a Volunteer in the Kildalkey I.R.A. Company in July 1921. Source: RO 496.

Harry O'Brien, Mountpoplar, Kldalkey, Co. Meath was a Volunteer in the Kildalkey I.R.A. Company in July 1921. In April 1921 he opened fire with a rifle on three Military Lorries passing through Kildalkey in the direction of Trim. The soldiers in the lorries returned fire without stopping. Sources: WS1660. RO 496

James O'Brien, Clonmore, Athboy, Co. Meath was a Volunteer in the Kildalkey I.R.A. Company in July 1921. In early September 1922 he was arrested following an attack on Athboy Barracks in which one of the Official Forces I.R.A. was killed, see page 62. He died before 1936. Source: RO 496. Faithful to Ireland by Tony Brady, page 78.

George Plunkett, Kildalkey, Co. Meath was born in Trim about 1897. In July 1921 he was a Volunteer in the Kildalkey I.R.A. Company but he was arrested and imprisoned in Mountjoy, Dublin for offences under the Restoration of Order in Ireland Regulations (ROIR). Sources: RO 496. MM9.1.1/KM79-YSM

Pat Potterton, Moyrath, Kildalkey, Co Meath was the Kildalkey Irish Volunteers Company Commanding Officer in December 1917. In July 1921 he was still the Kildalkey I.R.A. Company Commanding Officer but he was being held in prison. Sources: WS1660. RO 496.

Thomas Potterton, Moynath, Kildalkey, Co Meath was a Volunteer in the Kildalkey I.R.A. Company in July 1921. In May 1966 he attended the 1916 Commemoration in Kildalkey. Source: RO 496. Meath Chronicle dated 7th May 1966, page 9.

James Reilly, Kildalkey, Co. Meath was the Kildalkey I.R.A. Company 2nd Lieutenant in July 1921. He died before 1936. Source: RO 496

James (Jim) Reynolds, Corballis, Kildalkey, Co. Meath was a member of the Trim Senior Hurling Team in 1914. In 1915 he was on the Trim team that won the second in a row Meath Senior Football Championship. He was a Volunteer in the Kildalkey I.R.A. Company in July 1921. In May 1966 he attended the 1916 Commemoration in Kildalkey. Source: RO 496. Trim G.A.A. Team photographs - Seamus Brennan. Meath Chronicle dated 7th May 1966, page 9.

Joseph Reynolds, Corballis, Kildalkey, Co. Meath was the Kildalkey I.R.A. Company Engineer in July 1921. Source: RO 496

James Tyrrell, Neilstown, Kildalkey, Co. Meath was the Kildalkey I.R.A. Company 1st Lieutenant in July 1921. Source: RO 496

John Tyrrelll, Kildalkey, Co. Meath was the Quartermaster of the 3rd Battalion (Delvin), Meath Brigade, 1st Eastern Division, Irish Volunteers in 1918. In July 1921 he was the Quartermaster of the 4th Brigade, 1st Eastern Division. I.R.A. He died before 1936. Sources: WS1723. WS1623. WS1715. RO 494

Kilmainhamwood Company:

Coill Chille Maighneann
KILMAINHAMWOOD

Laurence Farrelly, Lisnagrent, Kilmainhamwood, Co. Meath was the Kilmainhamwood I.R.A. Company Quartermaster and the company 2nd Lieutenant for a period in 1921. Source: RO 489

Luke Lynch, Kilmainhamwood, Co. Meath was the Kilmainhamwood I.R.A. Company Adjutant in July 1921. Source: RO 489

Patrick O'Brien, Kilmainhamwood, Co. Meath was the Kilmainhamwood I.R.A. Company Commanding Officer in July 1921. Source: RO 489

Michael O'Hagan, was the Kilmainhamwood I.R.A. Company 1st Lieutenant in July 1921. Source: RO 489

Michael (Mick) Rooney, Kilmainhamwood was a Volunteer in the Kilmainhamwood I.R.A. Company about 1919. He died in August 1975 aged 79 years. Source: The Meath Chronicle dated 23rd August 1975, page 7

Kilmore Company:

In 1919 Kilmore Company ceased to exist. The Volunteers were transferred to Kiltale, Kilcloon and Dunshaughlin.

Jim McCann, Kilmore, Co. Meath was the Kilmore Company of Irish Volunteers Commanding Officer in 1917. In 1921 he was still involved in the Kilmore I.R.A. Company but I do not know at what rank. Jim McCann's premises became a main meeting place in Kilmore. The premises suffered numerous raids by British Forces accompanied by breakages and lootings. Source: WS0857.

David Hall, see Culmullin Company.

William Smith, see Culmullin Company.

Kiltale Company:

The Kiltale Company of Irish Volunteers was formed at the latter end of 1917. It was organised by Paddy Mooney and Seamus O'Higgins of Trim Company. In January 1919 the Irish Volunteers became the I.R.A. In 1919 Kilmore I.R.A. Company ceased to exist. The Volunteers were transferred to Kiltale, Kilcloon and Dunshaughlin. On 2nd November 1919 the Kiltale I.R.A. Company blocked all the roads in their area as part of the co-ordinated attack on Lismullen R.I.C. Barracks also known as Dillon's Bridge, see the story on page 37. In the summer of 1920 the Kiltale I.R.A. Company was attached to the 2nd Battalion, Meath Brigade. In

July 1921 the Kiltale I.R.A. Company had a strength of seventeen men. In July 1922 the company strength had diminished to two men. Sources: WS1696.

Patrick Bannon was a Volunteer in the Kiltale I.R.A. Company in July 1921. In 1936 he was serving in the Free State Army. Source: RO 485.

James Barry, Arodstown, Summerhill, Co. Meath was a Volunteer in the Kiltale I.R.A. Company in July 1921. Source: RO 485.

Christopher Cusack, Kiltale, Dunsany, Co. Meath was the Kiltale I.R.A. Company 2nd Lieutenant and 1st Lieutenant for a periods in 1921. Source: RO 485.

Patrick Dunne, Celbridge, Co. Kildare was a Volunteer in the Kiltale I.R.A. Company in July 1921. Source: RO 485.

Eugene Englishby, Killeen, Dunsany, Co. Meath was a Volunteer in the Kiltale I.R.A. Company in July 1921. In 1936 he attended a meeting to appoint a Brigade Committee for gathering information related to qualifying Volunteers for the Military Service Pensions. He died on 5th January 1972 at Our Lady's Hospital Navan. He also lived in Drumree, Dunboyne and Rathmolyn. He was buried in Dunboyne Cemetery. Source: RO 485. Irish Press dated 7th January 1972, Page 2.

Nicholas Gannon, Freffans, Trim, Co. Meath was a Volunteer in the Kiltale I.R.A. Company in July 1921. Source: RO 485.

John Hazel was a Volunteer in the Kiltale I.R.A. Company in July 1921. In 1936 he was serving in the Free State Army. Source: RO 485.

John Hynes, Kiltale, Dunsany, Co. Meath was the Kiltale Company Commanding Officer in July 1921. Source: RO 485.

John Madden, Kiltale, Dunsany, Co. Meath was a Volunteer in the Kiltale I.R.A. Company in July 1921. Source: RO 485.

Michael Madden, Kiltale, Dunsany, Co. Meath was the Kiltale Company Adjutant in July 1921. Source: RO 485.

Patrick Madden, Kiltale, Dunsany, Co. Meath was a Volunteer in the Kiltale I.R.A. Company in July 1921. Source: RO 485. Military Service Pension Collection, file reference No. MD-20522

Maurice Neville was a Volunteer in the Kiltale I.R.A. Company in July 1921. Source: RO 485.

John O'Neill, Arodstown, Summerhill, Enfield, Co. Meath was a Volunteer in the Kiltale I.R.A. Company in July 1921. Source: RO 485. Military Service Pension Collection, file reference No. 34-50818

Michael O'Neill, Freffans, Trim, Co. Meath was a Volunteer in the Kiltale I.R.A. Company in July 1921. Source: RO 485.

Thomas Scully, Kilcarty, Kilmessan, Co. Meath was the Kiltale Company Quartermaster in July 1921. Source: RO 485.

Michael Twomey, Galtrim, Enfield, Co. Meath was a Volunteer in the Kiltale I.R.A. Company in July 1921. Source: RO 485.

Matthew (Matt) Wallace, Batterstown, Co. Meath was a Volunteer in the Kiltale I.R.A. Company in 1917. At the time he worked on the roads for Meath County Council. He remained with the Kiltale I.R.A. Company right through to 1922. Sources: Oliver Coogan, Politics and War in Meath 1913-25, page 113 and RO 485.

James Walsh, Basketstown, Summerhill, Enfield, Co. Meath was a Volunteer in the Kiltale I.R.A. Company in July 1921. Source: RO 485.

Peter Walsh, Basketstown, Summerhill, Enfield, Co. Meath was a Volunteer in the Kiltale I.R.A. Company in July 1921. Source: RO 485.

Killyon Company:

In July 1921 the Killyon Company had a strength of thirteen men. In July 1922 there were no Volunteers so the Killyon Company ceased to exist. Source: RO 495

Patrick Colelough was a Volunteer in the Killyon Company of Irish Volunteers in 1916. After the failed Rising he got involved in mustering up disappointed Volunteers and trying to get them to regroup and reorganise. Source: WS0857.

Patrick Cunningham, Derrycommon, Ballivor, Co. Meath was a Volunteer in the Killyon I.R.A. Company in July 1921. Source: RO 495.

William Feely, Hill of Down, Co. Meath was a Volunteer in the Killyon I.R.A. Company in July 1921. In 1936 his address was given as Dublin. Source: RO 495.

Michael Gray was a Volunteer in the Killyon I.R.A. Company in July 1921. In 1936 he was a member of the Dublin Fire Brigade. Source: RO 495.

Patrick Henry, Fordstown, Navan, Co. Meath was a Volunteer in the Killyon I.R.A. Company in July 1921. Source: RO 495.

James Keegan, Clondalee Beg, Hill of Down, Co. Meath was a Volunteer in the Killyon I.R.A. Company in July 1921. Source: RO 495.

Michael Keegan, Clondalee Beg, Hill of Down, Co Meath was the Killyon I.R.A. Company 1st Lieutenant in July 1921. After the failed Rising he got involved in trying to bolster up disappointed Volunteers in an effort to get them to regroup and reorganise. Sources: WS0857. RO 495.

Patrick Keegan, Clondalee Beg, Hill of Down, Co Meath was the Killyon I.R.A. Company Quartermaster in July 1921. Source: RO 495.

Christopher Kelly, Cherrylane, Kinnegad, Ballivor, Co. Meath was a Volunteer in the Killyon I.R.A. Company in July 1921. Source: RO 495.

Stephen Kelly, Newtown, Hill of Down, Co. Meath was the Killyon I.R.A. Company Commanding Officer in July 1921. Source: RO 495.

William Kelly, Clondalee Beg, Hill of Down, Co Meath was a Volunteer in the Killyon I.R.A. Company in July 1921. Source: RO 495.

John Malone, Clondalee Beg, Hill of Down, Co Meath was the Killyon I.R.A. Company 2nd Lieutenant in July 1921. Source: RO 495.

James Mooney, Clondalee Beg, Hill of Down, Co Meath was a Volunteer in the Killyon I.R.A. Company in July 1921. Source: RO 495.

John Quinn, Ballasport, Hill of Down, Co Meath, was a Volunteer in the Killyon I.R.A. Company in July 1921. Source: RO 495.

William Reilly was the Killyon I.R.A. Company Adjutant in July 1921. Source: RO 495.

Lobinstown Company:

In July 1921 the Lobinstown Company had a strength of sixteen men. In July 1922 there were no Volunteers so the Lobinstown Company ceased to exist. Source: RO 487

Christopher Quail, Killeavy, Lobinstown, Slane Co. Meath was the Lobinstown I.R.A. Company Commanding Officer in 1921. Source: RO 487

Longwood Company:

On 31st October 1919 the Longwood Company were involved in the attack on the Ballivor R.I.C. Barracks. One R.I.C. man was shot dead in the melee before the garrison surrendered. All rifles and revolvers were seized during the attack, see the story on page 37. In November 1920 all below listed mem, with the exception of Michael Fagan, were involved in an attack on the Longwood R.I.C. Barracks. They did not secure any weapons during the attack, see the story on page 43. Source: WS1715. WS1060. WS01060.

Edward Bird, Longwood, Co. Meath was a Volunteer in the Longwood I.R.A. Company in 1920. See also page 43. Source: WS1060.

Christopher (Chris) Boylan, Longwood, Co. Meath was a Volunteer in the Longwood I.R.A. Company in 1920. See also page 43. Source: WS1060

P. Corrigan, Longwood, Co. Meath was a Volunteer in the Longwood I.R.A. Company in 1920. See also page 43. Source: WS1060.

John Costello, Longwood, Co. Meath was a Volunteer in the Longwood I.R.A. Company in 1920. See also page 43. His name is inscribed on a headstone in Longwood Cemetery, see page 379. Source: WS1060. Headstone inscription

Thomas Donnelly, Longwood was a Volunteer in the Longwood Company of Irish Volunteers in 1920. See also page 43. Source: WS1060.

Michael Fagan, Longwood, Co. Meath was involved in an attack on Lismullen R.I.C. Barracks at Halloween 1919, see page 37.
Source: Politics and War in Meath 1913-23 by Oliver Coogan, page 121.

Moss Fagan, Longwood, Co. Meath was a Volunteer in the Longwood Company of Irish Volunteers In 1919 and 1920. See also page 43. Source: WS1060.

Laurence (Larry) Giles, Brock, Longwood, Co. Meath was a Volunteer in the Longwood I.R.A. Company in 1919 and 1920. In September 1920 he was involved in the attack on the heavily fortified Trim R.I.C. Barracks, see the story on page 40. See also page 43. His name is inscribed on a headstone in Longwood Cemetery, see page 379. Sources: WS1060. WS0901. WS0858. Headstone Inscription.

Patrick (Pat) Giles, Brock, Longwood was born about 1899 or 1900. He was a member of the I.R.B. He was also a Volunteer in the Longwood I.R.A. Company in 1919. He was a Volunteer in the Trim I.R.A. Company in July 1920. In September 1920 he was involved in the attack on the heavily fortified Trim R.I.C. Barracks, see the story on page 40. See also page 43. He was linked to the Trim attack and as a wanted man he had to go "on the run". He was eventually arrested and served one year in jail in Perth, Scotland. He later progressed to company Commanding Officer of the Trim I.R.A. Company. In 1921 he was arrested and imprisoned in Mountjoy, Dublin for offences under the Restoration of Order in Ireland Regulations (ROIR) and for being in possession of ammunition. In 1922 he took the Pro-Treaty side. He served in the Free State Army and achieved the rank of Captain. In 1934 he was elected to Meath County Council. In 1937 he was elected a Fine Gael TD and he moved to a farm in Drumlargan near Summerhill. He held his seat untill 1960. Deputy Captain Patrick Giles TD died on 6th March 1965 aged 66 years and was buried in Coole Churchyard Cemetery, Garadice, see page 376.
Sources: WS1060. WS0901. WS0858. WS0857. MM9.1.1/KM79-TY9. MM9.1.1/KMQR-5GL. http://en.wikipedia.org/wiki/Patrick_Giles Headstone inscription.

John Grogan, Longwood, Co. Meath was a Volunteer in the Longwood I.R.A. Company in 1920. See also page 43. Source: WS1060.

Peter Grogan, Longwood, Co. Meath was a Volunteer in the Longwood I.R.A. Company in 1920. See also page 43. Source: WS1060.

P. Heavy, Longwood was a Volunteer in the Longwood I.R.A. Company in 1920. See also page 43. Source: WS1060.

C. McEvoy, Longwood, Co. Meath was a Volunteer in the Longwood I.R.A. Company in 1919 and 1920. See also page 43. Source: WS1060.

Michael McEvoy, Longwood, Co. Meath was a Volunteer in the Longwood I.R.A. Company in 1920. See also page 43. His name is engraved on a headstone in Longwood Cemetery, see page 380. Sources: WS1060. Headstone Inscription.

William Murray, Longwood, Co. Meath was a Volunteer in the Longwood I.R.A. Company in 1920. See also page 43. Source: WS1060

Martry Company:

The Martry Company of Irish Volunteers was in existence in 1914. See the Volunteers assembled outside "The Hall" in Oristown, Kells, Co. Meath on their way to the annual St. Kieran's Well Festival in Carnaross on 4th September 1914 on the next page. The original photograph was kindly provided by Sib Rooney, the proud owner and resident of "The Hall." In January 1919 the Irish Volunteers became the I.R.A. In July 1921 the Martry Company had a strength of 24 men. In July 1922 there were no Volunteers so the Martry Company ceased to exist. Source: RO 488. Photography kindly provided by Sib. Rooney.

William Battersby, Charlesfort, Kells, Co. Meath was a Volunteer in the Martry Company of Irish Volunteers in July 1921. He died on 1st February 1976 aged 73 years and was buried in Cortown Cemetery, see page 298. Source: RO 488. Headstone Inscription.

John (Johnny) Bennett, Ardbraccan, Navan, Co. Meath while working in Tullamore learning his trade as a stonecutter from 1917 to 1919 he joined the Irish Volunteers in Tullamore. On his return in 1919 he joined the Bohermeen I.R.A. Company until 1920 when he moved to Belfast to work for six months. Later he transferred to Martry Company where he became the company 2nd Lieutenant. In January 1921 he was Involved in the transportation of explosives from Martry to Moynalty. Source: WS1650. RO 488. Oliver Coogan P114

Patrick Coffey Ardbraccan, Navan, Co. Meath was a Volunteer in the Martry I.R.A. Company in July 1921. In 1925 he was a member of the Martry G.A.A. Football Team who won the Feis Cup that year. He died in the County Hospital Navan on 5th March 1946 aged 45 years. The funeral took place from Bohermeen Church to the new Cemetery, see page 318. Sources: RO 488. Royal and Loyal by Michael O'Brien page 93. The Meath Chronicle dated 9th March 1946 page 1. Headstone inscription.

Joseph (Joe) Coogan, Ardbraccan, Navan, Co. Meath was a Volunteer in the Martry Company of Irish Volunteers in July 1921. He was a brother of below Michael. In 1925 Joe was a member of the Martry G.A.A. Football Team who won the Feis Cup that year. He died on 25th October 1954 and was buried in Donaghpatrick Cemetery, see page 325 Sources: RO 488 & Royal and Loyal by Michael O'Brien page 93. Headstone Inscription.

Michael Coogan, Ardbraccan, Navan, Co. Meath was a Volunteer in the Martry I.R.A. Company in July 1921. He was a brother of above Joe. He later lived beside Bachelors Lodge on main Navan/Kells road. He died on 19th October 1952 and was buried in Donaghpatrick Cemetery, see page 325. Source: RO 488. Headstone Inscription. Personal interview with his Grandson, Stephen Ball, Ardbraccan in June 2015

William (Willie) Coogan, see Bohermeen Company.

John Farnan, Ardbraccan, Navan, Co. Meath was a Volunteer in the Martry Company of Irish Volunteers in July 1921. His name is engraved on a headstone in Bohermeen, see page 319. Source: RO 488. Headstone Inscription. Photo kindly provided by Stephen Ball, Bohermeen.

William Farnan, Ardbraccan, Navan, Co. Meath was a Volunteer in the Martry Company of Irish Volunteers in July 1921. In 1925 he was a member of the Martry G.A.A. Football Team who won the Feis Cup that year. He died on 5th November 1976 aged 77 years and was buried in Bohermeen Cemetery, see page 319. Sources: RO 488. Royal and Loyal by Michael O'Brien page 93. Headstone Inscription. Photo kindly provided by Stephen Ball, Bohermeen.

Patrick Kane, Balreask, Navan, Co. Meath was born in Balreask about 1896. In 1920 he was arrested and imprisoned in Mountjoy, Dublin for offences under the Defence of the Realm Regulations (DRR) and on a charge of having a revolver. In July 1921 he was a Volunteer in the Martry Company of Irish Volunteers. He died before 1935. Sources: RO 488. MM9.1.1/KMQR-G5C. MM9.1.1/KM79-R92.

James Keary, Kilmessan, Navan, Co. Meath was a Volunteer in the Martry I.R.A. Company of Irish Volunteers in July 1921. In 1935 his address was given as Kilmessan. Source: RO 488.

Patrick Keary, Navan, Co. Meath was a Volunteer in the Martry I.R.A. Company in July 1921. Source: RO 488.

Patrick Kelly was a Volunteer in the Martry I.R.A. Company in July 1921. Source: RO 488.

James Martin, Horan's Cross, Oristown, Kells, Co. Meath was the Martry I.R.A. Company 1st Lieutenant in July 1921. Source: RO 488

John McLoughlin, was a Volunteer in the Martry I.R.A. Company in July 1921. In 1921 he gave his address as Tankardstown, Donaghpatrick, Navan. He was buried in Donaghpatrick Cemetery but there are no dates on the headstone, see page 326. Source: RO 488. Headstone Inscription.

James Mitchell, Tankardstown, Donaghpatrick, Navan, Co. Meath was a Volunteer in the Martry I.R.A. Company in July 1921. His name is engraved on a headstone in Martry Cemetery. I am not sure if it is the same James Mitchell. The inscription says that James Mitchell died on 3rd January 1967 aged 66 years, see page 303. Source: RO 488. Headstone Inscription.

John Mitchell, Phoenixtown, Navan, Co. Meath was involved in the transportation of explosives from Martry to Moynalty in January 1921. In July 1921 he was a Volunteer in the Martry I.R.A. Company. Sources: WS1650. RO 488

Patrick (Sonny) Mitchell, Tankardstown, Donaghpatrick, Navan, Co. Meath was a Volunteer in the Martry I.R.A. Company in July 1921. Source: RO 488.

Richard (Dick) Mitchell, Tankardstown, Donaghpatrick, Navan, Co. Meath was a Volunteer in the Martry I.R.A. Company in July 1921. Source: RO 488.
Joe Murtagh, Boyerstown, Navan, Co. Meath was involved in the transportation of explosives from Martry to Moynalty in January 1921. In July 1921 he was the Martry Company Commanding Officer. Sources: WS1650. RO 488
Sam Rennicks, Ardbraccan, Navan, Co. Meath was a Volunteer in the Martry I.R.A. Company in July 1921. In 1925 he was a member of the Martry G.A.A. Football Team who won the Feis Cup that year. Source: RO 488. Royal and Loyal by Michael O'Brien page 93.
Thomas Rennicks, Ardbraccan, Navan, Co. Meath was a Volunteer in the Martry I.R.A. Company in July 1921. He died on 16th October 1939 aged 72 years and was buried in St. Mary's Cemetery, Navan, see page 343. Source: RO 488. Headstone Inscription.

William Rennicks, Ardbraccan, Navan, Co. Meath was a Volunteer in the Martry I.R.A. Company in July 1921. Source: RO 488.

Joseph (Joe) Smith, Neilstown, Bohermeen, Navan, Co. Meath worked with Meath County Council. He was also a Volunteer in the Martry I.R.A. Company in July 1921. He was involved in the Local Defence Force. A keen G.A.A. footballer he held a Senior Championship medal and in 1925 he was a member of the Martry G.A.A. Football Team who won the Feis Cup. He died on Christmas eve 1958 aged 59 years and his funeral took place from Bohermeen Church to Cortown Cemetery on St. Stephens Day 1958, see his headstone on page 298.
Source: RO 488. Royal and Loyal by Michael O'Brien page 93. Headstone Inscription.

William Smith, Neilstown, Bohermeen, Navan, Co. Meath was a Volunteer in the Martry I.R.A. Company in July 1921. In 1925 he was a member of the Martry G.A.A. Football Team who won the Feis Cup that year. Sources: RO 488, Royal and Loyal by Michael O'Brien page 93

Meath Hill Company:

In early 1918 the Meath Hill Company of Irish Volunteers was formed. In January 1919 the Irish Volunteers became the I.R.A. In early 1919 the I.R.A. reorganised their structures and the Meath Hill Company became attached to the 4th Battalion, Meath Brigade. Source: WS1625. WS1650.

Peter Boland, Meath Hill, Co. Meath was a Volunteer in the Meath Hill I.R.A. Company in July 1921 and 1922. Source: RO 489. RO 528

Peter Carolan, Meath Hill, Co. Meath was a Volunteer in the Meath Hill I.R.A. Company in July 1921 and 1922. He died on 22nd March 1976 and was buried in Drumconrath Cemetery, see page 275. Source: RO 489. RO 528. Headstone Inscription.

James Carry, Cloughreea, Drumconrath, Co. Meath was a Volunteer in the Meath Hill I.R.A. Company in July 1921. Source: RO 489.

Thomas Cruise, Meath Hill, Co. Meath was a Volunteer in the Meath Hill I.R.A. Company in July 1921 and 1922. He died on 2nd January 1968 aged 78 years and was buried in Drumconrath Cemetery, see page 275.
Source: RO 489. RO 528. Headstone Inscription.

James (Jimmy) Daly, Meath Hill, Co. Meath was the Meath Hill Company Commanding Officer in July 1921. In 1922 he was the 2nd Lieutenant. He died on 25th July 1998 aged 94 years and was buried in Drumconrath Cemetery, see page 276. Source: RO 489. RO 528. Headstone Inscription.

Eugene Foster, Rooskey, Drumconrath, Co. Meath was a Volunteer in the Meath Hill I.R.A. Company in July 1921. He was the company Commanding Officer in 1922. He was also Battalion Vice Commanding Officer. In 1936 his address was given as U.S.A. Source: RO 489. RO 528.

Thomas Foster, Rooskey, Drumconrath, Co. Meath was a Volunteer in the Meath Hill I.R.A. Company in July 1921. In 1936 his address was given as U.S.A. Source: RO 489.

Patrick Lambe was the Meath Hill Company 1st Lieutenant in July 1921. Source: RO 489.

John McElroy, Meath Hill, Co. Meath was a Volunteer in the Meath Hill I.R.A. Company in July 1921. Source: RO 489.

Thomas McGrath, Carragh, Kingscourt, Co. Cavan was a Volunteer in the Meath Hill I.R.A. Company in July 1921. Source: RO 489.

John McKenna, Meath Hill, Co. Meath was a Volunteer in the Meath Hill I.R.A. Company in July 1921 and 1922. Source: RO 489. RO 528

William McKenna, Meath Hill, Co. Meath was a Volunteer in the Meath Hill I.R.A. Company in July 1921. He was the 1st Lieutenant in 1922. He died on 19th February 1978 and was buried in Drumconrath Cemetery, see page 277.
Source: RO 489. Headstone Inscription.

James Sheevan, Cloughrea, Kingscourt, Co. Cavan was a Volunteer in the Meath Hill I.R.A. Company in July 1921 and 1922. Source: RO 489. RO 528

Patrick Tierney, Meath Hill, Co. Meath was a Volunteer in the Meath Hill I.R.A. Company in July 1921 and 1922. Source: RO 489. RO 528

Moylagh Company:

The Moylagh Company was formed about September 1920. When I.R.A. structures were reorganised in April 1921 the Moylough Company became attached to the 2nd Battalion, 3rd Brigade, 1st Eastern Division. In July 1921 the Moylagh Company had a strength of 26 men. In July 1922 the strength of the company was eleven men. Sources: RO 489. WS1627. WS1659

Edward Brady, Belleek, Dromone, Oldcastle, Co. Meath was a Volunteer in the Moylagh I.R.A. Company in July 1921. In 1936 his address was given as U.S.A.
Source: RO 489.

John Brady, Belleek, Dromone, Oldcastle, Co. Meath was a Volunteer in the Moylagh I.R.A. Company in July 1921. In 1936 his address was given as U.S.A.
Source: RO 489.

Peter Brady, Herbertstown, Killallon, Co. Meath was a Volunteer in the Moylagh I.R.A. Company in July 1921. In 1936 his address was given as U.S.A. Source: RO 489.

Thomas Brady, Herbertstown, Killallon, Co. Meath was a Volunteer in the Moylagh I.R.A. Company in July 1921. He took the Pro-Treaty side and he joined the Free State Army. In 1936 his address was given as U.S.A. He owned a Pub in the Catskill Mountains in the state of New York.
Sources: RO 489. Personal interview with Malachy Hand, Moylagh on 25th June and 30th June 2015.

Bernard (Benny) Briody, Bellaney, Oldcastle, Co. Meath had a shop in Bellaney. He used to trade in the sale of eggs. He traded in the collector and sale of eggs. He was also a Volunteer in the Moylagh I.R.A. Company in July 1921. He died on 1st February 1958 aged 71 years and was buried in Moylagh Church Cemetery, see page 354. Sources: RO 489. Headstone Inscription. Personal interview with Malachy Hand, Moylagh on 30th June 2015. Personal interview with Malachy Hand, Moylagh on 30th June 2015.

John Briody, Corstown, Oldcastle, Co. Meath was a Volunteer in the Moylagh I.R.A. Company in July 1921 and July 1922. He died on 12th August 1952 and was buried in Moylagh Cemetery, see page 354. Source: RO 489. Photo kindly provided by his Granddaughter Ann Briody. Personal interview with Malachy Hand, Moylagh on 30th June 2015.

John Chatten, Loughcrew, Oldcastle, Co. Meath was a Volunteer in the Moylagh I.R.A. Company in July 1921. In 1936 he was a member of An Garda Síochána. Source: RO 489.

Richard Connell, Dromone, Oldcastle, Co. Meath was a Volunteer in the Moylagh I.R.A. Company in July 1921. In 1936 his address was given as U.S.A. and he died and was buried in U.S.A. Source: RO 489. Personal interview with Malachy Hand, Moylagh on 30th June 2015.

Owen Cooke, Glenaward and Annagh, Dromone, Oldcastle, Co. Meath was a brother of below Patrick. He described himself as a farmer. He was a Volunteer in the Moylagh I.R.A. Company in July 1921 and July 1922. He died on 16th March 1959 aged 56 years and was buried in Moylagh Church Cemetery, see page 355. Sources: RO 489. Headstone Inscription.

Patrick Cooke, Glenaward, Dromone, Oldcastle, Co. Meath was a brother of above Owen. He was the Moylagh I.R.A. Company Adjutant in July 1921 and July 1922. He died on 7th September1963 aged 71 years and was buried in Moylagh Church Cemetery, see page 355. Source: RO 489.

Patrick Coyle, Gortloney, Dromone, Oldcastle, Co. Meath was a Volunteer in the Moylagh I.R.A. Company in July 1921. In 1936 his address was given as Canada. Source: RO 489.

Patrick Coyle, Gortloney, Dromone, Oldcastle, Co. Meath was a Volunteer in the Moylagh I.R.A. Company in July 1921. After the Treaty he joined the Civic Police. In 1936 his address was given as Canada. Source: RO 489. Personal interview with Malachy Hand, Moylagh on 25th June 2015

Edward Fanning, Dromone, Oldcastle, Co. Meath was a Volunteer in the Moylagh I.R.A. Company in July 1921 and July 1922. In 1936 his address was given as Canada. Source: RO 489.

James Fanning, Loughbawn, Crossdrum, Dromone, Oldcastle, Co. Meath was a Volunteer in the Moylagh I.R.A. Company in July 1921 and July 1922. Source: RO 489. Personal interview with Malachy Hand, Moylough on 25th June 2015.

Peter Gilsenan, Gortloney, Dromone, Oldcastle, Co. Meath was a Volunteer in the Moylagh I.R.A. Company in July 1921 and July 1922. In 1936 his address was given as U.S.A. He had a large family of between 14 and 16 children. He did return from U.S.A. and he died on 5th June 1973. He was buried in Moylagh Cemetery, see page 355. Sources: RO 489. Headstone Inscription.

Terence Gilsenan, Gortloney, Dromone, Oldcastle, Co. Meath was a Volunteer in the Moylagh I.R.A. Company in July 1921. In 1936 his address was given as U.S.A. It is probable that he did not return from U.S.A. as there is no living memory of him in Moylagh. Sources: RO 489. Personal interview with Malachy Hand, Moylough on 25th June 2015.

John (Jack) Hand, Bellaney, Oldcastle, Co. Meath was elected to the Oldcastle Rural District Council in June 1920 as a Sinn Fein Councillor representing Oldcastle. He was the Moylagh I.R.A. Company 1st Lieutenant in July 1921. He died on 17th December 1978 aged 86 years and was buried in Moylagh Church Cemetery, see page 355. Source: RO 489. Military Service Pension Collection, file reference No. MD-49582. Headstone Inscription. Personal interview with his son Malachy Hand, Moylagh on 30th June 2015 and photo kindly proviced also by Malachy.

Thomas Hand, Loughbawn, Dromone, Oldcastle, Co. Meath was a Volunteer in the Moylagh I.R.A. Company in July 1921. He later became a Civic Guard before the establishment of An Garda Síochána. He was also a farmer and he had one of the few Trashing Mills in the area. Source: RO 489. Military Service Pension Collection, file reference No. MD-48506. Personal interview with his nephew Malachy Hand, Moylagh in 30th June 2015 and photo kindly proviced also by Malachy.

John Haughan, Herbertstown, Killallon, Co. Meath was a Volunteer in the Moylagh I.R.A. Company in July 1921. Source: RO 489.

Patrick Kileen, Galmoyestown, Dromone, Oldcastle, Co. Meath was involved in Athletic Running. He set the handicaps on the running. He was also a Volunteer in the Moylagh I.R.A. Company in July 1921 and July 1922. In 1936 his address was given as U.S.A. His name is engraved on a headstone in Moylagh Church Cemetery. It says that Patrick Kileen died on 11th July 1963, see page 356. Sources: RO 489. Headstone Inscription. Personal interview with Malachy Hand, Moylagh on 30th June

John Loughlin, Herbertstown, Killallon was a Volunteer in the Moylagh I.R.A. Company in July 1922. Source: RO 489.

Michael Markey, Balintogher, Moylagh, Co. Meath was a Volunteer in the Moylagh I.R.A. Company in July 1921 he. He died before 1936. Source: RO 489. Personal interview with Malachy Hand, Moylagh on 30th June

Michael Martin, Bellaney, Dromone, Oldcastle, Co. Meath was a Volunteer in the Moylagh I.R.A. Company in July 1921. In 1936 his address was given as Canada. Source: RO 489.

James McGrath, Annagh, Dromone, Oldcastle, Co. Meath was a Volunteer in the Moylagh I.R.A. Company in July 1921. He was a farmer and he died on the Hill of Annagh on 23rd November 1948, see page 356. Source: RO 489. Headstone Inscription. Personal interview with Malachy Hand, Moylagh on 30th June 2015.

John Milia was a Volunteer in the Moylagh I.R.A. Company in July 1921. He died before 1936. Source: RO 489.

Michael Moore, Ratheven, Mountnugent, Co. Cavan was a Volunteer in the Moylagh I.R.A. Company in July 1922. Source: RO 489.

Patrick Reilly, Belleek, Dromone, Oldcastle, Co. Meath was a Volunteer in the Moylagh I.R.A. Company in July 1921. In 1936 his address was given as U.S.A. His name is engraved on a headstone in Moylagh Church Cemetery. It says that Patrick Reilly died on 3rd December 1973, see page 357. Sources: RO 489. Headstone Inscription.

Pádraig Mac Gabhann (Patrick Smith), Belleek, Dromone, Oldcastle, Co. Meath was the Moylagh Company Commanding Officer in July 1921 and July 1922. He died on 23rd November 1972 aged 83 years and was buried in Moylagh Cemetery, see page 357. Photo kindly provided by his Daughter Mairead. Source: RO 489. Headstone Inscription. Personal interview with Malachy Hand, Moylagh on 30th June

Thomas Smith, Gortloney, Dromone, Oldcastle, Co. Meath was a Volunteer in the Moylagh I.R.A. Company in July 1921 and July 1922. In 1936 his address was given as Canada. Source: RO 489.

Moynalty Company:

A company of National Volunteers was formed in Moynalty in the summer of 1914

and they had a strength of 38 men. The company drill Instructors were two ex-British soldiers named Garrigan and O'Reilly. The National Volunteers followed John Redmond's call and joined the Irish Regiment in the British Army and went to fight in World War One. Some of the Moynalty Volunteers did not agree with the move and left the National Volunteers. In 1916 they formed their own version of Volunteers but they had not made contact with the Irish Volunteers General Head Quarters (G.H.Q.) and they did not know anything about the Easter Rising. In 1917 the Moynalty Company of National Volunteers ceased to exist. The remaining few Volunteers in the area transferred to Irish Volunteers with assistance from Pádraig DeBurca of Kells, see Carnaross Company. The strength of the Moynalty Irish Volunteers Company was less than eighteen men at the time. In September 1917 a fair that was planned to be held in Mullagh was stopped by the Moynalty Company of Irish Volunteers, see page 34. In 1918 the Moynalty Irish Volunteers company had a strength of 25 or 26 men. Around October 1918 a flu epidemic crippled the country. Shops in Moynalty closed for a whole month. In January 1919 the Irish Volunteers became the I.R.A. They reorganised their structures and the Moynalty I.R.A. Company became attached to the 4th Battalion, Meath Brigade, I.R.A. In 1919 the Moynalty I.R.A. Company was involved in an attack and destruction of Moynalty Courthouse. In autumn 1919 they seized about 90 legally held privately owned guns in the area. In 1920 the company was involved in an ambush of Black and Tans at Salford, Moynalty and the burning of Moynalty R.I.C. Barracks. They blocked roads with felled trees, they destroyed Moynalty and Carlanstown bridges and they collected fines from people who helped enemy forces repair bridges and roads. On 23rd May 1920 the Drumconrath R.I.C. Barracks was burnt down by I.R.A. Volunteers from Moynalty and Newcastle to ensure the R.I.C. did not return. In the summer of 1920 a Sinn Fein court was set up in Moynalty. On the 11th June 1921 the whole Moynalty I.R.A. Company were involved in an ambush of Black and Tans at Maudlin Bridge, Kells. One Black and Tan was wounded and subsequently died.

In July 1921 the Moynalty I.R.A. Company had a strength of 27 men. They were involved in the destruction of Carlanstown Bridge on more than one occasion. In July 1922 the strength of the company was seventeen men. They were involved in the arrest of men in the Six Counties of the North and taking them prisoners. They were involved in an attack on Baileboro Barracks and an ambush of Free State Forces at Donore, Moynalty. Sources: WS1625. WS1715. RO 489. WS1650.

Michael Cahill was a native of Moynalty. In April 1920 he was appointed the Adjutant of the 4th Battalion (Kells), Meath Brigade, I.R.A. In March 1921 he was appointed I.R.A. Battalion Commanding Officer, 1st Battalion, 3rd Brigade, 1st Eastern Division. In April 1921 he was appointed I.R.A. Battalion Adjutant of the 1st Battalion, 3rd Brigade, 1st Eastern Division. He was a wanted man and by the end of June 1921 he was "on the run" and camped out in the open on Mullagh Hill with about 30 other mainly Battalion and Brigade Officers attached to the 3rd Brigade. They formed and became involved in an I.R.A. Active Service Unit (A.S.U.). In 1922 he joined An Garda Síochána. He was in charge of Ballinasloe Garda Station for fourteen years. He later served in Monaghan Town, in Newtownforbes, Co. Longford and at Carnew, Co. Wicklow. In 1936 his address was given as Garda Barracks, Ballinasloe. Garda Sergeant Michael Cahill died on 19th August 1953. The funeral took place from Moynalty Church to the family burial plot.
Sources: WS1715. WS1650. WS1060. WS1625. RO 484. RO 498. The Meath Chronicle dated 22nd August 1953 page 5. WS1627.

Bryan Carolan was a Volunteer in the Moynalty I.R.A. Company in July 1922.
Source RO 489.

Terence Carolan, Carlanstown, Kells, Co. Meath was a Volunteer in the Moynalty I.R.A. Company in July 1921 and July 1922.
Source RO 489. Military Service Pension Collection, file reference No. 34-SP-40533

Francis (Frank) Clarke, Donover, Moynalty, Kells, Co. Meath was the Moynalty I.R.A. Company 1st Lieutenant in July 1921. In January of that year he was involved in the rescue of arms and explosives from the R.I.C. in Moynalty. In May 1921 he was involved on a raid on Moynalty Post Office to seize telephone equipment. Source RO 489. WS1650.

Patrick Clarke, Donover, Moynalty, Kells, Co. Meath was a Moynalty I.R.A. Company Officer in July 1921 and July 1922. Source RO 489.

James Curran, Moynalty, Kells, Co. Meath was a Volunteer in the Moynalty I.R.A. Company in 1921. He was involved in the rescue of arms and explosives from the R.I.C. in Moynalty in January 1921. In February 1921 he was arrested and interned until December 1921. He continued as a Volunteer in the Moynalty I.R.A. Company. Sources: WS1625. WS1650. RO 489.

Patrick Curran, Moynalty, Kells, Co. Meath was a Volunteer in the Moynalty I.R.A. Company in July 1921. Source: RO 489.

Philip Daly, Moynalty, Kells, Co. Meath was a Volunteer in the Moynalty I.R.A. Company in July 1922. His name is engraved on a headstone in Moynalty Cemetery, see page 304. Sources: RO 489. Headstone Inscription.

William Daly, Moynalty, Kells, Co. Meath was a Volunteer in the Moynalty I.R.A. Company in July 1922. Source: RO 489.

Peter Fox, Harstown, Clonmellon, Co. Westmeath was a Volunteer in the Moynalty I.R.A. Company in July 1921 and July 1922. Source: RO 489.

? Garrigan was an ex-British Army man. In 1914 he was the Moynalty Company Commanding Officer, National Volunteers. Source: WS1625.

Edward (Ned) Govern, Reillystown, Moynalty, Kells, Co. Meath was a member of the Moynalty Irish National Volunteers in 1914. In March 1917 when the company became Irish Volunteers he was appointed Moynalty Company Adjutant. In January 1921 he was involved in the transportation of explosives from Martry to Moynalty. In that same month he was involved in the rescue of arms and explosives which had been seized by the R.I.C. in Moynalty. For a period in 1921 he was the Moynalty I.R.A. Company Quartermaster. In July 1922 he was the company Commanding Officer. Sources: WS1625. RO 489. WS1650.

James Govern, Donore, Moynalty, Kells, Co. Meath was a Moynalty I.R.A. Company Officer In July 1922. Source: RO 489.

Michael Govern was born in Reillystown, Moynalty, Kells, Co. Meath in 1892. In 1914 he was a Volunteer in the Moynalty Company of National Volunteers. He was a founder member of the Moynalty Irish Volunteers in 1917. In March 1917 when the company became Irish Volunteers he was appointed Moynalty Company Quartermaster. In 1920 he was appointed Battalion Quartermaster, 4th Battalion, Meath Brigade, I.R.A. In April 1920 he was Involved in the burning of Moynalty and Drumconrath R.I.C. Barracks and the destruction of Moynalty Courthouse. In summer 1920 he was appointed one of three Parish Justices for the area in the new Sinn Fein court in Moynalty. In January 1921 he was involved in the transportation of explosives from Martry to Moynalty. In that same month he was involved in the rescue of arms and explosives which had been seized by the R.I.C. in Moynalty. In March 1921 he was appointed I.R.A. Battalion Quartermaster, 1st Battalion, 3rd Brigade, 1st Eastern Division. Also in March 1921 he became a member of the I.R.B. He was a wanted man and by the end of June 1921 he was "on the run" and camped out in the open on Mullagh Hill with about 30 other mainly Battalion and Brigade Officers attached to the 3rd Brigade. They formed and became involved in an I.R.A. Active Service Unit (A.S.U.). In October 1921 he was the I.R.A. 4th Battalion (Kells) Quartermaster. In 1923 he was arrested by Pro-Treaty I.R.A. and interned in Mountjoy, Dublin. He later joined the Free State Army. He later lived in Clooney, Moynalty. He died at Our Lady's Hospital Navan on 16th February 1974 aged 82 years and was buried in Moynalty New Cemetery.

Sources: WS1625. WS01060. WS1650. RO 489. MM9.1.1/KM78-4YZ. WS1627. WS1715. Irish Press dated 18th February 1974, page 2. Headstone Inscription.

Peter Govern, Moynalty, Kells, Co. Meath was a Volunteer in the Moynalty I.R.A. Company in July 1921 and July 1922.
Source: RO 489. Military Service Pension Collection, file reference No MD-20251

Thomas Govern, Donore, Moynalty, Kells, Co. Meath was a native of Moynalty. He was interned in the Curragh in 1920 by the British Army. In January 1921 he was a Volunteer in the Moynalty I.R.A. Company. In February 1921 he was arrested and interned until December 1921. In July 1921 he was the I.R.A. Battalion Quartermaster but he resigned from that post after three months. The role of Battalion Quartermaster was taken over by Michael Govern. Thomas Govern died on 29th December 1971 aged 73 years and his funeral took place from St. Mary's Church Moynalty to the adjoining Cemetery.
Sources: WS1650. RO 489. The Meath Chronicle dated 8th January 1972, page 4. Headstone Inscription.

Thomas King, Ballincleva, Moynalty, Kells, Co. Meath was the Moynalty I.R.A. Company Commanding Officer in July 1921. In January 1921 he was involved in the transportation of explosives from Martry to Moynalty. Sources: WS1650. RO 489.

Edward Lynch, Kilbeg, Kells, Co. Meath was a Volunteer in the Moynalty I.R.A. Company in July 1921 and July 1922. Source: RO 489.

Michael McMahon, Shancannon, Moynalty, Kells, Co. Meath was a Volunteer in the Moynalty I.R.A. Company in July 1921. In 1936 his address was given as London, England. Source: RO 489.

Patrick McMahon was a Volunteer in the Moynalty Company of Irish Volunteers in July 1922. Source: RO 489.

Peter McMahon was the Moynalty I.R.A. Company 2nd Lieutenant In July 1921. He died before 1936. Source: RO 498

Thomas Morris, Castlemartin, Navan, Co. Meath was a Volunteer in the Moynalty I.R.A. Company in July 1921 and July 1922. In January 1921 he was involved in ambush of an R.I.C. patrol at Mullagh Lake. Source: WS1650.

James Mulvany was a Volunteer in the Moynalty I.R.A. Company In July 1922.
Source: RO 489.

William O'Brien was a Volunteer in the Moynalty I.R.A. Company in July 1921 and July 1922. In 1936 his address was given as U.S.A. Source: RO 489.

Eugene O'Reilly, Feagh, Moynalty, Co. Meath was the Moynalty National Volunteers company Vice Commanding Officer in 1914. He joined the British Army and he fought in the First World War. He died of the flu on 8th November 1918 when an epidemic spread across Europe killing thousands of people. The war ended three days later. He was buried in Moynalty Cemetery but I did not find his grave. Sources: WS1625. Faithful to Ireland by Tony Brady page 27.

Michael (Mick) O'Reilly, Kilbeg, Kells, Co. Meath was a member of the Moynalty Irish National Volunteers in 1914. In March 1917 when the company became Irish Volunteers he was appointed Moynalty Company 1st Lieutenant. In January 1921 he was still the company 1st Lieutenant. He was a brother of below Patrick. Mick died before 1957. Source: WS1625. WS1650.

Patrick O'Reilly was born in 1895. He was a brother of above Michael (Mick). Patrick was a member of the Moynalty National Volunteers in 1914. In March 1917 when the company became Irish Volunteers he was appointed the Moynalty Company Commanding Officer and he held that role through to 1921. In August 1920 he was Involved in an armed raid on the Northern Bank in Kells to seize two revolvers from the Bank. In September 1920 he attended the meeting in Carnaross which seen charges of mutiny being made, see the story on page 40. On 30th September 1920 he got married. In the 1st week of December 1920 he was involved in the blowing up of Moynalty Bridge. On 29th January 1921 he was involved in an ambush of an R.I.C. patrol at Mullagh Lake and he was involved in the rescue of arms and explosives which were seized by the R.I.C. in Moynalty. He was the Vice Commanding Officer in an I.R.A. A.S.U. in early 1921.
In April 1921 he was appointed Battalion Vice Commanding Officer of the 1st Battalion, 3rd Brigade, 1st Eastern Division, I.R.A. In May 1921 he was involved in a raid on Moynalty Post Office to seize telephone equipment. He is survived by his daughter Mrs. Farrelly of Mahonstown. Source: WS1625. WS1627. WS1650.

Edward (Ned) Reilly, Kilbeg, Kells, Co. Meath was involved in the rescue of arms and explosives which were seized by the R.I.C. in Moynalty in January 1921. In July 1921 he continued as a Volunteer in the Moynalty I.R.A. Company.
Source: WS1625. WS1650.

John Reilly, Kilbeg, Kells, Co. Meath was a Volunteer in the Moynalty I.R.A. Company in January 1921. In February 1921 he was arrested and interned until December 1921. Sources: WS1650. RO 489.

Michael Reilly, Kilbeg, Kells, Co. Meath was a Moynalty I.R.A. Company Commanding Officer in July 1921. In January 1921 he was involved in the transportation of explosives from Martry to Moynalty. Sources: WS1650. RO 489.

Michael (Senior) Reilly, Reillystown, Moynalty, Kells, Co. Meath was a Moynalty Company Adjutant In July 1921 and July 1922. In 1936 his address was given as U.S.A. Source: RO 489

Patrick Reilly, Bellair, Moynalty, Kells, Co. Meath was a Volunteer in the Moynalty I.R.A. Company in July 1921. Source: RO 489.

Thomas (Tom) Russell was a Volunteer in the Moynalty I.R.A. Company in January 1921. In February 1921 he was arrested and interned until December 1921. Sources: WS1650. RO 489

John Sheridan, Donore, Moynalty, Co. Meath was a Volunteer in the Moynalty I.R.A. Company of Irish Volunteers in July 1921 and July 1922. Source: WS1625.

Patrick Sheridan, Donore, Moynalty, Kells, Co. Meath was a Volunteer in the Moynalty I.R.A. Company in July 1921. In January 1921 he was involved in the transportation of explosives from Martry to Moynalty. In that same month he was involved in the rescue of arms and explosives from the R.I.C. in Moynalty. Sources: WS1650. RO 489.

Peter Smith, Rathgillan, Nobber, Co. Meath was a Volunteer in the Moynalty I.R.A. Company in July 1921. Source RO 489.

Thomas Smith, Ballincleva, Moynalty, Kells, Co. Meath was a Volunteer in the Moynalty I.R.A. Company in July 1921. In January 1921 he was involved in the transportation of explosives from Martry to Moynalty. Sources: WS1650 RO 489.

Navan Company: In July 1916 in an effort to reorganise after the failed Easter

Rising a small number of Irish Volunteers from Navan, Drumbaragh, Delvin and Athboy got together for a meeting in Larry Clarke's house at No. 13 Brews Hill Navan. This house became a main meeting place over the next few years. In 1917 the Navan Irish Volunteers company had a strength of twenty men. In January 1919 the Irish Volunteers became the I.R.A. In June 1919 the Navan I.R.A. Company had a strength of 30 men and was attached to the 6th Battalion, Meath Brigade. In November 1919 Volunteers from the Navan I.R.A. Battalion area attacked Lismullen R.I.C. Barracks, see the story on page 37. On 10th June 1920 one hundred additional British Troops were drafted into Navan. They were known as the 1st Battalion Cameronians. Old and sick people had to be moved from part of the Navan Workhouse to make room for them. This brings the overall British Troops in Navan up to four hundred and fifty men. Local girls were warned not to associate with them but according to *Dunderry A Folk History* at least one girl suffered hair chopping and was tarred and feathered for ignoring the warnings. In September 1920 the Navan I.R.A. Company played a fairly small but important role in the attack on the heavily fortified Trim R.I.C. Barracks, see the story on page 40. This was followed by a large scale round-up by military, R.I.C. Auxiliaries and Black and Tans on 5th October 1920 in which about twenty members of Navan I.R.A. Company and Battalion were arrested. These raids continued into the following year. The Navan I.R.A. Company strength now was twenty men. In February 1921 Mr. Hodgett, the Postmaster in Navan, was

abducted, executed and his body was thrown in the river Boyne, see the story on page 75. Also in February 1921 all of Navan I.R.A. Company and Battalion Officers were involved in the questioning and execution of a stranger in Navan suspected of being a spy, see the story on page 77. In April 1921 Navan Workhouse was occupied by a regiment of the British Army called the South Wales Borderers. In July 1921 the Navan I.R.A. Company had a strength of 30 men. In July 1922 the Navan Company had a strength of twenty men. For years the Commons area was in the Navan Company Area but when the Ardbraccan I.R.A. Company was formed around the end of 1920 it took in the area known as Commons and for that reason you will find I.R.A. Volunteers from Commons buried in Ardbraccan Cemetery.
Sources: WS0857. WS1060. WS1622. RO 488. WS1615. WS1624. WS1715. Dunderry A Folk History by Dunderry history Group and Johnny Keely

Joseph Bailey, Trimgate Street, Navan, Co. Meath was a Volunteer in the Navan I.R.A. Company in 1919. He was a native of Eskaroon, Dunderry, Navan. On 2nd November 1919 he was involved in an attack on Lismullen R.I.C. Barracks, see the story on page 37. In 1921 he was arrested and interned in Ballykinlar Internment Camp, Co. Down. He was held in Compound No 2 for a year.
Sources: RO 488. Prisoners of War by Liam O' Duibhir, page 314. Dunderry A Folk History by Dunderry History Group & Johnny Keely.

John Boland, Navan, Co. Meath was a Volunteer in the Navan I.R.A. Company in 1919. He was involved in an attack on Lismullen R.I.C. Barracks on 2nd November 1919, see the story on page 37. Source: Politics and War in Meath 1913-23 by Oliver Coogan, page 121. Dunderry A Folk History by Dunderry History Group & Johnny Keely.

William (Liam) Booth, 66 Vernon Avenue, Clontarf and a native of Mooretown, Hayes, Navan, Co. Meath. At some stage he also had an address at Proudstown, Navan. He was the Vice-Brigadier of the 2nd Brigade, 1st Eastern Division, I.R.A. in July 1921. He was appointed to that role in March or April 1921. On the 2nd July 1921, about two weeks before the Truce, he was involved in a failed attack on a troop train near Celbridge, see the story on page 51. In 1922 he took over control of the Navan Barracks from the British Forces. He joined the Free State Army and was promoted to 2nd in command of the Eastern Command. His address was given as McKee Barracks Dublin. He was later Military Governor of Arbour Hill. He retired in 1946 with the rank of Commandant, which he did not use. Captain William (Liam) Booth died on 23th August 1963 and he was buried in St. Fintan's Cemetery, Sutton. Source: WS0932. WS1622. WS1715. RO 484. The Meath Chronicle dated 31st August 1963 page 1. WS1696. Military Service Pension Collection, file reference No 24SP1392

Joseph Boyle, Flower Hill, Navan, Co. Meath was a painter in the town. In May 1920 he was involved in the arrest of a British Army sniper who was with a criminal gang who allegedly killed Mark Clinton, an I.R.A. Volunteer, see the story on page 70. In July 1920 he was a Volunteer in the Navan I.R.A. Company. At Christmas 1920 he was being held prisoner under the Restoration of Order Act.
Sources: WS1715. Politics and War in Meath 1913-23 by Oliver Coogan, page 149.

Peter Brady was a Volunteer in the Navan I.R.A. Company in July 1921. He died before 1935. Source: RO 488.

Robert (Bobby) Byrne was a barber in Navan and a Volunteer in the Navan Company of Irish Volunteers in 1918. He joined the Volunteers along with his buddy Tom Reilly. In 1919 and 1920 Bobby was a Volunteer in the Navan I.R.A. Company. He was buried in St. Mary's Cemetery, Navan, see page 336. Sources: Politics and War in Meath 1913-23 by Oliver Coogan, page 129 & 136. Headstone Inscription.

James Byrne, Dunmoe, Navan, Co. Meath was a member of the Navan I.R.A. Company in 1920. In September 1920 he was involved in the attack on the heavily fortified Trim R.I.C. Barracks, see the story on page 40. He was appointed the Navan I.R.A. Company 1st Lieutenant In October 1920. Sources: WS1622. RO 488. WS0858. WS1624.

Edward Cahill, No 38, St. Vincent's Terrace, Navan, Co. Meath. (St. Vincent's Terrace was the address stated in the prison record). Edward Cahill was born in Stillorgan, Dublin about 1899. In July 1922 he was a blacksmith and a Volunteer in the Navan I.R.A. Company. He became a member of a 30 man strong I.R.A. Active Service Unit who later became known as the Curraghtown A.S.U. On 5th July 1922 he was involved in the Battle of Curraghtown where he was arrested by the Free State Army, see the story on page 58. He was temporarily held in Trim and then interned in Dundalk, Co. Louth on 22nd July 1922. On 27th July 1922 he escaped from Dundalk Jail, see the story on page 59. On 28th July 1922 he was recaptured by Pro-Treaty I.R.A. and reinterned in Dundalk Jail. In 1935 his address was given as England. Sources: RO 488. MM9.1.1/KM3L-F2F. Louth County Archives http://www.louthcoco.ie/en/Services/Archives/Archive_Collections/ Dunderry A Folk History by Dunderry History Group & Johnny Keely.

Joseph Clarke, Gas House, Navan, Co. Meath was a Volunteer in the Navan I.R.A. Company in July 1922. Source: RO 488

Thomas Clarke, Navan, Co. Meath was a tailor. In July 1920 he was a Volunteer in the Navan I.R.A. Company. At Christmas 1920 he was being held prisoner under the Restoration of Order Act. Source: Politics and War in Meath 1913-23 by Oliver Coogan, page 149

Laurence (Larry) Clarke, No 13 Brews Hill, Navan was a Volunteer in the Navan Company of Irish Volunteers in July 1916 and July 1921. After the failed Rising he got involved in mustering up disappointed Volunteers and trying to get them to regroup and reorganise. Larry Clarke made his home available to the Volunteers for meetings and a resting place for Volunteers "on the run" Sources: WS0857. RO 488. Photo kindly provided by Mick O'Brien, Johnstown.

Patrick Clynch was a Volunteer in the Navan I.R.A. Company in 1920. In April 1920 he was being held prisoner in Mountjoy Jail when a hunger strike commenced. After public pressure he was released with about 70 other I.R.A. prisoners, see page 39. He continued as a Volunteer of the Navan I.R.A. Company in July 1921. In 1935 he was a member of An Garda Síochána and his address was given as Howth, Co. Dublin. His name is engraved on a headstone in the Church of the Nativity Cemetery in Kilmessan and it says that Patrick Clynch died on 12th March 1971, see page 285.

Source: RO 488. Dunderry A Folk History by Dunderry history Group and Johnny Keely. Headstone Inscription.

Christopher Cregan, Emmet Terrace, Navan, Co. Meath was born in Sandymount, Navan about 1900. In July 1921 and July 1922 he was a Volunteer in the Navan I.R.A. Company. In 1922 he was a labourer. He became a member of a 30 man strong I.R.A. Active Service Unit who later became known as the Curraghtown A.S.U. On 5th July 1922 he was involved in the Battle of Curraghtown where he was arrested by the Free State Army, see the story on page 58. He was temporarily held in Trim and then interned in Dundalk, Co. Louth on 22nd July 1922. On 27th July 1922 he escaped from Dundalk Jail, see the story on page 59. He was recaptured around 28th July 1922. Source: RO 488. MM9.1.1/KM3L-FKD. Louth County Archives http://www.louthcoco.ie/en/Services/Archives/Archive_Collections/ Dunderry A Folk History by Dunderry History Group & Johnny Keely.

Michael Cregan was a Volunteer in the Navan I.R.A. Company in July 1922. He died before 1935. Source: RO 488

Richard Doran, Kilcarne, Navan, Co. Meath was born in Kilcarne about 1901. In July 1921 and July 1922 he was a Volunteer in the Navan I.R.A. Company. In 1922 he was a labourer. He became a member of a 30 man strong I.R.A. Active Service Unit who later became known as the Curraghtown A.S.U. On 5th July 1922 he was involved in the Battle of Curraghtown where he was arrested by the Free State Army, see the story on page 58. He was temporarily held in Trim and then interned in Dundalk, Co. Louth on 22nd July 1922. On 27th July 1922 he escaped from Dundalk Jail, see the story on page 59. In 1935 his address was given as Bonmahon, Co. Waterford. Sources: RO 488. Louth County Archives http://www.louthcoco.ie/en/Services/Archives/Archive_Collections/ Dunderry A Folk History by Dunderry History Group & Johnny Keely.

Thomas Eamon Duffy was a Volunteer in the Navan I.R.A. Company. In October 1920 he replaced Ciaran O'Connell as I.R.A. Battalion Adjutant, 4th Battalion, 2nd Brigade. He also became the local Sinn Fein Court Registrar. In the summer of 1920 he set up a Sinn Fein court in Moynalty and Carnaross. In 1922 he was the I.R.A. Brigade Intelligence Officer, 4th Battalion, 2nd Brigade. He signed his name T.E. Duffy. In July 1922 he was arrested by the Free State Army and he was being held in Kells Barracks when he escaped along with four other prisoners. He died in October 1972 and was buried in St. Mary's Cemetery Navan, see page 337. Source: WS1622. RO 484. RO 488. WS1624. WS1625. Headstone Inscription. Meath Chronicle dated 22nd July 1922 page 1. Faithful to Ireland by Tony Brady, page 73. Photo kindly provided by Mick O'Brien, Johnstown.

Patrick Dunne was a Volunteer in the Navan I.R.A. Company in July 1921. In 1935 his address was given as Carlow Mental Home, Co Carlow. Source: RO 488.

Hugh Durr, Trimgate Street, Navan, Co. Meath was a Volunteer in the Navan I.R.A. Company in July 1921. In February 1921 he was a tailor in Trimgate Street, Navan. Also in February 1921 he was involved in the questioning of a stranger in Navan suspected of being a spy, see the story on page 77. Sources: RO 488. WS1622.

Joseph Egan was a Volunteer in the Navan I.R.A. Company in July 1922. He became a member of a 30 man strong I.R.A. Active Service Unit who later became known as the Curraghtown A.S.U. On 5th July 1922 he was involved in the Battle of Curraghtown where he was arrested by the Free State Army, see the story on page 58. He was temporarily held in Trim and then interned in Dundalk, Co. Louth on 22nd July 1922. In 1935 his address was given as U.S.A. Source: RO 488. Dunderry A Folk History by Dunderry History Group & Johnny Keely.

John Farrelly, Emmet Terrace, Navan, Co. Meath was born in New Lane, Navan, Co. Meath about 1902. In July 1922 he was a Volunteer in the Navan I.R.A. Company. His occupation was a sawyer (someone who saws wood). He became a member of a 30 man strong I.R.A. Active Service Unit who later became known as the Curraghtown A.S.U. On 5th July 1922 he was involved in the Battle of Curraghtown where he was arrested by the Free State Army, see the story on page 58. He was temporarily held in Trim and then interned in Dundalk, Co. Louth on 22nd July 1922. On 27th July 1922 he escaped from Dundalk Jail, see the story on page 59. Sources: RO 488. MM9.1.1/KM3L-FTG. Louth County Archives http://www.louthcoco.ie/en/Services/Archives/Archive_Collections/ Dunderry A Folk History by Dunderry History Group & Johnny Keely.

John Fay, c/o Clarke's, Commons Road, Navan, Co. Meath was a Volunteer in the Navan I.R.A. Company in July 1922. Source: RO 488

Andrew Finnerty, Trimgate Street, Navan, Co. Meath was a Volunteer in the Navan I.R.A. Company in July 1921. He was arrested and interned in Ballykinlar Internment Camp, Co Down. He was held in Compound No 2. Sources: RO 488. Prisoners of War by Liam O' Duibhir, page 315. Dunderry A Folk History by Dunderry history Group and Johnny Keely

Patrick (Pat) Fitzsimons, Trimgate St., Navan was a Volunteer in the Navan Company of Irish Volunteers in 1916. After the failed Rising he got involved in mustering up disappointed Volunteers and trying to get them to regroup and reorganise. On 2nd November 1919 he was involved in an attack on Lismullen R.I.C. Barracks, see the story on page 37. In October 1920 he took over as Battalion Commanding Officer from Pat Loughran who had been arrested. In February 1921 he was involved in the questioning of a stranger in Navan suspected of being a spy, see the story on page 77. On 28th March 1921 Pat Fitzsimons was succeeded by Patrick Kelly (see Johnstown Company). In 1924

Pat Fitzsimons was a member of the Navan Gaels G.A.A. Football Team. His name is engraved on a headstone in St. Mary's Cemetery, see page 337. Sources: WS0857. RO 488. Royal and Loyal by Michael O'Brien page 127. WS1622. Headstone inscription. Dunderry A Folk History by Dunderry History Group & Johnny Keely. Photo kindly provided by Mick O'Brien, Johnstown.

Tom Gavigan, Ludlow St., Navan, Co. Meath was born in Delvin about 1895. In July 1916 he was a Volunteer in the Navan Company of Irish Volunteers. After the failed Rising he got involved in trying to boldter up disappointed Volunteers in an effort to get them to regroup and reorganise. On 2nd November 1919 he was involved in an attack on Lismullen R.I.C. Barracks, see the story on page 37. He was arrested and imprisoned in Mountjoy, Dublin on a charge of discharging a loaded firearm. Sources: WS0857. MM9.1.1/KM79-GL4. Dunderry A Folk History by Dunderry History Group & Johnny Keely.

John Gaynor was a Volunteer in the Navan I.R.A. Company in July 1921 and July 1922. He became a member of a 30 man strong I.R.A. Active Service Unit who later became known as the Curraghtown A.S.U. On 5th July 1922 he was involved in the Battle of Curraghtown where he was arrested by the Free State Army, see the story on page 58. He was temporarily held in Trim and then interned in Dundalk, Co. Louth on 22nd July 1922. In 1935 his address was given as Dublin. Source: RO 488. Dunderry A Folk History by Dunderry History Group & Johnny Keely.

Michael Gaynor, St. Patrick's Terrace, Navan, Co. Meath was born in Navan about 1883. In July 1916 he was a Volunteer in the Navan Company of Irish Volunteers. After the failed Rising he got involved in trying to boost up disappointed Volunteers and in an effort to get them to regroup and reorganise. On 2nd November 1919 he was involved in an attack on Lismullen R.I.C. Barracks, see the story on page 37. In July 1921 he was a Volunteer in the Navan I.R.A. Company. He was arrested and interned in Ballykinlar Internment Camp, Co Down. He was held in Compound No 2. On his release he continued his role with the Navan I.R.A. Company. In 1922 he was a labourer. He became a member of a 30 man strong I.R.A. Active Service Unit who later became known as the Curraghtown A.S.U. On 5th July 1922 he was involved in the Battle of Curraghtown where he was arrested by the Free State Army, see the story on page 58. He was temporarily held in Trim and then interned in Dundalk, Co. Louth on 22nd July 1922. On 27th July 1922 he escaped from Dundalk Jail, see the story on page 59. On 28th July 1922 he was re-captured by Pro-Treaty I.R.A. and re-interned in Dundalk Jail. Sources: WS0857. Prisoners of War by Liam O' Duibhir, page 315. RO 488. MM9.1.1/KM3L-FKD. Louth County Archives http://www.louthcoco.ie/en/Services/Archives/Archive_Collections/ Dunderry A Folk History by Dunderry History Group & Johnny Keely.

John Giles, Newbridge, Navan, Co. Meath was a Volunteer in the Navan I.R.A. Company in July 1921. In the 1920s he was the Secretary of the Meath G.A.A. County Board. He died in November 1981 aged 89 years and was buried in St. Mary's Cemetery, see page 337. Sources: RO 488. Royal and Loyal by Mick O'Brien. Headstone Inscription.

Joseph Gleeson, Church View, Navan, Co. Meath was a Volunteer in the Navan I.R.A. Company in July 1921. He was arrested and interned in Ballykinlar Internment Camp, Co. Down. He was held in Compound No 2. In 1935 his address was given as Dublin. Source: RO 488 and Prisoners of War .E. Duffyby Liam O' Duibhir, page 315

James Gorman, St. Finian's Tce., Navan, Co. Meath was a Volunteer in the Navan I.R.A. Company in 1919. On 2nd November 1919 he was involved in an attack on Lismullen R.I.C. Barracks, see the story on page 37. He succeeded Mick Hilliard as the Navan I.R.A. Company Adjutant at the latter end of 1920 and he still held that post in July 1921. Sources: WS1622. RO 488. Dunderry A Folk History by Dunderry History Group & Johnny Keely.

Laurence Govern, Navan, Co. Meath was a Volunteer in the Navan I.R.A. Company in July 1921 and July 1922. He became a member of a 30 man strong I.R.A. Active Service Unit who later became known as the Curraghtown A.S.U. On 5th July 1922 he was involved in the Battle of Curraghtown where he was arrested by the Free State Army, see the story on page 58. He was temporarily held in Trim and then interned in Dundalk, Co. Louth on 22nd July 1922. On 27th July 1922 he escaped from Dundalk Jail, see the story on page 59. On 12th August 1922 he was re-captured at Wilkinstown, Navan. In 1935 his address was given as Moynalty, Kells. Source: RO 488. Dunderry A Folk History by Dunderry History Group & Johnny Keely.

Joseph Harte was a Volunteer in the Navan I.R.A. Company In July 1921. Source: RO 488

Peter Healy, Emmet Terrace, Navan, Co. Meath was a Volunteer in the Navan I.R.A. Company in July 1921. Source: RO 488

James Heany, Watergate Street, Navan, Co. Meath was a Volunteer in the Navan I.R.A. Company in July 1922. Source: RO 488

James Hilliard, Batterstown, Navan, Co. Meath was a brother of below Michael. He was a Volunteer in the Navan I.R.A. Company in 1919. On 2nd November 1919 he was involved in an attack on Lismullen R.I.C. Barracks, see the story on page 37. He was the I.R.A. Quartermaster of the 6th Battalion In 1920. He was the 4th Battalion Quartermaster, 2nd Brigade, 1st Eastern Division in April 1921 and 1922. He also gave his address as Clonmagadden, Navan, Co. Meath. He died in March 1973 and was buried in St. Mary's Cemetery, Navan, see page 337. Sources: WS1622. Headstone Inscription. Dunderry A Folk History by Dunderry History Group & Johnny Keely.

Michael (Mick) Hilliard, was born at 19 Flower Hill, Navan, in 1903. In September  1920 he was involved in blocking roads to Trim with fallen trees as part of the attack on the heavily fortified Trim R.I.C. Barracks, see the story on page 40. In October 1920 he was appointed Navan I.R.A. Company Adjutant. Soon afterwards he took over as company Commanding Officer from Patrick Stapleton and the role of Adjutant went to James Gorman. In February 1921 Mick was involved in the questioning of a stranger in Navan suspected of being a spy, see the story on page 77. In March / April 1921 Mick Hilliard was appointed I.R.A. 2nd Brigade Intelligence Officer. At the same time he continued as the Navan Company Commanding Officer. In July 1922 he was the I.R.A. Brigade Commanding Officer. He became a member of a 30 man strong I.R.A. Active Service Unit who later became known as the Curraghtown A.S.U. On 5th July 1922 he was involved in the Battle of Curraghtown where he was arrested by the Free State Army, see the story on page 58. He was temporarily held in Trim and then interned in Dundalk, Co. Louth on 22nd July 1922. His occupation was recorded in the prison records as a farmer's son. On 27th July 1922 he escaped from Dundalk Jail, see the story on page 59. On 28th July 1922 he was re-captured by Pro-Treaty I.R.A. and re-interned in Dundalk Jail. He escaped and went "on the run". On 8th January 1923 he was captured by the Free State Army in a shed at Peter McMahon's farm (see Moynalty Company). He faced a charge of being in possession of a revolver which carried the death sentence at the time. He had a lucky break when Captain Charles Conaty (see Stonefield Company) who was a former comrade of Mick Hilliard and was then a Free State Army Captain, said in his evidence to the court that the revolver might not have been in Hilliard's possession. Mick Hilliard survived to be elected to Dáil Éireann in 1943 as a Fianna Fail TD. He served as Minister for Posts and Telegraphs from 1959 to 1965. He was Minister for Defence from 1965 to 1969. He also lived at No 11 St. Enda's Villas, Navan, Co. Meath. He died in August 1982 aged 79 years and was buried in St. Mary's Cemetery, Navan, see page 338. Sources: WS1622. MM9.1.1/KM3L-FK5. Louth County Archives http://www.louthcoco.ie/en/Services/Archives/Archive_Collections/ WS1060. WS1696. Oireachtas Members Database. Retrieved 31 July 2012. ElectionsIreland.org. Retrieved 31 July 2012. Headstone Inscription. Dunderry A Folk History by Dunderry History Group & Johnny Keely. Faithful to Ireland by Tony Brady, pages 82 & 83. Photo from the Meath Chronicle.

Patrick Keating was a Volunteer in the Navan I.R.A. Company in 1919. On 2nd November 1919 he was involved in an attack on Lismullen R.I.C. Barracks, see the story on page 37. In May 1920 he was involved in the arrest of a British Army sniper who was part of a criminal gang who allegedly killed Mark Clinton, an I.R.A. Volunteer see the story on page 70. In September 1920 he was involved in the attack on the heavily fortified Trim R.I.C. Barracks, see the story on page 40. He was recorded as a member of the I.R.A. in July 1921 and July 1922. In 1935 his address was given as U.S.A. Source: WS1715. WS0858. RO 488. Dunderry A Folk History by Dunderry History Group & Johnny Keely.

Patrick (Bustie) Keelan, Railway Street, Navan, Co. Meath was a Volunteer in the Navan I.R.A. Company in July 1921. In 1924 he was Captain of the Navan Gaels G.A.A. Football Team. He was known as Patrick 'Bustie' Keelan. At the Annual Convention of the Navan and District Old I.R.A. Association in the CYMS Hall in Navan in February 1953 Patrick Keelan was appointed Treasurer. He died in November 1969 aged 74 and was buried in St. Mary's Cemetery, Navan, see page 339. Sources: RO 488, Royal and Loyal by Michael O'Brien page 127. The Meath Chronicle dated 7th March 1953, page 8. Headstone Inscription.

Thomas Killoran, Navan, Co. Meath was appointed I.R.A. Battalion Intelligence Officer, 4th Battalion, 2nd Brigade, 1st Eastern Division in April 1921. In 1921 and 1922 he continued in that role. In 1935 his address was given as Dublin. He died in June 1976 and was buried in St. Mary's Cemetery, Navan, see page 339. Sources: WS1622. RO 488. Headstone Inscription.

James Kinsella, Bridge Street, Navan, Co. Meath was a brother of below Thomas. He was a Volunteer in the Navan I.R.A. Company in July 1921. He died in December 1948 and was buried in St. Mary's Cemetery, Navan, see page 339. Sources: RO 488. Headstone Inscription.

Thomas Kinsella, Bridge Street, Navan, Co. Meath was a brother of above James. He was born in Celbridge, Co. Kildare about 1901. In 1919 he was a Volunteer in the Navan I.R.A. Company. On 2nd November 1919 he was involved in an attack on Lismullen R.I.C. Barracks, see the story on page 37. In July 1921 he was the Navan I.R.A. Company Quartermaster. In July 1922 he was a woodturner and he continued as a member of the Navan I.R.A. Company. He became a member of a 30 man strong I.R.A. Active Service Unit who later became known as the Curraghtown A.S.U. On 5th July 1922 he was involved in the Battle of Curraghtown where he was arrested by the Free State Army, see the story on page 58. He was temporarily held in Trim and then interned in Dundalk, Co. Louth on 22nd July 1922. On 27th July 1922 he escaped from Dundalk Jail, see the story on page 59. He died in October 1966 and was buried in St. Mary's Cemetery, Navan, see page 339. Source: RO 488. MM9.1.1/KM3L-FTR. Louth County Archives http://www.louthcoco.ie/en/Services/Archives/Archive_Collections/ Headstone Inscription. Dunderry A Folk History by Dunderry History Group & Johnny Keely.

John Lawlor, Dean Hill, Navan, Co. Meath was the Battalion Engineer in 1921. He died in Our Lady's Hospital Navan on 11th February 1959. His funeral took place from Yellow Furze Church to Painstown. Patrick Loughran conducted the funeral parade and M. Hyland was in charge of the firing party. Sources: RO 486. The Meath Chronicle 21st February 1959, page 1

John William Leer was a Volunteer in the Navan I.R.A. Company in July 1922. In July 1922 he was arrested by the Free State Army. He was being held in Kells Barracks when he escaped along with four other prisoners. He had previously been imprisoned in Mountjoy during a portion of the Anglo-Irish war. In 1935 his address was given as Dublin. His name is marked on a grave in St Mary's Cemetery, Navan but without dates, see page 339.

Source: RO 488. Headstone Inscription. Meath Chronicle dated 22nd July 1922 page 1. Faithful to Ireland by Tony Brady, page 73.

Arthur Levins was appointed the 6th Battalion (Navan) Vice Commanding Officer, Meath Brigade, I.R.A. around April 1920. In March 1921 he was the I.R.A. Division Organising Officer and Captain. Sources: WS1060. WS1696. WS1715.

Matthew Loughran, Navan, Co. Meath was a Volunteer in the Navan I.R.A. Company in 1919. He was involved in an attack on Lismullen R.I.C. Barracks on 2nd November 1919, see the story on page 37. Source: Politics and War in Meath 1913-23 by Oliver Coogan, page 121. Dunderry A Folk History by Dunderry History Group & Johnny Keely.

Patrick (Pat) Loughran, Market Square, Navan, Co. Meath was born in Shambo,

Navan in 1894. He went to school in Robinstown and in Navan. In 1911 he became an apprentice draper. He went to Tralee to learn his trade. While in Tralee he joined the local Irish Volunteers. From 1914 to 1916 he worked in Dublin where he joined the Dublin Irish Volunteers in 1915. He moved back to Navan and in July 1916 he was Volunteer in the Navan Company of Irish Volunteers. After the failed Rising he got involved in mustering up disappointed Volunteers and trying to get them to regroup and reorganise. In July 1917 he took over the role of Navan Company of Irish Volunteers Commanding Officer from Seamus

Patrick Loughran, photo kindly provided by Ethna Cantwell, Navan

Ryan. He also became a member of the I.R.B. at the end of 1918. On 2nd November 1919 he was involved in an attack on Lismullen R.I.C. Barracks, see the story on page 37. In April 1920 Pat was appointed I.R.A. Battalion Commanding Officer of the 6th Battalion, Meath Brigade. In May 1920 Patrick Loughran was proprietor of a drapery shop in Market Street, Navan called Loughran & Woods. During May - June period of 1920 he was involved in the arrest and imprisonment of a criminal gang who were operating in North Meath and who allegedly killed Mark Clinton, an I.R.A. Volunteer, see the story on page 70. He stood as a Sinn Fein Candidate in the 1920 Navan Urban Elections but failed to get elected. On 1st December 1920 he was arrested following an attack on Trim R.I.C. Barracks and Pat Fitzsimons took over the role as 6th Battalion (Navan) Commanding Officer. Pat Loughran was held in Navan for four days and then transferred to

Collinstown Aerodrome where he spent a fortnight and was later taken to Arbour Hill Barracks, Dublin, until mid-February. He was taken by boat to Belfast and on to Ballykinlar where he was interned and held in Compound No 2, Ballykinlar until after the Truce in July 1921. In November 1936 he attended a meeting to appoint a Brigade Committee to gather information related to qualifying Volunteers for the Military Service Pensions where he was appointed Secretary of the Committee. In 1957 his address was given as Cannon Row, Navan. He died on 1st January 1970 and was buried in St. Mary's Cemetery, Navan, see page 340. Sources: WS0857. WS1624. RO 488. Prisoners of War by Liam O' Duibhir, page 315. WS1060. WS1622. WS1624. WS1715. Headstone Inscription. Dunderry A Folk History by Dunderry History Group & Johnny Keely.

William Loughran, Brews Hill, Navan, Co. Meath was a Volunteer in the Navan I.R.A. Company in 1919. On 2nd November 1919 he was involved in an attack on Lismullen R.I.C. Barracks, see the story on page 37. He continued as a member of the Navan Company in July 1921.
Source: RO 488. Dunderry A Folk History by Dunderry History Group & Johnny Keely.

James Lynch, St. Finian's Terrace, Navan, Co. Meath was born in Navan, Co. Meath about 1901. In 1919 he was a Volunteer in the Navan I.R.A. Company. On 2nd November 1919 he was involved in an attack on Lismullen R.I.C. Barracks, see the story on page 37. In July 1921 and July 1922 he continued as a Volunteer in the Navan I.R.A. Company. In 1922 he was described as a Woodturner. He became a member of a 30 man strong I.R.A. Active Service Unit who later became known as the Curraghtown A.S.U. On 5th July 1922 he was involved in the Battle of Curraghtown where he was arrested by the Free State Army, see the story on page 58. He was temporarily held in Trim and then interned in Dundalk, Co. Louth on 22nd July 1922. The prison records state his address as St. Finian's Terrace, Navan. On 27th July 1922 he escaped from Dundalk Jail, see the story on page 59. He died in May 1966 and was buried in St. Mary's Cemetery, Navan, Co. Meath, see page 340. Sources: RO 488. MM9.1.1/KM3L-F2L. Louth County Archives http://www.louthcoco.ie/en/Services/Archives/Archive_Collections/ Headstone Inscription. Dunderry A Folk History by Dunderry History Group & Johnny Keely.

James Mackey was a Volunteer in the Navan I.R.A. Company in 1919. On 2nd November 1919 he was involved in an attack on Lismullen R.I.C. Barracks, see the story on page 37. He was involved in the arrest and imprisonment of a criminal gang who were operating in North Meath and who allegedly killed Mark Clinton, an I.R.A. Volunteer during May - June period of 1920, see the story on page 70. In July 1921 he continued as a Volunteer in the Navan I.R.A. Company. In 1935 his address was given as U.S.A.
Sources: RO 488 WS1060. Dunderry A Folk History by Dunderry History Group & Johnny Keely.

John Mahony, Emmet Terrace, Navan, Co. Meath was a Volunteer in the Navan I.R.A. Company in July 1922. He died on 6th January 1962 and was buried in St. Mary's Cemetery, Navan, see page 340. Source: RO 488. Headstone Inscription.

Richard McCabe, Brews Hill, Navan, Co. Meath was the Quartermaster of the 2nd Battalion, 2nd Brigade, 1st Eastern Division I.R.A. in July 1921. Source: RO 486

Hugh McGee, Kilcarne, Navan, Co. Meath was a Volunteer in the Navan I.R.A. Company in 1920. At the latter end of 1920 he became the Navan I.R.A. Company 1st Lieutenant. He continued to hold that post in July 1921 and July 1922. In February 1921 he was involved in the questioning of a stranger in Navan suspected of being a spy, see the story on page 77. In 1922 his address was given as Balreask, Navan. Sources: WS1622. RO 488.

McGovern, see Govern

Leo McKenna was the Navan I.R.A. Company Quartermaster in June 1919. Between October and December 1920 he was arrested in the follow up to the attack on Trim R.I.C. Barracks, which is described on page 40. He was interned in Ballykinlar Internment Camp, Co. Down. He was held in Compound No 2. In December 1920 he was appointed I.R.A. 6th Battalion (Navan) Quartermaster and he still held that position in July 1921. In 1935 he was serving with the Free State Army. Sources: WS1622. RO 488. Prisoners of War by Liam O' Duibhir, page 315. WS1060.

Michael McKeon, New Lane, Navan, Co. Meath was born in Navan about 1898. In 1919 he was a Volunteer in the Navan I.R.A. Company. On 2nd November 1919 he was involved in an attack on Lismullen R.I.C. Barracks, see the story on page 37. In 1920 he was arrested and imprisoned in Mountjoy, Dublin for offences under the Restoration of Order in Ireland Regulations (ROIR) and for being in possession of documents. During May - June period of 1920 he was involved in the arrest and imprisonment of a criminal gang who were operating in North Meath and who allegedly killed Mark Clinton, an I.R.A. Volunteer, see the story on page 70. In July 1921 he continued as a Volunteer in the Navan I.R.A. Company. He became a member of a 30 man strong I.R.A. Active Service Unit who later became known as the Curraghtown A.S.U. On 5th July 1922 he was involved in the Battle of Curraghtown where he was arrested by the Free State Army, see the story on page 58. He was temporarily held in Trim and then interned in Dundalk, Co. Louth on 22nd July 1922. On 27th July 1922 he escaped from Dundalk Jail, see the story on page 59. He was re-captured on 12th August at Wilkinstown, Navan. The prison records state his address as Flower Hill, Navan. Sources: RO 488. MM9.1.1/KMQR-5QH. MM9.1.1/KM79-T7R. MM9.1.1/KM3L-FY7. Louth County Archives http://www.louthcoco.ie/en/Services/Archives/Archive_Collections/ WS1060. Dunderry A Folk History by Dunderry History Group & Johnny Keely.

Laurence McKeon, New Lane, Navan, Co. Meath was a Volunteer in the Navan I.R.A. Company in July 1922. Source: RO 488

John McLoughlin was born in Navan, Co. Meath about 1902. In 1920 he was a Volunteer in the Navan I.R.A. Company. At the latter end of 1920 he was appointed the Navan I.R.A. Company 2nd Lieutenant. He held that role in July 1921 and July 1922. In February 1921 he was working in a pub in Navan when a stranger asked him questions about local I.R.A. The Navan I.R.A. Company shot the stranger that evening as a spy, see the story on page 77. In 1922 John was described as a shop assistant. He became a member of a 30 man strong I.R.A. Active Service Unit who later became known as the Curraghtown A.S.U. On 5th July 1922 he was involved in the Battle of Curraghtown where he was arrested by the Free State Army, see the story on page 58. He was temporarily held in Trim and then interned in Dundalk, Co. Louth on 22nd July 1922. On 27th July 1922 he escaped from Dundalk Jail, see the story on page 59. In 1935 his address was given as U.S.A. Sources: WS1622. RO 488. MM9.1.1/KM3L-FKH. Louth County Archives http://www.louthcoco.ie/en/Services/Archives/Archive_Collections/. Faithful to Ireland by Tony Brady, page 73.

Cornelius (Con) McMahon, Navan, Co. Meath was a native of Clooney, Co. Clare. He was an Insurance Salesman and after the Rising he travelled round Meath mustering up disappointed Volunteers and trying to get them to regroup under the guise that he was selling insurance. In 1918 he was a Lieutenant in the Navan Company of Irish Volunteers. In August 1918 he was in charge of an operation to derail a train near Navan, see the story on page 35. In April 1921 he was the Battalion Commanding Officer of the 6th Battalion, Meath Brigade. He took the Anti-Treaty side. He returned back to his native Co. Clare where he became Commanding officer of the 1st Battalion Mid Clare Brigade. He directed the activities of an A.S.U. and he was arrested in possession of arms. In February 1922 he was taken from his cell in Limerick Prison and executed by the Irish Free State Army. Source: WS0857. WS1624. Politics & War in Meath 1913-23 by Oliver Coogan. Page 322. http://freepages.genealogy.rootsweb.ancestry.com/~ccfgpw/ban-191.jpg

Peter McNellis was a draper's assistant. In July 1920 he was a Volunteer in the Navan I.R.A. Company. At Christmas 1920 he was being held prisoner under the Restoration of Order Act. Source: Politics and War in Meath 1913-23 by Oliver Coogan, page 149

Hugh Mulligan, St. Finian's Tce., Navan, Co. Meath was a Volunteer in the Navan I.R.A. Company in July 1921. Source: RO 488

Edward Mulvaney was born in Academy Street, Navan, Co. Meath about 1901. In July 1921 and July 1922 he was a Volunteer in the Navan I.R.A. Company. In 1922 he was a Slater. He became a member of a 30 man strong I.R.A. Active Service Unit who later became known as the Curraghtown A.S.U. On 5th July 1922 he was involved in the Battle of Curraghtown where he was arrested by the Free State Army, see the story on page 58. He was temporarily held in Trim and then interned in Dundalk, Co. Louth on 22nd July 1922. On 27th July 1922 he escaped from Dundalk Jail, see the story on page 59.

Sources: RO 488. MM9.1.1/KM3L-F29. Louth County Archives http://www.louthcoco.ie/en/Services/Archives/Archive_Collections/

Nicholas Naulty, Railway Street, Navan, Co. Meath was a Volunteer in the Navan I.R.A. Company in July 1921 and July 1922. He became a member of a 30 man strong I.R.A. Active Service Unit who later became known as the Curraghtown A.S.U. On 5th July 1922 he was involved in the Battle of Curraghtown where he was arrested by the Free State Army, see the story on page 58. He was temporarily held in Trim and then interned in Dundalk, Co. Louth on 22nd July 1922. He died in January 1960 and was buried in St. Mary's Cemetery, Navan, see page 341.

Source: RO 488. Headstone Inscription. Dunderry A Folk History by Dunderry History Group & Johnny Keely.

Patrick Nellis was a Volunteer in the Navan I.R.A. Company in July 1921. Source: RO 488

Patrick O'Brien, Watergate Street, Navan, Co. Meath was the Engineer of the 4th Battalion, 2nd Brigade, 1st Eastern Division, I.R.A. in July 1922. At the Annual Convention of the Navan and District Old I.R.A. Association in the CYMS Hall in Navan in February 1953 Patrick O'Brien was appointed Secretary.

Source: RO 488. The Meath Chronicle dated 7th March 1953, page 8

Ciaran O'Connell, Boyerstown, Navan, Co. Meath was born in Bawnmore, Co. Kilkenny, about 1894. In late 1918 or early 1919 he was appointed 6th Battalion (Navan) Adjutant. Between October and December 1920 he was arrested following the attack on Trim R.I.C. Barracks and his role was taken over by Tom Duffy. Ciaran O'Connell was imprisoned in Mountjoy, Dublin for offences under the Restoration of Order in Ireland Regulations (ROIR). In 1921 he was arrested again and imprisoned in Mountjoy, Dublin on a charge of having documents in his possession. (The type of documents was not specified in the record). In July 1922 he was arrested by the Free State Army and held in Kells Barracks where he escaped along with four other prisoners. In November 1936 he attended a meeting to appoint a Brigade Committee to gather information related to qualifying Volunteers for the Military Service Pensions and he was appointed to the Committee. He died in January 1963 and was buried in St. Mary's Cemetery

Navan. Source: RO 488. MM9.1.1/KM79-T9C. MM9.1.1/KMQR-5M5. The Meath Chronicle dated 9th January 1963, page 4. WS1622. WS1624. WS1715. Meath Chronicle dated 22nd July 1922 page 1. Faithful to Ireland by Tony Brady, page 73.

Eugene O'Gorman, Dunmoe, Navan, Co. Meath was born in Brews Hill, Navan about 1896. In July 1921 and July 1922 he was a Volunteer in the Navan I.R.A. Company. In 1921 he was arrested and imprisoned in Mountjoy, Dublin for offences under the Restoration of Order in Ireland Regulations (ROIR) and for being in possession of firearms. The prison record gives his address as Brews Hill, Navan. In 1922 he was a labourer. He became a member of a 30 man strong I.R.A. Active Service Unit who later became known as the Curraghtown A.S.U. On 5th July 1922 he was involved in the Battle of Curraghtown where he was arrested by the Free State Army, see the story on page 58. He was temporarily held in Trim and then interned in Dundalk, Co. Louth on 22nd July 1922. On 27th July 1922 he escaped from Dundalk Jail, see the story on page 59. On 28th July 1922 he was re-captured by Pro-Treaty I.R.A. and re-interned in Dundalk Jail. Sources: RO 488. MM9.1.1/KMQR-5GH. MM9.1.1/KM79-T12. MM9.1.1/KM3L-F2M. Louth County Archives http://www.louthcoco.ie/en/Services/Archives/Archive_Collections/

Richard O'Gorman was born in Brews Hill, Navan, Co. Meath about 1890. In July 1921 he was a Volunteer in the Navan I.R.A. Company but he was arrested and imprisoned in Mountjoy, Dublin for offences under the Restoration of Order in Ireland Regulations (ROIR) and for being in possession of firearms.
Source: RO 488 MM9.1.1/KMQR-5G8. MM9.1.1/KM79-T1V.

Donal O'Sullivan, was born in Caherdaniel, Co. Kerry about 1902. In July 1922 he lived in Navan, Co Meath. His occupation was recorded as teacher and I.R.A. Soldier. He was the Quartermaster of the 2nd Brigade, 1st Eastern Division. He became a member of a 30 man strong I.R.A. Active Service Unit who later became known as the Curraghtown A.S.U. On 5th July 1922 he was involved in the Battle of Curraghtown where he was arrested by the Free State Army, see the story on page 58. He was temporarily held in Trim and then interned in Dundalk, Co. Louth on 22nd July 1922. On 27th July 1922 he escaped from Dundalk Jail, see the story on page 59. On 28th July 1922 he was re-captured at Kilberry, Navan and re-interned in Dundalk Jail. In 1936 his address was given as U.S.A. Sources: RO 484. MM9.1.1/KM3L-FKT. Louth County Archives http://www.louthcoco.ie/en/Services/Archives/Archive_Collections/

James (Seamus) Perry, 11-12 Watergate Street, Navan, Co. Meath was a Water Inspector with Navan Urban Council. He was interned in the 1950's and when released he was not reinstated in his post as water inspector. The Meath Chronicle dated 21st February 1959, page 1 reports that the Meath Brigade Executive of the Federation of Old I.R.A. (1916-1921) would suggest that the organisation take the necessary steps to bring the case before an International Tribunal. He died on 19th April 1973 and was buried in St. Mary's Cemetery, Navan, see page 342.
Source: The Meath Chronicle dated 21st February 1959, page 1. Headstone Inscription.

Patrick Quilty, Bridge Street, Navan, Co. Meath was a Volunteer in the Navan I.R.A. Company in July 1921. He died on 26th November 1960 and was buried in St. Mary's Cemetery, Navan, see page 342. Sources: RO 488. Headstone Inscription.

Donal Quinn, see Rathkenny Company.

Thomas (Tom) Reilly, Market Square, Navan, Co. Meath became a Volunteer in the Navan I.R.A. Company in 1919 along with his buddy Bobby Byrne.
Source: Politics and War in Meath 1913-23 by Oliver Coogan

Seamus Ryan, a native of Tipperary was the 1st Commanding Officer in the Navan Company of Irish Volunteers in 1917. He was employed in a Navan furniture factory. In July 1917 he was succeeded by Patrick Loughran as Navan Company Commanding Officer, Irish Volunteers. Sources: WS1715. WS1624.

Peter Sheridan, Trimgate Street, Navan, Co. Meath was a Volunteer in the Navan I.R.A. Company in July 1921. Source: RO 488

Patrick Stapleton was born in Commons, Navan about 1892 and he became a Volunteer in the Commons Irish Volunteers. He was a Volunteer in the Navan I.R.A. Company in 1919. On 2nd November 1919 he was involved in an attack on Lismullen R.I.C. Barracks, see the story on page 37. In October 1920 he took over the role of Navan I.R.A. Company Commanding Officer from Joe Woods. Around the end of 1920 the Ardbraccan I.R.A. Company was formed and the Commons Area incorporated into the Ardbraccan Area. Patrick Stapleton transferred to the Ardbraccan I.R.A. Company also as the Commanding Officer there. He was replaced in the Navan I.R.A. Company by Michael Hilliard at the latter end of 1920. In April 1921 Patrick Stapleton was appointed I.R.A. Battalion Vice Commanding Officer, 4th Battalion, 2nd Brigade, 1st Eastern Division. In July 1921, just days before the Truce, he sent men from the Navan I.R.A. Company to a failed attack of a troop train at Celbridge. He was unable to attend the operation himself, see the story on page 51. In 1922 he described himself as a Farmer. He became a member of a 30 man strong I.R.A. Active Service Unit who later became known as the Curraghtown A.S.U. On 5th July 1922 he was involved in the Battle of Curraghtown where he was arrested by the Free State Army, see the story on page 58. He was temporarily held in Trim and then interned in Dundalk, Co. Louth on 22nd July 1922. On 27th July 1922 he escaped from Dundalk Jail, see the story on page 59. On 28th July 1922 he was re-captured by Pro-Treaty I.R.A. and re-interned in Dundalk Jail. In 1936 his address was given as Dunmoe Navan. He attended a meeting to appoint a Brigade Committee to gather information related to qualifying Volunteers for the Military Service Pensions where he was appointed to the Committee. He died on 18th November 1974 and was buried in Donaghmore Cemetery in Navan, see page 324. Sources: WS1622. MM9.1.1/KM3L-FKG.
http://www.louthcoco.ie/en/Services/Archives/Archive_Collections/ WS0932. Dunderry A Folk History by Dunderry History Group & Johnny Keely. Headstone Inscription.

Michael Sullivan was a Volunteer in the Navan I.R.A. Company in July 1921 and July 1922. In 1935 his address was given as Ardee, Co. Louth. Source: RO 488

William Sullivan was born in Sligo about 1904. In July 1922 he was a Volunteer in the Navan I.R.A. Company. He was employed as a sawyer (someone who saws wood). He became a member of a 30 man strong I.R.A. Active Service Unit who later became known as the Curraghtown A.S.U. On 5th July 1922 he was involved in the Battle of Curraghtown where he was arrested by the Free State Army, see the story on page 58. He was temporarily held in Trim and then interned in Dundalk, Co. Louth on 22nd July 1922. He was eighteen years of age. On 27th July 1922 he escaped from Dundalk Jail, see the story on page 59. On 28th July 1922 he was re-captured by Pro-Treaty I.R.A. and re-interned in Dundalk Jail. In 1935 his address was given as Ardee, Co. Louth. Sources: RO 488. MM9.1.1/KM3L-FKN. Louth County Archives http://www.louthcoco.ie/en/Services/Archives/Archive_Collections/ Dunderry A Folk History by Dunderry History Group & Johnny Keely.

Frank Swan, Balreask, Navan, Co. Meath was a Volunteer in the Navan I.R.A. Company in July 1921. Source: RO 488

Joseph Woods was born in Co. Louth. He was a drapers assistant and he lived at No 46, Trimgate Street, Navan. He was a Volunteer in the Navan Company of Irish

Joe Woods.

Volunteers in July 1916. After the failed Rising he got involved in mustering up disappointed Volunteers and trying to get them to regroup and reorganise. In June 1919 he was the Navan I.R.A. Company Commanding Officer. On 2nd November 1919 he was involved in an attack on Lismullen R.I.C. Barracks, see the story on page 37. Between October and December 1920 he was arrested following an attack on Trim R.I.C. Barracks and Patrick Stapleton took over the role as the company Commanding Officer. In 1921 Joseph Woods was arrested again and imprisoned in Mountjoy, Dublin on a charge of having documents in his possession. He died on 22nd October 1981 and was buried in St. Mary's Cemetery, Navan, see page 347.

Sources: RO 488. WS0857. WS1622. MM9.1.1/KMQR-5MP. Headstone Inscription. Dunderry A Folk History by Dunderry History Group & Johnny Keely.

Newcastle Company:

In early 1919 the I.R.A. reorganised their structures and the Newcastle Company became attached to the 4th Battalion, Meath Brigade. On 12th May 1920 the Mullagh R.I.C. Barracks was burnt down by I.R.A. Volunteers from Mullagh and Newcastle to ensure the R.I.C. did not return. On 23rd May 1920 the Drumconrath R.I.C. Barracks was also burnt down by Moynalty and Newcastle I.R.A. Volunteers. In 1921 the Newcastle Company was involved in an attack on British Forces at Mullagh Lake, an attempted ambush at Moynalty and an attack on Nobber R.I.C. Barracks. In July 1921 the Newcastle Company had a strength of 35 men. In July 1922 the company had a strength of four men. Sources: RO 489. WS1650.

Patrick Cahill, Diralagh, Moynalty, Co. Meath was a Volunteer in the Newcastle I.R.A. Company in July 1921. Source: RO 489

Stephen Cahill, Diralagh, Moynalty, Kells, Co. Meath was the Newcastle Company 1st Lieutenant in July 1921. Source: RO 489

Bernard Carolan, Drominiskin, Moynalty, Kells, Co. Meath was a Volunteer in the Newcastle I.R.A. Company in July 1921 and July 1922. Source: RO 489

Hugh Carolan was a Volunteer in the Newcastle I.R.A. Company in July 1921. In 1936 he was a member of An Garda Síochána and his address was given as Clara, Co. Offaly. Source: RO 489

Peter Clinton, Cluffa, Mullagh, Co. Cavan was a Volunteer in the Newcastle I.R.A. Company in July 1921. Source: RO 489

Eugene Daly, Diralagh, Mullagh, Co. Cavan was a Volunteer in the Newcastle I.R.A. Company in July 1921. Source: RO 489. Military Service Pension Collection, file reference No. MD-20257

Philip Daly, Diralagh, Mullagh, Co. Cavan was a Volunteer in the Newcastle I.R.A. Company in July 1921. Source: RO 489

James Ennis, Lustown, Batterstown, Navan, Co. Meath was a Brigade Transport Officer, 1st Brigade, 1st Eastern Division in July 1921. He died before 1936. Source: RO 479

John Gallagher was a Volunteer in the Newcastle I.R.A. Company in July 1921. In 1936 he was a member of An Garda Síochána. Source: RO 489. Military Service Pension Collection, file reference No. MD-5931

Patrick Gallagher, Newcastle was born in Slane, Co. Meath about 1898. In 1922 he was an Engineer of the 3rd Battalion, 1st Brigade (Meath), I.R.A. He became a member of a 30 man strong I.R.A. Active Service Unit who later became known as the Curraghtown A.S.U. On 5th July 1922 he was involved in the Battle of Curraghtown where he was arrested by the Free State Army, see the story on page 58. He was temporarily held in Trim and then interned in Dundalk, Co. Louth on 22nd July 1922. On 27th July 1922 he escaped from Dundalk Jail, see the story on page 59. On 28th July 1922 he was re-captured by Pro-Treaty I.R.A. and re-interned in Dundalk Jail. Sources: RO 479. MM9.1.1/KM3L-FKX. Louth County Archives http://www.louthcoco.ie/en/Services/Archives/Archive_Collections/

Patrick Geraghty, Drominiskin, Moynalty was a Volunteer in the Newcastle I.R.A. Company in July 1921. His name is engraved on a headstone in Saint Bridget Cemetery, Oldcastle, see page 360. Source: RO 489. Military Service Pension Collection, file reference No. 24-SP-43724, 29/6/70. Headstone inscription.

James Lynch, Drominiskin, Moynalty, Kells, Co. Meath was a Volunteer in the Newcastle I.R.A. Company in July 1921. In 1936 his address was given as U.S.A. Source: RO 489

John Lynch, Mosney, Laytown, Co. Meath was the Newcastle Company Commanding Officer in 1921. In January 1921 he was involved in ambush of an R.I.C. patrol at Mullagh Lake. Sources: WS1650. RO 489

John P. Lynch, Newcastle, Mullagh, Co. Cavan was the Newcastle Company Adjutant in July 1921. In 1936 his address was given as U.S.A. Source: RO 489

Patrick Lynch Drominiskin, Moynalty, Kells, Co. Meath was a Volunteer in the Newcastle I.R.A. Company in July 1921. In 1936 his address was given as U.S.A. His name is engraved on a headstone in St. Mary's Cemetery Moynalty. The inscription says that Patrick Lynch died on 1st June 1962, see page 305. Sources: RO 489. Headstone inscription.

Patrick Lynch, Diralagh, Mullagh, Co. Cavan was a Volunteer in the Newcastle I.R.A. Company in July 1921. In 1936 his address was given as U.S.A. He died on 3rd July 1962 and was buried in St Mary's Cemetery Mullagh, see page 305. Sources: RO 489. Headstone Inscription.

Peter Lynch, Newcastle, Mullagh, Co. Cavan was a Volunteer in the Newcastle I.R.A. Company in July 1921. In 1936 his address was given as U.S.A. Source: RO 489

Stephen Lynch, Newcastle, Mullagh, Co. Cavan was a Volunteer in the Newcastle I.R.A. Company in July 1921. In 1936 his address was given as U.S.A. Source: RO 489

Thomas Lynch, Newcastle was appointed I.R.A. Battalion Adjutant, 1st Battalion, 3rd Brigade, 1st Eastern Division in March 1921. He was a wanted man and by the end of June 1921 he was "on the run" and camped out in the open on Mullagh Hill with about 30 other mainly Battalion and Brigade Officers attached to the 3rd Brigade. They formed and became involved in an I.R.A. Active Service Unit (A.S.U.). In July 1922 he had joined the Free State Army. In 1936 his address was given as U.S.A. Sources: RO 489. WS1625. WS1627.

Thomas Lynch, Diralagh, Mullagh, Co. Cavan was a Volunteer in the Newcastle I.R.A. Company in July 1921. Source: RO 489

John McKenna, Lislin, Mullagh, Co. Cavan was a Volunteer in the Newcastle I.R.A. Company in July 1921. Source: RO 489

Patrick McMahon, Diralagh, Mullagh, Co. Cavan was the Newcastle Company 2nd Lieutenant in July 1921. In July 1922 he was the company Commanding Officer. Source: RO 489

Peter McMahon, Maio, Tierworker, Bailieborough, Co. Cavan was the Newcastle I.R.A. Company Engineer in early 1921. In March 1921 he was appointed I.R.A. Battalion Engineer, 1st Battalion, 3rd Brigade, 1st Eastern Division. He was a wanted man and by the end of June 1921 he was "on the run" and camped out in the open on Mullagh Hill with about 30 other mainly Battalion and Brigade Officers attached to the 3rd Brigade. They formed and became involved in an I.R.A. Active Service Unit (A.S.U.). In September 1922 he was appointed I.R.A. Battalion Commanding Officer, 3rd Battalion, 2nd Brigade. He later joined the Free State Army. Sources: RO 489. WS1625.

Philip McMahon, Drominiskin, Moynalty, Co. Meath was a Volunteer in the Newcastle I.R.A. Company in July 1921. Source: RO 489

James Mulvany, Drominiskin, Moynalty, Co. Meath was a Volunteer in the Newcastle I.R.A. Company in July 1921. In July 1922 he was a company officer. Source: RO 489

Richard O'Connor, Coolnahinch, Moynalty, Co. Meath was a Volunteer in the Newcastle I.R.A. Company in July 1921. Source: RO 489

Patrick R. O'Reilly, The Park, Mullagh, Co. Cavan was a Volunteer in the Newcastle I.R.A. Company in July 1921. He was a retired postman when he died in October 1974 and his address at that time was Rosehill, Mullagh. Sources: RO 489. The Meath Chronicle dated 19th October 1974, page 4

Peter Reilly, Leitrim, Upper Mullagh, Kells Co. Meath was involved in the 1916 Rising. His name appears in the Irish Military Archives Alphabetical List of 1916 Veterans. He was a native of Ardmore, Dungarven, Co. Waterford. In April or May 1921 as part of a re-structuring plan he was appointed Battalion Police Officer, 2nd Battalion, 3rd Brigade, 1st Eastern Division. He was paid £4:10:0 per week. He was a wanted man and by the end of June 1921 he was "on the run" and camped out in the open on Mullagh Hill with about 30 other mainly Battalion and Brigade Officers attached to the 3rd Brigade. They formed and became involved in an I.R.A. Active Service Unit (A.S.U.). He became the Commanding Officer of an A.S.U. In July 1921 he was the I.R.A. Brigade Intelligence Officer. In March 1922 he joined the Free State Army aged 31. On 5th July 1922 he engaged Anti-Treaty I.R.A. at the Battle of Curraghtown House, Dunderry where two men were killed, see the story on page 58. In October 1922 he joined An Garda Síochána. He was stationed in Raheny where he became Sergeant. In June 1927 his Military Pension of £23:13:04 per year was approved from 1st October 1924, ref file No SP10148. In 1936 he was serving in An Garda Síochána and his address was given as Raheny, Dublin. In 1948 he was discharged from An Garda Síochána as a Garda Sergeant with a pension. In April 1948 his address was given as Turlough, 432 Howth Road, Dublin. In February 1976 he died aged 86 Years. His address was given as 638 Howth Road, Raheny, Co. Dublin. He was buried in Mount Jerome Cemetery,

Harold's Cross, Dublin. Source: WS1659. WS1627. RO 489. RO 494. Military Service Pension Collection, file reference 24SP10148. Irish Press dated 10th February 1976 page 2.

Hugh Reilly was a Volunteer in the Newcastle I.R.A. Company in July 1921. In 1936 he was a member of An Garda Síochána and his address was given as Clara, Co. Offaly. Source: RO 489

John Reilly, Feach, Mullagh, Co. Cavan was a Volunteer in the Newcastle I.R.A. Company in July 1921 but he was arrested and held prisoner. Source: RO 489

Patrick Reilly, Lenenavara, Mullagh, Co. Cavan was a Volunteer in the Newcastle I.R.A. Company in July 1921. Source: RO 489

Samuel Russell, Nobber, Co. Meath was a Volunteer in the Newcastle I.R.A. Company in July 1921. Source: RO 489

Thomas Russell, Feach, Mullagh, Co. Cavan was a Volunteer in the Newcastle I.R.A. Company in July 1921 but he was arrested and held prisoner. In July 1922 he was a company officer. Source: RO 489

James Sheridan was a Volunteer in the Newcastle I.R.A. Company in July 1921. In 1936 he was serving with the Free State Army. Source: RO 489

Philip Sheridan was a Volunteer in the Newcastle I.R.A. Company in July 1921. Source: RO 489

Mark Tully was a Volunteer in the Newcastle I.R.A. Company in July 1921. In 1935 he was a member of An Garda Síochána. Source: RO 489

Laurence Walsh, Carrickspringan, Moynalty, Kells, Co. Meath was a Volunteer in the Newcastle I.R.A. Company in July 1921. Source: RO 489

Nobber Company:

In early 1918 the Nobber Company of Irish Volunteers was formed. In January 1919 the Irish Volunteers became the I.R.A. In early 1919 the I.R.A. reorganised their structures and the Nobber Company became attached to the 4th Battalion, Meath Brigade. In July 1921 the Nobber Company had a strength of 23 men. In July 1922 they had a strength of four men. Source: RO 489. WS1625. WS1650.

Alfred Carry, Rothlogan, Drumconrath, Co. Meath was a Volunteer in the Nobber I.R.A. Company in July 1921. Source: RO 489

James Carry, Cloughrea, Drumconrath, Co. Meath was a Volunteer in the Nobber I.R.A. Company in July 1921. Source: RO 489

John Cassidy, College, Nobber, Co. Meath was a Volunteer in the Nobber I.R.A. Company in July 1921. Source: RO 489

Michael Cassidy was a member of the Castletown G.A.A. Senior Football Team who became Champions in 1908. In July 1921 he was a Volunteer in the Nobber I.R.A. Company. In 1936 his address was given as Cheshire, England. Source: RO 489

John Fitzsimons, Cootehill, Co. Cavan was the Nobber Company 1st Lieutenant for a period in 1921 but he was arrested and held prisoner. In 1936 he was a member of An Garda Síochána. Source: RO 489

Patrick Foylen, Posseckstown, Nobber, see Drumconrath Company

John Hickey, Summerhill, Drumconrath, Co. Meath was a Volunteer in the Nobber I.R.A. Company from 1918 to 1922. He died on 12th December 1974 and was buried in Drumconrath Cemetery, see page 276. Source: RO 489. Headstone Inscription.

Frank Marron, College, Nobber, Co. Meath was a Volunteer in the Nobber I.R.A. Company in July 1921. Source: RO 489

James Marron, College, Nobber, Co. Meath was a Volunteer in the Nobber I.R.A. Company in July 1921. In July 1922 he was the company Commanding Officer. Source: RO 489. Military Service Pension Collection, file reference No. 34-SP-47502

James Martin, Main Street, Nobber, Co. Meath was a Volunteer in the Nobber I.R.A. Company in July 1921. Source: RO 489

Patrick Martin, Edmondstown, Ardee, see Drumconrath Company

Richard Martin, Main Street, Nobber, Co. Meath was a Volunteer in the Nobber I.R.A. Company in July 1921. Source: RO 489

James McDonald, Dunroe, Nobber, Co. Meath was a Volunteer in the Nobber I.R.A. Company in July 1921. On 11th June 1939 James McDonald from Carrickleck, aged 45 years, was killed when his bicycle was involved in a collision with a car. Source: RO 489. The Meath Chronicle dated 6th September 1939. The Meath Chronicle dated 14th October 1939, page 6.

Thomas McGrath, Carrickleck, Kingscourt, Co. Cavan was a Volunteer in the Nobber I.R.A. Company in July 1921. Source: RO 489

John McGuire, Cnegg, Nobber, Co. Meath was the Nobber I.R.A. Company Representative in July 1921. Source: RO 489

Patrick McGuire, Carrickleck, Kingscourt, Co. Cavan was a Volunteer in the Nobber I.R.A. Company in July 1921. Source: RO 489

Hugh McMahon, Anigil, Nobber, Co. Meath was a Volunteer in the Nobber I.R.A. Company in July 1921 and 1922. Source: RO 489

Patrick McMahon, Anigil, Nobber, Co. Meath was the Nobber I.R.A. Company Commanding Officer for a period in 1921 but he was arrested and interned in Ballykinlar Internment Camp, Co. Down. He was held in Compound No 2. In July 1922 he was still involved in the Nobber I.R.A. Company but I don't know at what rank. Source: RO 489. Prisoners of War by Liam O' Duibhir, page 315

Thomas McMahon, Anigil, Nobber, Co. Meath was a Volunteer in the Nobber I.R.A. Company in July 1921 and 1922. Source: RO 489

Patrick Rourke, Cruicetown, Kilmainhamwood, Co. Meath was a Volunteer in the Nobber I.R.A. Company in July 1921. Source: RO 489

James Ward, Ballyhaise, Co Cavan, see Drumconrath Company
John Ward was born in Cloughmacoo, Nobber, Co. Meath about 1902. In 1920 he was arrested and imprisoned in Mountjoy, Dublin for offences under the Restoration of Order in Ireland Regulations (ROIR). His address was given as Rolagh, Nobber, Co. Meath. For a period in 1921 he was the Nobber I.R.A. Company Commanding Officer but he was arrested and held prisoner. In 1936 his address was given as Cheshire, England. Source: RO 489. MM9.1.1/KM79-T63.
Francis Watters, Drumconrath, see Drumconrath Company

Oldcastle Company:

In 1902 Liam Sheridan, Michael Grace, Charlie Fox and Paddy Bartley from

Mountnugent launched a Sinn Fein newspaper in Oldcastle. After the 1916 Rising Charlie Fox and Michael Grace were arrested and imprisoned for a short time.
In 1917 the Oldcastle Company of Irish Volunteers was organised by two Dublin men, Harry Murray and John Kavanagh. Prior to arriving in Oldcastle both men had been involved in the 1916 Easter Rising and they had been interned for several months. They stayed in Charlie Fox's in Oldcastle. Charlie Fox was a local merchant in Oldcastle and later supplied clothes to two German prisoners who escaped from Oldcastle Internment Camp. He assisted Owen Clarke, see below, to get rid of blood stained clothes on the night that Seamus Cogan (see Stonefield Company) was killed, see the story of Seamus Cogan's death on page 72. The Oldcastle Irish Volunteers company strength in 1917 was 20 or 25 men. In January 1919 the Irish Volunteers became the I.R.A. In 1920 the Oldcastle I.R.A. Company was attached to the 5th Battalion, Meath Brigade. In April or May 1920 the Stonefield Company raided the Income Tax Offices in Oldcastle while the Oldcastle Company used their knowledge of the area and the people to provide security while the raid was in progress. All documents, ledgers and correspondence were seized and were burned on the outskirts of the town. The old workhouse in Oldcastle had been used by the British authorities as an Internment Camp for German Prisoners Of War during World War One. In May 1920 I.R.A. Intelligence indicated that the old workhouse was to be re-occupied by the British Military and used as a blockhouse. The Oldcastle and Stonefield I.R.A. companies burned the Workhouse to the ground to prevent it being re-occupied. In July 1921 the Oldcastle Company had a strength

of 37 men. In July 1922 the company had a strength of seventeen men. Sources: Oliver
Coogan's Politics and War in Meath 1913-23, Page 113. RO 489. WS1627. WS1659.

Thomas Bardon, Summerbank, Oldcastle, Co. Meath was born in Boley, Oldcastle
about 1893. He was a champion weight thrower and G.A.A. football player.
Immediately after a shootout with British Troops in Oldcastle on 22nd July 1920, in
which I.R.A. Commandant Seamus Cogan was killed, he was arrested at the "safe
house" in which Seamus Cogan and the I.R.A. Police were taking their prisoner,
see the story on page 72. He was charged with being in possession of arms and
ammunition, including a six chamber revolver, an offence under the Defence of
the Realm Regulations. On 13th August he was found guilty and sentenced to two
years hard labour and he was imprisoned in Mountjoy, Dublin. In July 1921 and
1922 he was recorded as a Volunteer in the Oldcastle I.R.A. Company. His name is
engraved on a headstone in Saint Bridget Cemetery, Oldcastle, see page 359.
Sources: RO 489. MM9.1.1/KMQR-G28. MM9.1.1/KM79-51Y. Headstone Inscription. Faithful to Ireland by Tony Brady, page 42

Patrick Bradley was a Volunteer in the Oldcastle I.R.A. Company in July 1921.
Source: RO 489

Thomas (Redney) Callan, Mountdutton, Oldcastle, Co. Meath was involved in the
burning of the Oldcastle Workhouse to the ground to prevent it being re-occupied
by British Troops In May 1920. In July 1921 he was the Oldcastle Company
Commanding Officer. Source: WS1659. RO 489.

Owen Clarke, The Square, Oldcastle, Co. Meath was born 1898 in Belturbet. In
1916 he came to Oldcastle to work in Charlie Fox's store. In 1917 he was a
Volunteer in the Oldcastle Company of Irish Volunteers. Around 1917 or 1918 he
took over the role of Oldcastle Company Commanding Officer from Tommy
Harpur. In July 1920 he was involved in a shootout with British Troops in Oldcastle
in which I.R.A. Commandant Seamus Cogan was killed, see the story on page 72.
In 1921 he was arrested and interned in Ballykinlar Internment Camp, Co Down.
He was held in Compound No 2 for three months. On his release he continued as
the Oldcastle I.R.A. Company Commanding Officer through 1922. In the 1940's he
ran a very modern Cinema in Oldcastle. He also built up a successful Wholesale
and Retail Business in Oldcastle. His name is engraved on a headstone in Saint
Bridget Cemetery, Oldcastle, see page 359. Sources: Oliver Coogan's Politics and War in Meath 1913-23
Page 113. WS1615. RO 489. Headstone Inscription. Dunderry A Folk History by Dunderry history Group and Johnny Keely. Personal
Interview with Sean Craughan, Oldcastle.

William Devine was a Volunteer in the Oldcastle I.R.A. Company in July 1922. In
1936 his address was given as Dublin. Source: RO 489

Joseph (Joe) Fagan, Oldcastle, Co. Meath was a Volunteer in the Oldcastle I.R.A.
Company in July 1921. He was arrested and interned in Ballykinlar Internment
Camp, Co. Down. He was held in Compound No 2.
Sources: RO 489. Prisoners of War by Liam O' Duibhir, page 315

Hugh Foley, Oldcastle, Co. Meath was a Volunteer in the Oldcastle I.R.A. Company
in July 1921 and 1922. In 1936 his address was given as Ballinseary, Castlepollard,
Co. Westmeath. Source: RO 489. Military Service Pension Collection, file reference No. MD-20450

John Foley, Oldcastle, Co. Meath was a Volunteer in the Oldcastle I.R.A. Company in July 1921. In 1936 his address was given as U.S.A. Source: RO 489

Thomas Foley, Oldcastle, Co. Meath was a Volunteer in the Oldcastle I.R.A. Company In July 1921 and 1922. He died on 2nd June 1980 aged 93 years and was buried in Ballinacree Cemetery, see page 352. Source: RO 489. Headstone Inscription. Photo kindly provided by the Ballinacree Community Centre, thanks to Seamus Smith, Ballinacree.

Matthew Gargan, Baltrasna, Oldcastle, Co. Meath was the Oldcastle Company 1st Lieutenant in July 1921 and 1922. In 1936 his address was given as 159 Church Street, Orange City, U.S.A. Source: RO 489

James Garrigan (called himself Gargan), Baltrasna, Oldcastle, Co. Meath was a Volunteer in the Oldcastle I.R.A. Company in July 1921 and 1922. He was a son of below John and a brother of below Patrick. In 1936 his address was given as Hillside, New Jersey, U.S.A. He died on the 8th January 1949 and was buried in Moylagh Churchyard Cemetery, see page 355. Source: RO 489. Headstone inscription. Personal Interview with Sean Craughan in Moylagh Cemetery.

John Garrigan (called himself Gargan) was a Volunteer in the Oldcastle I.R.A. Company in 1922. He was the Father of above James and below Patrick. He died on 28th October 1930 and was buried in Moylagh Churchyard Cemetery, see page 355. Source: RO 489. Headstone inscription. Personal Interview with Sean Craughan in Moylagh Cemetery.

Patrick Garrigan (called himself Gargan), Baltrasna, Oldcastle, Co. Meath was a Volunteer in the Oldcastle I.R.A. Company in July 1921 and 1922. He was the son of above John and a brother of above James. He died on 5th January 1966 and was buried in Moylagh Churchyard Cemetery, see page 355. Source: RO 489. Headstone inscription. Personal Interview with Sean Craughan in Moylagh Cemetery.

Edward Gavin, Crossdrum, Oldcastle, Co. Meath was a Volunteer in the Oldcastle I.R.A. Company in July 1921. Source: RO 489

Thomas Gavin, Chapel Street Oldcastle, Co. Meath and also of Crossdrum, Oldcastle, Co. Meath was a Volunteer in the Oldcastle I.R.A. Company in July 1921 and 1922. In 1936 his address was given as Greenview, Oldcastle, Co. Meath. Source: RO 489. Military Service Pension Collection, file reference No MSP34REF50373.

Matthew Gibney Castle Street, Oldcastle, Co. Meath was a Volunteer in the Oldcastle I.R.A. Company in July 1921 and 1922. He was arrested and interned in Ballykinlar Internment Camp, Co. Down. He was held in Compound No 2. Source: RO 489 and Prisoners of War by Liam O' Duibhir, page 314

Philip Glennon, Linnor, Oldcastle, Co. Meath was a Volunteer in the Oldcastle I.R.A. Company in July 1921. Source: RO 489

Michael Grace was a brother of below William. He was a Civil Engineer by profession. Along with building up a considerable private practice he also carried out work for Oldcastle Board of Guardians and the Oldcastle Rural District Council. He had a great love for the Irish Language. He was one of four men who founded the Sinn Fein Newspaper in Oldcastle in 1902. He was Vice-President of the local Total Abstinence Society. He was Chairman of the North Meath Executive Sinn Fein. Along with Pádraig DeBurca, see Carnaross Company, he proposed Liam Mellows to stand for election as the Sinn Fein Candidate in North Meath in 1918.
Source: Sean Craughan, Oldcastle.

William Grace, Castle Street, Oldcastle, Co. Meath was a brother of above Michael. William was an active I.R.A. man in the Oldcastle area. In July 1920 William was one of the men travelling with Seamus Cogan in a car through Oldcastle when Cogan was shot dead during an exchange of gunfire with British Troops, see the story on page 72. In July 1921 he was a Volunteer in the Oldcastle I.R.A. Company. He was arrested and interned in Ballykinlar Internment Camp, Co. Down where he was held in Compound No 2. Before 1936 he had moved to Drumconrath, Dublin. He died in St. Vincent's Hospital Dublin in January 1958 and was buried in Glasnevin Cemetery, Dublin.
Source: RO 489 and Prisoners of War by Liam O' Duibhir, page 315 and The Meath Chronicle dated 25th January 1958, page 1

Michael Greally, The Square, Oldcastle, Co. Meath worked in Grace's which is now known as Gibney's shop at the square in Oldcastle. He was a Volunteer in the Oldcastle I.R.A. Company in July 1921. In February 1923 he was executed by the Free State Army for being involved in an armed raid on a Bank in Oldcastle, see the story on page 67.
Sources: RO 489. http://www.irishmedals.org/anti-treaty-killed.html Personal Interview with Sean Craughan, Oldcastle.

Thomas (Tommy) Harpur was the Oldcastle Company of Irish Volunteers Commanding Officer in 1917. Around 1917 or 1918 Owen Clarke took over the role as company commanding Officer. In April 1920 Thomas was involved in a raid on the Income Tax Office in Oldcastle. In May 1920 he was involved in the burning of the Oldcastle Workhouse to prevent it being re-occupied by British Troops. He was still in the Oldcastle I.R.A. Company in July 1921. In 1936 he was serving in the Free State Army and his address was given as Collins Barracks, Co. Cork. Sources: Oliver Coogan's Politics and War in Meath 1913-23 Page 113. WS1659. RO 489. Sean Craughan, Oldcastle.

Leo Herbstreit, The Square, Oldcastle, Co. Meath had a ladies and gents hair salon and a confectionary and stationary shop in Oldcastle. He was also a Volunteer in the Oldcastle I.R.A. Company in July 1921. In 1936 his address was given as Cloghan Street, Oldcastle. He died on 18the September 1977 and was buried in St. Bridget's Cemetery Oldcastle, see page 360. Source: RO 489. Headstone Inscription. Personal Interview with Sean Craughan, Oldcastle on 30th June 2015.

John Husband, Baltrasna, Oldcastle, Co. Meath was a Volunteer in the Oldcastle I.R.A. Company in July 1921. He was arrested and interned in Ballykinlar Internment Camp, Co. Down. He was held in Compound No 2. He died on 4th

December 1957 aged 72 years and was buried in Moylagh Church Cemetery, Oldcastle, see page 356. Source: RO 489. Prisoners of War by Liam O' Duibhir, page 315. Headstone Inscription.

Patrick Keenan, Cavan Street, Oldcastle, Co. Meath was a Volunteer in the Oldcastle I.R.A. Company in July 1921. In 1936 his address was given as U.S.A. Source: RO 489

Peter Lynch, Crossdrum, Oldcastle, Co. Meath was a Volunteer in the Oldcastle I.R.A. Company in July 1921. In 1936 his address was given as U.S.A. Source: RO 489

Richard Lynch, Castle Street, Oldcastle, Co. Meath was a Volunteer in the Oldcastle I.R.A. Company in July 1921. He was arrested and interned in Ballykinlar Internment Camp, Co. Down and he was held in Compound No 2. In 1936 his address was given as Tonagh, Mountnugent, Co. Cavan. Source: RO 489. Prisoners of War by Liam O' Duibhir, page 315.

Thomas Lynch, The Square, Oldcastle, Co. Meath was involved in a shootout with British Troops in Oldcastle in which I.R.A. Commandant Seamus Cogan was killed in July 1920, see the story on page 72. In July 1921 he was the Oldcastle I.R.A. Company 2nd Lieutenant. In 1936 his address was given as Newcastle, Mullagh. Sources: RO 489. WS1615.

John (Jack) McGinn, Tubride, Oldcastle, Co. Meath was a Volunteer in the Oldcastle I.R.A. Company in July 1921. He died in May 1997 and was buried in Saint Bridget Cemetery, Oldcastle, see page 361. Source: RO 489. Headstone Inscription.

James McGinn, Tubride, Oldcastle, Co. Meath was arrested and interned in Ballykinlar Internment Camp, Co. Down In 1921. He was held in Compound No 2. According to Internment Camp records his address was Castle Street, Oldcastle. He does not appear to have been a member of the Irish Volunteers at the time and he would have been interned without trial. In July 1922 he was a Volunteer in the Oldcastle Company of Irish Volunteers. In 1936 his address was given as U.S.A. Sources: RO 489 and Prisoners of War by Liam O' Duibhir, page 315

William McGinn, Cloghan Street, Oldcastle, Co. Meath was a Volunteer in the Oldcastle I.R.A. Company in July 1921. Source: RO 489

James (The Blog) McNamee, Baltrasna, Oldcastle, Co. Meath was a Volunteer in the Oldcastle I.R.A. Company in July 1921 and July 1922. In 1922 his address was given as Milltown, Oldcastle. He was buried in Loughcrew Old Cemetery. Sources: RO 489. Personal Interview with Sean Craughan, Oldcastle.

Michael Monaghan, Oldcastle, Co. Meath was the Engineer of the 3rd Brigade (Meath), 1st Eastern Division in July 1921. In 1936 he was serving in the Free State Army. Source: RO 494

Michael Morne, Redeaven, Oldcastle, Co. Meath was a Volunteer in the Oldcastle I.R.A. Company in July 1921. Source: RO 489

Frank Reilly, Bolies, Oldcastle, Co. Meath was a Volunteer in the Oldcastle I.R.A. Company in July 1921 and July 1922. He died on 5th November 1966 aged 79 years and was buried in Saint Bridget's Cemetery, Oldcastle, see page 361. Source: RO 489. Headstone Inscription.

John Reilly, Crossdrum, Oldcastle, Co. Meath was a Volunteer in the Oldcastle I.R.A. Company in July 1921 and July 1922. In 1936 his address was given as U.S.A. Source: RO 489

Harry Sheridan, Oldcastle, Co. Meath was a Volunteer in the Oldcastle I.R.A. Company in 1920. In July 1920 he was wounded in the leg during a shootout with British Troops in Oldcastle in which I.R.A. Commandant Seamus Cogan was killed, see the story on page 72. Harry spent some time in the Mater Hospital being treated for a gunshot wound to the shin bone. He was still a member of the Oldcastle I.R.A. company in July 1921. In 1936 he was a member of An Garda Síochána and his address was given as Garda Barracks, Skryne, Co. Meath. Sources: WS1615. RO 489.

Patrick Timmons, Tubride, Oldcastle, Co. Meath was a Volunteer in the Oldcastle I.R.A. Company in July 1921. He was arrested and interned in Ballykinlar Internment Camp, Co. Down. He was held in Compound No 2. In July 1922 he continued as a Volunteer with the Oldcastle Company. He was a Carpenter by trade and he emigrated to America. In 1936 his address was given as New York, U.S.A. Sources: RO 489 and Prisoners of War by Liam O' Duibhir, page 315. Sean Craughan, Oldcastle.

Brian Tuite, Newcastle, Oldcastle, Co. Meath was a brother of below James. He was a Volunteer in the Oldcastle I.R.A. Company in July 1921. In 1936 his address was given as Dunancney, Newcastle, Virginia, Co. Cavan. Source: RO 489. Personal Interview with Sean Craughan, Oldcastle on 30th June 2015.

James (Jim) Tuite, Newcastle, Oldcastle, Co. Meath was a brother of above Brian. He worked as a caretaker in the Gilson Endowed School. He was a Volunteer in the Oldcastle I.R.A. Company in July 1921 and July 1922. He was married to a sister of above Tom Foley. He died on 14th April 1976 and was buried in St. Bridget's Cemetery, Oldcastle. Source: RO 489. Headstone Inscription. Personal Interview with Sean Craughan, Oldcastle on 30th June 2015.

Peter Tuite, Cogan Street, Oldcastle, Co. Meath was a Volunteer in the Oldcastle I.R.A. Company in July 1921. In 1936 his address was given as U.S.A. Source: RO 489

Peter Tully was a Volunteer in the Oldcastle I.R.A. Company in July 1921. He died on 24th February 1924 and was buried in Saint Bridget Cemetery, Oldcastle, see page 362. Source: RO 489. Headstone Inscription.

Patrick Walsh, Milbrook, Oldcastle, Co. Meath provided training to the Oldcastle Company of Irish Volunteers in 1917 and for many years after that. He was a Volunteer in the Oldcastle I.R.A. Company in July 1921. He died on 17th November 1975 aged 77 years and was buried in Moylagh Church Cemetery,

Oldcastle, see page 357. Source: RO 489 Source: Military Service Pension Collection, file reference No MSP34REF50373. Headstone Inscription. Personal Interview with Sean Craughan, Oldcastle on 30th June 2015.

Rathkenny Company:

In July 1921 the Rathkenny Company had a strength of seventeen Men. In July 1922 the company had no Volunteers so it ceased to exist. Sources: RO 487

James Allen, Mullaha, Navan, Co. Meath was a Volunteer in the Rathkenny I.R.A. Company prior to July 1921. In 1935 his address was given as Co. Kildare. Source: RO 487

Patrick Callan was a Volunteer in the Rathkenny I.R.A. Company in July 1921. In 1935 his address was given as U.S.A. His name is engraved on a headstone in Rathkenny Old Cemetery see page 369. Source: RO 487. Headstone inscription.

L. Carroll, Dublin was a Volunteer in the Rathkenny I.R.A. Company in July 1921. Source: RO 487

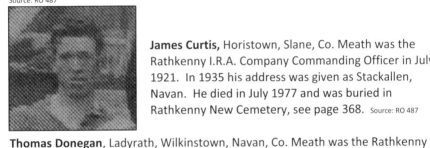

James Curtis, Horistown, Slane, Co. Meath was the Rathkenny I.R.A. Company Commanding Officer in July 1921. In 1935 his address was given as Stackallen, Navan. He died in July 1977 and was buried in Rathkenny New Cemetery, see page 368. Source: RO 487

Thomas Donegan, Ladyrath, Wilkinstown, Navan, Co. Meath was the Rathkenny I.R.A. Company Intelligence Officer in July 1921. He died in November 1979 and was buried in Ladyrath New Cemetery, see page 368. Source: RO 487

James Ginnity, Kells, Co. Meath was a brother of below Matthew. He was a native of Gernonstown, near Slane Co. Meath. He was a Volunteer in the Rathkenny I.R.A. Company in July 1921 he but he was arrested and interned by the British in Ballykinlar Internment Camp, Co. Down during that time. He was held in Compound No 2. He was the only one from the company who was interned at the time. The records from the Internment Camp gives his address as College Hill, Slane. In July 1922 he was an I.R.A. Battalion Commanding Officer. He was a member of Meath County Council and he was Chairman of the Navan Rural Council. In 1936 he was a member of An Garda Síochána and his address was given as Dundalk Garda Station. Sources: A letter from Jim Reilly to Pensions Board on 13/03/1935. RO 484. RO 487 Prisoners of War by Liam O' Duibhir, page 315. Meath Chronicle dated 28th July 1923, page 1

Matthew Ginnity, Stackallen, Navan, Co. Meath was a Lieutenant in the Rathkenny I.R.A. Company in July 1922. He was a native of Gernonstown, near Slane Co. Meath. He was a brother of above James. He took the Anti-Treaty side and he became a member of a 30 man strong I.R.A. Active Service Unit who later became known as the Curraghtown A.S.U. On 5th July 1922 he was involved in the Battle of Curraghtown where he was arrested by the Free State Army, see the story on page 58. He was temporarily held in Trim and then interned in Dundalk, Co. Louth on 22nd July 1922. On 27th July 1922 he escaped from Dundalk Jail, see the story on page 59. Around September 1922 he was re-captured by the Free State Army at Balsaw Hill and he was interned in the Curragh Camp in Kildare. He died in the Internment Camp on 23rd July 1923 aged 32 years. He was buried in Gernonstown Cemetery, near Slane Co. Meath, see page 363. Sources: Dunderry A Folk History by Dunderry History Group & Johnny Keely. Meath Chronicle dated 28th July 1923, page 1. Meath Chronicle 15th April 1933, page 5. Meath Chronicle dated 27th April 1935, page 5. Headstone Inscription.

Joseph (Joe) Hughes of Ladyrath, Wilkinstown was a keen Irish language speaker. In April 1920 he was appointed I.R.A. 6th Battalion (Navan) Engineer, Meath Brigade. In March or April 1921 he was appointed I.R.A. 2nd Brigade Engineer, 1st Eastern Division. He was also a Brigade Intelligence Officer for a period. In November 1936 he attended a meeting to appoint a Brigade Committee to gather information related to qualifying Volunteers for the Military Service Pensions and he was appointed to the Committee. He died in July 1960 and his funeral took place from Rathkenny Church to the neighbouring Cemetery. Sources: WS1715. WS1060. WS1622. WS1715. RO 484. RO 487. WS1624. WS1696.

Michael Keelan was a Volunteer in the Rathkenny I.R.A. Company in July 1921. In 1935 his address was given as New Jersey, U.S.A. Source: RO 487

Tom Keelan, Creewood, Slane, Co. Meath was a Volunteer in the Rathkenny I.R.A. Company prior to July 1921. Source: RO 487

P. Lambe, Rathkenny, Slane, Co. Meath was a Volunteer in the Rathkenny I.R.A. Company in July 1921. Source: RO 487

Patrick Lynch, Bornafooka, Rathkenny, Slane, Co. Meath was a Volunteer in the Rathkenny I.R.A. Company in July 1921. Source: RO 487

Eugene Monahan was a Volunteer in the Rathkenny I.R.A. Company in July 1921. In 1935 his address was given as U.S.A. Source: RO 487

Michael Monahan was a Volunteer in the Rathkenny I.R.A. Company in July 1921. In 1935 his address was given as Dublin and he worked in the Park. His name is engraved on a headstone in Rathkenny Old Cemetery, see 370. Sources: RO 487. Headstone Inscription.

James Murray, Rathkenny, Slane, Co. Meath was a Volunteer in the Rathkenny I.R.A. Company in July 1921. Source: RO 487

Donal Quinn, Flower Hill, Navan, Co. Meath was a Volunteer in the Rathkenny I.R.A. Company in July 1921. He was born in Navan, Co. Meath about 1902. In July 1922 he transferred from the Rathkenny I.R.A. Company to the Navan I.R.A.

Company. He was an Irish teacher. He became a member of a 30 man strong I.R.A. Active Service Unit who later became known as the Curraghtown A.S.U. On 5th July 1922 he was involved in the Battle of Curraghtown where he was arrested by the Free State Army, see the story on page 58. He was temporarily held in Trim and then interned in Dundalk, Co. Louth on 22nd July 1922. On 27th July 1922 he escaped from Dundalk Jail, see the story on page 59. Source: RO 487. RO 488. Louth County Archives http://www.louthcoco.ie/en/Services/Archives/Archive_Collections/ Dunderry A Folk History by Dunderry History Group & Johnny Keely.

Bernard Reilly, Creewood, Slane, Co. Meath was a Volunteer in the Rathkenny I.R.A. Company in July 1921. His name is engraved on a headstone in Rathkenny Old Cemetery, see page 370. Sources: RO 487. Headstone Inscription.

James Reilly, Rathkenny, Slane, Co. Meath was a member of the Rathkenny G.A.A. Football Team who won the Feis Cup in 1920. Prior to July 1921 he was a Volunteer in the Rathkenny I.R.A. Company. In 1922 he was a member of the Rathkenny G.A.A. Senior Football Team who became Champions that year.
Sources: RO 487. Royal and Loyal by Michael O'Brien page 113 and page 118

Tim Reilly, Rathkenny, Slane, Co. Meath was the Rathkenny I.R.A. Company 1st Lieutenant in 1920 and July 1921. In 1920 he was a member of the Rathkenny G.A.A. Football Team who won the Feis Cup that year.
Source: RO 487. Royal and Loyal by Michael O'Brien page 113

Michael Sheridan, Ladyrath, Wilkinstown, Navan, Co. Meath was a Volunteer in the Rathkenny I.R.A. Company prior to July 1921. Source: RO 487

Walter Smyth, Kilbride, Co. Dublin was a Volunteer in the Rathkenny Company of Irish Volunteers prior to July 1921. Source: RO 487

Ratoath Company:

In July 1921 the Ratoath Company had a strength of twelve men. In July 1922 the company's strength was still twelve men. Sources: RO 481

Patrick Caffrey, Pacetown, Ratoath, Co. Meath was a Volunteer in the Ratoath I.R.A. Company in July 1921 and July 1922. Source: RO 481

James Casey, Pacetown, Ratoath, Co. Meath was a Volunteer in the Ratoath I.R.A. Company in July 1921 and July 1922. Source: RO 481

Christopher Donnelly, Lagore, Ratoath, Co. Meath was the Ratoath I.R.A. Company Commanding Officer in July 1921 and July 1922. He died before 1936.
Source: RO 481

William Eiffe, Ratoath, Co. Meath was a Volunteer in the Ratoath I.R.A. Company in July 1921 and July 1922. Source: RO 481

Francis Fortune, Ratoath, Co. Meath was a Volunteer in the Ratoath I.R.A. Company in July 1921 and July 1922. Source: RO 481

Thomas Heague, Pace, Dunboyne, Co. Meath was the Ratoath I.R.A. Company Quartermaster in July 1921 and July 1922. Source: RO 481

William Heague Ratoath, Co. Meath was the Ratoath I.R.A. Company 2nd Lieutenant in July 1921 and July 1922. Source: RO 481

John Hessman, Ratoath, Co. Meath was the Ratoath I.R.A. Company 1st Lieutenant in July 1921 and July 1922. In 1936 his address was given as Pennsylvania, U.S.A. Source: RO 481

John Lynch, Tankardstown, Ratoath, Co. Meath was a Volunteer in the Ratoath I.R.A. Company in July 1921 and July 1922. Source: RO 481

Patrick Morgan, Ratoath, Co. Meath was the Ratoath I.R.A. Company Adjutant in July 1921 and July 1922. Source: RO 481

Laurence Nolan, Curraghstown, Navan, Co. Meath was a Volunteer in the Ratoath I.R.A. Company in July 1921 and July 1922. Source: RO 481

Thomas Smith, Larch Hill, Kilcock, Co Meath was a Volunteer in the Ratoath I.R.A. Company in July 1921 and July 1922. Source: RO 481

Skryne and Killeen Company:

In July 1921 the Skryne and Killeen Company had a strength of eighteen men. In July 1922 the company had a strength of sixteen men. Sources: RO 481

Michael Cahalan, Killeen, Dunshaughlin, Co. Meath was a Volunteer in the Skryne and Killeen I.R.A. Company in July 1921 and July 1922. Source: RO 481

Patrick Connor, Dunshaughlin, Co. Meath was a Volunteer in the Skryne and Killeen I.R.A. Company in July 1921 and July 1922. Source: RO 481

James Dolan, Oberstown, Tara, Co. Meath was a son of below Martin. He was the Skryne and Killeen Company of Irish Volunteers Commanding Officer in 1917. He was still the I.R.A. Company Commanding Officer in July 1921 and July 1922. He died on 11th May 1965 and was buried in Saint Colmcille's Churchyard, Skryne, Tara, see page 335. Sources: Oliver Coogan's Politics and War in Meath 1913-23, page 113. RO 481. Headstone Inscription.

Martin Dolan, Oberstown, Tara, Co. Meath was the father of above James. He was the Skryne and Killeen I.R.A. Company Quartermaster in July 1921 and 1922. In 1936 he was serving with the Free State Army. He died on 27th March 1936 and was buried in Saint Colmcille's Churchyard, Skryne, Tara, see page 335. Source: RO 481. Headstone Inscription.

Michael Dunphy was a Volunteer in the Skryne and Killeen I.R.A. Company in July 1921 and July 1922. In 1936 his address was given as Co. Cork. Source: RO 481

Patrick Dunphy was a Volunteer in the Skryne and Killeen I.R.A. Company in July 1921 and July 1922. In 1936 his address was given as Co. Sligo. Source: RO 481

Patrick English, Ross, Tara, Co. Meath was the Skryne and Killeen I.R.A. Company Adjutant in July 1921 and July 1922. Source: RO 481

John Farrell, Knockmark, Drumree, Co. Meath was a Volunteer in the Skryne and Killeen I.R.A. Company in July 1921 and July 1922. Source: RO 481

Bartle Fitzsimons, Oberstown, Tara, Co. Meath was a Volunteer in the Skryne and Killeen I.R.A. Company, a member of Meath County Council and Chairman of Dunshaughlin District Council in July 1921. Sources: RO 481. WS1060.

James Griffin, Bohermeen, Navan, Co. Meath was the Skryne and Killeen I.R.A. Company 1st Lieutenant in July 1921 and July 1922. Source: RO 481

Christopher Hughes was a Volunteer in the Skryne and Killeen I.R.A. Company in July 1921. In 1936 his address was given as Cabra, Dublin. Source: RO 481

Christopher Martin, Ballinagh, Dunsany, Co. Meath was a Volunteer in the Skryne and Killeen I.R.A. Company in July 1921 and July 1922. He died before 1936. Source: RO 481

Maurice Mulvaney, Killeen, Dunshaughlin, Co. Meath was a Volunteer in the Skryne and Killeen I.R.A. Company in July 1921 and July 1922. Source: RO 481

James (The Yank) O'Connell was born in New York in 1901 where he lived until he was ten years of age. In 1917 he joined the Skryne and Killeen Company of Irish Volunteers. In July 1921 and July 1922 he was still a Volunteer in the I.R.A. Company. Sources: Oliver Coogan's Politics and War in Meath 1913-25, page 113 and RO 481

Matthew O'Neill, Termonfeckin, Drogheda, Co. Louth was the Skryne and Killeen I.R.A. Company Commanding Officer in July 1921 and July 1922. In 1936 he was serving in the Free State Army. Source: RO 481

John Reilly, Skryne, Tara, Co. Meath was a Volunteer in the Skryne and Killeen I.R.A. Company in July 1921 and July 1922. Source: RO 481

Patrick Stoney, Killeen, Dunshaughlin, Co. Meath was a Volunteer in the Skryne and Killeen I.R.A. Company in July 1921 and July 1922. In 1936 he was serving in the Free State Army. Source: RO 481

Joseph Webb, Killeen, Dunshaughlin, Co. Meath was a Volunteer in the Skryne and Killeen I.R.A. Company in July 1921 and July 1922. He died in July 1985 aged 81 years and was buried in St. Loman's Cemetery, see page 384. Source: RO 481. Headstone Inscription.

Slane Company:

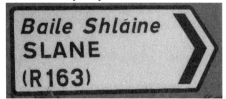

Nicholas Clarke, Monknewtown, Slane, Co. Meath was a Volunteer in the Slane I.R.A. "G" Company in July 1921. He died on 9th March 1966 aged 78 years and was buried in Monknewtown Cemetery, see page 366. Source: RO 526. Headstone Inscription

Thomas Clarke, Monknewtown, Slane, Co. Meath was the Slane I.R.A. "G" Company Quartermaster in July 1921 and 1922. He died on 9th September 1965 aged 80 years and was buried in Monknewtown Cemetery, see page 366. Source: RO 526. Headstone Inscription.

W. Clarke, Monknewtown, Slane, Co. Meath was a Volunteer in the Slane I.R.A. "G" Company in July 1922. Source: RO 526.

Vincent Gerrard, Monknewtown, Slane, Co. Meath was the Slane I.R.A. "G" Company Commanding Officer in July 1921. Source: RO 526.

James Madden, England, was a Volunteer in the Slane I.R.A. "G" Company in July 1921. He died on 22nd February 1936. Source: RO 526.

J. Marry, Kellystown, Slane, Co. Meath was the Slane I.R.A. "G" Company 1st Lieutenant in July 1921. In 1922 he was the company Commanding Officer. Source: RO 526.

J. Martin, Monknewtown, Slane, Co. Meath was a Volunteer in the Slane I.R.A. "G" Company in July 1921 and 1922. Source: RO 526.

L. O'Brien, Newgrange, Slane, Co. Meath was a Volunteer in the Slane I.R.A. "G" Company in July 1921. Source: RO 526.

T. O'Brien, Monknewtown, Slane, Co. Meath was a Volunteer in the Slane I.R.A. "G" Company in July 1922. Source: RO 526.

J. Reilly, Kellystown, Slane, Co. Meath was the Slane I.R.A. "G" Company 2nd Lieutenant in July 1921 and 1922. There is a cross in Monknewtown Cemetery bearing the name James (Jemmie) Reilly, late of Kellystown, Slane. There is no dates or any other information on the cross so I can't be sure if it is the same J. Reilly, see page 367. Source: RO 526. Headstone Inscription.

W. Smyth, Kellystown, Slane, Co. Meath was a Volunteer in the Slane I.R.A. "G" Company in July 1921. Source: RO 526.

Owen Briody, Slane, Co. Meath was the Slane I.R.A. "H" Company Adjutant in July 1921. Source: RO 526.

Leo Clarke, Balgathern, Drogheda, Co. Louth was the Slane I.R.A. "H" Company Quartermaster in July 1921. Source: RO 526.

Frank Feely was a Volunteer in the Slane I.R.A. "H" Company in July 1921. He died before 1936. Source: RO 526.

Andrew Gallagher, Slane, Co. Meath was a Volunteer in the Slane I.R.A. "H" Company in July 1921. Source: RO 526.

Patrick Gallagher, Slane, Co. Meath was a Volunteer in the Slane I.R.A. "H" Company in July 1921. Source: RO 526.

Patrick Lane, Slane, Co. Meath was the Slane I.R.A. "H" Company 1st Lieutenant in July 1921. Source: RO 526.

Joseph Ledwidge, Slane, Co. Meath was the Slane I.R.A. "H" Company Commanding Officer in July 1921. He died in 1980 and was buried in Slane Cemetery, see page 364. Source: RO 526. Headstone Inscription

Patrick Tiernan, Slane, Co. Meath was a Volunteer in the Slane I.R.A. "H" Company in July 1921. He died on 24th February 1981 and was buried in Slane Cemetery, see page 364. Source: RO 526. Headstone Inscription.

John Vaughey, Barristown, Slane, Co. Meath was a Volunteer in the Slane I.R.A. "H" Company in July 1921. The Vaughey family plot is in Slane Cemetery, see page 365. Source: RO 526. Inscription on grave.

Stackallen Company:

Patrick Loughran said in his Witness Statement that at the latter end of 1918 the Navan Company helped to establish and organise the Stackallen Company of Irish Volunteers. In January 1919 the Irish Volunteers became the I.R.A. In 1919 the Stackallen I.R.A. Company was part of the 6th Battalion. I found no further record of their existence or its members. Source: WS1624. .

Stonefield Company:

In 1917 Seamus Cogan got a few lads together and formed the Stonefield Company of Irish Volunteers. He carried out all training and drilling duties, there were no other officers in the company. They had one Lee Enfield Rifle and a couple of revolvers. In 1918 the strength of the Stonefield Company of Irish Volunteers increased to 25 men due to the threat of conscription into the British Army. In January 1919 the Irish Volunteers became the I.R.A. In 1919 the Stonefield I.R.A. Company had a strength of ten men with two rifles between them. In 1920 the Stonefield I.R.A. Company was attached to the 5th Battalion,

Meath Brigade. In May 1920 the Stonefield I.R.A. Company raided the Income Tax Offices in Oldcastle while the Oldcastle Company used their knowledge of the area and the people to provide security while the raid was in progress. All documents, ledgers and correspondence were seized and were burned on the outskirts of the town. The old workhouse in Oldcastle had been used by the British authorities as an Internment Camp for German Prisoners of War during the World War One. In May 1920 I.R.A. Intelligence indicated that the Workhouse was to be re-occupied by the British Military and used as a blockhouse. The Oldcastle and Stonefield I.R.A. companies burned down the Workhouse to prevent it being re-occupied. Also in May 1920 the Stonefield Company spent weeks on guard duty at Boltown House, Kilskyre, Kells guarding members of the Cormeen Gang who had been arrested by the I.R.A., see the story on page 70. In September 1920 Stonefield was the venue for the court-martial of 5th Battalion Officers which resulted in three officers being found guilty of mutiny, see the story on page 40. When I.R.A. structures were reorganised in April 1921 the Stonefield Company became attached to the 2nd Battalion, 3rd Brigade, 1st Eastern Division. In July 1922 the company was involved in an ambush of a military truck at Sylvan Park Kells, see the story on page 47. In July 1921 the company had a strength of 19 men and in July 1922 the company had a strength of eleven men.

Sources: WS1627. WS1659. WS01060. RO 489.

Michael (Mick) Bennett was a Volunteer in the Stonefield I.R.A. Company in July 1921. In April 1921 he and Peter Smith conducted an opportunistic ambush on two R.I.C. men in Stonefield. Source: WS1659.

Michael (Mick) Boylan, Virginia Road, Lisduff, Kells, Co. Meath was a brother of below Patrick and he was an I.R.A. Volunteer in the Stonefield Company in July 1921 and July 1922. On 1st April 1921 he was involved in an ambush of a military truck at Sylvan Park, Kells, see the story on page 47. He died 29th November 1976 and was buried in Ballinlough Cemetery, see page 290.

Sources: RO 489. WS1060. Headstone Inscription.

Patrick Boylan was a brother of above Michael and he was a Volunteer in the Stonefield I.R.A. Company in July 1921 and July 1922. In 1936 his address was given as London, England. He died on 17th April 1972 and was buried in Ballinlough cemetery, see page 290. Source: RO 489. Headstone Inscription

Seamus Cogan, Lisduff, Kells, Co. Meath was born in November 1893. He was from the townland of Clonasillagh. He was the first cousin of below Peter O'Connell. In 1917 he formed the Stonefield Company of Irish Volunteers and he

became the company Commanding Officer. In May 1920 he was appointed 5th Battalion Commanding Officer, Meath Brigade, I.R.A. In July 1920 he was killed in action in an exchange of gunfire with British Troops in Oldcastle, see the story on page 72. Commandant Seamus Cogan was buried in a Republican plot in Balinlough, see page 290. The roll of Battalion Commanding Officer went to Padraig McDonnell from Stonefield, see Ballinlough Company. Sources: WS1659. WS1615. WS1627. Politics and War in Meath 1913-23 by Oliver Coogan. Inscription on Monument in Oldcastle. Inscription on Headstone on grave. WS1715. WS1734.

Charles Conaty, Ballyhist, Carnaross, Kells was born in 1901. In 1916 he worked on the Everard Estate in Randlestown, Navan as Assistant Land Steward. In 1919 he joined the Stonefield I.R.A. Company. In May 1920 he was the Stonefield I.R.A. Company 1st Lieutenant and he spent a week on guard duty at Boltown House, Kilskyre, Kells guarding members of the Cormeen Gang who had been arrested by the I.R.A. see the story on page 70. On 1st April 1921 he was involved in an ambush of a military truck at Sylvan Park, Kells see the story on page 47. In April 1921 when Sean Keogh was arrested again and as part of an overall reorganising of I.R.A. structures Charles Conaty was appointed I.R.A. Battalion Commanding Officer, 2nd Battalion, 3rd Brigade, 1st Eastern Division. He was a wanted man and by the end of June 1921 he was "on the run" and camped out in the open on Mullagh Hill with about 30 other mainly Battalion and Brigade Officers attached to the 3rd Brigade. They formed and became involved in an I.R.A. Active Service Unit (A.S.U.). In 1922 he took the Pro-treaty side and he joined the Free State Army where he was appointed a Captain. On 8th January 1923 he was involved in the capture of a former comrade Mick Hilliard (see Navan Company) in a shed at Peter McMahon's farm (see Moynalty Company). Mick Hilliard faced a charge of being in possession of a revolver which carried the death sentence at the time. Captain Charles Conaty said in his evidence to the court that the revolver might not have been in Hilliard's possession which spared Mick Hilliard's life. On 6th April 1986 he died at his residence. He was buried in Ballinlough Cemetery. Sources: WS1627. WS1060. Irish Press, dated 7th April 1986, Page 2. Faithful to Ireland by Tony Brady, pages 82 & 83.

Matthew Duffy, Gallon, Lisduff, Kells, Co. Meath was a Volunteer in the Stonefield I.R.A. Company in July 1921. Source: RO 489

Matthew Gargan, Lisduff, Kells, Co. Meath was a Volunteer in the Stonefield I.R.A. Company in July 1921 and July 1922. Source: RO 489

Mick Gillic, Lisnagon, Lisduff, Kells, Co. Meath was a Volunteer in the Stonefield I.R.A. Company in July 1921. Source: RO 489

John Greene, Clonasillagh, Lisduff, Kells, Co. Meath was a Volunteer in the Stonefield I.R.A. Company in July 1921. Source: RO 489

Patrick Green, Drumbaragh, Kells, Co. Meath was the Stonefield I.R.A. Company Quartermaster in July 1921. Source: RO 489

James (Jim) Keenan, Clonasillagh, Lisduff, Kells, Co. Meath was a Volunteer in the Stonefield I.R.A. Company in July 1921 and July 1922. Source: RO 489

Matthew Malloy, Lisduff, Kells, Co. Meath was a Volunteer in the Stonefield I.R.A. Company in July 1921 and July 1922. He died before 1936. Source: RO 489

James Masterson, Kingsmountain, Lisduff, Kells, Co. Meath was a Volunteer in the Stonefield I.R.A. Company in July 1921. Source: RO 489

Owen Masterson, Ballyhist, Kells, Co. Meath was a Volunteer in the Stonefield I.R.A. Company in July 1921 and July 1922. Source: RO 489

Ultan McCabe, Lisduff, Kells, Co. Meath was a Volunteer in the Stonefield I.R.A. Company in July 1921. Source: RO 489. Military Service Pension Collection, file reference No. MD-44218

William McCabe, Lisduff, Kells, Co. Meath was a Volunteer in the Stonefield I.R.A. Company in July 1921. Source: RO 489

Matthew McEnroe, Ballinlough, Kells, Co. Meath was a Volunteer in the Stonefield I.R.A. Company in July 1921 and July 1922. Source: RO 489

William Miller was a Volunteer in the Stonefield I.R.A. Company in July 1921. In 1936 his address was given as London, England. Source: RO 489

Michael Mooney was a Volunteer in the Stonefield I.R.A. Company in July 1921. In 1936 his address was given U.S.A. Source: RO 489

Thomas Mulvany, Lisduff, Maghera, Kells was the Stonefield I.R.A. Company 1st Lieutenant in July 1921 and July 1922. On 1st April 1921 he was involved in an ambush of a military truck at Sylvan Park, Kells, see the story on page 47.
Sources: WS1627. RO 489. WS1060.

Peter O'Connell, Fartagh, Virginia, Co. Cavan was born in 1900 and he was a brother of below Thomas and first cousin of above Seamus Cogan. In 1917 he

joined the Stonefield Company of Irish Volunteers. In April or May 1920 he was Involved in a raid on the Income Tax Office in Oldcastle. In May 1920 he was involved in the burning of the Oldcastle Workhouse to prevent it being re-occupied by British Troops. Also in May 1920 he and other members of the Stonefield Company spent some weeks on guard duty at Boltown House, Kilskyre, Kells guarding members of the Cormeen Gang who had been arrested by the I.R.A. see the story on page 70. In September 1920 he succeeded Peter O'Higgins, see Ballinlough Company, as the

Battalion Adjutant, 5th Battalion (Oldcastle), Meath Brigade. Peter O'Higgins had been removed from this post by Sean Boylan on a charge of Mutiny, see that story on page 40. On 1st April 1921 Peter O'Connell was involved in an ambush of a military truck at Sylvan Park, Kells, see the story on page 47. Along with other members of the Stonefield Company he was involved in the burning down of Crossakiel R.I.C. Barracks. In April or May 1921 as part of a re-structuring plan he was appointed I.R.A. Battalion Adjutant, 2nd Battalion, 3rd Brigade, 1st Eastern Division. He was a wanted man and by the end of June 1921 he was "on the run" and camped out in the open on Mullagh Hill with about 30 other mainly Battalion and Brigade Officers attached to the 3rd Brigade. They formed and became involved in an I.R.A. Active Service Unit (A.S.U.). In 1936 his address was given as Glendon, Scots Flat, Singleton, New South Wales, Australia. His name is engraved on a headstone in Ballinlough Cemetery, see page 292.

Sources: WS1659. WS1734. WS1060. WS1627. WS1615. WS1715. Faithful to Ireland by Tony Brady. Headstone Inscription.

Thomas O'Connell, Fartagh, Lisduff, Kells, Co. Meath was a brother of above Peter. On 1st April 1921 he was involved in an ambush of a military truck at Sylvan Park, Kells, see the story on page 47. In July 1921 he was a Volunteer in the Stonefield I.R.A. Company. Source: WS1659.

Peter Smith was a Volunteer in the Stonefield I.R.A. Company in July 1921. In April 1921 he and Mick Bennett conducted an opportunistic ambush on two R.I.C. men in Stonefield. His name is engraved on a headstone in Ballinlough Cemetery, see page 292. Source: WS1659.

Matthew Smyth, Enagh, Lisduff, Kells, Co. Meath was a Volunteer in the Stonefield I.R.A. Company in July 1922. Source: RO 489

Matthew (Matt) Tobin, Tandera was a Volunteer in the Stonefield Company of Irish Volunteers in 1917. On 1st April 1921 he was involved in an ambush of a military truck at Sylvan Park, Kells, see the story on page 47. Source: WS1659.

Michael (Mick) Wynne, Clonasillagh, Virginia Road, Kells, Co. Meath was the Stonefield I.R.A. Company 1st Lieutenant in May 1919. In May 1920 he was appointed Stonefield I.R.A. Company Commanding Officer when Seamus Cogan was promoted to I.R.A. Battalion Commanding Officer. On 1st April 1921 he was involved in an ambush of a military truck at Sylvan Park, Kells, see the story on page 47. In April or May 1921 as part of a re-structuring plan he was appointed Battalion Vice Commanding Officer, 2nd Battalion, 3rd Brigade, 1st Eastern Division and he still held that role in July 1922. In July 1921 his address was given as Lisduff, Co Cavan. He was a wanted man and by the end of June 1921 he was "on the run" and camped out in the open on Mullagh Hill with about 30 other mainly Battalion and Brigade Officers attached to the 3rd Brigade. They formed and became involved in an I.R.A. Active Service Unit (A.S.U.). In 1936 his address was given as Clonasillagh, Kells, Co. Meath. Sources: WS1627. WS1659. WS1060. RO 489.

Patrick Wynne, Clonasillagh, Virginia Road, Kells, Co. Meath was the Stonefield I.R.A. Company 2nd Lieutenant in July 1921. Source: RO 489

Peter Wynne, Clonasillagh, Lisduff, Kells, Co. Meath was the Stonefield I.R.A. Company Commanding Officer in July 1921 and July 1922. Source: RO 489

Summerhill Company:

Towards the end of 1918 Michael Collins visited Summerhill where he spoke at a concert and later attended an Irish Volunteers Brigade Council Meeting. In January 1919 the Irish Volunteers became the I.R.A. In 1921 the Summerhill I.R.A. Company ceased to exist and the remaining Volunteers transferred to the Kilcloon Company. By Easter Sunday 4th April 1920 the R.I.C. had evacuated the Summerhill Barracks due to attacks and R.I.C. men had moved to the safety of bigger towns. The barracks was burnt down by local volunteers to ensure the R.I.C. did not return. In 1920 there were no Volunteers in the Summerhill I.R.A. Company. Sean Boylan said in his Witness Statement that in the Spring of 1921 Michael Collins men intercepted a coded message to Dublin Castle which indicated that Auxiliaries were about to occupy Summerhill Castle, the property of Lord Langford. Lord Langford was a Unionist M.P. and an absentee Landlord. This was seen as a viable threat and Summerhill Castle was burned down to prevent the Auxiliaries from moving in. See below Patrick Cole said he was one of the Volunteers who was involved in that operation. In 1922 the company had a strength of fourteen men. Sources: WS1723. RO 480. WS0901. WS1715.

James Barry, Arodstown, Summerhill, Co. Meath was a Volunteer in the Summerhill I.R.A. Company in July 1922. Source: RO 480

John Barry, College Park, Summerhill, Co. Meath was a Volunteer in the Summerhill I.R.A. Company in July 1922. His name is inscribed on a headstone in Summerhill New Cemetery, see page 371. Source: RO 480. Headstone Inscription

Joseph Cole, Arodstown, Summerhill, Co. Meath was a Volunteer in the Summerhill I.R.A. Company in July 1922. Source: RO 480

Patrick Cole from Arodstown, Summerhill, Co. Meath was one of the few Meath men who were involved in the 1916 Rising. His name appears in the Irish Military Archives Alphabetical List of 1916 Veterans. He was born in 1895. In 1915 and 1916 he worked in Aughrim Street, Dublin and became a member of D Company (The Grocers), 2nd Battalion, Dublin Brigade. He mobilised himself on Tuesday 24th April but could not get to his company who were in Jacobs. He took part in fighting in North King's Street, Church Street and the Bridewell. After the surrender he was interned in Frongoch until Christmas 1916. In 1917 and 1918 he was a Volunteer in the Dunboyne Company Volunteers. In 1919 and 1921 he was the 1st Lieutenant of the Kilmore Company. In July 1922 he was in the Summerhill Company of Irish Volunteers. In his submission to the Pension Board he claimed to have been involved in the burning of Lord Langford's House in Summerhill. In 1936 his address was given as Mullagh, Kilcock. After lengthy deliberation he was eventually awarded a Military Pension 1942. He died 26th February 1965. Sources: RO 480. www.militaryarchives.ie/fileadmin/user_upload/MSPC/WENTIRELISTRELEASE1.pdf Military Archives File No MSP34REF4992

Eamon Cullen was a Volunteer in the Summerhill Company of Irish Volunteers in 1916 and 1917. After the failed Rising he got involved in mustering up disappointed Volunteers and trying to get them to regroup and reorganise. In 1918 he was the Summerhill I.R.A. Company Commanding Officer. In the summer of 1920 he was appointed I.R.A. Battalion Engineer, 2nd Battalion, Meath Brigade. He later became Brigade Engineer, Meath Brigade. As Brigade Engineer he gave classes and instructions on how to make crude hand grenades. In January 1921 he was busy making land mines for road ambushes and destruction of bridges. Carlanstown bridge was blown up under his command, see page 44. In March 1921 he was promoted to Colonel Commandant and he became Divisional Vice Commanding Officer and Engineer, I.R.A. He set up small bomb factories in almost all Brigade areas of Meath, Westmeath, Cavan. In February 1921 he ordered a raid on Kells Post Office to remove a Telegraph Machine that was being used by the R.I.C, see the story on page 46. In June 1921 his name was high on the most wanted list and several raids were conducted by the British Army in the in Ballyhist, Carnaross area looking for him. In December 1922 he was a Garda Chief Superintendent. Later in his career be became the Deputy Commissioner of An Garda Síochána. Sources: WS1663. WS0857. WS1715. WS1060. WS1696. WS1659. Garda Síochána Historical Society Irish Police History website http://www.policehistory.com/issues.html WS1627 Bureau of Military Service Pension Collection, file reference No MSP34REF38375 of Mary Connell, Lustown, Batterstown, Co Meath.

Peter Dolan, Summerhill was a member of the I.R.B. In October 1919 he was a Volunteer in the Summerhill I.R.A. Company and he was involved in a failed attack on Summerhill R.I.C. Barracks. The R.I.C. subsequently evacuated the barracks and moved to the safety of bigger towns. The barracks were burnt down by local Volunteers to ensure the R.I.C. did not return. In July 1921 he was the Battalion Vice Commanding Officer. In 1936 his address was gives as U.S.A. Source: WS0901. WS1723. RO 479. RO 4083.

Joseph Farrell, Moynalvy, Summerhill, Co. Meath was a Volunteer in the Summerhill I.R.A. Company in July 1922. He transferred to the Kilcloon Company in 1921 because the Summerhill Company failed to exist. See also the Kilcloon Company. Source: RO 480

Joseph Fitzsimons, Moynalvy, Summerhill, Co. Meath was a Volunteer in the Summerhill I.R.A. Company in July 1922. Source: RO 480

John Gannon, Galtrim, Summerhill, Co. Meath was a Volunteer in the Summerhill I.R.A. Company in July 1922. Source: RO 480

Edward Gill, Derrypatrick, Drumree, Co. Meath was a Volunteer in the Summerhill I.R.A. Company in July 1922. Source: RO 480

Michael Graham was a member of the I.R.B. In the autumn of 1919 he was a Volunteer with the Summerhill Company I.R.A. and he was involved in a failed attack on Summerhill R.I.C. Barracks. The R.I.C. subsequently evacuated the barracks and moved to the safety of bigger towns. The barracks were burnt down by local Volunteers to ensure the R.I.C. did not return. In 1921 he was the Summerhill Company Commanding officer.
Source: Politics and War in Meath 1913-23 by Oliver Coogan. WS0901. WS1723.

Michael Grehan, Summerhill, Co. Meath was born about 1895. He was a Volunteer in the Summerhill I.R.A. Company in October 1919. He died in October 1970 aged 75 years and was buried in Summerhill New Cemetery, see page 371.
Sources: WS0901. Headstone Inscription

Patrick Grogan, Summerhill, Co. Meath was a member of the I.R.B. In October 1919 he was a Volunteer in the Summerhill I.R.A. Company and he was involved in a failed attack on Summerhill R.I.C. Barracks. The R.I.C. subsequently evacuated the barracks and moved to the safety of bigger towns. The barracks were burnt down by local Volunteers to ensure the R.I.C. did not return. Sources: WS0901. WS1723.

Edward Kearney, Summerhill was a member of the I.R.B. In October 1919 he was a Volunteer in the Summerhill I.R.A. Company and he was involved in a failed attack on Summerhill R.I.C. Barracks. The R.I.C. subsequently evacuated the barracks and moved to the safety of bigger towns. The barracks were burnt down by local Volunteers to ensure the R.I.C. did not return. Source: WS0901. WS1723.

James Malone, Moynalvy, Summerhill, Co. Meath was a Volunteer in the Summerhill I.R.A. Company in July 1922. Source: RO 480

James Powderly, Deerpark, Garlow Cross, Navan, Co. Meath was a Volunteer in the Summerhill I.R.A. Company in July 1922. Source: RO 480

Christopher Sheridan, Cloneymeath, Summerhill, Co. Meath was a Volunteer in the Summerhill I.R.A. Company in July 1922. Source: RO 480

Matthew Sheridan, Maudlins, Trim, Co. Meath was a Volunteer in the Summerhill I.R.A. Company in July 1922. Source: RO 480

Patrick Thompson, Kilmore, Kilcock, Co. Meath was a Volunteer in the Summerhill I.R.A. Company in July 1922. Source: RO 480

Patrick Troy, Cloneymeath, Summerhill, Co. Meath was a Volunteer in the Summerhill I.R.A. Company in July 1922. Source: RO 480

Trim Company:

In the summer of 1920 the Trim I.R.A. Company was attached to the 2nd Battalion, Meath Brigade. In September 1920 the Trim Company was involved in an attack on the heavily fortified Trim R.I.C. Barracks

which is now the Castle Court Hotel. That night British Troops retaliated by attacking the town, see the story on page 40. Many of the I.R.A. Volunteers were arrested and interned and the rest of them had to go "On The Run." While "on the run" some of them became involved in an Active Service Unit (A.S.U.). In 1921 the Volunteers were still "on the run" and the local people formed a 2nd Trim I.R.A. Company in the town. On 9th February 1921 a curfew was imposed on the town from 10pm to 5am nightly. No one was allowed out on the streets during these hours except Doctors, Nurses and Clergy. Trim was the only town in Co. Meath that had a curfew. 11th February 1921 a company of Auxiliaries were drafted into Trim and they occupied the Industrial School which now is the Convent of Mercy Secondary School. In July 1921 the Trim I.R.A. Company had a strength of 23 men. In July 1922 the company had a strength of eighteen men.
Source: RO 485. WS1696. Dunderry A Folk History by Dunderry History Group & Johnny Keely

Christopher Andrews, Trim, Co Meath was a Volunteer in the Trim Company of Irish Volunteers in 1918. He was a Volunteer in the Trim I.R.A. Company in 1920. In September 1920 he was involved in an attack on the heavily fortified Trim R.I.C. Barracks, see the story on page 40. Sources: RO 485. WS0858.

Matthew Andrews, Trim, Co. Meath was a Volunteer in the Trim Company of Irish Volunteers In 1918. He was a Volunteer in the Trim I.R.A. Company in 1920. In September 1920 he was involved in an attack on the heavily fortified Trim R.I.C. Barracks, see the story on page 40. Source: RO 485. WS0858.

John Bishop, No 9, Castle Street, Trim, Co. Meath was a Volunteer in the Trim Company of Irish Volunteers in 1917. He was a Volunteer in the Trim I.R.A. Company in 1919 and 1922. He died in February 1955 and was buried in St. Loman's Cemetery, Trim, see page 381. Source: RO 485. Headstone Inscription

William (Billy) Carter, Trim, Co. Meath was involved in setting up another company of Irish Volunteers in Trim while the 1st company was "on the run" in 1921. Source: WS1696.

Walter (Wally) Carter, Haggard Street, Trim, Co. Meath was involved in setting up another company of Irish Volunteers in Trim in 1921 while the 1st company was "on the run". He died in January 1975 aged 73 years and was buried in St. Loman's Cemetery, Trim, see page 381. Sources: WS1696. RO 485. Headstone Inscription.

James Cowley was a Volunteer in the Trim I.R.A. Company in July 1922. In 1936 his address was given as The Asylum, Mullingar, Co. Westmeath. Source: RO 485

Thomas Creighton was a Volunteer in the Trim I.R.A. Company in July 1922. He died before 1936. Source: RO 485

Michael Doggett, Trimblestown, Trim, Co. Meath was a Volunteer in the Trim I.R.A. Company in July 1921. Source: RO 485

Philip (Phil) Doggett, Trim, Co. Meath was involved in an attack on the heavily fortified Trim R.I.C. Barracks in September 1920, see the story on page 40. His name is engraved on a headstone in St. Loman's Cemetery, see page 382.

Source: WS0858. Politics and War in Meath 1913-23 by Oliver Coogan, page 139

Patrick Duignan was born in Trim, Co. Meath about 1900. After the failed Rising of 1916 he got involved in mustering up disappointed Volunteers and trying to get them to regroup and reorganise. In 1917 he was a Volunteer in the Trim Company of Irish Volunteers. In the summer of 1920 he was appointed I.R.A. Battalion Quartermaster, 2nd Battalion, Meath Brigade. In September 1920 he was involved in an attack on the heavily fortified Trim R.I.C. Barracks, see the story on page 40. As a wanted man he had to go "on the run". In March 1921 he was still "on the run" but he was eventually arrested and imprisoned in Mountjoy, Dublin for offences under the Restoration of Order in Ireland Regulations (ROIR). Sources: RO 485. WS0857. MM9.1.1/KM79-TTT. WS1696.

? Duignan, Trim, Co. Meath. This was Pat's brother. In 1921 he was a Volunteer in the Trim I.R.A. Company and he was also "on the run". Source: WS1696.

? Duignan, Trim, Co. Meath. This was Pat's Sister. In 1921 she was wanted by British Authorities and she was also "on the run". Source: WS1696.

Patrick Fay, Kilbride, Trim, Co. Meath was the Trim Company of Irish Volunteers 1st Lieutenant in 1917. In October 1919 he was involved in an attack on Ballivor R.I.C. Barracks in which one R.I.C. man was shot dead, see the story on page 37. In September 1920 he was involved in an attack on the heavily fortified Trim R.I.C. Barracks, see the story on page 40. The local word in Kilbride is that at one stage Patrick was aware that he was being followed by a British Army under cover spy. He lured the spy into an ambush where he was shot dead. In 1921 Patrick was involved in setting up another company of Irish Volunteers in Trim while the 1st company was "on the run"
Sources: WS0901. WS0858. WS1696. Dunderry A Folk History by Dunderry History Group & Johnny Keely.

Michael (Mick) Giles, a native of Longwood, Co. Meath was born about 1897. In 1915 he was on the Trim team that won the second in a row Meath Senior Hurling  Championship. In 1917 he was a Volunteer in the Trim Company of Irish Volunteers. In December he was the company 1st Lieutenant. In September 1920 he was involved in an attack on the heavily fortified Trim R.I.C. Barracks, see the story on page 40. As a wanted man he had to go "On The Run." He was eventually arrested and imprisoned in Mountjoy, Dublin for offences under the Restoration of Order in Ireland Regulations (ROIR) and for being in possession of documents. The prison records say that his residential address was Main Street, Trim. In July 1921 he was still the Trim I.R.A. Company 1st Lieutenant. His name is inscribed on a headstone in Longwood, see age 380 Sources: WS0857. WS0858. RO 485. MM9.1.1/KMQR-5QQ. MM9.1.1/KM79-TZ1. Trim G.A.A. Team photographs ndly provided by Seamus Brennan, Trim. Headstone Inscription.

Nicholas (Nick) Giles, Trim Co. Meath got involved in trying to bolster up disappointed Volunteers in an effort to get them to regroup and reorganise after the failed Rising of 1916. He was a Volunteer in the Trim I.R.A. Company in July 1920. In September 1920 he was involved in an attack on the heavily fortified Trim R.I.C. Barracks, see the story on page 40. As a wanted man he had to go "on the run". Source: WS0857.

Richard Hamon, Emmet Street, Trim, Co. Meath was a Volunteer in the Trim Company of Irish Volunteers in 1917. He was a Volunteer in the Trim I.R.A. Company in 1920 and July 1922. Source: RO 485

John (Jack) Healy was born in Kells, Co. Meath about 1902. In September 1920 he was involved in an attack on the heavily fortified Trim R.I.C. Barracks, see the story on page 40. He was arrested and imprisoned in Mountjoy, Dublin for offences under the Restoration of Order in Ireland Regulations (ROIR). In 1921 he was a Volunteer in the Trim Company of Irish Volunteers. In 1936 his address was given as U.S.A. He died in 1985 and was buried in St. Loman's cemetery, see page 382. Sources: RO 485. MM9.1.1/KM79-TTP. Headstone Inscription.

Higgins – See O'Higgins

Michael (Mick) Hynes Tullyard, Trim, Co. Meath was born about 1882 and

described himself as a small farmer. In the early 1900 he was a prominent player on the Bohermeen G.A.A. football team and the Trim hurling team. In 1915 he was on the Trim team that won the second in a row Meath Senior Hurling Championship. He got involved in trying to boost up disappointed Volunteers and trying to get them to regroup and reorganise after the failed Rising of 1916. In January or February 1917 he was the Trim Company 1st Lieutenant Irish Volunteers. In late 1918 or early 1919 he was appointed Irish Volunteers Battalion Quartermaster. In the summer of 1920 he was appointed I.R.A. Battalion Commanding Officer, 2nd Battalion, Meath Brigade. In September 1920 he was involved in an attack on the heavily fortified Trim R.I.C. Barracks. Michael Hynes and Paddy Mooney were jointly in charge of the actual attack, see the story on page 40. In October 1920 Mick Hynes was "on the run", however he was involved in an I.R.A. Active Service Unit (A.S.U.). At the end of 1920 he was the I.R.A. 2nd Battalion (Trim) Commanding Officer. He was appointed I.R.A. Brigade Quartermaster of 2nd Brigade in March or April 1921. In 1922 he took the Free

State side and served in the Free State Army until 1924. In November 1936 he attended a meeting to gather information related to qualifying Volunteers for the Military Service Pensions where he was appointed Chairman of the Brigade Committee. He died in 1956 and he was buried with full military honours in Moymet Graveyard, Kilbride, Trim, see page 377. For some unknown reason he was not buried in the Hynes family plot which is in the same graveyard. His name is not marked on his grave and despite local requests to political representatives over the years to have the grave properly identified it has not happened. Will it be done for the 2016 Centenary?

Sources: WS1715. WS0858. WS0857. WS1622. WS1696. WS1060. RO 484. Personal Interview with Sean Fay, Moymet, Kilbride on 27/01/15. Obituary in Meath Chronicle, 1956. Trim G.A.A. Team photographs kindly provided by Seamus Brennan, Trim.

Patrick (Pat) Hynes, Tullyard, Trim Co. Meath was involved in an attack on the heavily fortified Trim R.I.C. Barracks in September 1920, see the story on page 40. In October 1920, as a wanted man, he had to go "on the run", however he was involved in an Active Service Unit (A.S.U.). In early 1921 he was still "on the run" and involved in an A.S.U. that took part in an ambush of a military foot patrol at Haggard Street, Trim, see the story on page 43. He continued with the Trim Company throughout 1921. Sources: WS1060. RO 487. WS0858.

Joe (Poultice) Kelly was on the Trim team that won the second in a row Meath

Senior Hurling Championship in 1915. He was a Volunteer in the Trim I.R.A. Company in 1920. In September 1920 he was involved in an attack on the heavily fortified Trim R.I.C. Barracks, see the story on page 40. In October 1920, as a wanted man, he had to go "on the run", however he was involved in an Active Service Unit (A.S.U.). In early 1921 he was still "on the run" and involved in an A.S.U. that took part in an ambush of a military foot patrol at Haggard Street, Trim, see the story on page 43. He continued with the Trim Company throughout 1921. His name is engraved on a headstone in St. Loman's Cemetery, see page 382. Sources: WS1060. RO 485. Trim G.A.A. Team photographs kindly provided by Seamus Brennan, Trim.

George Lawlor was a Volunteer in the Trim Company of Irish Volunteers in 1917. He was a Volunteer in the Trim I.R.A. Company in 1919 and July 1922. In 1936 his address was given as Cooloney, Co. Sligo. Source: RO 485

Joseph Lalor, Trim Co. Meath got involved in trying to strengthen disappointed Volunteers and trying to get them to regroup and reorganise after the failed Rising of 1916. In 1917 he was a Volunteer in the Trim Company of Irish Volunteers. In October 1919 he was the Trim I.R.A. Company 1st Lieutenant. In September 1920 he was involved in an attack on the heavily fortified Trim R.I.C. Barracks, see the story on page 40. As a wanted man, he had to go "on the run". In July 1922 he was an I.R.A. Battalion Commanding Officer and there was no other Battalion Staff. His address was given as c/o B. McGinley, Finglas, Dublin. Sources: WS0857. WS0901. WS0858. RO 485.

Mark Lawlor was a Volunteer in the Trim I.R.A. Company in 1922. In 1936 he was a member of An Garda Síochána and his address was given as Dublin. Source: RO 485

Patrick Lalor was a Volunteer in the Trim Company of Irish Volunteers In 1917. He was a Volunteer in the Trim I.R.A. Company in October 1919 and 1920. In September 1920 he was involved in an attack on the heavily fortified Trim R.I.C. Barracks, see the story on page 40. In 1936 he was a member of An Garda Síochána and his address was given as Dublin. Sources: RO 485. WS0901. WS0858.

William J. Lawlor, Mill House, Trim, Co. Meath was a Volunteer in the Trim I.R.A. Company in July 1922. Source: RO 485

Matthew (Matty) Matthews, Oakstown, Trim, Co. Meath aged sixteen was involved in an attack on the heavily fortified Trim R.I.C. Barracks in September 1920, see the story on page 40. In July 1921 he was a Volunteer in the Trim I.R.A. Company. He died in December 1978 aged 74 and was buried in St. Loman's Cemetery, see page 382. Sources: RO 485. WS0858.

Peter Matthews, Trim, Co. Meath was a Volunteer in the Trim I.R.A. Company in July 1921. Source: RO 485

Michael (The Gale) McArdle, Trim, Co. Meath was ex-British Army sniper. In March 1921 he was a Volunteer in the Trim I.R.A. Company. As a wanted man, he had to go "on the run", however he was involved in an I.R.A. Active Service Unit (A.S.U.). In early 1921 he and the A.S.U. took part in an ambush of a military foot patrol at Haggard Street, Trim, see the story on page 43. While the original Trim I.R.A. Company were "on the run" he helped the local people to form a 2nd company in the town. He was appointed the company Commanding Officer of this 2nd Trim I.R.A. Company in 1921. He died in August 1973 aged 77 years and was buried in St. Loman's Cemetery, see page 383.
Sources: WS1060. RO 485. Headstone Inscription. Dunderry A Folk History by Dunderry History Group & Johnny Keely.

James McCormack, Connally Ave., Navan, Co. Meath was a Volunteer in the Trim I.R.A. Company in July 1922. Source: RO 485

John McCormack was a Volunteer in the Trim I.R.A. Company in July 1922. In 1936 his address was given as London, England. Source: RO 485

Robert McCormack was a Volunteer in the Trim I.R.A. Company in July 1922. In 1936 his address was given as Blackrock College, Dublin. Source: RO 485

William McCormack was a Volunteer in the Trim I.R.A. Company in July 1922. In 1936 his address was given as Chester, England. Source: RO 485

Patrick McCullagh was a Volunteer in the Trim Company of Irish Volunteers in 1917. He was a Volunteer in the Trim I.R.A. Company in 1920. In 1936 his address was given as Carlow. Source: RO 485

John Mooney was a Volunteer in the Trim I.R.A. Company in July 1919 and July 1921. He was a brother of below Patrick. In September 1920 he was involved in an attack on the heavily fortified Trim R.I.C. Barracks, see the story on page 40. In 1936 his address was given as England. Sources: RO 485. WS0858.

Patrick (Pat) Mooney, Trim Co Meath was on the Trim team that won the second in a row Meath Senior Hurling Championship in 1915. He got involved in mustering up disappointed Volunteers and trying to get them to regroup and reorganise after the failed Rising of 1916. He was a  brother of above John. In 1917 he was the Trim Company Commanding Officer. He was involved in organising the Bective Company of Irish Volunteers and he became their drill instructor. In October 1919 Pat led an attack on Ballivor R.I.C. Barracks in which one R.I.C. man was shot dead, see the story on page 37. In the summer of 1920 he was appointed I.R.A. Battalion Vice Commanding Officer, 2nd Battalion, Meath Brigade. In September 1920 he was involved in an attack on the heavily fortified Trim R.I.C. Barracks, see the story on page 40. Michael Hynes and Paddy Mooney were jointly in charge of the actual attack. In October 1920 he was the Battalion Vice Commanding Officer but he was "on the run". He stayed out of sight in Patrick O'Reilly's house in Moynalty for a while, however he was involved in an Active Service Unit (A.S.U.). In December 1920 he was the Brigade Training Officer and Division Assistant. In March 1921 he was "on the run". In early 1921 he was still "on the run" and involved in an A.S.U. that took part in an ambush of a military foot patrol at Haggard Street, Trim, see the story on page 43. Also in April 1921 he was appointed Battalion Commanding Officer. On the 2nd July 1921, about two weeks before the Truce, he was involved in a failed attack on a troop train near Celbridge, see the story on page 51. In 1921 his address was given as Dublin. He died in September 1961 aged 83 and was buried in St. Loman's Cemetery, see page 383. Sources: WS0857. WS1715. WS0858. WS0932. WS1060. WS1696. WS1715. Trim G.A.A. Team photographs kindly provided by Seamus Brennan, Trim.

James (Seamus) Moore, Market Street, Trim, Co. Meath was a Volunteer prior to 1919. He was also a member of the local Hurling Team. He died at his residence on 16th March 1919 aged 24 years from Sceptic Pneumonia as a result of Influenza. This was caused by a flu epidemic that spread across Europe killing thousands of people in late 1918 early 1919. He was buried in Moymet Cemetery, Kilbride, Trim, see page 377.
Source: The Meath Chronicle dated around March 1919 (date on paper is smudged). Headstone Inscription.

Joseph Nolan, Trim, Co. Meath was involved in an attack on the heavily fortified Trim R.I.C. Barracks in September 1920, see the story on page 40. In July 1921 he was a Volunteer in the Trim I.R.A. Company. Sources: RO 485. WS0858.

John O'Dore, Newhaggard Road, Trim, Co. Meath was a Volunteer in the Trim I.R.A. Company in July 1922. Source: RO 485

Harry O'Hagan, Trim, Co. Meath got involved in trying to bolster up disappointed Volunteers in an effort to get them to regroup and reorganise after the failed Rising of 1916. In 1917 and October 1919 he was the Trim Company 2nd Lieutenant. In September 1920 he was involved in an attack on the heavily fortified Trim R.I.C. Barracks, see the story on page 40. He died in December 1981 and was buried in St. Loman's Cemetery, see page 383.
Sources: RO 485. WS0857. WS0858. Headstone Inscription.

James H. O'Hagan, Trim, Co. Meath was the Trim I.R.A. Company Commanding Officer in July 1922. Source: RO 485

Patrick (Pat) (Sap) O'Hagan, Emmet St. Trim, Co. Meath was on the Trim team that won the second in a row Meath Senior Hurling Championship in 1915. He got involved in trying to boost up disappointed Volunteers and trying to get them to regroup and reorganise after the failed Rising of 1916. In 1917 he was a Volunteer in the Trim Company of Irish Volunteers. In 1920 and July 1922 he was a Volunteer in the Trim I.R.A. Company. In September 1920 he was involved in an attack on the heavily fortified Trim R.I.C. Barracks, see the story on page 40. Sources: RO 485. WS0857. WS0858. Trim G.A.A. Team photographs kindly provided by Seamus Brennan, Trim. Dunderry A Folk History by Dunderry History Group & Johnny Keely.

Patrick (Pat) O'Hara, Trim, Co. Meath was involved in an attack on the heavily fortified Trim R.I.C. Barracks in September 1920, see the story on page 40.
Sources: Politics and War in Meath 1913-23 by Oliver Coogan, page 139. WS0858.

Seamus (Jim) O'Higgins was born in Trim, Co. Meath about 1894. He was a member of the Trim Senior Hurling Team in 1914. In 1915 he was on the Trim

team that won the second in a row Meath Senior Hurling Championship. He was a brother of below Sean. In 1916 he was a Volunteer in the Trim Company of Irish Volunteers. After the failed Rising he got involved in trying to strengthen disappointed Volunteers and trying to get them to regroup and reorganise. He was involved in organising the Bective Company of Irish Volunteers. In January or February 1917 he

Seamus O'Higgins. Photo kindly provided by Seamus Brennan, Trim.

became the company Commanding Officer. On 24th January 1918 he addressed a public meeting in Ballivor to start a Sinn Fein Club, fifty men

enrolled. In early 1919 he was arrested and imprisoned in Mountjoy, Dublin for offences under the Defence of the Realm Regulations (DRR). He took part in a hunger strike. When released he had to go "on the run" again. He was in poor health after the hunger strike and went to Kilcormac Co. Offaly to recuperate. In August 1919 Seamus Higgins resumed activities after returning from Co. Offaly and he was appointed Brigade Quartermaster, Meath Brigade, I.R.A. As a wanted man in 1920, he had to continue "on the run", however he was involved in an Active Service Unit (A.S.U.). On Sunday 30th September 1920 he was involved in the attack on the heavily fortified Trim R.I.C. Barracks as a member of the A.S.U., see the story on page 40. In early 1921 he was still "on the run" and involved in an A.S.U. that took part in an ambush of a military foot patrol at Haggard Street, Trim, see the story on page 43. In March 1921 he was appointed Division Quartermaster and he became a Colonel Commandant. Sources: WS0901. WS1060. WS0857. WS1696. MM9.1.1/KM79-G89. WS0858. WS1715. Trim G.A.A. Team photographs kindly provided by Seamus Brennan, Trim. The Meath Chronicle dated 9th Feb 1918

Sean O'Higgins, Trim, Co. Meath was a brother of above Seamus. He got involved in mustering up disappointed Volunteers and trying to get them to regroup and reorganise after the failed Rising of 1916. In the summer of 1920 he was appointed I.R.A. Battalion Adjutant, 2nd Battalion, Meath Brigade. As a wanted man he was "on the run", however he was involved in an Active Service Unit (A.S.U.). In September 1920 he was involved in an attack on the heavily fortified Trim R.I.C. Barracks as part of the A.S.U., see the story on page 40. In early 1921 he was still "on the run" and involved in an A.S.U. that took part in an ambush of a military foot patrol at Haggard Street, Trim, see the story on page 43. He died before 1936. Sources: WS0857. WS1060. WS1696. WS1715. RO 485

Michael Plunkett was born in Trim, Co. Meath about 1901. In July 1921 he was a Volunteer in the Trim I.R.A. Company but he was arrested and imprisoned in Mountjoy, Dublin for offences under the under the Restoration of Order in Ireland Regulations (ROIR). Sources: RO 485. MM9.1.1/KM79-TY3.

Patrick Proctor was a Volunteer in the Trim Company of Irish Volunteers in 1917. In 1920 and July 1922 he was a Volunteer in the Trim I.R.A. Company. In September 1920 he was involved in an attack on the heavily fortified Trim R.I.C. Barracks, see the story on page 40. In 1921 we was a member of Trim Urban Council. In 1936 he gave his address as Town Hall, Trim, Co. Meath.
Sources: RO 485. WS0858. WS1060.

Michael Rogers was a Volunteer in the Trim I.R.A. Company in July 1922. In 1936 his address was given as Emmet Terrace, Navan, Co. Meath. Source: RO 485

Patrick Scfton, Trim Co. Meath was a Volunteer in the Trim I.R.A. Company. He emigrated to Australia sometime after 1921. He died in 1937 in Sydney Australia.
Source: The Meath Chronicle dated 9th September 1939, page 4

Edward (Ned) Sherry, The Rock, Trim, Co. Meath was a Volunteer in the Trim I.R.A. Company in July 1921. Source: RO 485

James (Jim) Sherry was a brother of below John. In 1920 and July 1921 he was a Volunteer in the Trim I.R.A. Company. In September 1920 he was involved in an attack on the heavily fortified Trim R.I.C. Barracks, see the story on page 40. In October 1920, as a wanted man, he had to go "on the run", however he was involved in an Active Service Unit (A.S.U.). In 1936 his address was given as England. Sources: WS1696. RO 485.

John Sherry was a brother of above Jim. In 1920 he was a Volunteer in the Trim I.R.A. Company. In September 1920 he was involved in an attack on the heavily fortified Trim R.I.C. Barracks, see the story on page 40. In October 1920, as a wanted man, he had to go "on the run", however he was involved in an Active Service Unit (A.S.U.). Sources: WS1696.

Luke Sherry, Kildalkey, Co. Meath was involved in an attack on the heavily fortified Trim R.I.C. Barracks in September 1920, see the story on page 40. In July 1921 he was a Volunteer in the Trim I.R.A. Company. Sources: RO 485. WS0858

Stephen Sherry was a Volunteer in the Trim I.R.A. Company in October 1919. In September 1920 he was involved in the attack on the heavily fortified Trim R.I.C. Barracks, see the story on page 40. Sources: WS0858. WS0901.

Thomas (Tom) Sherry, Scurlogstown, Trim and formally of Emmet Street, Trim and formally of Grangeboyne, Trim was involved in an attack on the heavily fortified Trim R.I.C. Barracks in September 1920, see the story on page 40. He was a Volunteer in the Trim I.R.A. Company in July 1921 and July 1922. He died in May 1943. His name is inscribed on a headstone in St. Loman's Cemetery, see page 384. Sources: RO 485. The Meath Chronicle dated 29th May 1943, page 5. WS0858. Headstone Inscription.

William (Bill) Sherry, Dogstown, Trim, Co. Meath was a Volunteer in the Trim I.R.A. Company in July 1921. There was a William Sherry in Dunderry Company of Irish Volunteers in 1919. I do not know if this is the same William Sherry, see Dunderry Company. Source: RO 485

Edward Smyth, Kiltoome, Trim, Co. Meath helped the local people of Trim to form a 2nd I.R.A. company in the town while the original company was "on the run" in June 1921. He was a Volunteer in this 2nd company. Sources: WS1696. RO 485

Patrick Ward, Kilnagross, Trim, Co. Meath was a Volunteer in the Trim I.R.A. Company in July 1921. Source: RO 485

Thomas Waters was a Volunteer in the Trim Company of Irish Volunteers in 1918. In July 1920 he was a Volunteer in the Trim I.R.A. Company. He died before 1936. Source: RO 485

Whitegate Company:

The Whitegate I.R.A. Company was formed about September 1920. When I.R.A. structures were reorganised in April 1921 the Whitegate Company became attached to the 2nd Battalion, 3rd Brigade, 1st Eastern Division. In July 1921 the Whitegate I.R.A. Company had a strength of 29 men. In July 1922 there were no Volunteers so the company ceased to exist. Sources: RO 489. WS1627. WS1659.

Michael Bennett, Fartagh, Lisduff, Kells, Co. Meath was a Volunteer in the Whitegate I.R.A. Company in July 1921. Source: RO 489

Patrick Bennett, Fartagh, Lisduff, Kells, Co. Meath was a Volunteer in the Whitegate I.R.A. Company in July 1921. Source: RO 489

Andy Brady, Fartagh, Lisduff, Kells, Co. Meath was a Volunteer in the Whitegate I.R.A. Company in July 1921. Source: RO 489

Bernard Brady, Stramatt, Lisduff, Kells, Co. Meath was a Volunteer in the Whitegate I.R.A. Company in July 1921. Source: RO 489

Mick Cahill, Bruse, Lisduff, Kells, Co. Meath was a Volunteer in the Whitegate I.R.A. Company in July 1921. Source: RO 489

Philip Cahill, Edenburt, Lisduff, Kells, Co. Meath was a Volunteer in the Whitegate I.R.A. Company in July 1921. Source: RO 489

Harry Carroll, Edenburt, Lisduff, Kells, Co. Meath was a Volunteer in the Whitegate I.R.A. Company in July 1921. Source: RO 489

Joe Carroll, Edenburt, Lisduff, Kells, Co. Meath was a Volunteer in the Whitegate I.R.A. Company in July 1921. Source: RO 489

Philip Carroll, Edenburt, Lisduff, Kells, Co. Meath was a Volunteer in the Whitegate I.R.A. Company in July 1921. Source: RO 489

Thomas Carroll, Edenburt, Lisduff, Kells, Co. Meath was a Volunteer in the Whitegate I.R.A. Company in July 1921. Source: RO 489

Bryan Daly, Fartagh, Lisduff, Kells, Co. Meath was a Volunteer in the Whitegate I.R.A. Company in July 1921. Source: RO 489

John Madden, Whitegate, Lisduff, Kells, Co. Meath was a Volunteer in the Whitegate I.R.A. Company in July 1921. Source: RO 489

John McFadden, Cloughbally, Mullagh, Co. Cavan was a Volunteer in the Whitegate I.R.A. Company in July 1921. Source: RO 489

Bryan McGivna, Dervor, Carnaross, Kells, Co. Meath was a Volunteer in the Whitegate I.R.A. Company in July 1921. Source: RO 489

Thomas Mooney, Dervor, Carnaross, Kells, Co. Meath was a Volunteer in the Whitegate I.R.A. Company in July 1921. Source: RO 489

Thomas Morris, Fartagh, Lisduff, Kells, Co. Meath was a Volunteer in the Whitegate I.R.A. Company in July 1921. Source: RO 489

Mick Murtagh was a Volunteer in the Whitegate Company of Irish Volunteers in July 1921. In 1936 his address was given as 126 North Circular Rd, Dublin. Source: RO 489

John O'Reilly, Cloughbally, Mullagh, Co. Cavan was a Volunteer in the Whitegate I.R.A. Company in July 1921. Source: RO 489

Patrick J. O'Reilly, Cloughbally, Mullagh, Co. Cavan was a Volunteer in the Whitegate I.R.A. Company in July 1921. In 1936 he was serving in the Free State Army. Source: RO 489.

Andy Reilly, Enagh, Lisduff, Kells, Co. Meath was a Volunteer in the Whitegate I.R.A. Company in July 1921. In 1936 his address was given as Co. Monaghan. Source: RO 489

Charles Reilly, Fartagh, Lisduff, Kells, Co. Meath was a Volunteer in the Whitegate I.R.A. Company in July 1921. Source: RO 489

James Reilly, Cloughbally Mullagh, Co. Cavan was the Whitegate I.R.A. Company Quartermaster in July 1921. In 1936 his address was given as U.S.A. Source: RO 489

James Reilly, Bruse, Lisduff, Kells, Co. Meath was a Volunteer in the Whitegate I.R.A. Company in July 1921. In 1936 his address was given as Australia. Source: RO 489

Patrick Reilly, Fartagh, Lisduff, Kells, Co. Meath was the Whitegate I.R.A. Company Adjutant in July 1921. Source: RO 489

Peter Smith, Cloughbally Mullagh, Co. Cavan was the Whitegate I.R.A. Company Commanding Officer in July 1921. Source: RO 489

Edward (Ned) Tobin, Drumbaragh, Kells, Co. Meath was a Volunteer in the Whitegate I.R.A. Company in July 1921. Source: RO 489

Patrick Tobin, Drumbaragh, Kells, Co. Meath was involved in an ambush of a military truck at Sylvan Park, Kells on 1st April 1921, see the story on page 47. In July 1921 he was the Whitegate I.R.A. Company 1st Lieutenant. Sources: WS1060. WS1627. WS1659.

James Tuite was a Volunteer in the Whitegate I.R.A. Company in July 1921. In 1936 his address was given as Brixton, London, England. Source: RO 489.

Yellow Furze Company:

The Yellow Furze I.R.A. Company was formed about early 1919 and became part of the 6th Battalion. In July 1921 the Yellow Furze I.R.A. Company had a strength of 25 men. Days before the Truce the Yellow Furze Company was involved in failed attack on a troop train at Celbridge, see the story on page 51. In July 1922 there were no Volunteers so the company ceased to exist. Sources: WS1060. RO 486. WS1624.

James Bowens, Smithstown, Hayes, Navan, Co. Meath was a Volunteer in the Yellow Furze I.R.A. Company in July 1921.
Source: RO 486. Military Service Pension Collection, file reference No. 34-SP-41324

Edward Byrne, was a Volunteer in the Yellow Furze I.R.A. Company in July 1921. In 1936 he was serving in the Free State Army. Source: RO 486

Peter Byrne was the Yellow Furze Company Engineer in July 1921. In 1936 his address was given as England. Source: RO 486

Richard Carter, Brownstown, Navan, Co. Meath was a Volunteer in the Yellow Furze I.R.A. Company in July 1921.
Source: RO 486 Military Service Pension Collection, file reference No. 348-P-40389

Christopher Collins, Greenhills, Beauparc, Navan was the Yellow Furze I.R.A. Company Commanding Officer in July 1921. On the 2nd July 1921, about two weeks before the Truce, he was involved in a failed attack on a troop train near Celbridge, see the story on page 51. He died before 1936. Source: WS0932. RO 486

Patrick Collins, Greenhills Beauparc, Navan was the Yellow Furze I.R.A. Company Quartermaster in July 1921. On the 2nd July 1921, about two weeks before the Truce, he was involved in a failed attack on a troop train near Celbridge, see the story on page 51. He died on 4th November 1935 and was buried in Ardmulchan Cemetery, Navan, see page 316.
Source: WS0932. RO 486. Military Service Pension Collection, file reference No. 34-SP-41889. Headstone Inscription.

John Cusack, Stackallen, Navan, Co. Meath was a Volunteer in the Yellow Furze I.R.A. Company in July 1921. His name is engraved on a headstone in Ardmulchan Cemetery, Navan, see page 316. Source: RO 486. Headstone Inscription.

James Farrell, Hayes, Navan, Co. Meath was a Volunteer in the Yellow Furze I.R.A. Company in July 1921. Source: RO 486

Laurence Farrelly, Yellow Furze, Navan, Co. Meath was a Volunteer in the Yellow Furze I.R.A. Company in July 1921. Source: RO 486

Patrick Healy, Juneville, Slane, Co. Meath was a Volunteer in the Yellow Furze I.R.A. Company in July 1921. Source: RO 486. Military Service Pension Collection, file reference No. MD-3183

Joseph Hickey, Hayes, Navan, Co. Meath was the Yellow Furze Company 1st Lieutenant in July 1921. Source: RO 486

Patrick Hickey, Stackallen, Navan, Co. Meath was a Volunteer in the Yellow Furze I.R.A. Company in July 1921. Source: RO 486

James McNally, Follistown, Navan, Co. Meath was a Volunteer in the Yellow Furze I.R.A. Company in July 1921. Source: RO 486

Laurence O'Hare was a Volunteer in the Yellow Furze Company of Irish Volunteers in July 1921. He died before 1936. Source: RO 486

Thomas O'Hare, Ballinlough, Beauparc, Navan, Co. Meath was a Volunteer in the Yellow Furze I.R.A. Company in July 1921. Source: RO 486

Michael O'Toole, Hayes, Navan, Co. Meath was the Yellow Furze Company 2nd Lieutenant in July 1921. Source: RO 486. Military Service Pension Collection, file reference No. MD-3569

Patrick Power was a Volunteer in the Yellow Furze I.R.A. Company in July 1921. In 1936 his address was given as Redhill, Surrey, England. Source: RO 486

Thomas Power was the Yellow Furze I.R.A. Company Adjutant in July 1921. In 1936 he was a member of An Garda Síochána. Source: RO 486

Joseph Quigley was a Volunteer in the Yellow Furze I.R.A. Company in July 1921. In 1936 he was serving in the Free State Army. He achieved the rank of Captain which he held when he retired. He died on 10th November 1975 and was buried in Moynalty Cemetery, see page 305. Sources: RO 486. Inscription on headstone in Moynalty Cemetery.

Joseph Quinn was a Volunteer in the Yellow Furze I.R.A. Company in July 1921. In 1936 his address was given as Hilltown, Drogheda, Co. Louth. His name is engraved on a headstone in St. Mary's Cemetery, Navan, see page 342. Source: RO 486. Headstone Inscription.

James Raleigh, Stackallen, Navan, Co. Meath was a Volunteer in the Yellow Furze I.R.A. Company in July 1921. Source: RO 486. Military Service Pension Collection, file reference No. MD-6567

Thomas Sheridan was a Volunteer in the Yellow Furze I.R.A. Company in July 1921. In 1936 his address was given as Hilltown, Drogheda, Co. Louth. Source: RO 486

James Synnott, Beauparc, Navan, Co. Meath was a Volunteer in the Yellow Furze I.R.A. Company in July 1921. Source: RO 486. Military Service Pension Collection, file reference No. MD-886

Matthew Vaughey, Barristown, Slane, Co. Meath was a Volunteer in the Yellow Furze I.R.A. Company in July 1921. Source: RO 486

Chapter 8
Final Resting Place

During months of visiting graveyards all over Co. Meath I came across the
following poem in a graveyard.   I have since found out the name of the author
and I think it is fitting to quote it here:

The Ancestors by Walter Butler Palmer

Your tombstone stands among the rest neglected and alone.

The names and dates are chiselled out on polished marble stone.

It reaches out to all who care; it is too late to mourn.

You did not know that we existed, you died and we were born.

Yet each of us is a cell of you in flesh, in blood, in bone.

Our blood contracts and beats a pulse, entirely not our own.

Dear Ancestors, the place you filled one hundred years ago

Spreads out among the ones you left who would have loved you so.

I wonder if you lived and loved, I wonder if you knew

That someday we would find this spot and come to visit you.

Ashbourne - Kilbride Cemetery:

Bruton, Michael   Kilbride Company   *Smyth, Frank   Kilbride Company*

Athboy - Church of Ireland Churchyard Cemetery:

Doherty, Martin   Athboy Company

Athboy - Saint James's Cemetery

Callery, John Athboy Company

Devine, Thomas Athboy Company

Athboy - Saint James's Cemetery Cont'd.

Doyle, James   Athboy Company

Eustace, Matthew   Athboy Company

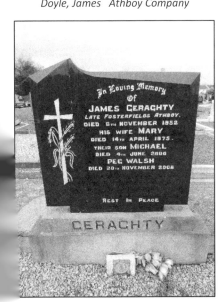

Geraghty, James   Athboy Company

Holland, Patrick   Athboy Company

Athboy - Saint James's Cemetery Cont'd.

Martin, John   Athboy Company

Martin, Joseph   Athboy Company

Monaghan, Patrick
Athboy Company

Athboy – Rathmore - Saint Lawrence's Cemetery:

Farrelly, Patrick
Athboy Company

Batterstown - Ballymaglassan Churchyard Cemetery:

Daly, Robert
Kilbride Company

Drumconrath Cemetery:

Carolan, Peter
Meath Hill Company

Cruise, Thomas
Meath Hill Company

Drumconrath Cemetery Cont'd.

Daly, James Meath Hill

Fay, John Drumconrath Company

Hickey, John
Nobber Company

Keelan, Christopher
Drumconrath Company

Drumconrath Cemetery Cont'd.

McKenna, William Meath Hill Company

Ward, Matthew Drumconrath Company

Watters, Francis
Drumconrath Company

Dunboyne - Loughsallagh Cemetery:

Boylan, Edward, Peter & Sean
Dunboyne Company

Byrne, Peter
Dunboyne Company

Dunboyne - Loughsallagh Cemetery Cont'd.:

Kelly, John   Dunboyne Company

Kelly, Michael   Dunboyne Company

King, Owen
Dunboyne Company

O'Broin, Giolla Chriost
Dunboyne Company

Dunboyne - Loughsallagh Cemetery Cont'd.:

Reilly, William
Dunboyne Company

Dunboyne - Rooske Cemetery:

Baker, Christopher
Battalion Adjutant
see Dunshaughlin Company

Keating, Christopher and James
Dunboyne Company

Dunboyne - Rooske Cemetery Cont'd.

Leonard, John Dunboyne Company

Maguire, James Brigade Quartermaster see Dunboyne Company

Maguire, William Dunboyne Company

Manning, Michael Battalion vice Commanding Officer see Dunshaughlin Company

Dunboyne - Rooske Cemetery Cont'd.

Manning, Thomas   Kilbride Company

Moran, Nicholas Snr. Dunboyne Company
Moran, Nicholas Jnr. Dunboyne Company

Moran, Peter   Dunboyne Company

Woods, Patrick Dunboyne Company

Dunshaughlin Churchyard Cemetery

Kenny, Daniel & Patrick
Dunshaughlin Company

Dunshaughlin – Kilmessan – Church of the Nativity

Clynch, Patrick Navan Company

Farrelly, Sean
Brigade vice Commanding Officer,
see Carnaross Company

Dunshaughlin – Kilmessan – Church of the Nativity Cont'd.

Horan, James
Bective & Kilmessan Company

Losty, Edward
Bective & Kilmessan Company

Loughran, Frank
Bective & Kilmessan Company

McCabe, Patrick
Bective & Kilmessan Company

Dunshaughlin – Kilmessan – Church of the Nativity Cont'd.

Moran, Christopher & Joseph
Bective & Kilmessan Company

Quinn, James & Patrick
Bective & Kilmessan Company

Whelan, Christopher
Bective & Kilmessan Company

Dunshaughlin – Knockmark Cemetery

Fox, James   Irish Citizen Army
see details in Chapter 3

McCormack, James & Nicholas
Culmullin Company

Dunshaughlin – Knockmark Cemetery Cont'd.

McCormack, John
Culmullin Company

Rattigan, Michael
Culmullin Company

Wildridge, James Culmullin Company

Kells – Ballinlough – Church of Assumption Cemetery:

Boylan, Michael and Patrick
Stonefield Company

Cogan, Seamus
Stonefield Company

Kells – Ballinlough – Church of Assumption Cemetery Contd.

McDonnell, Patrick
Ballinlough Company

Keogh, Sean
Ballinlough Company

McDonnell, Thomas
Ballinlough Company

McNamee, James
Carnaross Company

Kells – Ballinlough – Church of Assumption Cemetery Contd.

McNamee, William   Carnaross Company

O'Connell, Peter   Stonefield Company

Smith, Peter   Stonefield Company

Kells – Carnaross Cemetery:

Dunne, Christopher & Patrick
Carnaross Company

Farnan, Laurence
Carnaross Company

Kells – Carnaross Cemetery Cont'd

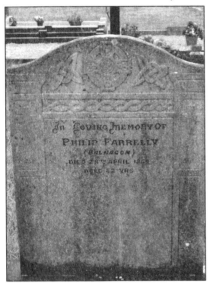

Farrelly, Philip Carnaross Company

Farrelly Thomas, Carnaross Company

Lynch, Joseph & Thomas
Carnaross Company

Lynch, John (Jack)
Carnaross Company

Kells – Carnaross Cemetery Cont'd

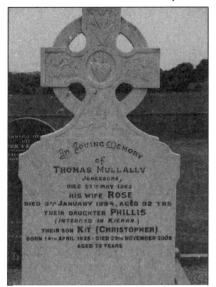

Mullally, Thomas Carnaross Company

O'Connor, Edward Carnaross Company

Reilly, Bernard Carnaross Company

Tevlin, John Carnaross Company

Kells – Carnaross Cemetery Cont'd

Yore, Thomas
Carnaross Company

Kells – Carnaross - Dulane Cemetery:

Boylan, James Kells Company

Kells – Cortown Cemetery:

Battersby, William Martry Company

Smith, Joseph Martry Company

Kells – Fordstown - Girley Old Cemetery:

*Bradley, Luke Irish Citizen Army & Irish Volunteers,
see Fordstown Company on page 162*

Kells – Kilskyre Churchyard Cemetery:

Farrelly, Christie Ballinlough Company

Matthews, Philip Ballinlough Company

Kells – Kilskyre Churchyard Cemetery Cont'd.

Reilly, Matthew
Ballinlough Company

Kells – Martry Graveyard

Coogan, William Bohermeen Company

Mallon, Patrick Bohermeen Company

Kells – Martry Graveyard

Mallon, Thomas Bohermeen Company

Mitchell, James Martry Company

Kells – Moynalty – Saint Mary's Cemetery:

Daly, Philip
Moynalty Company

Govern, Michael
Moynalty Company

Kells – Moynalty – Saint Mary's Cemetery:

Govern, Thomas
Moynalty Company

Lynch, Patrick
Newcastle Company

Lynch, Patrick
Newcastle Company

Quigley, Joseph
Yellow Furze Company

Kells - Saint Colmcille's Cemetery

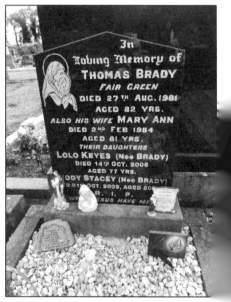

Black, William Kells Company (but not buried here, see Saint Columba's Cemetery)

Brady, Thomas Kells Company

Kells - Saint Colmcille's Cemetery Cont'd.

Connell, James Kells Company

Donagh, Michael Kells Company

Caffrey, William
Kells Company

Carolan, Bernard
Kells Company

Kells - Saint Colmcille's Cemetery Cont'd.

Flynn, Bernard   Kells Company

Flynn, Patrick   Kells Company

Heraghty, John
Kells Company

Maguire, Patrick
Kells Company

Kells - Saint Colmcille's Cemetery Cont'd

Mooney, Thomas
Carnaross Company

Morris, Thomas
Kells Company

Murray, Thomas
Kells Company

Reilly, Thomas
Kells Company

Kells - Saint Colmcille's Cemetery Cont'd

Joseph Smyth from Ethelstown, Kells, Co Meath lost his life at Athboy on 7th September 1922. The events that surround his death are detailed on page 57 and 62.

Smyth, Joseph   Official Forces I.R.A.

Smith, Patrick
Kells Company

Tully, Patrick
Kells Company

Kells - Saint Colmcille's Cemetery Cont'd

Tully, Farrell
Kells Company

Kells - Saint John's Cemetery

Carry, Patrick Kells Company

Grace, James Kells Company

Kells – Stahalmog Cemetery:

Mooney, Patrick
Kilbeg Company

313

Navan - Ardbraccan Churchyard Cemetery (also Includes R.I.C.)

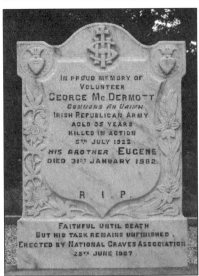

IN PROUD MEMORY OF
VOLUNTEER
GEORGE McDERMOTT
COMMONS AN UAIMH
IRISH REPUBLICAN ARMY
AGED 35 YEARS
KILLED IN ACTION
5TH JULY 1922
HIS BROTHER EUGENE
DIED 31ST JANUARY 1982

R I P

FAITHFUL UNTIL DEATH
BUT HIS TASK REMAINS UNFINISHED
ERECTED BY NATIONAL GRAVES ASSOCIATION
25TH JUNE 1987

McDermott, George
Ardbraccan Company

Rennicks, Sam
Martry Company

Rennicks, Arthur
Bohermeen Company

Smyth, Harry R.I.C. District Inspector

Inscription:
In memory of Harry Smyth D.I.
Royal Irish Constabulary
Youngest son of Hugh Smyth Baldock, Herts
Killed in Action at Ashbourne
28th April 1916 aged 41 years.

Harry Smyth
R.I.C. District Inspector

The incident referred to above
is the Battle of Ashbourne,
see the story on page ???

Photo from ahttp://www.irishmedals.org/r-i-c-and-d-m-p-killed.html

Navan - Ardmulchan Churchyard Cemetery:

Collins, Patrick
Yellow Furze Company

Cusack, John
Yellow Furze Company

316

Navan - Bohermeen Churchyard Cemetery:

Bennett, John
Bohermeen Company

Bennett, Patrick (Patsy)
Ardbraccan Company

Navan - Bohermeen Church Cemetery Cont'd

Bishop, Peter
Bohermeen Company

Coffey, Francis
Ardbraccan Company

Coffey, Patrick
Martry Company

Navan - Bohermeen Church Cemetery Cont'd.

Coogan, Patrick Ardbraccan Company

Farnan, john Martry Company

Gibbons, Joseph
Bohermeen Company

Farnan, William
Martry Company

Navan - Bohermeen Church Cemetery Cont'd.

Gibney, Thomas
Battalion Commanding Officer
see Bohermeen Company

Harmon, Nicholas
Bohermeen Company

Harte, Edward Bohermeen Company

Mallon, Edward Bohermeen Company

Nally, John
Bohermeen Company

Navan - Boyerstown Cemetery:

Harte, Patrick
Bohermeen Company

Hyland, Patrick
Ardbraccan Company

Navan - Castletown Kilpatrick Cemetery:

Hoey, Patrick
Castletown Company

Markey, Patrick
Castletown Company

323

Navan – Donaghmore Cemetery:

Carolan, Christopher
Dunmoe Company

Stapleton, Nicholas & Patrick
Ardbraccan Company & Navan Company

Navan – Donaghpatrick Churchyard Cemetery:

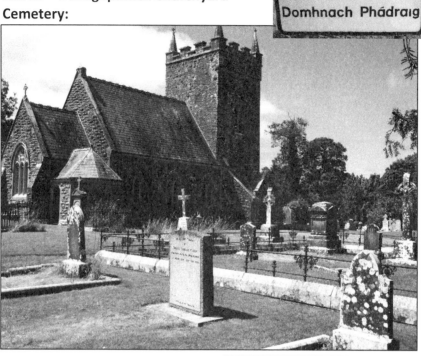

Domhnach Phádraig

Coogan, Joe & Michael
Martry Company

Crahan Philip
possibly Clongill Company

McLoughlin, John
Martry Company

Navan – Dunderry Cemetery:

Hyland, James Dunderry Company

Mulligan, Patrick Dunderry Company

327

Navan – Dunderry Cemetery Cont'd.

Yore, Richard
Dunderry Company

Navan – Dunderry – Churchtown Cemetery:

Conway, John Dunderry Company

Loughran, Bernard Dunderry Company

Navan - Kentstown Churchyard Cemetery:

Traynor, Nicholas
Kentstown Company

330

Navan – Kilberry Cemetery:

Crahan, Thomas
Clongill Company

Bray, Nicholas Kilberry Company

Navan – Kilberry Cemetery Cont'd

Doran, Thomas Kilberry Company

Fitzsimons, Patrick Dunmoe Company

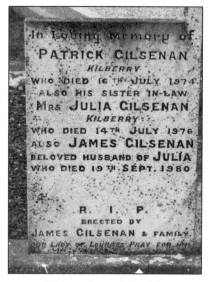

Gilsenan James & Patrick
Kilberry Company

Heaney, Owen
Kilberry Company

Navan – Kilcarne Cemetery

The unmarrked burial place of Thomas Coyle (Johnstown Company) outside the gates of the cemetery. He was not allowed inside the Cemetery because of his apparent suicide, see page 165.

Navan – Kilcarne Cemetery Cont'd.

Kelly, Patrick
Johnstown Company

O'Brien, John
Johnstown Company

O'Neill, William
Johnstown Company

Smith, James
Johnstown Company

Navan – Skryne - Saint Colmcille Churchyard Cemetery

Dolan, James & Martin
Skreene & Kileen Company

O'Hare, Patrick
Kentstown Company

Navan - Saint Mary's Cemetery   (Also includes R.I.C.)

Collins, Laurence (Larry)
Commons Company

Byrne, Robert
Navan Company

Navan - Saint Mary's Cemetery Cont'd.

Duffy, Thomas Eamonn
Navan Company

Fitzsimons, Patrick
Navan Company

Giles, John
Navan Company

Hilliard, James
Navan Company

Navan - Saint Mary's Cemetery Cont'd.

*Hilliard, Michael Brigade Commanding
Officer. see Navan Company*

*Hyland, Michael   Battalion Engineer
see Ardbraccan Company*

*Kavanagh, James
Dunmoe Company*

*Kavanagh, Michael   Battalion Adjutant
see Dunmoe Company*

Navan - Saint Mary's Cemetery Cont'd.

Keelan, Patrick   Navan Company

Killoran, Thomas   Navan Company

Kinsella, James & Thomas
Navan Company

Leer, John William
Navan Company

Navan - Saint Mary's Cemetery Cont'd.

Loughran, Patrick   Navan Company

Lynch, James
Navan Company

Mahoney, John
Navan Company

Mathews, John
Kentstown Company

Navan - Saint Mary's Cemetery Cont'd.

Moran, William
Bective or Kilmessan Company

Naulty, Nicholas
Navan Company

Nulty, Thomas
Dunderry Company

O'Donoghue, Thomas
R.I.C.

Navan - Saint Mary's Cemetery Cont'd.

Perry, Seamus
Navan Company

Quilty, Patrick
Navan Company

Quinn, Joseph
Yellow Furze Company

Navan - Saint Mary's Cemetery Cont'd.

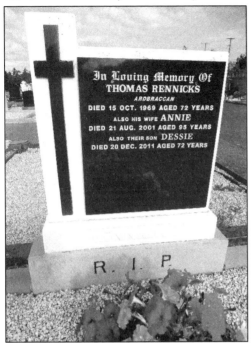

Rennicks, Thomas
Martry Company

The Republican Plot contains the graves of Volunteer Laurence Sheeky and Volunteer Terence Brady, see the story on page 64.

Navan - Saint Mary's Cemetery Cont'd.   Republican Plot.

Beautifully carved stone Monument in the Republican Plot

The Inscription is in Irish.   Translated it reads: *In memory of the Republican Soldiers who fought for Irish Freedom and were executed by the Free State Government in 1922 - 23.*
Name: Laurence Sheeky.   Died in Portobello on 8th January 1923.
Name: Terence Brady.   Died in Portobello on 8th January 1923.
Name: Thomas Murray.   Died in Dundalk on 13th January 1923.
Lord have mercy on their souls.   This monument was erected by the Meath Commemoration Committee in 1936.

Navan - Saint Mary's Cemetery Cont'd.

Roberts, John
R.I.C.

Smyth, Laurence,
Clongill Company

Walsh, Thomas
Dunmoe Company

Waters, Patrick
Ardbraccan Company

346

Navan - Saint Mary's Cemetery Cont'd

Woods, Joseph
Navan Company

Navan - Saint Mary's Cemetery Cont'd

Constable James Gormley from Balintogher Co. Sligo. His brother was an active Irish Volunteer in Balintogher. Local Irish Volunteers attended his funeral in Navan as a mark of respect. Source: http://irishconstabulary.com/reply /5443/Easter-Monday-1916#reply-5443

Inscription is difficult to read but it says:

"Sergeant John Young, Constable James Hickey, Constable James Gormley, Constable Richard McHale who died on 23rd April 1916 from wounds received while gallantly doing their duty as members of the Royal Irish Constabulary. Erected by their sorrowing families and by the subscriptions of the Irish Police and Constabulary Recognition Fund".

The incident referred to in the above inscription is the Battle of Ashbourne, see page 25 for details.

Navan – Wilkinstown – Fletcherstown Cemetery:

Allen, Matthew
Clongill Company

Swan, Seamus
Clongill Company

Navan – Wilkinstown – Fletcherstown Cemetery Cont'd.

Carberry, Thomas   Castletown Company

Meehan, Tom
Castletown Company

Navan – Wilkinstown – Fletcherstown Cemetery Cont'd.

Sweeney, Patrick
Clongill Company

Oldcastle - Ballinacree Churchyard Cemetery:

Balfe, John and Patrick
Ballinacree Company

Foley, Thomas
Oldcastle Company

Oldcastle - Ballinacree Churchyard Cemetery Cont'd

Kelly, Edward   Ballinacree Company

Murtagh, Thomas
Ballinacree Company

Reilly, Thomas
Ballinacree Company

Oldcastle - Moylagh Churchyard Cemetery:

Briody, Benny
Moylagh Company

Briody, John
Moylagh Company

Oldcastle - Moylagh Churchyard Cemetery Cont'd

Cooke, Owen & Patrick
Moylagh Company

Garrigan, James, John & Pat
Oldcastle Company

Gilsenan, Peter
Moylagh Company

Hand, John
Moylagh Company

Oldcastle - Moylagh Churchyard Cemetery Cont'd

Hand, Thomas Moylagh Company

Husband, John Oldcastle Company

*Kileen, Patrick
Moylagh Company*

*McGrath, James
Moylagh Company*

Oldcastle - Moylagh Churchyard Cemetery Cont'd

Reilly, Patrick Moylagh Company

Smith, Patrick
Moylagh Company

Walsh, Patrick
Oldcastle Company

Oldcastle – Old Loughcrew Cemetery

McNamee, James   Oldcastle Company

Oldcastle - Saint Bridget's Cemetery

Bardon, Thomas
Oldcastle Company

Clarke, Owen
Oldcastle Company

Oldcastle - Saint Bridget Cemetery Cont'd.

Geraghty, Patrick
Newcastle Company

Herbstreit, Leo
Oldcastle Company

Oldcastle - Saint Bridget Cemetery Cont'd.

McGinn, John   Oldcastle Company

Reilly, Frank
Oldcastle Company

Tuite, James
Oldcastle Company

Oldcastle - Saint Bridget Cemetery Cont'd.

Tully, Peter
Oldcastle Company

Slane – Gernonstown Graveyard:

Doggett, John
Kilberry Company

Ginnity, Matthew
Rathkenny Company

Slane – Hill of Slane Cemetery:

Ledwidge, Joseph
Slane Company

Tiernan, Patrick
Slane Company

Slane – Hill of Slane Cemetery Cont'd.

Vaughey, John
Slane Company

Slane – Monknewtown Cemetery

Clarke, Thomas   Slane Company.
Clarke, Nicholas   Slane Company.

Inscription also says:
Philip Clarke I.C.A. killed in action Dublin Easter Week 1916 aged 41 years.

I.C.A. means Irish Citizen Army and the events that surrounded Philip Clarke's death are detailed in Chapter 3. This is obviously the family plot of Philip Clarke but he is not buried here.   He is buried in St Brigid's Cemetery Glasnevin.

Slane – Monknewtown Cemetery Cont'd

Very limited information on this grave so I am not sure if this is the same J. Reilly that was in Slane Company.

Reilly, J. Slane Company

Slane - Rathkenny New Churchyard Cemetery

Curtis, James
Rathkenny Company

Donegan, Thomas
Rathkenny Company

Slane - Rathkenny Old Cemetery:

Callan, Patrick
Rathkenny Company

Slane - Rathkenny Old Cemetery Cont'd.

Monahan Michael   Rathkenny Company

Reilly, Bernard
Rathkenny Company

Summerhill New Churchyard Cemetery:

Barry, John   Summerhill Company

Grehan, Michael Summerhill Company

Trim – Ballivor - Killaconnigan Cemetery   (also includes R.I.C.)

Brown, Thomas
Ballivor Company

Cunningham, John
Ballivor Company

Trim – Ballivor - Killaconnigan Cemetery Cont'd.:

Dixon, Patrick   Ballivor Company

Kiernan, Peter   Ballivor Company

McDonnell, Thomas
Ballivor Company

McGearty, John
R.I.C.

373

Trim – Ballivor - New Cemetery:

Bracken, John   Ballivor Company

Connor, Dan   Ballivor Company

Trim - Ballivor - New Cemetery Cont'd.

Grey, Philip
Ballivor Company

Loughlin, Patrick
Ballivor Company

Trim – Garadice – Coole Churchyard Cemetery:

Captain Patrick Giles TD
see Longwood Company

Trim – Kilbride - Moymet Cemetery:

Hynes, Michael
Trim Company

Moore, Seamus
Trim Company

Trim – Longwood – Kilglass Graveyard:

Lieutenant Thomas Allen from the parish of Moyvalley, Longwood, Co. Meath. He lost his life on 28th April 1916 during the Easter Rising.   The events that surround his death are detailed on pages 19 and 29.

Trim - Longwood – Saint Mary's Cemetery:

Costello, John
Longwood Company

Giles, Laurence
Longwood Company

Trim - Longwood – Saint Mary's Cemetery Cont'd.:

Giles, Michael   Trim Company

McEvoy, Michael
Longwood Company

Regan, John   Ballivor Company

Trim - Saint Loman's Cemetery

Bishop, John
Trim Company

Carter, Walter (Wally)
Trim Company

Trim - Saint Loman's Cemetery Cont'd.

Doggett, Philip   Trim Company

Healy, John   Trim Company

Kelly, Joseph (Joe)
Trim Company

Matthews, Matthew
Trim Company

Trim - Saint Loman's Cemetery Cont'd.

McArdle, Michael   Trim Company

Mooney, Patrick   Trim Company

O'Hagan, Harry
Trim Company

Rickard, Luke   Boardsmill Company

Sherry, Thomas (Tom)   Trim Company

Webb, Joseph
Skryne & Kileen Company

Looking for someone?

Name	Go to section	Name	Go to section
Allen, Christopher	Kilberry Company	Bishop, John	Trim Company
Allen, James	Rathkenny Co.	Bishop, Peter	Bohermeen Co.
Allen, M	Clongill Company	Bissett, John	Curragha Co.
Allen, Thomas	Kilglass Cemetery	Black, William	Kells Company
Andrews, Christopher	Trim Company	Blake, Michael	Dunshaughlin Co.
Andrews, John	Ardcath Company	Blake, Patrick	Dunshaughlin Co.
Andrews, Matthew	Trim Company	Bligh, Michael	Ballivor Company
Bailey, Joseph	Navan Company	Boland, John	Navan Company
Baker, Christopher	Dunshaughlin Co.	Boland, Peter	Meath Hill Co.
Balfe, John	Ballinacree Co.	Boland, Thomas	Fordstown Co.
Balfe, Patrick	Ballinacree Co.	Booth, William	Navan Company
Bannon, Patrick	Kiltale Company	Bough, George	Ballinlough Co.
Bardon, Thomas	Oldcastle Co.	Bough, Michael	Ballinlough Co.
Barker, Christopher	Dunshaughlin Co.	Bowens, James	Yellow Furze Co.
Barrett, Thomas	Athboy Company	Boyd, Patrick	Julianstown & Laytown
Barry, James	Kilcloon Company	Boylan, Christopher	Longwood Co.
Barry, James	Kiltale Company	Boylan, Edward	Dunboyne Co.
Barry, James	Summerhill Co.	Boylan, Hugh	Cloncurry Co.
Barry, John	Kilcloon Company	Boylan, James	Johnstown Co
Barry, John	Summerhill Co.	Boylan, James	Kells Company
Barry, Matthew	Johnstown Co.	Boylan, Michael	Bohermeen Co.
Battersby, Joseph	Dunboyne Co.	Boylan, Mick	Stonefield Co.
Battersby, William	Martry Company	Boylan, Patrick	Kilcloon Company
Beehan, Christopher	Kilbride Company	Boylan, Patrick	Stonefield Co.
Beggan, George	Ballinlough Co.	Boylan, Peter	Dunboyne Co.
Beggan, James	Ballinlough Co.	Boylan, Seán	Dunboyne Co.
Bennett, John	Dunmoe Co.	Boyle, John	Johnstown Co
Bennett, John	Kilbeg Company	Boyle, Joseph	Navan Company
Bennett, John (Johnny)	Bohermeen Co.	Boyle, Matthew	Bective / Kilmessan
Bennett, Michael	Whitegate Co.	Boyle, Patrick	Ardbracken Co.
Bennett, Mick	Stonefield Co.	Boyle, Patrick	Johnstown Co
Bennett, Patrick	Ardbracken Co.	Brackin, John	Ballivor Company
Bennitt, Patrick	Whitegate Co.	Bradley, Luke	Fordstown Co.
Berrill, Joseph	Kells Company	Bradley, Patrick	Fordstown Co.
Bird, Edward	Longwood Co.	Bradley, Patrick	Oldcastle Co.

385

Name	Go to section	Name	Go to section
Brady, Andrew	Whitegate Co.	Buchannon, Michael	Ardbracken Co.
Brady, Bernard	Whitegate Co.	Butler, Patrick	Cloncurry Co.
Brady, Edward	Moylagh Co.	Butterfield, George	Athboy Company
Brady, Hugh	Ballinlough Co.	Butterfield, Patrick	Athboy Company
Brady, James	Ballinlough Co.	Byrne, Edward	Yellow Furze Co.
Brady, James	Carnaross Co.	Byrne, Gerald (Gary)	Drumbaragh Co.
Brady, John	Dunboyne Co.	Byrne, James	Ardbracken Co.
Brady, John	Kells Company	Byrne, James	Navan Company
Brady, John	Moylagh Co.	Byrne, Laurence	Ardbracken Co.
Brady, Laurence	Dunmoe Co.	Byrne, Matthew	Boardsmill Co.
Brady, Leo	Kells Company	Byrne, Michael	Boardsmill Co.
Brady, Michael	Bective / Kilmessan	Byrne, Patrick	Kentstown Co.
Brady, Patrick	Kells Company	Byrne, Peter	Dunboyne Co.
Brady, Peter	Moylagh Co.	Byrne, Peter	Yellow Furze Co.
Brady, Peter	Navan Company	Byrne, Richard	Ardbracken Co.
Brady, Stephen	Bective / Kilmessan	Byrne, Robert	Navan Company
Brady, Terence	Castletown Co. & St. Mary's Cemetery, Navan	Byrne, Thomas	Ballivor Company
Brady, Thomas	Kells Company	Byrne, William	Drumbaragh Co.
Brady, Thomas	Moylagh Co.	Caddell, Christopher	Curragha Co.
Bratton, Eugene (R.I.C.)	Page 26, 27, 28	Caffrey, Christopher	Bective / Kilmessan
Bray, Nicholas	Kilberry Company	Caffrey, Christopher	Kells Company
Bray, Peter	Ardbracken Co.	Caffrey, John	Dunderry Co.
Brennan, Andrew	Ballivor Company	Caffrey, L	Kells Company
Brien, James	Johnstown Co.	Caffrey, Patrick	Ratoath Company
Brien, John	Johnstown Co.	Caffrey, William	Kells Company
Brien, Peter	Johnstown Co.	Cahalan, Michael	Skryne & Killeen Co.
Brilly, Christopher	Cloncurry Co.	Cahill, Edward	Navan Company
Briody, Benjamin	Moylagh Co.	Cahill, Michael	Moynalty Co.
Briody, John	Moylagh Co.	Cahill, Mick	Whitegate Co.
Briody, Owen	Slane Company	Cahill, Patrick	Newcastle Co.
Brodrick, John	Athboy Company	Cahill, Philip	Whitegate Co.
Brown, John	Ballinacree Co.	Cahill, Stephen	Newcastle Co.
Brown, Thomas	Ballivor Company	Callaghan, J	Clongill Company
Browne, Matthew	Kildalkey Co.	Callaghan, Patrick	Kilcloon Company
Bruton, Michael	Culmullin Co.	Callaghan, Peter	Kilcloon Company
Bruton, Michael	Kilbride Company	Callan, Patrick	Rathkenny Co.

Name	Go to section	Name	Go to section
Callan, Thomas	Oldcastle Co.	Cassidy, James	Athboy Company
Callen, Vincent	Johnstown Co.	Cassidy, John	Athboy Company
Callery, John	Athboy Company	Cassidy, John	Creewood Rathkenny
Carberry, T	Castletown Co.	Cassidy, John	Nobber Company
Carey, Patrick	Athboy Company	Cassidy, Michael	Nobber Company
Carey, William	Curragha Co.	Cassidy, Thomas	Creewood Rathkenny
Carolan, Bernard	Kells Company	Chatten, John	Moylagh Co.
Carolan, Bernard	Newcastle Co.	Clarke, Andrew	Creewood Rathkenny
Carolan, Brien	Moynalty Co.	Clarke, Annie	Page 35 & 37
Carolan, Christopher	Castletown Co.	Clarke, Edward	Carnaross Co.
Carolan, Christopher	Duleek Company	Clarke, Francis	Moynalty Co.
Carolan, Christopher	Dunmoe Co.	Clarke, G	Castletown Co.
Carolan, Francis	Kilcloon Company	Clarke, James	Kilberry Company
Carolan, Frank	Dunboyne Co.	Clarke, John	Kilberry Company
Carolan, Hugh	Newcastle Co.	Clarke, Joseph	Kildalkey Co.
Carolan, Peter	Meath Hill Co.	Clarke, Joseph	Navan Company
Carolan, Terence	Moynalty Co.	Clarke, Laurence	Navan Company
Carroll, James	Dunboyne Co.	Clarke, Leo	Slane Company
Carroll, Bartle	Athboy Company	Clarke, Nicholas	Slane Company
Carroll, Harry	Whitegate Co.	Clarke, Owen	Oldcastle Co.
Carroll, Joseph	Whitegate Co.	Clarke, Patrick	Carnaross Co.
Carroll, L	Rathkenny Co.	Clarke, Patrick	Kells Company
Carroll, Patrick	Johnstown Co.	Clarke, Patrick	Kilbeg Company
Carroll, Philip	Whitegate Co.	Clarke, Patrick	Moynalty Co.
Carroll, Thomas	Johnstown Co.	Clarke, PcH	Carnaross Co.
Carroll, Thomas	Whitegate Co.	Clarke, Peter	Ballinacree Co.
Carry, Alfred	Nobber Company	Clarke, Philip (ICA)	Monknewtown Cemetery
Carry, James	Meath Hill Co.	Clarke, Thomas	Creewood Rathkenny
Carry, James	Nobber Company	Clarke, Thomas	Navan Company
Carry, Patrick	Kells Company	Clarke, Thomas	Slane Company
Carter, Billy	Trim Company	Clarke, W.	Slane Company
Carter, Richard	Yellow Furze Co.	Clery, Joseph	Curragha Co.
Carter, Walter	Trim Company	Clery, Peter	Curragha Co.
Casey, Bernard	Drumcondrath Co.	Clery, Peter T.	Curragha Co.
Casey, James	Ratoath Company	Clinton, John	Julianstown & Laytown
Casserly, Christopher	Ballivor Company	Clinton, Mark	Page 71, 72

Name	Go to section	Name	Go to section
Clinton, Patrick	Dunboyne Co.	Connor, Thomas	Kilbeg Company
Clinton, Peter	Newcastle Co.	Connor, William	Dunderry Co.
Cluskey, James	Kilbeg Company	Conway, John	Dunderry Co.
Clynch, Patrick	Navan Company	Conway, Patrick	Ballinlough Co.
Coffey, Christopher	Dunderry Co.	Coogan, Joseph	Martry Company
Coffey, Francis	Ardbracken Co.	Coogan, Michael	Martry Company
Coffey, Patrick	Martry Company	Coogan, Patrick	Ardbracken Co.
Cogan, Seamus	Stonefield Co.	Coogan, William	Bohermeen Co.
Cole, Joseph	Summerhill Co.	Cooke, Owen	Moylagh Co.
Cole, Patrick	Summerhill Co.	Cooke, Patrick	Moylagh Co.
Collier, Richard	Duleek Company	Corrigan, John	Kildalkey Co.
Collins, Christopher	Yellow Furze Co.	Corrigan, P	Longwood Co.
Collins, John	Duleek Company	Corrigan, Thomas	Kildalkey Co.
Collins, Laurence	Commons Co.	Costello, John	Longwood Co.
Collins, M.	Boardsmill Co.	Costigan, John	Athboy Company
Collins, Patrick	Curragha Co.	Cowley, James	Trim Company
Collins, Patrick	Yellow Furze Co.	Cowley, John	Ballinlough Co.
Colman, James	Culmullin Co.	Cox, Thomas	Ardcath Company
Cols, Joseph	Kilcloon Company	Coyle, Patrick	Bohermeen Co.
Cols, Patrick	Kilcloon Company	Coyle, Patrick	Moylagh Co.
Commons, Joseph	Creewood Rathkenny	Coyle, Thomas	Johnstown Co.
Conaty, Charles	Stonefield Co.	Crahan, ?	Clongill Company
Conaty, Thomas	Fennor Company	Crahan, Philip	Clongill Company
Conlon, Anthony	Kells Company	Crahan, Thomas	Clongill Company
Connell, Edward	Carnaross Co.	Crean, Aidan	Dunboyne Co.
Connell, James	Duleek Company	Cregan, Christopher	Navan Company
Connell, James	Kells Company	Cregan, Michael	Navan Company
Connell, Leo	Kells Company	Creighton, Thomas	Trim Company
Connell, Nicholas	Duleek Company	Crosby, P	Clongill Company
Connell, Patrick	Duleek Company	Crosby, Patrick	Fordstown Co.
Connell, Peter	Ballinacree Co.	Cruice, Thomas	Meath Hill Co.
Connell, Richard	Moylagh Co.	Cudden, G	Castletown Co.
Connell, William	Kells Company	Cullen, Eamonn	Summerhill Co.
Connor, Daniel	Ballivor Company	Cullen, Michael	Athboy Company
Connor, Patrick	Skryne & Killeen Co.	Cumiskey, James	Kells Company
Michael Collins	Chapter 5	Cumiskey, Michael	Kells Company

Name	Go to section	Name	Go to section
Cunningham, John	Ballivor Company	Doherty, Martin	Athboy Company
Cunningham, Joseph	Ballivor Company	Dolan, James	Skryne & Killeen Co.
Cunningham, Patrick	Kilyon Company	Dolan, Martin	Skryne & Killeen Co.
Curran, James	Moynalty Co.	Dolan, Patrick	Kells Company
Curran, Patrick	Moynalty Co.	Dolan, Peter	Summerhill Co.
Curren, Patrick	Fordstown Co.	Dolan, Peter	Summerhill Co.
Curtis, James	Rathkenny Co.	Donagh, Michael	Kells Company
Cusack, Christopher	Kiltale Company	Donegan, Thomas	Rathkenny Co.
Cusack, John	Yellow Furze Co.	Donegan, William	Kells Company
Dalton, James	Ardbracken Co.	Donnelly, Christopher	Ratoath Co.
Dalton, John	Dunshaughlin Co.	Donnelly, Thomas	Longwood Co.
Daly, Brien	Carnaross Co.	Donoghue, James	Ballinacree Co.
Daly, Brien	Whitegate Co.	Donohue, Patrick	Ballivor Company
Daly, Eugene	Newcastle Co.	Doran, Patrick	Kilberry Company
Daly, James	Meath Hill Co.	Doran, Richard	Navan Company
Daly, John	Carnaross Co.	Doran, Thomas	Kilberry Company
Daly, Owen	Fennor Company	Dowling, Fir in	Ardcath Company
Daly, Pat	Carnaross Co.	Downes, Patrick	Duleek Company
Daly, Patrick	Fennor Company	Doyle, James	Athboy Company
Daly, Philip	Moynalty Co.	Doyle, James	Boardsmill Co.
Daly, Philip	Newcastle Co.	Doyle, Peter	Boardsmill Co.
Daly, Robert	Kilbride Company	Doyle, William	Athboy Company
Daly, William	Moynalty Co.	Drumm, John	Johnstown Co.
Darcy, Stephen	Kilcloon Company	Duffy, Joseph	Carnaross Co.
Dardis, Sean	Carnaross-Drumbaragh	Duffy, Matthew	Stonefield Co.
Davis, James	Kildalkey Co.	Duffy, Patrick	Culmullin Co.
De Burca, Padraig	Carnaross Co.	Duffy, Patrick	Dunshaughlin Co.
Delany, Michael	Dunmoe Co.	Duffy, Thomas Eamonn	Navan Cemetery
Dempsey, Louis	Ardbracken Co.	Duggan, Denis	Enfield Company
Devine, Thomas	Athboy Company	Duignan,	Trim Company
Devine, William	Oldcastle Co.	Duignan, ?	Trim Company
Dixon, Patrick	Ballivor Company	Duignan, Edward	Kells Company
Doggett, John	Kilberry Company	Duignan, Patrick	Trim Company
Doggett, Michael	Trim Company	Dungan, Michael	Johnstown Co
Doggett, Philip	Trim Company	Dungan, Thomas	Dunshaughlin Co.
Doherty, John	Julianstown & Laytown	Dunly, John	Johnstown Co

Name	Go to section	Name	Go to section
Dunly, Nicholas	Johnstown Co	Fagan, Christopher	Kildalkey Co.
Dunne, Bernard	Dunboyne Co.	Fagan, Joseph	Oldcastle Co.
Dunne, Bnjaminnie	Carnaross Co.	Fagan, Maurice	Longwood Co.
Dunne, Christopher	Carnaross Co.	Falkner, Peter	Athboy Company
Dunne, George	Carnaross Co.	Fanning, Edward	Moylagh Co.
Dunne, James	Ardcath Company	Fanning, James	Moylagh Co.
Dunne, James	Carnaross Co.	Farley, Bernard	Carnaross Co.
Dunne, John	Carnaross Co.	Farley, Bernard	Carnaross Co.
Dunne, John	Duleek Company	Farley, Michael	Carnaross Co.
Dunne, Michael	Drumcondrath Co.	Farley, Philip	Carnaross Co.
Dunne, Mick	Carnaross Co.	Farnan, Bernard	Ballinacree Co.
Dunne, Pat	Carnaross Co.	Farnan, Christopher	Bective / Kilmessan
Dunne, Patrick	Kiltale Company	Farnan, John	Martry Company
Dunne, Patrick	Navan Cemetery	Farnan, Laurence	Carnaross Co.
Dunne, Peter	Carnaross Co.	Farnan, William	Martry Company
Dunne, Thomas	Carnaross Co.	Farrell, Christopher	Ballinlough Co.
Dunne, Thomas	Enfield Company	Farrell, F	Dunboyne Co.
Dunphy, Michael	Skryne & Killeen Co.	Farrell, Francis	Dunboyne Co.
Dunphy, Patrick	Skryne & Killeen Co.	Farrell, Hugh	Dunboyne Co.
Durr, Hugh	Navan Cemetery	Farrell, James	Dunboyne Co.
Durrin, Thomas	Bective / Kilmessan	Farrell, James	Yellow Furze
Egan, J.	Boardsmill Co.	Farrell, John	Skryne & Killeen Co.
Egan, Joseph	Navan Cemetery	Farrell, Joseph	Summerhill Co.
Eiffe, William	Ratoath Company	Farrell, Thomas	Dunboyne Co.
Elliott, Patrick	Creewood Rathkenny	Farrell, William	Julianstown & Laytown
English, Patrick	Skryne & Killeen Co.	Farrelly, Brien	Carnaross Co.
Englishby, Eugene	Kiltale Company	Farrelly, Christopher	Ballinlough Co.
Englishby, James	Drumcondrath Co.	Farrelly, Hugh	Kilbeg Company
Englishby, Laurence	Johnstown Co	Farrelly, James	Kildalkey Co.
Ennis, Christopher	Dunboyne Co.	Farrelly, John	Navan Cemetery
Ennis, Jack	Enfield Company	Farrelly, Laurence	Kilmainhamwood
Ennis, Joseph	Cloncurry Co.	Farrelly, Laurence	Yellow Furze
Ennis, Patrick	Cloncurry Co.	Farrelly, Michael	Ballinlough Co.
Ennis, Thomas	Dunboyne Co.	Farrelly, Michael	Kildalkey Co.
Ennis, William	Enfield Company	Farrelly, Nicholas	Ballinlough Co.
Eustace, Matthew	Athboy Company	Farrelly, Patrick	Athboy Company

Name	Go to section	Name	Go to section
Farrelly, Patrick	Ballinlough Co.	Fitzsimons, Thomas	Cloncurry Co.
Farrelly, Patrick	Dunderry Co.	Flanagan, Michael	Ballivor Company
Farrelly, Patrick (Pat)	Carnaross Co.	Flanagan, Patrick	Kilbeg Company
Farrelly, Philip	Ballinlough Co.	Flanigan, Michael	Kells Company
Farrelly, Philip	Carnaross Co.	Fleming, Peter	Creewood Rathkenny
Farrelly, Philip	Kildalkey Co.	Flood, Bernard	Ballinlough Co.
Farrelly, Sean	Carnaross Co.	Flood, Joseph	Ballinlough Co.
Farrelly, Thomas	Carnaross Co.	Flood, Matthew	Ballinlough Co.
Fay, John	Drumcondrath Co.	Flood, Thomas	Ballinlough Co.
Fay, John	Navan Cemetery	Flynn, Bernard	Kells Company
Fay, Patrick	Kilcloon Company	Flynn, Patrick	Kells Company
Fay, Patrick	Trim Company	Foley, Hugh	Oldcastle Co.
Fay, William	Johnstown Co	Foley, John	Oldcastle Co.
Feely, Frank	Slane Company	Foley, Michael	Ardbracken Co.
Feely, William	Kilyon Company	Foley, Thomas	Bohermeen Co.
Feeney,	Carnaross Co.	Foley, Thomas	Oldcastle Co.
Feeney, John	Cloncurry Co.	Foley, William	Bective / Kilmessan
Feeney, Lawrence	Cloncurry Co.	Foran, Thomas	Dunmoe Co
Feeney, Patrick	Cloncurry Co.	Fortune, Francis	Ratoath Company
Feeney, Thomas	Cloncurry Co.	Foster, Eugene	Meath Hill Co.
Finn, Michael	Athboy Company	Foster, Thomas	Meath Hill Co.
Finn, Seamus	Athboy Company	Fox, James (ICA)	Knockmark Cemetery
Finnegan, John	Athboy Company	Fox, Michael	Culmullin Co.
Finnegan, John	Fordstown Co.	Fox, Michael	Kells Company
Finnerty, Andrew	Navan Cemetery	Fox, Peter	Moynalty Co.
Fitzgerald, John	Ballinlough Co.	Foylan, Patrick	Drumcondrath Co.
Fitzgerald, Patrick	Ballinlough Co.	Foylan, Patrick	Drumcondrath Co.
Fitzpatrick, Bartley	Johnstown Co	Friary, Patrick	Ballinlough Co.
Fitzsimons, Bartle	Skryne & Killeen Co.	Gaffney, James	Kildalkey Co.
Fitzsimons, Edward	Cloncurry Co.	Gaffney, Peter	Kildalkey Co.
Fitzsimons, James	Dunderry Co.	Gallagher, Andrew	Slane Company
Fitzsimons, John	Nobber Company	Gallagher, John	Newcastle Co.
Fitzsimons, Joseph	Kilcloon Company	Gallagher, Patrick	Slane Company
Fitzsimons, Joseph	Summerhill Co.	Gannon, Ambrose	Cloncurry Co.
Fitzsimons, Patrick	Dunmoe Co.	Gannon, John	Kilcloon Company
Fitzsimons, Patrick	Navan Cemetery	Gannon, John	Summerhill Co.

Name	Go to section	Name	Go to section
Gannon, Nicholas	Kiltale Company	Gill, Edward	Summerhill Co.
Gannon, Thomas	Culmullin Co.	Gill, Thomas	Dunderry Co.
Gargan, John	Ballinlough Co.	Gilleran, Peter	Kildalkey Co.
Gargan, Matthew	Stonefield Co.	Gillic, James	Ballinlough Co.
Garrigan,	Moynalty Co.	Gillic, Larry	Ballinlough Co.
Garrigan, James	Oldcastle Co.	Gillic, Mick	Stonefield Co.
Garrigan, John	Oldcastle Co.	Gillie, Augustine	Dunshaughlin Co.
Garrigan, Matthew	Oldcastle Co.	Gilligan, Andrew	Cloncurry Co.
Garrigan, Patrick	Oldcastle Co.	Gilligan, James	Kildalkey Co.
Garry, John	Ballinlough Co.	Gilsenan, James	Kilberry Company
Garry, Owen	Fennor Company	Gilsenan, Patrick	Ballinlough Co.
Garry, Richard	Kilcloon Company	Gilsenan, Patrick	Kilberry Company
Gartland, Francis	Kilberry Company	Gilsenan, Peter	Moylagh Co.
Gavigan, Tom	Navan Cemetery	Gilsenan, Terence	Moylagh Co.
Gavin, Edward	Oldcastle Co.	Gilsenan, Thomas	Clongill Company
Gavin, Thomas	Oldcastle Co.	Ginnitty, James	Rathkenny Co.
Gaynor, John	Navan Cemetery	Ginnitty, Matthew	Rathkenny Co.
Gaynor, Joseph	Dunboyne Co.	Gleeson, Joseph	Navan Cemetery
Gaynor, Michael	Navan Cemetery	Glennon, Patrick	Bohermeen Co.
Gaynor, Nicholas	Ballinlough Co.	Glennon, Philip	Oldcastle Co.
Geeicle, Christopher	Enfield Company	Gogarty, B.	Boardsmill Co.
Geeicle, Terrence	Enfield Company	Gogarty, J	Castletown Co.
Geraghty, James	Athboy Company	Golden, Gerry	Page 27
Geraghty, Patrick	Newcastle Co.	Goodwin, Thomas	Kilcloon Company
Gerrard, Michael	Ardbracken Co.	Goodwin, William	Kilcloon Company
Gerrard, Vincent	Slane Company	Gordan, Michael	Johnstown Co
Gibbons, Joseph	Bohermeen Co.	Gorman, Eugene	Navan Cemetery
Gibney, Matthew	Oldcastle Co.	Gorman, James	Navan Cemetery
Gibney, Patrick	Kilbeg Company	Gorman, Richard	Navan Cemetery
Gibney, Thomas	Bohermeen Co.	Gormley, James (RIC)	Navan Cemetery
Giles, John	Navan Cemetery	Gough, John	Julianstown & Laytown
Giles, Laurence	Longwood Co.	Gough, Michael	Curragha Co.
Giles, Michael	Trim Company	Gough, Patrick	Curragha Co.
Giles, Nicholas	Trim Company	Govern, Edward	Moynalty Co.
Giles, Patrick (Pat)	Longwood Co.	Govern, James	Moynalty Co.
Gill, Edward	Kilcloon Company	Govern, Laurence	Navan Cemetery

Name	Go to section	Name	Go to section
Govern, Michael	Moynalty Co.	Hand, Thomas	Moylagh Co.
Govern, Peter	Moynalty Co.	Hanly, Michael	Enfield Company
Govern, Thomas	Moynalty Co.	Harmon, John	Julianstown & Laytown
Grace, James	Kells Company	Harmon, Nicholas	Bohermeen Co.
Grace, William	Oldcastle Co.	Harpur, Thomas	Oldcastle Co.
Gray, Michael	Kilyon Company	Harris, Bernard	Bective / Kilmessan
Greely, Michael	Oldcastle Co.	Harris, John	Bective / Kilmessan
Green, James	Kentstown Co.	Harte, Bernard	Ballinlough Co.
Green, John	Stonefield Co.	Harte, Edward	Bohermeen Co.
Green, Patrick	Stonefield Co.	Harte, Joseph	Navan Cemetery
Gregan, John	Kilbride Company	Harte, Patrick	Ballinlough Co.
Gregan, William	Kilbride Company	Harte, Patrick	Bohermeen Co.
Grehan, Michael	Summerhill Co.	Haughan, John	Moylagh Co.
Greville, Albert	Enfield Company	Hayes, John	Drumbaragh Co.
Grey, Philip	Ballivor Company	Hazel, John	Kiltale Company
Griffin, James	Bective / Kilmessan	Heague, Thomas	Ratoath Company
Griffin, James	Skryne & Killeen Co.	Heague, William	Ratoath Company
Griffith, Arthur	Page 35, 55, 69	Healy, John	Trim Company
Grogan, John	Longwood Co.	Healy, Patrick	Yellow Furze
Grogan, Patrick	Enfield Company	Healy, Peter	Navan Cemetery
Grogan, Patrick	Summerhill Co.	Healy, Thomas	Enfield Company
Grogan, Peter	Longwood Co.	Heaney, B	Kilberry Company
Halford, J	Clongill Company	Heaney, James	Kilberry Company
Halford, T	Clongill Company	Heaney, Owen	Kilberry Company
Hall, David	Culmullin Co.	Heany, James	Navan Cemetery
Halligan, James	Athboy Company	Heany, P	Kilberry Company
Halligan, Michael	Kildalkey Co.	Heatherton, Thomas	Longwood Co.
Halpin, Andrew	Ardbracken Co.	Heavy, P	Ballinacree Co.
Halpin, Brian	Fennor Company	Heery, James	Ballinacree Co.
Halpin, James	Enfield Company	Heery, James	Ballinacree Co.
Hamill, Brian	Kilbeg Company	Heery, John	Boardsmill Co.
Hamilton, David	Enfield Company	Heery, Michael	Ballinacree Co.
Hamilton, James	Enfield Company	Heffernan, Christopher	Kilberry Company
Hamon, Richard	Trim Company	Hegarty, John	Kells Company
Hand, Francis	Clongill Company	Hennessy, Patrick	Ballinacree Co.
Hand, John	Moylagh Co.	Henry, Patrick	Kilyon Company

393

Name	Go to section	Name	Go to section
Heny, James	Ballivor Company	Hynes, John	Kiltale Company
Herbstreit, Leo	Oldcastle Co.	Hynes, Michael	Trim Company
Hesnan, Michael	Kildalkey Co.	Hynes, Patrick	Trim Company
Hessman, John	Ratoath Company	Isdale, James	Kilbride Company
Hickey, James	Kilbride Company	James, Peter	Dunboyne Co.
Hickey, James (RIC)	Navan Cemetery	Kane, Patrick	Martry Company
Hickey, John	Nobber Company	Kane, Peter	Dunderry Co.
Hickey, Joseph	Yellow Furze	Kavanagh, James	Dunmoe Co.
Hickey, Patrick	Yellow Furze	Kavanagh, Michael	Dunmoe Co.
Higgins, Francis	Ballinlough Co.	Kavanagh, Peter	Fennor Company
Higgins, John	Trim Company	Kavanagh, Thomas	Dunmoe Co.
Hillard, James	Navan Cemetery	Kealy, Patrick	Creewood Rathkenny
Hillard, Michael	Navan Cemetery	Keane, Patrick	Bohermeen Co.
Hiney, Michael	Kilcloon Company	Keane, Thomas	Athboy Company
Hodgett, Mr.	Page 75, 76	Kearney, Edward	Enfield Company
Hoey, John	Clongill Company	Kearney, Edward	Summerhill Co.
Hoey, M	Clongill Company	Kearney, Patrick	Kildalkey Co.
Hoey, Michael	Athboy Company	Keary, James	Martry Company
Hoey, P	Castletown Co.	Keary, Patrick	Martry Company
Holland, Patrick	Athboy Company	Keating, Christopher	Dunboyne Co.
Hollywood, Matthew	Dunboyne Co.	Keating, James	Dunboyne Co.
Holten, Anthony	Johnstown Co	Keating, Mr.	Page 26, 28
Holten, Bartley	Johnstown Co	Keating, Patrick	Navan Cemetery
Horan, James	Bective / Kilmessan	Keating, Peter	Dunboyne Co.
Horan, John	Kilbride Company	Keegan, James	Kilyon Company
Horan, Nicholas	Dunboyne Co.	Keegan, James	Stonefield Co.
Hudson, Dominick	Enfield Company	Keegan, Michael	Kilyon Company
Hughes, Christopher	Skryne & Killeen Co.	Keegan, Patrick	Kilyon Company
Hughes, James	Ardbracken Co.	Keelan, Brien	Carnaross Co.
Hughes, Joseph	Rathkenny Co.	Keelan, Christopher	Drumcondrath Co.
Husband, John	Oldcastle Co.	Keelan, Michael	Rathkenny Co.
Hyland, James	Dunderry Co.	Keelan, Mick	Creewood Rathkenny
Hyland, John	Ardbracken Co.	Keelan, Patrick	Kells Company
Hyland, Michael	Ardbracken Co.	Keelan, Patrick	Navan Cemetery
Hyland, Patrick	Ardbracken Co.	Keelan, Peter	Duleek Company
Hyland, Thomas	Carnaross Co.	Keelan, Richard	Drumcondrath Co.

Name	Go to section	Name	Go to section
Keelan, Thomas	Rathkenny Co.	King, John	Dunboyne Co.
Keenan, Patrick	Oldcastle Co.	King, John	Dunshaughlin Co.
Keenan, Thomas	Ardcath Company	King, Owen	Dunboyne Co.
Keirnan, Terrence	Fennor Company	King, Thomas	Moynalty Co.
Kelly, Arthur	Kentstown Co.	Kinsella, James	Navan Cemetery
Kelly, Christopher	Kilyon Company	Kinsella, Thomas	Navan Cemetery
Kelly, Edward	Ballinacree Co.	Lalor, Joseph	Trim Company
Kelly, H	Castletown Co.	Lalor, Patrick	Trim Company
Kelly, Hugh	Athboy Company	Lambe, P	Rathkenny Co.
Kelly, James	Ardcath Company	Lambe, Patrick	Meath Hill Co.
Kelly, James	Julianstown & Laytown	Landy, James	Bective / Kilmessan
Kelly, Joe	Trim Company	Lane, Patrick	Slane Company
Kelly, John	Dunboyne Co.	Larkin, Michael	Dunboyne Co.
Kelly, Joseph	Culmullin Co.	Lawlor, George	Trim Company
Kelly, Michael	Dunboyne Co.	Lawlor, John	Navan Cemetery
Kelly, Patrck	Martry Company	Lawlor, Mark	Trim Company
Kelly, Patrick	Johnstown Co	Lawlor, William	Trim Company
Kelly, Peter	Cloncurry Co.	Lear, John	Navan Cemetery
Kelly, Samuel	Kildalkey Co.	Lear, Robert	Kells Company
Kelly, Stephen	Kilyon Company	Leddy, Bernard	Carnaross Co.
Kelly, Thomas	Johnstown Co	Leddy, John	Kells Company
Kelly, William	Kilyon Company	Ledwedge, Andrew	Cloncurry Co.
Kennedy, James	Julianstown & Laytown	Ledwedge, Edward	Cloncurry Co.
Kennedy, Kevin	Dunmoe Co.	Ledwedge, Patrick	Enfield Company
Kenny, Daniel	Dunshaughlin Co.	Ledwidge, J.	Slane Company
Kenny, James	Dunshaughlin Co.	Ledwith, Joseph	Kildalkey Co.
Kenny, Patrick	Dunshaughlin Co.	Ledwith, Matthew	Kildalkey Co.
Keogh, James	Dunshaughlin Co.	Lee, Henry	Ballinlough Co.
Keogh, John	Ballinlough Co.	Lee, James	Ballinlough Co.
Keogh, Matthew	Dunshaughlin Co.	Lee, John	Duleek Company
Keogh, Patrick	Dunshaughlin Co.	Lee, Patrick	Duleek Company
Kiernan, Michael	Dunderry Co.	Lee, Peter	Dunboyne Co.
Kiernan, Peter	Ballivor Company	Lenehan, Bernard	Bective / Kilmessan
Kileen, Patrick	Moylagh Co.	Lenehan, Edward	Fordstown Co.
Killoren, Thomas	Navan Cemetery	Lenehan, James	Kentstown Co.
King, George	Julianstown & Laytown	Lenehan, Patrick	Kentstown Co.

Name	Go to section	Name	Go to section
Leonard, John	Dunboyne Co.	Lynch, Joseph	Dunshaughlin Co.
Leonard, Thomas	Dunboyne Co.	Lynch, Joseph	Johnstown Co
Levins, Arthur	Navan Cemetery	Lynch, Joseph	Kells Company
Levins, Michael	Julianstown & Laytown	Lynch, Laurence	Carnaross Co.
Levins, Peter	Julianstown & Laytown	Lynch, Laurence	Dunderry Co.
Lillieropn, Fredrick	Curragha Co.	Lynch, Luke	Kilmainhamwood
Losty, Edward	Bective / Kilmessan	Lynch, Michael	Carnaross Co.
Loughlin, John	Moylagh Co.	Lynch, Michael	Dunderry Co.
Loughlin, Patrick	Ballivor Company	Lynch, P	Clongill Company
Loughran, Bernard	Dunderry Co.	Lynch, Patrick	Dunderry Co.
Loughran, Frank	Bective / Kilmessan	Lynch, Patrick	Dunshaughlin Co.
Loughran, James	Bohermeen Co.	Lynch, Patrick	Dunshaughlin Co.
Loughran, Matthew	Navan Cemetery	Lynch, Patrick	Johnstown Co
Loughran, Patrick	Navan Cemetery	Lynch, Patrick	Kilberry Company
Loughran, Thomas	Bective / Kilmessan	Lynch, Patrick	Newcastle Co.
Loughran, William	Navan Cemetery	Lynch, Patrick	Newcastle Co.
Lowndes, Francis	Dunboyne Co.	Lynch, Patrick	Rathkenny Co.
Lynam, Christopher	Dunboyne Co.	Lynch, Peter	Newcastle Co.
Lynam, James	Enfield Company	Lynch, Peter	Oldcastle Co.
Lynam, John	Enfield Company	Lynch, Richard	Oldcastle Co.
Lynch, Daniel	Fordstown Co.	Lynch, Stephen	Newcastle Co.
Lynch, Edward	Dunderry Co.	Lynch, Thomas	Carnaross Co.
Lynch, Edward	Moynalty Co.	Lynch, Thomas	Newcastle Co.
Lynch, James	Carnaross Co.	Lynch, Thomas	Newcastle Co.
Lynch, James	Kilberry Company	Lynch, Thomas	Oldcastle Co.
Lynch, James	Navan Cemetery	Lyons, William	Julianstown & Laytown
Lynch, James	Newcastle Co.	Mackey, James	Navan Cemetery
Lynch, John	Carnaross Co.	Madden, Daniel	Dunboyne Co.
Lynch, John	Carnaross Co.	Madden, James	Slane Company
Lynch, John	Dunshaughlin Co.	Madden, John	Kiltale Company
Lynch, John	Kildalkey Co.	Madden, John	Whitegate Co.
Lynch, John	Newcastle Co.	Madden, Michael	Kiltale Company
Lynch, John	Newcastle Co.	Madden, Patrick	Kiltale Company
Lynch, John	Ratoath Company	Magher, Thomas	Bective / Kilmessan
Lynch, Joseph	Carnaross Co.	Magher, William	Bective / Kilmessan
Lynch, Joseph	Culmullin Co.	Maguire, James	Dunboyne Co.

Name	Go to section	Name	Go to section
Maguire, Patrick	Johnstown Co	Martin, James	Martry Company
Maguire, Patrick	Kells Company	Martin, James	Nobber Company
Maguire, Thomas	Ballivor Company	Martin, John	Athboy Company
Maguire, William	Dunboyne Co.	Martin, Joseph	Athboy Company
Mahon, Christopher	Athboy Company	Martin, Joseph	Bohermeen Co.
Mahony, John	Navan Cemetery	Martin, Michael	Moylagh Co.
Mallon, Edward	Bohermeen Co.	Martin, Patrick	Carnaross Co.
Mallon, James	Bohermeen Co.	Martin, Patrick	Drumcondrath Co.
Mallon, Patrck	Bohermeen Co.	Martin, Richard	Nobber Company
Mallon, Thomas	Bohermeen Co.	Martin, Thomas	Athboy Company
Malloy, Matthew	Stonefield Co.	Martin, William	Ardbracken Co.
Malone, James	Kilcloon Company	Masterson, James	Stonefield Co.
Malone, James	Summerhill Co.	Masterson, John	Dunderry Co.
Malone, John	Kilyon Company	Masterson, Owen	Stonefield Co.
Mangan, John	Bective / Kilmessan	Mathews, Michael	Ballinlough Co.
Manning, Christopher	Kilbride Company	Mathews, Peter	Ballinlough Co.
Manning, John	Enfield Company	Mathews, Philip	Ballinlough Co.
Manning, John	Kilbride Company	Matthews, John	Kentstown Co.
Manning, Michael	Dunshaughlin Co.	Matthews, Laurence	Dunmoe Co.
Manning, Michael	Kilbride Company	Matthews, Matthew	Trim Company
Manning, Patrick	Ballinlough Co.	Matthews, Peter	Trim Company
Manning, Richard	Kilbride Company	Matthews, William	Dunmoe Co.
Manning, Thomas	Ballinlough Co.	McArdle, Michael	Trim Company
Manning, Tom	Kilbride Company	McCabe, Bernard	Ballivor Company
Markey, G	Castletown Co.	McCabe, Bernard	Dunmoe Co.
Markey, H	Castletown Co.	McCabe, Edward	Ballivor Company
Markey, Micael	Moylagh Co.	McCabe, J	Clongill Company
Markey, Michael	Ardbracken Co.	McCabe, James	Dunmoe Co.
Markey, Michael	Creewood Rat'kenny	McCabe, Patrick	Bective / Kilmessan
Markey, Patrick	Castletown Co.	McCabe, Richard	Navan Cemetery
Markey, William	Creewood Rat'kenny	McCabe, Ultan	Stonefield Co.
Marron, Francis	Nobber Company	McCabe, William	Stonefield Co.
Marron, James	Nobber Company	McCaffrey, John	Kilberry Company
Marry, J.	Slane Company	McCann, James	Kilmore Co.
Martin, Christopher	Skryne & Killeen Co.	McCannon, Matthew	Creewood Rat'kenny
Martin, J.	Slane Company	McClorey, Thomas	Dunshaughlin Co.

397

Name	Go to section	Name	Go to section
McConnell, Bernard	Athboy Company	McGinn, William	Oldcastle Co.
McCormack, Christopher	Athboy Company	McGivna, Brien	Whitegate Co.
McCormack, James	Culmullin Co.	McGovern, Joseph	Kilbride Company
McCormack, James	Trim Company	McGovern, Patrick	Kilbride Company
McCormack, John	Ardcath Company	McGovern, Philip	Dunboyne Co.
McCormack, John	Culmullin Co.	McGrane, Henry	Bective / Kilmessan
McCormack, John	Trim Company	McGrane, John	Julianstown & Laytown
McCormack, Nicholas	Culmullin Co.	McGrane, Michael	Ballinlough Co.
McCormack, Robert	Trim Company	McGrane, Robert	Julianstown & Laytown
McCormack, William	Trim Company	McGrath, James	Moylagh Co.
McCourt, Francis	Duleek Company	McGrath, Peter	Curragha Co.
McCullagh, Patrick	Trim Company	McGrath, Thomas	Meath Hill Co.
McDermott, George	Ardbracken Co.	McGrath, Thomas	Nobber Company
McDonald, James	Nobber Company	McGuinness, Daniel	Ballinlough Co.
McDonald, Patrick	Johnstown Co	McGuinness, James	Ardcath Company
McDonnell, James	Kells Company	McGuinness, John	Fordstown Co.
McDonnell, James	Kildalkey Co.	McGuinness, Patrick	Carnaross Co.
McDonnell, John	Ballivor Company	McGuinness, T	Clongill Company
McDonnell, Patrick	Ballinlough Co.	McGuinness, Thomas	Athboy Company
McDonnell, Thomas	Ballinlough Co.	McGuire, James	Ballinlough Co.
McDonnell, Thomas	Ballivor Company	McGuire, John	Kells Company
McElroy, John	Meath Hill Co.	McGuire, John	Nobber Company
McEnroe, Jack	Fennor Company	McGuire, Patrick	Nobber Company
McEnroe, Matthew	Stonefield Co.	McGuirk, William	Ardbracken Co.
McEvoy, C.	Longwood Co.	McGurl, John	Athboy Company
McEvoy, Michael	Longwood Co.	McGurl, Patrick	Athboy Company
McFadden, John	Whitegate Co.	McHale, Richard (RIC)	Navan Cemetery
McGearty, John (RIC)	Killaconnigan Cemetery	McHugh, James	Kilberry Company
McGee, Hugh	Navan Cemetery	McHugh, Thomas	Kilberry Company
McGillic, John	Kells Company	McInerney, Matthew	Carnaross Co.
McGillic, Owen	Kells Company	McInerney, Michael	Carnaross Co.
McGillick, James	Kilbeg Company	McInerney, Robert	Carnaross Co.
McGillick, Patrick	Kilbeg Company	McKenna, James	Ardbracken Co.
McGinn, James	Oldcastle Co.	McKenna, John	Athboy Company
McGinn, John	Oldcastle Co.	McKenna, John	Meath Hill Co.
McGinn, Richard	Ballinacree Co.	McKenna, John	Newcastle Co.

Name	Go to section	Name	Go to section
McKenna, Leo	Navan Cemetery	Miggan, Thomas	Kildalkey Co.
McKenna, William	Meath Hill Co.	Milia, John	Moylagh Co.
McKeon, Laurence	Navan Cemetery	Miller, William	Stonefield Co.
McKeon, Michael	Navan Cemetery	Mitchell, James	Martry Company
McKeown, Bernard	Ballinlough Co.	Mitchell, John	Martry Company
McKeown, Brian	Ballinlough Co.	Mitchell, Patrick	Martry Company
McKeown, Patrick	Ballinlough Co.	Mitchell, Richard	Martry Company
McKoen, John	Kilberry Company	Monaghan, Bernard	Ardbracken Co.
McLoughlin, John	Martry Company	Monaghan, James	Julianstown & Laytown
McLoughlin, John	Navan Cemetery	Monaghan, John	Kilcloon Company
McLoughlin, Patrick	Dunshaughlin Co.	Monaghan, John	Kilcloon Company
McMahon, Cornelius	Navan Cemetery	Monaghan, Joseph	Athboy Company
McMahon, Hugh	Nobber Company	Monaghan, Joseph	Ballivor Company
McMahon, Michael	Moynalty Co.	Monaghan, Matthew	Athboy Company
McMahon, Patrick	Moynalty Co.	Monaghan, Michael	Ardbracken Co.
McMahon, Patrick	Newcastle Co.	Monaghan, Michael	Johnstown Co
McMahon, Patrick	Nobber Company	Monaghan, Michael	Oldcastle Co.
McMahon, Peter	Moynalty Co.	Monaghan, Patrick	Athboy Company
McMahon, Peter	Newcastle Co.	Monaghan, Patrick	Kells Company
McMahon, Philip	Newcastle Co.	Monaghan, Thomas	Kells Company
McMahon, Thomas	Kilbride Company	Monahan, Eugene	Rathkenny Co.
McMahon, Thomas	Nobber Company	Monahan, Michael	Rathkenny Co.
McNally, James	Yellow Furze	Mongan, Michael	Johnstown Co
McNamee, James	Carnaross Co.	Mongey, James	Kilberry Company
McNamee, James	Oldcastle Co.	Mooney, James	Kilyon Company
McNamee, Patrick	Carnaross Co.	Mooney, John	Trim Company
McNamee, William	Carnaross Co.	Mooney, Michael	Stonefield Co.
McNellis, Peter	Navan Cemetery	Mooney, Paddy	Trim Company
McNulty, Matthew	Kilbride Company	Mooney, Patrick	Kilbeg Company
Meade, Bernard	Castletown Co.	Mooney, Patrick	Trim Company
Meade, G	Castletown Co.	Mooney, Thomas	Carnaross Co.
Meade, P	Castletown Co.	Mooney, Thomas	Whitegate Co.
Meade, Patrick	Drumcondrath Co.	Moore, James	Trim Company
Meehan, T	Castletown Co.	Moore, Joseph	Ballinlough Co.
Melady, Francis	Dunmoe Co.	Moore, Michael	Moylagh Co.
Miggan, James	Ballivor Company	Moore, Patrick	Ardcath Company

Name	Go to section	Name	Go to section
Moore, Peter	Ardcath Company	Mulvany, James	Athboy Company
Moore, William	Ardbracken Co.	Mulvany, James	Moynalty Co.
Moran, Christopher	Bective / Kilmessan	Mulvany, James	Newcastle Co.
Moran, Joseph	Bective / Kilmessan	Mulvany, Thomas	Stonefield Co.
Moran, Nicholas	Dunboyne Co.	Murphy, Anthony	Dunshaughlin Co.
Moran, Nicholas	Dunboyne Co.	Murray, A	Clongill Company
Moran, Peter	Dunboyne Co.	Murray, Alexander	Dunboyne Co.
Moran, Thomas	Johnstown Co	Murray, James	Rathkenny Co.
Moran, William	Bective / Kilmessan	Murray, John	Kildalkey Co.
Morgan, James	Boardsmill Co.	Murray, Michael	Cloncurry Co.
Morgan, Patrick	Ratoath Company	Murray, P	Kells Company
Morgan, Robert	Boardsmill Co.	Murray, Patrick	Athboy Company
Morne, Michael	Oldcastle Co.	Murray, Samuel	Johnstown Co
Morris, John	Kells Company	Murray, Thomas	Kells Company
Morris, Joseph	Kells Company	Murray, Thomas	Navan Cemetery
Morris, Thomas	Dunderry Co.	Murray, William	Kildalkey Co.
Morris, Thomas	Kells Company	Murray, William	Longwood Co.
Morris, Thomas	Moynalty Co.	Murtagh, Edward	Kilbeg Company
Morris, Thomas	Whitegate Co.	Murtagh, James	Dunboyne Co.
Mulcahy, Richard	Page 25, 26, 27, 30, 36, 63, 64	Murtagh, John	Martry Company
Muldoon, Charles	Dunboyne Co.	Murtagh, Laurence	Dunboyne Co.
Muldoon, Edward	Ballinlough Co.	Murtagh, Michael	Whitegate Co.
Muldoon, James	Ballinlough Co.	Murtagh, Richard	Ballinacree Co.
Mullally, Pat	Carnaross Co.	Murtagh, Thomas	Ballinacree Co.
Mullally, Thomas	Carnaross Co.	Nally, John	Bohermeen Co.
Mullally, William	Carnaross Co.	Nally, Thomas	Bohermeen Co.
Mullaly, James	Dunboyne Co.	Naulty, Nicholas	Navan Cemetery
Mullaly, Patrick	Dunboyne Co.	Neill, Patrick	Johnstown Co
Mullen, Robert	Kells Company	Nellis, Patrick	Navan Cemetery
Mulligan, Hugh	Navan Cemetery	Neville, Maurice	Kiltale Company
Mulligan, Patrick	Dunderry Co.	Nevin, Thomas	Carnaross Co.
Mulvaney, Edward	Navan Cemetery	Newman, James	Bohermeen Co.
Mulvaney, James	Kildalkey Co.	Newman, John	Bohermeen Co.
Mulvaney, Maurice	Skryne & Killeen Co.	Newman, Peter	Dunboyne Co.
Mulvaney, Thomas	Fennor Company	Newman, Thomas	Dunmoe Co.
Mulvaney, William	Kildalkey Co.	Nixon, William	Kilcloon Company

Name	Go to section	Name	Go to section
Nolan, Joseph	Trim Company	O'Hagan, Michael	Kilmainhamwood
Nolan, Laurence	Ratoath Company	O'Hagan, Patrick	Trim Company
Norris, Christopher	Kilcloon Company	O'Hannigan, Donal	Chapter 3
Norris, Patrick	Bective / Kilmessan	O'Hara, Patrick	Trim Company
Nugent, Bernard	Dunderry Co.	O'Hare, Laurence	Yellow Furze
Nugent, J	Clongill Company	O'Hare, Patrick	Kentstown Co.
Nulty, Eugene	Ballinlough Co.	O'Hare, Thomas	Yellow Furze
Nulty, John	Fordstown Co.	O'Higgins, Francis	Drumbaragh
Nulty, Thomas	Dunderry Co.	O'Higgins, John	Trim Company
O'Brien, Gerald	Dunboyne Co.	O'Higgins, Peter	Ballinlough Co.
O'Brien, Giolla Chriost	Dunboyne Co.	O'Higgins, Seamus	Trim Company
O'Brien, Harold	Kildalkey Co.	O'Neill, Henry	Julianstown & Laytown
O'Brien, Jack	Bective / Kilmessan	O'Neill, James	Ballinlough Co.
O'Brien, James	Kildalkey Co.	O'Neill, James	Carnaross-Drumbaragh
O'Brien, John	Johnstown Co	O'Neill, John	Kiltale Company
O'Brien, L.	Slane Company	O'Neill, Matthew	Skryne & Killeen Co.
O'Brien, Patrick	Kilmainhamwood	O'Neill, Michael	Athboy Company
O'Brien, Patrick	Navan Cemetery	O'Neill, Michael	Kiltale Company
O'Brien, T.	Slane Company	O'Neill, Thomas	Dunboyne Co.
O'Brien, William	Dunboyne Co.	O'Neill, William	Johnstown Co
O'Brien, William	Moynalty Co.	O'Reilly,	Moynalty Co.
O'Byrne, Christopher	Dunboyne Co.	O'Reilly, Bernard	Dunboyne Co.
O'Byrne, Gilchrist	Athboy Company	O'Reilly, Gerald	Bohermeen Co.
O'Byrne, Peter	Dunboyne Co.	O'Reilly, John	Whitegate Co.
O'Connell, Ciaran	Navan Cemetery	O'Reilly, Michael	Moynalty Co.
O'Connell, James	Skryne & Killeen Co.	O'Reilly, Patrick	Moynalty Co.
O'Connell, Peter	Stonefield Co.	O'Reilly, Patrick	Newcastle Co.
O'Connell, Thomas	Stonefield Co.	O'Reilly, Patrick	Whitegate Co.
O'Connor, Edward	Carnaross Co.	O'Sullivan, Daniel	Navan Cemetery
O'Connor, Richard	Newcastle Co.	O'Toole, Michael	Yellow Furze
O'Donohue, Tom (RIC)	Navan Cemetery	Parke, William	Enfield Company
O'Dore, John	Trim Company	Perry, James	Navan Cemetery
O'Grady, John	Athboy Company	Phillips, Barney	Drumcondrath Co.
O'Growney, Patrick	Athboy Company	Phoenix, James	Kilcloon Company
O'Hagan, Harold	Trim Company	Phoenix, Michael	Kilcloon Company
O'Hagan, James	Trim Company	Phoenix, Richard	Kilcloon Company

Name	Go to section	Name	Go to section
Pickett, John	Johnstown Co	Reilly, Andrew	Dunshaughlin Co.
Pierce, James	Dunmoe Co.	Reilly, Andrew	Whitegate Co.
Plunkett, George	Kildalkey Co.	Reilly, Bartle	Kilbeg Company
Plunkett, James	Curragha Co.	Reilly, Bernard	Ballinlough Co.
Plunkett, James	Dunshaughlin Co.	Reilly, Bernard	Carnaross Co.
Plunkett, Michael	Trim Company	Reilly, Bernard	Carnaross Co.
Pollin, Christopher	Dunboyne Co.	Reilly, Bernard	Dunboyne Co.
Potterton, Patrick	Kildalkey Co.	Reilly, Bernard	Rathkenny Co.
Potterton, Thomas	Kildalkey Co.	Reilly, Charles	Carnaross Co.
Powderly, James	Kilcloon Company	Reilly, Charles	Whitegate Co.
Powderly, James	Summerhill Co.	Reilly, Christopher	Yellow Furze
Power, Joseph	Carnaross-Drumbaragh	Reilly, Edward	Kilbeg Company
Power, Patrick	Yellow Furze	Reilly, Edward	Moynalty Co.
Power, Thomas	Yellow Furze	Reilly, Francis	Oldcastle Co.
Price, Michael	Carnaross-Drumbaragh	Reilly, Hugh	Enfield Company
Price, T	Castletown Co.	Reilly, Hugh	Newcastle Co.
Proctor, Patrick	Trim Company	Reilly, J.	Slane Company
Purcell, Patrick	Cloncurry Co.	Reilly, James	Dunboyne Co.
Quail, Christopher	Lobinstown Co.	Reilly, James	Kilbeg Company
Quigley, Joseph	Yellow Furze	Reilly, James	Kildalkey Co.
Quilty, Patrick	Navan Cemetery	Reilly, James	Rathkenny Co.
Quinn, Donald	Rathkenny Co.	Reilly, James	Whitegate Co.
Quinn, James	Bective / Kilmessan	Reilly, James	Whitegate Co.
Quinn, John	Bective / Kilmessan	Reilly, John	Ballinlough Co.
Quinn, John	Kilbride Company	Reilly, John	Bohermeen Co.
Quinn, John	Kilyon Company	Reilly, John	Moynalty Co.
Quinn, Joseph	Yellow Furze	Reilly, John	Newcastle Co.
Quinn, Patrick	Bective / Kilmessan	Reilly, John	Oldcastle Co.
Rafferty, Edward	Curragha Co.	Reilly, John	Skryne & Killeen Co.
Rafferty, James	Boardsmill Co.	Reilly, Leo	Athboy Company
Rafferty, John	Curragha Co.	Reilly, Matthew	Ballinlough Co.
Rafferty, William	Dunshaughlin Co.	Reilly, Matthew	Johnstown Co
Raleigh, James	Yellow Furze	Reilly, Michael	Moynalty Co.
Rattigans, Michael	Culmullin Co.	Reilly, Michael	Moynalty Co.
Regan, John	Ballivor Company	Reilly, Patrick	Carnaross Co.
Reid, Christopher	Bective / Kilmessan	Reilly, Patrick	Fennor Company

Name	Go to section	Name	Go to section
Reilly, Patrick	Moylagh Co.	Ruddy, Laurence	Kentstown Co.
Reilly, Patrick	Moynalty Co.	Russell, John	Julianstown & Laytown
Reilly, Patrick	Newcastle Co.	Russell, Matthew	Kilcloon Company
Reilly, Patrick	Whitegate Co.	Russell, Samuel	Newcastle Co.
Reilly, Peter	Athboy Company	Russell, Thomas	Newcastle Co.
Reilly, Peter	Newcastle Co.	Russell, Tom	Moynalty Co.
Reilly, T	Castletown Co.	Russell, William	Kilcloon Company
Reilly, Thomas	Ballinacree Co.	Ryan, James	Navan Cemetery
Reilly, Thomas	Kells Company	Ryan, Joseph	Kilberry Company
Reilly, Thomas	Navan Cemetery	Scfton, Patrick	Trim Company
Reilly, Timothy	Rathkenny Co.	Scully, Patrick	Bective / Kilmessan
Reilly, William	Dunboyne Co.	Scully, Thomas	Kiltale Company
Reilly, William	Kilyon Company	Seerey, Joseph	Athboy Company
Rennicks, Arthur	Bohermeen Co.	Shanaher, Srgnt. (R.I.C.)	Page 26, 27
Rennicks, Sam	Martry Company	Sheeky, Laurence	Navan Cemetery
Rennicks, Thomas	Martry Company	Sheevan, James	Meath Hill Co.
Rennicks, William	Martry Company	Sheilds, Peter	Kilberry Company
Reynolds, James	Kildalkey Co.	Sheils, John	Kentstown Co.
Reynolds, Joseph	Fordstown Co.	Sheridan, Christopher	Kilcloon Company
Reynolds, Joseph	Kildalkey Co.	Sheridan, Christopher	Summerhill Co.
Reynolds, Peter	Kells Company	Sheridan, Harry	Oldcastle Co.
Richardson, John	Kilcloon Company	Sheridan, James	Newcastle Co.
Rickard, James	Ballivor Company	Sheridan, John	Moynalty Co.
Rickard, James	Ballivor Company	Sheridan, M	Castletown Co.
Rickard, Luke	Boardsmill Co.	Sheridan, Matthew	Kilcloon Company
Rispin,	Athboy Company	Sheridan, Matthew	Summerhill Co.
Roberts, John (RIC)	Navan Cemetery	Sheridan, Michael	Kells Company
Rock, Owen	Carnaross Co.	Sheridan, Michael	Rathkenny Co.
Rogers, Michael	Trim Company	Sheridan, Nicholas	Fordstown Co.
Rooney, Patrick	Culmullin Co.	Sheridan, Patrick	Fordstown Co.
Rooney, R	Culmullin Co.	Sheridan, Patrick	Moynalty Co.
Rooney, Richard	Culmullin Co.	Sheridan, Peter	Navan Cemetery
Rooney, William	Ardbracken Co.	Sheridan, Philip	Newcastle Co.
Rourke, Loughlin	Ardbracken Co.	Sheridan, Thomas	Yellow Furze
Rourke, Michael	Ballinlough Co.	Sherlock, Laurence	Athboy Company
Rourke, Patrick	Nobber Company	Sherry, C	Kilberry Company

Name	Go to section	Name	Go to section
Sherry, Christopher	Johnstown Co	Smith, William	Bective / Kilmessan
Sherry, Edward	Trim Company	Smith, William	Dunshaughlin Co.
Sherry, James	Trim Company	Smith, William	Martry Company
Sherry, John	Trim Company	Smyth Harry (R.I.C.)	Ardbraccen Cemetery
Sherry, Luke	Trim Company	Smyth Joseph (OFIRA)	Kells Cemetery
Sherry, Stephen	Dunderry Co.	Smyth,	Trim Company
Sherry, Stephen	Trim Company	Smyth, Edward	Culmullin Co.
Sherry, Thomas	Trim Company	Smyth, Francis	Kilbride Company
Sherry, William	Trim Company	Smyth, Harry (R.I.C.)	Page 26, 27
Shiels, Joseph	Kentstown Co.	Smyth, John	Culmullin Co.
Shiels, William	Johnstown Co	Smyth, John	Curragha Co.
Skelly, Michael	Kells Company	Smyth, John	Dunboyne Co.
Slevin, James	Dunderry Co.	Smyth, John	Johnstown Co
Slevin, Joseph	Dunderry Co.	Smyth, John	Kilbeg Company
Smith, Hugh	Carnaross-Drumbaragh	Smyth, Joseph	Page 62
Smith, James	Johnstown Co	Smyth, L	Clongill Company
Smith, John	Bective / Kilmessan	Smyth, Matthew	Stonefield Co.
Smith, John	Culmullin Co.	Smyth, Patrick	Cloncurry Co.
Smith, John	Dunshaughlin Co.	Smyth, Peter	Fordstown Co.
Smith, John	Fennor Company	Smyth, Peter	Kilbride Company
Smith, Joseph	Martry Company	Smyth, W.	Slane Company
Smith, Luke	Carnaross Co.	Smyth, Walter	Rathkenny Co.
Smith, Matthew	Carnaross Co.	Smyth, William	Culmullin Co.
Smith, Owen	Dunderry Co.	Stapleton, Nicholas	Ardbracken Co.
Smith, Patrick	Dunderry Co.	Stapleton, Patrick	Navan Cemetery
Smith, Patrick	Kells Company	Stapleton, Valentine	Ardbracken Co.
Smith, Patrick	Moylagh Co.	Stoney, Patrick	Skryne & Killeen Co.
Smith, Peter	Fennor Company	Sullivan, Daniel	Kells Company
Smith, Peter	Johnstown Co	Sullivan, Michael	Navan Cemetery
Smith, Peter	Moynalty Co.	Sullivan, William	Navan Cemetery
Smith, Peter	Stonefield Co.	Swan, Francis	Navan Cemetery
Smith, Peter	Whitegate Co.	Swan, James	Clongill Company
Smith, Thomas	Dunderry Co.	Swan, Michael	Clongill Company
Smith, Thomas	Moylagh Co.	Sweeney, James	Kells Company
Smith, Thomas	Moynalty Co.	Sweeney, Michael	Carnaross Co.
Smith, Thomas	Ratoath Company	Sweeny, John	Clongill Company

Name	Go to section	Name	Go to section
Sweeny, Patrick	Clongill Company	Twomey, Michael	Kiltale Company
Sweeny, Patrick	Kilbride Company	Tyrell, John	Carnaross Co.
Synnott, James	Yellow Furze	Tyrrell, James	Kildalkey Co.
Tevlin, John	Carnaross Co.	Tyrrell, John	Kildalkey Co.
Tevlin, Matthew	Carnaross Co.	Vaughey, John	Slane Company
Tevlin, Philip	Carnaross Co.	Vaughey, Matthew	Yellow Furze
Thomson, Patrick	Kilcloon Company	Wall, Thomas	Ardcath Company
Thomson, Patrick	Summerhill Co.	Wallace, James	Culmullin Co.
Thornton, Edward	Athboy Company	Wallace, Matthew	Culmullin Co.
Tiernan, Patrick	Slane Company	Walsh, John	Cloncurry Co.
Tierney, Patrick	Meath Hill Co.	Walsh, Laurence	Newcastle Co.
Timmons, Patrick	Fordstown Co.	Walsh, Patrick	Ardcath Company
Timmons, Patrick	Oldcastle Co.	Walsh, Patrick	Kilbride Company
Timmons, Thomas	Kilbeg Company	Walsh, Patrick	Oldcastle Co.
Tobin,	Stonefield Co.	Walsh, Peter	Ardcath Company
Tobin, Edward	Whitegate Co.	Walsh, Peter	Kiltale Company
Tobin, Patrick	Whitegate Co.	Walsh, Richard	Kilcloon Company
Tormey, Bernard	Enfield Company	Walsh, Thomas	Dunmoe Co.
Trainor, James	Drumcondrath Co.	Walshe, Thomas	Ardbracken Co.
Traynor, Nicholas	Kentstown Co.	Ward, James	Athboy Company
Troy, Patrick	Summerhill Co.	Ward, James	Drumcondrath Co.
Tuite, Brian	Oldcastle Co.	Ward, John	Nobber Company
Tuite, James	Whitegate Co.	Ward, Matthew	Drumcondrath Co.
Tuite, Jim	Oldcastle Co.	Ward, Patrick	Trim Company
Tuite, Michael	Fennor Company	Ward, William	Drumcondrath Co.
Tuite, Peter	Oldcastle Co.	Waters, Francis	Nobber Company
Tully, Bernard	Fennor Company	Waters, Patrick	Ardbracken Co.
Tully, Farrell	Kells Company	Waters, Patrick	Carnaross Co.
Tully, John	Kilbeg Company	Waters, Peter	Kentstown Co.
Tully, Mark	Newcastle Co.	Waters, Thomas	Trim Company
Tully, Michael	Carnaross Co.	Watters, Francis	Drumcondrath Co.
Tully, Nicholas	Kells Company	Watters, James	Drumcondrath Co.
Tully, Patrick	Kells Company	Webb, Joseph	Skryne & Killeen Co.
Tully, Peter	Oldcastle Co.	Wheelan, Christopher	Bective / Kilmessan
Tully, Thomas	Fennor Company	Wheelan, Edward	Bective / Kilmessan
Twomey, James	Bective / Kilmessan	White, H	Clongill Company

Name	Go to section	Name	Go to section
Wallace, Matthew	Kiltale Company	Wiseman, Patrick	Julianstown & Laytown
Wallace, Thomas	Culmullin Co.	Woods, Edward	Fordstown Co.
Walsh, James	Kilcloon Company	Woods, Joseph	Navan Cemetery
Walsh, James	Kiltale Company	Woods, Patrick	Dunboyne Co.
White, J	Clongill Company	Woods, Robert	Fordstown Co.
White, John	Kilbride Company	Wynne, Michael	Stonefield Co.
White, Joseph	Creewood Rathkenny	Wynne, Patrick	Stonefield Co.
White, Michael	Curragha Co.	Wynne, Peter	Stonefield Co.
White, Patrick	Clongill Company	Yore, Richard	Dunderry Co.
White, R	Clongill Company	Yore, Thomas	Carnaross Co.
White, Samuel	Curragha Co.	Young, John (RIC)	Navan Cemetery
Wildridge, James	Culmullin Co.		

Owen McFadden

Love to hear your feedback:

Your feedback and constructive opinion of this book is welcome so here is your opportunity. No matter whether you like or dislike the book your opinion will be read and I will make every effort to take your view on board for future publications. Send your e-mail to mcfadden@outlook.ie and thank you.